For Ali and
Stev

Lily

A Most Unsettled Man

A biography of George Matcham

Lily Style

Historium Press

Cover design by White Rabbit Arts

Follow the author at
www. thehistoricalfictioncompany. com/hp-authors/lily-style

www.lilystyle.co.uk

www.emmahamiltonsociety.co.uk

EBOOK ISBN: 978-1-962465-49-6
PAPERBACK ISBN: 978-1-962465-48-9
HARDCOVER ISBN: 978-1-962465-47-2

Published by Historium Press 2024
New York, NY / Macon, GA USA

Dedicated to Alison Huntingford who founded
South Hams Authors' Network and empowered me to write.

Contents

A Most Unsettled Man:
A Biography of George Matcham

Introduction

Dubbed "the most unsettled man alive"[1] George Matcham (1753–1833) reached maturity in colonial Bombay with a single lung, and a dauntlessly curious mind, the latter coaxing him to undertake uncharted, long distance overland adventures, despite his doctor's opinion about his state of health. George's restlessness was stilled by his marriage to the youngest sister of Horatio Nelson, who he witnessed rising to become Britain's most celebrated naval hero. After marriage, George's lively curiosity turned to sedate problem-solving, which resulted in him patenting two inventions of benefit to the Royal Navy and, apparently, designing the lake in Saint James's Park, London, that's been credited to architect, John Nash.

There are frequent mentions of George Matcham in biographies of Horatio Nelson and his equally famous paramour, Emma, Lady Hamilton, but, other than a 421-word entry in the Dictionary of National Biography, no account has focused on George's own life and, with this, his perspective on the dramatic events he witnessed, and was centrally involved with.

Mentions of George in disparate texts, combined with his own direct quotes, have rendered him into a three-dimensional human being with a warm personality, kind heart, adventurous spirit, steady loyalty and, perhaps most endearingly, a cheeky sense of humour (examples include trying to fool his new wife that an article about her beloved brother, Horatio Nelson was about someone else, and, when George was an old man, playfully harassing his handyman, Noyce, to be his guinea pig in Heath Robinson-style experiments).

This biography charts George Matcham's life from his British East India Company-ruled childhood in Bombay, journeys alongside him during his three, epic, overland crossings of the Middle Eastern peninsula, to his English country gentleman idyll and his relationship with Horatio Nelson and Emma Hamilton, whom he supported when she was spurned after Nelson's death. George's story finishes, good-naturedly, with his ambling final years, during which time he revelled in the company of his grandchildren.

As an author, my perspective is coloured by kinship. I'm the 4th great-granddaughter of both George and Kitty Matcham and of Nelson and

Emma Hamilton, through the marriage of their grandchildren –George and Kitty's granddaughter Tori Blanckley married Nelson and Emma's grandson William George Ward. The protective affection I feel towards all of them has informed my interpretation of available data. Nelson and Emma's fame is a mixed blessing because, on the one hand, there are myriad portraits and historical records, plus an incalculable quantity of detailed research carried out by others but, on the other hand, the sheer volume of entrenched and passionate opinions about them has hampered my ability to connect to them on a family level.

My interest as an historical author is in piecing together real people from dry data. My sense of family-relationship makes me hyper-vigilant when I read others' accounts of my ancestors. For example, in *England's mistress* –Kate Williams's best selling biography of Emma Hamilton– George Matcham is portrayed as a penniless scrounger forever sponging off kind-hearted Emma. Conversely, in Winifred Gérin's biography of Emma and Nelson's only child, Horatia, George is portrayed as a hero, but Emma is painted as malevolent. Both negative accounts irked me, and neither has stood up to scrutiny: George wasn't a penniless scrounger and Emma wasn't evil; although George, unlike his wife and children, adhered to mainstream society's view that Lady Hamilton had hauled hapless Horace, as his family named him, from holy matrimony.

This is George Matcham's story, so people and places are described as and when George encountered them. For example, his father-in-law, Reverend Edmund Nelson isn't described until George first met him in the city of Bath.

I've transcribed contemporary press reports because these would have provided George with initial information about his brother-in-law, Horatio Nelson's rise to fame and, after this, Nelson and Emma Hamilton's famous romance.

George's story is so tightly entwined with Nelson and Emma's that his perspective retells their oft-repeated tale in a new light. George scoured the press for news of Nelson before, and after, his rise to superstardom; was intimately involved in Nelson's final days; and –after this– it was the Matchams who supported Emma until her bitter end and then rescued her and Nelson's orphaned daughter, Horatia.

It's thanks to the Matchams' prolific letter-keeping and their descendant, Mary Eyre-Matcham, compiling a batch of their hoard into a book –The Nelsons of Burnham Thorpe– that rich details exist of George and his family's personal feelings, and engagements, during those dramatic years. George's prissy East India Company upbringing gifted him a cynicism towards Emma Hamilton which matched society's damning and, frankly, misogynistic view; whilst George's wife and children's unswerving loyalty towards her fills in gaps formed by historical censorship (early Nelson biographies entirely omitted his love letters to Emma).[2] George's perspective, therefore, is uniquely angled to recount the story of Nelson and Emma, not just as it unravelled to the British public, but close up and "warts and all".

Here, then, is my account of their extraordinary and intertwined lives.

Part One:
Early Years
in Bombay
and London
(1753–1777)

Chapter One: Childhood in Bombay

1753 – c. 1763

George Matcham was born in Bombay on the 30th of November 1753 but, curiously, there's no trace of his christening in Bombay's parish register, despite the chaplain later attesting that he'd baptised him on the 7th of February 1754. [3]

The subcontinental island of Bombay had been under British control for the best part of a century. The colony was a fortified garrison which the East India Company rented from the British monarchy for £10 a year. A 1754 watercolour by Jan van Ryne, entitled "Bombay on the Malabar Coast belonging to the East India Company of England" depicts it as predominantly rural. Rolling, scrub-covered hills rise green behind blocky European buildings clustering the shore. A grand, two-storey, grey-stone warehouse dominates the left-hand side of the image. The "Bunder Pier" (later named the "Apollo Bunder", then "Wellington Pier") protrudes from this into the sea. Behind it peeks St. Thomas's, looking every bit like a rural, English parish church. A group of red-roofed buildings to the church's right are the homes of the East Imdia Company's executive chiefs. In front of them are grey, crenelated fortifications guarding the harbour.

A visitor to Bombay in the 1780s said, "This island is very beautiful". [4] Another, who'd visited four decades earlier, noted that the peaks of the Western Ghats on the mainland:

"were in full view, at a trifling distance, and is so situate, as, together with the winding of other islands along that continent, to form one of the most commodious bays perhaps in the world... the harbour is spacious enough to contain any number of ships ; has excellent anchoring-ground, and by its circular position, can afford them a land-locked shelter against any winds, to which the mouth of it is exposed. It is also admirably situated for a center of dominion and commerce, the Gulf of Persia, the Red Sea, and the whole trade of that side of the great Indian Peninsula, and northern parts adjoining to it". [5]

High in those mountains, and cloud-cooled, perched Puna, the seat of the warlike Maratha people, who were preventing the British in Bombay from expanding eastwards into the Indian mainland. At the same time, the seas around Bombay swarmed with pirates and hostile French and Dutch ships.

George's father, Simon Matcham, was a captain of the Bombay Marine tasked with policing the Company's trade across the breadth of the Indian Ocean and, sometimes, eastwards, circumnavigating the subcontinent into the Bay of Bengal.

George and his elder brother —named Simon for their father— would have been familiar with their parents' stories about their south-west English heritage. Their father, baptised in 1711, was, according to Matcham family tradition, fifth "in descent from Thomas Macham, gentleman purchaser of the manor of Up Wimborne, co. Dorset, in 1547". [6] Their mother, baptised Elizabeth Peirce Bidwell, would have told George and his brother that her parents, Hugh and Hannah Bidwell, had been Presbyterian followers of Calvin. Her maternal grandfather, James Peirce M.D., had been a famous —or infamous— dissenting preacher, who'd authored many Presbyterian pamphlets. [7]

George's grandfather had been lured to Bombay by career opportunities in the predominantly Presbyterian East India Company, which fervently upheld their faith's core principals of the right to bear arms and exercise free trade (principles which went on to form the bedrock of the American Constitution). [8]

George's mother had arrived in Bombay as a tiny baby, [9] with her parents and four older sisters. At this time, Bombay Fort was controlled by a Presbyterian governor, Robert Cowan, [10] under whom George's grandfather, Hugh Bidwell, had been quickly promoted to senior merchant.

However, the Bidwells' fortunes were fickle and George's grandmother died in 1734, after which his grandfather, Hugh Bidwell, succumbed to consumption in '38. The orphaned Bidwell girls remained in Bombay and married expatriates. The last wedding was that of George's mother to Captain Simon Matcham of the Bombay Marine, which took place in 1751.

George's brother, Simon, had been born at some point in 1752 but, like George, had no baptism noted in Bombay's parish register. A simple explanation is that the relevant pages were lost, but contemporary baptisms are there to be seen. Another explanation is that the Matchams' Presbyterian faith had driven them to baptise both boys privately. George's mother, in fact, had been privately baptised by her preacher grandfather, James Peirce. [11]

Peculiarly, despite the predominance of Presbyterianism within the

East India Company, no Presbyterian minister had been officially appointed to Bombay,[12] so babies born to Presbyterian residents would have been privately baptised, or had their baptisms delayed until their families relocated elsewhere. Delaying baptism was no hardship for Presbyterians, for Calvin, whose evangelical philosophy they followed, believed that the children of Christians were automatically Christian too, so baptism wasn't essential.[13]

The only East India Company approved place of worship in mid eighteenth century Bombay was St Thomas's Anglican church. A 1758 French plan of Bombay Fort shows it in the southern part of the island labelled *le temple* by the cartographer (who, being French, likely had a poor view of non-Catholic churches). According to a 1757 travelogue:

"The only English Church at Bombay, and which is full sufficient for any possible congregation of them at it, is a building, which if it has nothing to boast of as to its architecture, is however extremely neat, commodious, and airy, being situate on what is called the Green, a spacious area that continues from the fort[ified harbour] thereto, and is pleasantly laid out in walks planted with trees, round which are mostly the houses of the English inhabitants."[14]

By the mid eighteenth-century, Bombay's population was nearing three hundred thousand,[15] though the British enclave, which accounted for a small fraction of this, didn't mingle with non-Europeans.[16]

Much of the uninhabited part of Bombay island was planted with *oarts* (coconut groves) which, when merged, were called "the woods". Roads and paths criss-crossed through the *oart* woods, forming a tempting labyrinth for young boys, like George, to run through, "where one is pleasantly defended from the sun at all hours of the day." Periodically flooded rice fields were also common and, nearer to the coast, *brab-trees* (wild palms) were found. The *Brab-trees* dangled with intricate toddy-bird nests and "an insipid kind of fruit, about the bigness of a common pear", but were prized for their sap, called *toddy* (hence the nesting birds' name) which, if tapped and brewed, made the finest, alcoholic *arrack*.[17]

On the French map, a large building named *"Le government"* (Government House) stands to the left of St. Thomas's. To the right of the church are the *maisons des chefs decadres* (houses of the executive chiefs) set back from the hustle of the dock. This would have been where the Matchams lived. A 1750 publication tells that these houses were constructed from wood, with tiled roofs.[18] In Van Ryne's 1754 watercolour the British residences, which cluster beneath a scrubby hillock, have white walls and red roofs. A 1740s account tells that they were single-storeyed "after the roman fashion [and] substantially built with stone, lime and smooth plastered on the outside [and] often kept white-washed, which has a very neat air, but very offensive to the eyes from the glare of the sun." In place of glass, most of the windows were pained with square-cut, transparent seashells which had "the singular property of transmitting the light full sufficiently, at the same time that they exclude the violence of its glare, and have besides a cool look."

Flooring was commonly "composed of a kind of loam or stucco, called Chunam, being a lime made of burnt shells, which have been well tempered [and] is extremely hard and lasting, and takes so smooth a polish, that one may literally see one's face in it." *Chunam* was rarely used on walls and outside terraces because, unless it was properly prepared – which was expensive– it spoiled and discoloured "because of saline particles in the lime".

The majority of English homes had courtyards, front and back, in which were "the offices and out-houses." Most houses also had a "convenience", not known in England, "called in the Portugueze [sic] Lingua-franca *Verandas*". These were "either round, or on particular sides of the house [to] afford a pleasing shelter against the sun," as well as keeping "the inner apartments refreshed by the draught of air under them"[19]

The French 1758 plan marks a Catholic chapel on the other side of Government House from St Thomas's Anglican church. Catholic *Popishness* was viewed with hostile suspicion by Presbyterians. The 1689 ousting of England's Catholic King James II by his Protestant daughter, Mary, and her husband, William of Orange, was still in living memory.

The Catholic chapel was a new and unwelcome addition to the fort. In 1748, the East India Company had told relevant parties:

"there is a Romish priest ... who wants to come hither to take up his residence on this island in quality of a Bishop, it is agreed that the Chief and Factors be ordered peremptorily to refuse him a passage on any of our ships till they have orders from us to the contrary. In case at any time any Romish priest should want to touch here for proceeding elsewhere they are to permit thereof if they think it proper."[20]

Religious prejudice didn't extend to "the common men" of the military, of whom some, known as, *Topazzes*, were "mostly black, or of a mixed breed from the Portuguese, to whom, and indeed to all the Roman-catholicks in the military service, there is not the least objection made, or molestation given on account of their religion, of which they have the freest exercise imaginable".[21]

Beyond this, East India Company rule was strict. In 1770, Bombay officers were reminded, "All gaming is strictly forbid [sic] on pain of severe punishment."[22]

Other killjoy diktats issued by the Governor of Bombay included:

"21st August 1768: The commanding officer is very much concerned that the young officers should pay so little attention to the orders given... The wearing of a red coat, and carelessly mounting a few guards, does not, will not, cannot constitute the good officer...

24th August 1768: discipline cannot be carried on, nor a proper subordination be kept up, while the non-commissioned officers keep on a free and intimate footing with the soldiers as at present; it is positively forbid that any non-commissioned officer keeps company or drinks with a private soldier farther than at the head of the mess, where it is supposed he is always on duty to keep up order, decency and regularity...

...When the troops are ordered to parade for church, an officer of each company is to attend and march with the men; they are to march in the same regular manner as they do from the parade, filing off by the right and left, and take up seats in the side aisles..."[23]

Although these rules didn't apply to officers' children, they paint a picture of an environment in which correct deportment was paramount, and fun was deemed unnecessary and sinful. Corporal punishment, however, would have been rarely used on children. In the eighteenth century, the traditional view that children were born with original sin that needed to be beaten out of them had been supplanted by John Locke's 1695 book, *some thoughts concerning education*, in which he proposed that bad behaviour should be coldly ignored and good behaviour praised, and that children were individuals whose creativity and curiosity should be nurtured. In place of the "be seen and not heard" ethos that marked the centuries either side, wealthy eighteenth-century parents placed value on answering their children's questions.[24]

Common children's toys included hoops, cup-and-balls, marbles, drums, windmills, skittles, pull-toys and toy soldiers.[25]

There were limited leisure options in mid-eighteenth century Bombay. There was no town hall or other space for public functions.[26] One of the few leisure activities permitted was day-tripping to the nearby island of Colaba, due south of Bombay fort.[27]

Though records of recreation in eighteenth-century, colonial India are scant, a glimpse is provided by a full-page notice of forthcoming sales, published in the Calcutta Gazette on the 26th July 1787, which lists, under "Sundries":

> "*Cricket batts and wicketts,*
> *Batts and balls,*
> *Ques and maces,*
> *Ivory billiard balls...* "[28]

The game of cricket had become popular in early eighteenth-century England and been quickly introduced to India by East India Company crewmen,[29] where it was "almost wholly a sport played by British military men and civil servants in all white clubs and gymkhanas."[30]

As the British population was small, the Matcham boys would have been well acquainted with the other officers' sons in the fort. Thomas Hallet Hodges, born on the 4th of November 1753 (less than a month before George) was the son of Thomas Hodges Esquire, who became Governor of Bombay in 1767.[31] Archibald, son of Sir James Foulis, Baronet, by Lady Mary his wife, was baptised in St Thomas's in 1755; two years after his father became Major of the Bombay European Regiment. [32]

George would also have been acquainted with William Hough, who was two years his junior and the son of Samuel Hough Esquire, who became Superintendent of the Bombay Marine in 1754,[33] making him Simon Matcham's superior. Below them in the hierarchy, their ships' crews "were chiefly manned with English, or European deserters from other nations".[34]

The southern part of Bombay island was interspersed with gardens,[35] of which "two very pleasant ones, belonging to the company, [were] cultivated in the European manner.[36]

The Green, between the church and English residencies, had fallen into disrepair over the course of the eighteenth-century, becoming "a mere receptacle for rubbish",[37] but would have provided an excellent, improvised cricket pitch for young boys in Bombay Fort.

It seems, however, that George and his brother were kept out of the sunshine –under their veranda, or within their shell-windowed bungalow, with its mirror-like *chunam* floors– because they're described as "pasty-faced" in a pair of Indian miniature portraits "each set in gold with a rim of pale Indian rubies" that was passed down to later generations of Matchams.[38]

Boys, like the Matcham lads, were cared for by ayahs (Indian nannies).

The cost of servants in eighteenth-century India was about eight times cheaper than in England. As a result, East India Company settlers tended to employ large numbers of domestic servants, including ayahs.[39]

The uncomfortable truth of slave-ownership is revealed in George's father's will, in which he decrees "that all my slaves without Exception are free and at liberty to go where they please to provide for themselves in one Twelve Months after my Decease".[40]

As a captain of the Bombay Marine, Simon Matcham would have been closely connected with the East India Company's practice of purchasing slaves in Zanzibar and transporting them to Bombay for holding before shipping them to Company factories in the East Indies.[41]

Bombay's governor, Thomas Hodges Esq., had two slaves baptised, Thomas and Sophia, in 1755: the same year that his own son, Archibald, was baptised in expectation of a life of racial and cultural privilege. Young Archibald Hodges, and other officers' children, would have dressed up for formal occasions like George and his brother, whose miniature portraits showed them attired in "precocious dress of velvet coat, laced waistcoat, frills and velvet ribbon." [42]

Eighteenth century Bombay was shamelessly racist. Indian families, no matter how wealthy, were segregated to the northern part of the island, [43] as far as possible from British homes. Even worse, the practice of keeping enslaved people was far from uncommon. George's attitude to slavery isn't known. It's unlikely that he'd have questioned his father's beliefs, though George seems to have been less ethnically blinkered than contemporary East India Company-men. He had a long-lasting friendship with an impoverished Indo-Armenian and was accompanied "only by Arabs"[44] during one of his three, epic overland treks across the Middle East.

According to an English visitor, who came to Bombay during the 1780s, the majority of the non-white population was Parsee:

"This island... is as populous for its size as any in the world ; merchants and others coming to settle here from the different parts of [India, including Gujarat] amongst those of the latter place, are many Persee; these are descended from the ancient [zoroastrian] Gubres, or worshippers of fire: most of the country merchants, as well as the menial servants of the island, are of this faith."[45]

In many ways, the society in Bombay Fort was similar to that of the garrisoned enclave of Gibraltar, which Britain still holds (much to Spain's chagrin). In modern-day Gibraltar, shops and restaurants, on the ground floors of English-style buildings, sell English-style food, such as fish &

chips, whilst the streets throng with the long-standing, multi-ethnic Gibraltarian population.

George's childhood took place in a melting pot, not just because of the climate, but because of the intermingling of cultures he was exposed to. Eighteenth-century Bombay was a magnet for traders from around the subcontinent and the population was swelled with migrant merchants and artisans, including goldsmiths and weavers.[46] The settlement was "rich with intrigue, interlopers, pirates, country powers, fortifications and land reclamation".[47] Although land reclamation didn't commence until 1784,[48] it was a hot topic and George acquired a lasting fascination with aquatic engineering.

George's mother amused herself by collecting exotic nick-nacks[49] whilst his father, Captain Simon Matcham of the Bombay Marine, brought home equally exotic tales from his patrols of the Indian Ocean. One of his stories, which was later recounted by a Scot named James Forbes, was of shoaling mermaids which tasted like fishy pork:

"Mr. Matcham, a gentleman of great respectability, and at that time superintendent of the Company's marine at Bombay. I have heard him declare, that when in command of a trading vessel at Mozambique, Mombaz, and Melinda, three of the principal sea-ports on the east coast of Africa, he frequently saw these extraordinary animals from six to twelve feet long; the head and mouth resembling the human, except about the nose and mouth, which were rather more like a hog's snout ; the skin fair and smooth ; the head covered with dark glossy hair of considerable length ; the neck, breasts, and body of the female, as low as the hips, appeared like a well-formed woman ; from thence to the extremity of the tail they were perfect fish. The shoulders and arms were in good proportion, but from the elbow tapered to a fin, like the turtle or penguin. These animals were daily cut up, and sold by weight in the fish markets of Mombaz ; nor was the flesh easily distinguished from the fishy pork with which those who have resided at Calicut or Anjengo are so well acquainted."[50]

The Matchams, and the other British residents of Bombay, may have eaten similarly to Company merchants in Yemen who, in 1720, sent a list of food purchases to the East India Company's council in Bombay: "greens, salt, beef, onions, limes, mutton... fresh fish... fowls, chicken, pigeons and eggs [and] spice."[51]

In 1756, when George was a toddler, he'd have sensed, but not understood, the anxiety that flooded Bombay after Britain and France took opposite sides in a war between Austria and Prussia that had resulted in the

British and French East India Companies being at war too.

The northern province of Bengal was vulnerable because the French East India Company had spent the previous decade vying for Bengalese supremacy over its British counterpart. In a flurry of panic, the British Company began fortifying Fort William, their enclave in Bengalese Calcutta (Kolkata).

Things quickly escalated. Bengal's newly-ascended *nawab* (ruler), Sirāj al-Dawlah, preferred the French[52] and ordered the British to cease reinforcing Fort William, but the British ignored his authority. The nawab, who'd already been enraged by the British Company's refusal to pay him taxes, stormed Fort William in June 1756. Some of the fleeing British were caught and thrown into a cell in Fort William that was nicknamed *the black hole* because it was a mere 18 feet long by 14 feet wide. Though the captured British were only locked in *the black hole* for one night, the cramping was so severe that –according to a British report– out of 146 prisoners, only twenty-three survived.[53]

The *black hole of Calcutta* massacre shocked and outraged Britons everywhere. The British press accused the *nawab* of "exercising most inhuman Cruelties",[54] and another paper termed it "The late amazing Catastrophe of Fort William and the City of Calcutta in Bengal".[55]

The British East India Company retaliated aggressively by despatching a flotilla of armed ships from their *presidencies* (military settlements) of Bombay and Madras which, as a captain of the Bombay Marine, George's father was part of:

"The Presidencies of Fort St. George [Madras] and Bombay, finding themselves in a Condition to send some immediate Assistance to Bengal, have each detached a large Number of Men, in conjunction with his Majesty's Squadron under Admiral Watson, to re-establish the Settlement of Fort William, in which they have great hopes of succeeding."[56]

News from Bengal was slow to reach Bombay, let alone England, to which subcontinental news took at least six-months to wend its way around Africa's Cape of Good Hope.

In June 1757, the British press published "a Letter from Bengal to a Gentleman in Bombay" which told that *the Moors* (the nawab's army) had taken six British East India Company ships, and their captains with them. [57]

This would have been a very worrying time for George's mother, as well as the families of other officers and crew.

During this time, George's father, Captain Simon Matcham, remained away at sea, separated from his family by both thousands of nautical miles, and the painstakingly slow, and unreliable, lines of communication that inched between them, slow as a snail.

By and large, the intelligence that sailed, sporadically, into Bombay from Bengal and Madras was good. The British East India Company's army leader, Lord Clive, was ably wresting Bengal back from Nawab Sirāj al-Dawlah and the French. There was a great battle at Plassey (Palashi), in June 1757, in which the *nawab* was killed. Britain's East India Company was now the supreme rulers of Bengal.

Young George's knowledge of events would have been bound to the mood in Bombay. Frowns in place of smiles. Panicked crowds running to the harbour as soon as tall masts were sighted to the south. Squirmily long, solemn services in the church. Of all these signs, his mother's mood would have impacted George most deeply. And his brother's sudden vanishment.

In Bombay, privilege and pampering weren't enough to save Britons from premature death. George's brother, Simon Matcham was buried in 1758 on an unspecified date. George was five and his mother's grief would have heightened his own. Why had his big brother vanished? Only one, lonely pair of children's feet now scuffed the *chunam* floors.

But what of George's papa? Did he still live?

News may, or may not, have reached Bombay that Simon Matcham's ship was lost. If George's mother did hear of it, she may, or may not, have also heard that her husband was taken onto a Bengal-bound ship, named Hardwicke,[58] during the winter of 1757-58, and that he'd been in such a poor state of health that he wrote his will, saying he knew "death is a debt all must pay sooner or later".[59]

Fresh anxiety would have ricochetted to George from his mother when rumour reached Bombay that the Hardwicke had been taken too.[60] Conflict continued as if Plassey hadn't happened.

The tide of incoming anxieties was relentless. Mrs. Elizabeth Matcham would have wrung her hands all the harder when a fresh dispatch, penned in March 1758, brought news that:

"The English Troops in the District of Bengal have lost upwards of twelve hundred Men by Sickness, and the Remainder are in a very bad Way. Most of their officers are dead".[61]

Then the happy, yearned for day arrived when a tall ship, first sighted to the south, docked in Bombay Harbour and Captain Simon Matcham disembarked, alive.

George's new brother, Charles Matcham, was born in October 1761, and family life was maybe happy again until, in June 1763, baby Charles died. No cause of death was recorded for either of George's brothers, but contemporary travellers reported "deadly illnesses they encountered in Bombay".[62]

Unlike later generations (who escaped to Puna), the British in 1760s Bombay had no place to retreat to during the hottest time of the year.[63] [64]

An English priest visiting Bombay in the late 1600s lamented that the climate was "very pernicious to the health of the European because the excess of earthly vapours after the rains ferment the air [weakening them to] those fevers and fluxes into which it casts them."[65]

Another traveller, John Henry Grose, who visited in the 1740s, noted that Bombay had once been called the "Burying-ground of the English", but that mortality rates had since decreased. He said that bloody fluxes were still endemic, but caused "much less ravage than they used to do."

According to Grose, one of the most common disorders in Bombay was "fevers, to which muscular strong men [were] more subject that those of laxer fibres." Other diseases were the "Barbeers, a violent disorder, generally ending in rendering all the limbs paralytic; and mordechin, which is a fit of violent vomiting and purging, that often proves fatal [both these being] distempers hardly now known on the island."[66]

A 1759 publication expanded that *barbeers* was one of the distempers affecting Europeans in India, and that the inability to "move either hand or foot" arose "sometimes from the neglect of guarding the limbs from the cold vapours of the night, and moisture of those nocturnal mists". The most effectual remedy for *barbeers* was "to frequent the hot baths", whilst *mordechin* had, apparently, "been cured by a red-hot iron clapped to the heel of the patient, till he feels the smart ; but some die of it."[67]

Whether or not Bombay still merited the nickname of "the burying ground of the English", Captain and Mrs. Matcham had no wish to lose their only remaining child. It was time to send George to England.

Chapter Two: English School Days

c. 1764 – 1771

George was nine when, having survived two brothers and "the putridness in the air",[68] his parents sent him to boarding school in England's healthier climes. There were, though, problems.

Firstly, the only route from India to England was by sea, and English ships were being picked off by Southern Indian *Mallivans* allied with the French. The peril is outlined in a letter sent to England from Bombay in April 1763:

> *"We are much pestered by Mallivans at Gariah, on the coast of Malabar, as they have got a large Fleet and some Thousand French in their service : they have taken two Ships and several Trading Vessels this season and increased their force fast ; so I imagine we shall be obliged to send the Bombay [Marine] against Gariah".*[69]

As a captain of the Bombay Marine, George's father would have been acutely aware of this danger. For him, and George's mother, to want to send George to England, despite the risk, suggests that they thought his remaining in Bombay would be even more dangerous.

Little George, like his ill-fated brothers, may have contracted a major, tropical illness. Evidence for this is circumstantial, and based on an account of him, aged forty-five, contracting a "bilious" fever with the peculiar, *barbeers*-like symptom of losing all use of his limbs,[70] and could have been a relapse of a childhood infection he contracted in Bombay.

A second problem was that the route to England around the Cape of Good Hope took half-a-year or more,[71] so was an inconceivably long voyage for a nine-year-old boy to undertake on his own. His mother could, perhaps, have accompanied him, but the journey-length would have separated her from her husband for over a year. This was, perhaps, a sacrifice they were willing to make to see their only surviving child safely established in a good English school. However, hints from the scant records that exist suggest that a trusted family friend, Henry Savage, accompanied George to England.

Henry Savage had been an East India Company agent in Gambroon, on the Iranian coast, from 1746 until 1752.[72] After this, he'd moved to Bombay where his son, also named Henry Savage, was baptised, "aged about two", on the 14th of November.[73] Tragically, Henry Savage junior died a few months after his baptism and was buried in Bombay on the 1st of March 1753, shortly before George Matcham's birth. The inherited family story is that Henry Savage senior was George's guardian,[74] which is understandable given the timings of Henry Savage's son's death and George's birth. Henry Savage was voted onto the London-based East India Company's board of directors in April 1764,[75] fitting with him having sailed from Bombay shortly after the death of George's baby brother the year before.

In her 1911 book, the Nelsons of Burnham Thorpe, George's great granddaughter, Mary Eyre Matcham, comments:

"Mr. Savage's portrait, with horse and groom, still hangs [in Newhouse, Wiltshire] near that of his favourite ward".[76]

In the portrait described, Henry Savage gazes, thoughtfully, towards the viewer wearing a dark grey, long-collared jacket, a tricorn hat, cream-coloured breeches, chestnut red garters, and knee-high black boots with brown top-bands. Savage's furrowed brow makes him look world-weary and hyper-vigilant.

In 1763, the Court of Directors of the East India Company allocated three brand-new East Indiamen to Bombay.[77] These were East India Company ships constructed to serve the triple purposes of being trading vessels, men-of-war, and passenger carriers.[78]

In true East India Company capitalist fashion, their ships maximised cargo space. Additionally, such large numbers of poultry and livestock, including cows, pigs, and sheep, were squeezed in that East Indiamen were dubbed "floating farmyards". As a result, conditions on board were cramped for all classes of passenger, and captains made fortunes from private passengers' fares. Even the most expensive cabins were boxy rooms that measured no more than seven-feet long by six-feet wide. At the turn of the nineteenth century, use of these tiny, "best" cabins cost £250 (£11,500 in modern money).[79]

Whilst poorer passengers endured the journey in cramped, unsegregated spaces, George would have enjoyed the relative comfort of a cabin. Did he share this minuscule room with Savage, or did he wake up on his tenth birthday alone in that tiny space with only the rocking of the ocean for company? When the ship passed Mombassa, did he stand on deck to scour the deep blue waves for the shoaling mermaids of his father's tales?

Daniel Defoe's Robinson Crusoe was a popular book for boys of this era. How deeply did Africa's passing coastline capture George's young imagination? What adventures, or treasures, did he daydream of as the ship glided and pitched, slowly, ever onwards past the mysterious African shores?

For passengers and crew alike, the journey from India to England was simultaneously monotonous and fraught with anxiety about disease and attack from hostile ships.[80] Decorum was important and printed regulations were distributed to every passenger, regardless of the accommodation they'd afforded. Commanders were tasked with modelling calm, sober behaviour and resolving disputes.[81]

Wealthy passengers, like George and Henry Savage, dined at the captain's table. The main meal was served in the afternoon, at about two o'clock, after which games were played. A dinner menu from a late eighteenth-century East Indianman comprised "pea soup, roast leg of mutton, hogs' puddings, two fowl, two hams, two ducks, corned round of beef, mutton pies, mutton chops, stewed cabbages and potatoes, followed by an enormous plum pudding and washed down with porter, spruce beer, port, wine, sherry, gin, and rum."[82]

East Indiamen stopped at the island of St Helena, in the South Atlantic, where news could be exchanged between outbound and homebound vessels. For example, when the *Royal Captain* arrived at Portsmouth from Bombay, in July 1763, its captain brought the news that, when he left "St. Helena, which was the 4th of April, the following Ships [and captains] were there, viz. the Royal Charlotte, Clements ; Harcourt, Morrison ; True Briton, Creichton ; Horsendon, Marter ; the Essex, Jackson, and the Albion, Larkins, from China [but the Elizabeth] blew up by Accident in Canton River, and the greatest Part of the Crew perished".[83]

George enrolled at Charterhouse School, near Smithfield in East London, and lodged there as a fee-paying *Saunderite*[84] (boarder in the house of the headmaster) who, at that time, was Samuel Berdmore.[85]

The school was a prestigious institution occupying monastic buildings that had been closed by Henry VIII.[86] Boarders as young as eight were admitted during the eighteenth-century.[87] However, the "Charterhouse Register 1769-1872" records the date that George left, but not when he arrived (presumably because he'd enrolled prior to the register's commencement).

William Makepeace Thackeray – author of *Vanity Fair* – was a Charterhouse pupil in the early 1800s. Thackeray's fictional Grey Friars school in his 1855 novel, *the Newcomes*, provides a vivid description of the real Charterhouse:

"an ancient foundation of the time of James I., still subsisting in the heart of London city... There is an old hall, a beautiful specimen of the architecture of James's time. An old hall? Many old halls, old staircases, old passages, old chambers decorated with old portraits, walking in the midst of which we walk, as it were, in the early seventeenth century". [88]

The beautiful, old hall described by Thackeray was where the scholars dined beneath a ceiling "adorned with arabesque shields and scrolls".[89] A grand, Elizabethan stone fireplace made English winters much more tolerable for students, like George, who were unaccustomed to the cold.

Another former Charterhouse student recollected:

"Food was very good; and on Fridays (perhaps as a protest against Roman Catholicism) we fared especially well [and] had roast lamb and currant tart, or roast pork and apple tart, according

to the season of the year".[90]

Eighteenth-century culture was strongly influenced by ancient Greek texts, such as those of Aristotle and Plato, which informed everything from medicine to mathematics. Consequently, classics featured heavily in school curriculums, in which Greek and Latin were staples alongside the "three Rs" of reading, 'riting, and 'rithmetic. Geography and logic were commonly taught too.[91]

A former pupil recalled, "Cricket was the chief game in the summer quarter; during the rest of the year we had football and hockey". [92]

Every school had its own version of football[93] which, along with hockey and cricket, would have provided vital, physical release for the pupils, whose freedom was strictly limited:

"We were locked up in our bedrooms at night, the windows of which were further secured by iron bars. The doors were unfastened at seven o'clock, and school began at eight... The upper form boys were allowed the privilege of going out from Saturday afternoon till Sunday evening, at nine p.m., provided they received an invitation from parents or friends, which invitation had to be submitted for approval to the headmaster. The lower forms were allowed the same privilege every alternate Saturday."[94]

One of the friends George made at Charterhouse was a Somerset preacher's son,[95] named Charles Warre Malet, who was exactly one month younger than George.

Boarders were permitted to stay during holidays, which were short and infrequent, but "those that could go to relatives would undoubtedly have preferred to do so."[96]

With round trips from England to Bombay taking a year (six months there and six months back) George would have been unable to visit his parents during his enrolment at Charterhouse. He possibly visited Matcham and Bidwell relatives in the west-country. As a young adult, he spoke to his mother about their abundance of fractious, poor relations, whom he hoped would "heal their little differences and renew their affection".[97]

However much he may, or may not, have been acquainted with his west-country kin, George's ever attentive guardian was Henry Savage. [98]

George left Charterhouse in December 1769,[99] aged sixteen, and immediately attached himself to a tutor named J. Sharpe who resided in the Middlesex parish of Bromley-by-Bow: an area east of London that would, later, become infamous for its slums.

At the time of teenaged George's stay, Bromley-by-Bow was a pleasant, rural neighbourhood. There was a scattering of country retreats, some dating back to the early seventeenth century when a Jacobean hunting lodge had been built that had since been converted into two houses. A row of four brick-built almshouses, with a central chapel, had been constructed in 1706.[100]

George spent a year under Sharpe's tutelage mastering double-entry bookkeeping and mathematics, which were specific skills that the East India Company demanded of new recruits. The first quill-written sheet of George's application for East India Company employment is a testimony from his tutor:

"These are to certify that Master George Matcham has been under my care and instruction since Christmas last 1769 & that he has gone through the practical rules of arithmetic & a regular set of Merchant's Accounts, according to the Italian method of Book Keeping by double entry & I believe he understands what he has learnt as well as most young men of his age and experience.
Bromley by Bow
October 29th 1770
J. Sharpe"

The next page of George's application highlights the Company's preference for grovelingly humble recruits:

"To the Honourable the Court of Directors of the United East India Company
The humble petition of George Matcham
Sheweth
That your petitioner having been educated in Writing and Accounts humbly hopes himself qualified to serve your Honours

abroad

And therefore humbly prays your Honours to admit him a Writer in your Service in India wherein he promises to behave himself with all possible Diligence & Fidelity and to give such security as your Honours shall require.

And your petitioner shall ever pray &c
George Matcham"

The final page attached to George's application is a testimony from J. Horwell, Chaplain of Bombay:

"This is to certify who it may concern that George the Son of Simon Matcham by Elizabeth his wife was born the 30th of November 1753 and was baptized the 7th of February 1754 as appears from the parish register of Bombay, given under my hand in Bombay, where no stampt paper is to be had, the 27th day of November 1769" [101]

If George's baptism had been a private Presbyterian ceremony, as it seems to have been, Horwell's testimony was false. Perhaps this was a commonly-used white lie concocted to bypass an impasse between, on the one hand, there having been no Presbyterian minister appointed to Bombay and, on the other hand, a Company stipulation for recruits to prove that they'd been baptised.

George's recruitment application was successful and he returned to Bombay Fort to commence his Company career. His fifty-nine-year-old father, Simon Matcham, had been working as Master Attendant[102] (harbour master)[103] since 1765.

Bombay's harbour was described by a British resident of Bengal, who visited during the 1780s:

"The harbour is capable of containing three hundred sail of ships, with the greatest safety: there is also a most excellent dock, in which ships of his Majesty's squadron, and others, are repaired, refitted, and completely equipped for sea. They build also here all sorts of vessels; and the workmen in the yard are very ingenious and dexterous, not yielding to our best shipwrights in England." [104]

George, who'd grown into a "handsome, enterprising, well-spoken man",[105] quickly progressed upwards through the Company's ranks. In 1771, a year after graduating from his East End tutor, he was listed as a writer living at home.[106] How cosy it would have been to be back in Bombay, and in his family's bungalow, with his father, now the harbour master, present every night. The glass-like *chunam* floors brightened with the exotic fabrics his mother's aesthetic, eagle-eye had swooped into their nest.

Whilst there, George befriended an Indo-Armenian traveler, named Émïn. His portrait shows him with dark skin, black hair neatly swept back from an oval face with pronounced check bones, a dark jacket, and an immaculately white, high collar.[107] [108]

However much George may have relished spending time with his parents, the Company had need of its elite, well-educated recruits, and George was permitted scant time to luxuriate in Bombay. Within a year, the Company jumped him two stages up their hierarchy by making him a senior merchant.[109] This was the highest rank in the Company's commercial service: their ranks being senior merchant, junior merchant, factor then, at the bottom, writer.[110]

The East India Company, originally named "the Company of Merchants of London Trading into the East-Indies"[111] was, at heart, a royally sanctioned merchants' club which protected their interests with a private army and navy (the Bombay Marine).

The 1862 Chambers Dictionary says of them:

"Properly speaking, the Company were only merchants: sending out bullion, lead, quicksilver, woollens, hardware, and other goods to India ; and bringing home calicoes, silk, diamonds, tea, porcelain, pepper, drugs, saltpetre, &c., from thence."[112]

The East India Company was expanding rapidly, both in terms of power and territory. Their private army's 1757 victory at Plassey had paved the way for their domination of Bengal.[113]

Historian, William Dalrymple, noted that, after the Mughal emperor ceded to them in 1765, "the East India Company… ceased to be a conventional corporation, trading [in] silks and spices, and became something much more unusual. Within a few years, 250 company clerks backed by the military force of 20,000 locally recruited Indian soldiers had become the effective rulers of Bengal. An international corporation was transforming itself into an aggressive colonial power."[114]

Chapter Three: East India Company Career

1771 – 1777

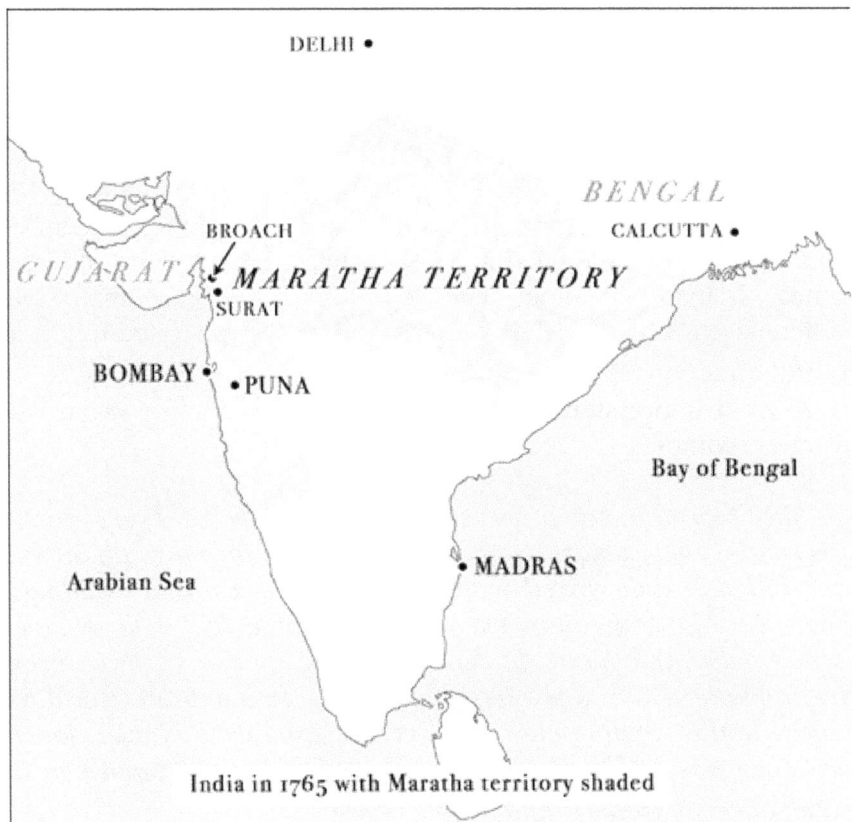

India in 1765 with Maratha territory shaded

George was one of fifty-eight senior merchants listed in Bombay in 1771. Part of their remit was the administration of outlying *factories* (warehouses) in places such as Surat: the key export centre for textiles from the state of Gujarat, north of Bombay, to Europe.

In neighbouring Bengal, a young London man, named Anselm Beaumont, who'd arrived in Calcutta as a lowly free merchant in 1753, was a senior merchant and provincial military storekeeper by 1759, and was resident (governor) of Midnapore by '63, where he was responsible for building a fort.[115]

In Bombay, the main block to the British East India Company claiming mainland territories was the Marathas. The Marathas were an indigenous Hindu culture whose subcontinental Maharashtra empire had displaced the Moguls, then, much to Marathas' own chagrin, their empire had been displaced in turn by the Europeans. [116] In the mid seventeen-hundreds, control of the weakened Maharashtra empire was inherited by a young *peshwa* (ruler) named Madhav Rao – rao being a title equivalent to raja.

Though sickly, Madhav managed to rekindle his empire's former strength by granting autonomy to its dispersed military leaders.[117] Madhav's ploy of delegating power enabled two men –a warrior named Mahadji Scindia and an administrator named Nana Fadnavis– to resurrect Maratha power via conglomerated might and skillful direction.[118]

A vivid impression of the Maratha's military might is provided by an eyewitness:

"the Maratha camp [was] an assemblage of every sort of covering of every shape and colour, spreading for miles on all sides over hill and dale mixed with tents, flags, trees, and buildings... When the Marathas marched, a sea of horse foot and dragoons poured over the country fifteen miles long by two or three broad. Here and there were a few horse with a flag and a drum, mixed with a loose and straggling mass of camels, elephants, bullocks, dancing girls, beggars and buffaloes, troops and followers, lancemen and matchlockmen, traders, and agents".[119]

In 1771, Scindia directed the Maratha war machine to wrest Delhi from Afghan control, then tarried there to set a puppet Mogul on Delhi's throne.[120]

In the meantime, the Maratha's young peshwa, Madhav, became so ill with tuberculosis that he retreated to a Hindu temple close to Puna, in the Western Ghat mountains overlooking Bombay. Madhav died there in 1772[121] leaving a chaos of instability in his wake. With Scindia and the Maratha army still 825 miles away in Delhi, Madhav's successor, Narayan, lasted a mere nine-months until, on the 30th of August 1773, he was assassinated by a rival contender named Raghunath.[122]

The British East India Company was quick to take advantage of the Marathas' temporary weakness. Two-months after Narayan's assassination they set out to capture the fortified port town of Broach (now known as Bharuch), in south-east Gujarat.

George, and his fellows in Bombay, would have been excited to read the colourful, eye-witness account of the Company's November 1773 campaign to seize Broach:

"The army sailed from Bombay on the 1st of November and was landed, together with its stores, and an exceedingly fine train of artillery, within a few miles of Broach on the 12th. It consisted of five and twenty hundred men, Europeans and Seapoys [native soldiers] included, and was commanded by Brigad. Gen. Weddenburn. On the 13th, the General made his approach close to the walls, under cover of the suburbs, and in the course of that day surrounded the town, secured its several gates, and began to erect his batteries : But unfortunately, the day following the 14th, while reconnoitring, he was killed by a shot from the walls. By unhappy accident, the command of the army devolved on Colonel Robert Gordon, then on duty at a detached post. The Colonel, the moment he received the melancholy news of the General's death, repaired to the place where the batteries were erected, and ordered the same works to be carried on, and the same posts to be maintained, which had been by him established. Early on the 16th, three twenty-four pound batteries were opened, which soon silenced the towers that annoyed us most, and after dismantling their defences, the guns were pointed to batter in the breach. On the 18th, the breach being reported practicable, two different attacks were ordered ; and, at the same time, directions were given for a feint being made by the different posts on the remote side of the town, in order to occasion a diversion, and to draw off the attention of the enemy ; and previous to the assault, an incessant fire of shot, shells, and grape were directed towards those places where we supposed the enemy might be lodged : Under cover of this fire, our officers and men mounted

the breach with the most undaunted courage and resolution ; they marched up briskly, and with a surprising alertness and intrepidity, drove the enemy from behind their defences, and afterwards pursued them through the streets, till they drove them entirely out of the town, at a gate on the opposite side to that where we assaulted, and through which the unfortunate Nabob himself made his escape, the moment he perceived our troops on top of the breach. Our loss in storming proved far less than we had reason to expect ; only one officer was killed, and one wounded. During the siege only six officers were killed, and six wounded, and 150 private men killed and wounded."

In conclusion:

"The treasure and effects found in the place belonging to the Nabob and his adherents, will turn out to be very considerable, and the town is well situated for trade, and strongly fortified by nature, so that whether the Company shall keep it, or dispose of it, it may justly be a considered a very valuable acquisition. The Marattahas have an interest in this place [as do] the Governor and Council of Bombay, whose decision we now wait for."[123]

With the Maratha army the better part of a thousand miles away in Delhi, the Company decided to keep Broach. This necessitated the installation of a trusted man as their resident there. East India Company residents were political agents who indirectly controlled regional states, such as Broach and its surrounds, by "advising" its prince, or chief.[124] The man they chose for this job was nineteen-year-old George.[125] This was an enormous responsibility for a teenager. It wasn't long after this that the Company was attacked by Whig politician, Edmund Burke, for "the rapid succession of young boys who govern India."[126]

George's life had been mapped and pinned down from the moment his parents sent him to school in England. His further education in the Company's required subjects of double-entry bookkeeping and mathematics had been part of his preordained career. When he'd returned home to Bombay, the Company viewed him as a freshly-milled cog to strengthen the workings of their ever-expanding, capitalist empire machine.

Unlike Anselm Beaumont, who rose from free merchant to Governor of Midnapore, George didn't need to battle his way up the ranks. The East India Company was not a meritocracy and posts were awarded on a 'who you knew' basis and, with George's mentor, Henry Savage, being one of the East India Company's directors, he certainly knew the right people.

Fresh, young, well-connected men, like George, made the best, new residents because they provided forty, or even fifty years of ongoing service, motivated by the insanely large rewards their residencies generated. So, George was duly packed onto a north-bound ship, bristling with arms, for the nine-day, 207 mile/333 kilometre sail through pirate riddled seas[127] and up the river Narmada to Broach where, as a teen, he became the port town's effective king.

Picturing India as an inverted triangle with teardrop-shaped Sri Lanka on the bottom right, and the Kathiawar peninsula, shaped like an elephant's ear, extending into the Arabian Sea on the top left, Broach is on the west coast, not far south from where the Kathiawar peninsula splits off.

In ancient times, in the days of the Egyptian pharaohs, the chief exports from Broach were wheat, teak and ebony harvested from the thick forests of the Narmada valley[128] which were populated with "wolves, leopards, bears, pangolins, hyenas, flying squirrels, blackbucks, cheetahs, and tigers".[129]

In more recent history, Broach's prolific production of calico had attracted British interest a hundred-and-fifty-years before George's residency, when, "on 19 January 1618 the English factors at Surat seconded that if trade be followed betwixt [Broach] and Surat, a residence will be absolutely necessary."[130]

A French traveler named Thévenot, who visited in the late 1600s when trade was controlled by the Dutch, noted:

"The fortress of Broach is large and square, standing on a Hill, which makes it to be seen a great distance. It is one of the chief strengths of the Kingdom [of Gujarat], and has had heretofore a very large Jurisdiction. The Town lies upon the side, and at the foot of the Hill, looking towards the River Nerdaba [sic]. It is environed

with Stone-Walls about three Fathom high, which are flanked by large round Towers at Thirty or Thirty five paces distant from one another... The Hill being high and hard to be mounted, it might be a very easie matter to put the fortress in a condition not to fear Attack, but at present it is so much slighted that there are several great breaches in the walls to the Land side, which no body thinks of repairing. "[131]

In the words of a mid-eighteenth-century East India Company man, identified only as "Mr. Tayler":

"Broach is the key to the rich kingdom of Gujarat where most of our Europe investment is provided, and from whence all the best cotton is brought for the consumption of India and China. Behind Gujarat lie the extensive provinces of Ajmer and Jaisalmer, which formerly took up a large quantity of our woolens and other European Commodities". [132]

Of Gujarat's fine cottons, the most prized European export was *bafta*, which was unique to Broach.[133] Bafta production is mentioned in Thévenot's journal: "The *Bazards* or Market-places are in a great Street at the foot of the Hill ; and there it is that those Cotton-Stuffs are made, which are called Baftas, and which are sold in so great plenty in the Indies... The River-water is excellent for the whitening of Cloaths [sic], and they are brought from all parts to be whitened there."[134]

Like it or not, and overwhelmed or not, the Company had catapulted George into Broach for the purposes of maximising profit from the local workforce and, indirectly, influencing decisions made by the ruling Marathas.[135]

George –whose skill was in accountancy not war– wouldn't have forgotten that Scindia wanted Broach. Scindia had recently reminded everyone in the Subcontinent of his mettle by chasing the Afghans out of Delhi. The contingent of East India Company army assigned to Broach would be hard-pushed to withstand the Maratha's army when Scindia brought them back to India's west shore.

With Scindia's imminent return hovering as an ever-present

black cloud, George set about overseeing the profitability of Broach's calico production. This may, initially, have felt like an easy option compared with facing the Maratha army. However, the cloth-making process required the labour of thousands of local workers[136] to churn out piece-goods in a similar fashion to present-day sweatshops. Though mercantile and privileged, George was deeply moved by "the misery of the people, and waste of fine agricultural land." He filled journals with ambitious plans to improve conditions for Broach's cotton workers.[137]

On top of this, when not worried for the local workforce or the thunderous approach of Scindia's elephants, young George likely felt bored stiff of being stuck, month after month, and year after year, in the backwater of Broach. After all, he was so innately restless that, in later years, Horatio Nelson's wife described him as "ever the most unsettled man alive".[138]

An alleviation of George's compound headache came through Raghunath, the man who'd made himself peshwa by assassinating Narayan. Raghunath was keen to ally with the British because Narayan's widow had borne a posthumous son. An alliance of twelve Maratha ministers had declared Narayan's infant son peshwa in Raghunath's stead and made themselves regents. One of these twelve new regents was Nana Fadnavis, the man who'd worked with Scindia to resurrect the Marathas' power. Deposed, Raghunath had fled the Maratha capital of Puna and gone into hiding.[139] Neither Nana nor Scindia supported British rule, making the ousted Raghunath Rao a useful political ally for the Company. What happened next is described in a 1779 publication, entitled *an analysis of the political history of India:*

"The English presidency of Bombay took part with Raganout-Row in consequence of his solicitations, and entered into an alliance with him. The cessions he made to the Company by that treaty were indisputably great, and in such light were they seen by the directors of the Company in England".[140]

This bonanza of cessions Raghunath handed the Company entailed several drafts, put forward by both parties, and culminated with the Treaty of Surat, which was signed on the 6th of March

1775.[141]

No record has come to light of George witnessing Raghunath signing the treaty. But, as Resident of Broach, the Company would likely have ordered George to attend the signing at Surat –which was a short sail south from Broach– because one of the "indisputably great" cessions was for the Company to receive revenue from Broach, as well as from the host port of Surat.

A British travelogue, published in 1772, describes Surat in detail:

"SURAT is situate on the continent, a little to the northward of Bombay, about fifteen miles up the river Tappee, on the right-hand side as you go up. The river itself is nothing remarkable ; but the city on the banks of it is perhaps one of the greatest instances in the known world, of the power of trade to bring in so little time wealth, arts and population, to any spot where it can be brought to settle [the town of Surat is] one of the most considerable in the world, not only for trade but size, being almost as large, and populous as London, within the walls, and contains many good houses, according to the Indian architecture. A wall was soon, after its taking the form of a town, built around it, to defend it from the insults of the Morattoes [Marathas], who had twice pillaged".[142]

Raghunath was forty years old and, according to a portrait that's believed to have been painted during his lifetime, if not from life, slim with a long nose and a neatly trimmed moustache. His biceps and neck are shown adorned with strings of dark beads. His head is covered by a small, white turban. He has a ceremonial axe in his right-hand and is sitting cross-legged with a ramrod-straight back that doesn't look like it needs any support but, nonetheless, is cushioned by a large bolster.

The treaty's signing wouldn't have been as grand an affair as the Anglo-Indian ones that were painted for posterity, such as –fifteen years later– George's school chum, Charles Warre Malet, signing a treaty in Puna with the peshwa of the day. Now, in 1775, Raghunath was deposed so he had no great court to attend him. However, being peshwa/rao/raj/king –call it what you will– was all important to him, and he'd have presented himself, cross-legged, with as much pomp and regal dignity as he could muster.

Raghunath's reality, though, was that of a weakened loser. His own people had deposed him and the British wrung far more from him than they gave. In addition to revenue from Broach and Surat, Raghunath ceded "Bassein, Salsette, Jambusar, Olpad and [other] small islands adjacent to Bombay" in perpetuity to the British.[143] In return, the Company granted him 2,500 men to retake Puna from Nana Fadnavis and the eleven other regents.[144] [145]

As George sailed back to Broach, "a small Way to the Northward of Surat",[146] he'd have felt immense relief, not least because Raghunath had been granted 2,500 British soldiers to keep Scindia at bay.

The Company –both the Council of Bombay and Court of Directors in London– were absolutely delighted to have made such a good deal with Raghunath, especially with regard to land gains. Alas, though, the Company in Bengal had other ideas and Raghunath's days were numbered.

As put by the 1779 *analysis of the political history of India:*

"the Government-general of Bengal, viewing matters through a different medium… disapproved under every circumstance of the treaty concluded with Raganout-Row [and] ordered it to be destroyed ; and had even sent Colonel Upton to Poonah [Puna], who concluded a fresh treaty with the opposite party.

The English forces were in consequence recalled ; and Raganout-Row, deserted by all, and particularly by the English". [147]

The Council of Bombay were outraged when, on the 1st of March 1776 –less than a year after their Surat Treaty had been signed– Bengal's Colonel Upton signed a counter treaty with Raghunath's enemy, Nana Fadnavi, the Maratha regent in Puna.

In London, the Court of Directors were far from happy too and sent a strongly worded missive to Calcutta:

"We cannot but disapprove of your mode of interfering by sending an ambassador directly to Poona, without first consulting the Governor and Council of Bombay and of your determination to disavow and invalidate the Treaty concluded by them." [148]

George knew it was only a matter of time until Scindia seized Broach. Never having claimed a military inclination, it would be understandable if he felt queasy imagining Scindia charging Broach's walls with his trumpeting war elephants and a valley-wide army of angry Marathas.

In fact, as it was at about this time that George fell severely ill, the stress may have weakened his immune system.

Part Two:
Overland Journeys
(1777–1785)

Chapter Four: First Overland Journey:
The Persian Gulf to Egypt

1777 – 1780

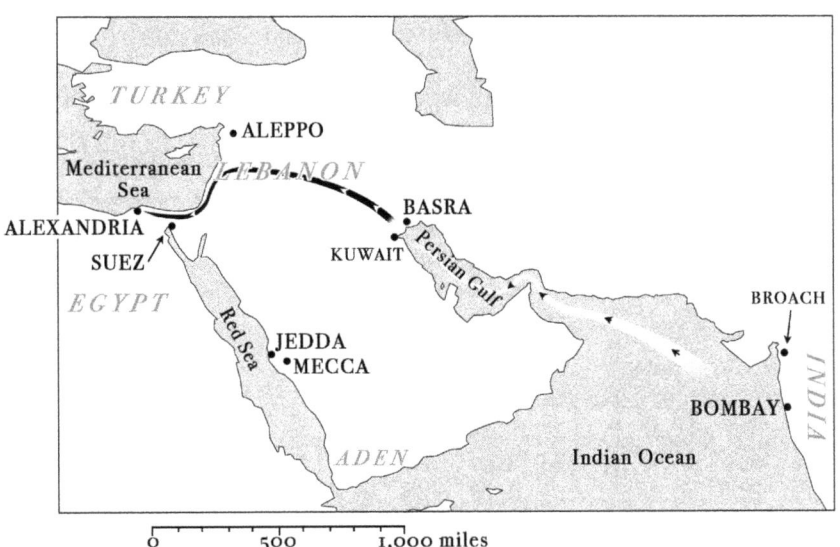

George's father, Simon Matcham's career peaked in 1774 when, aged sixty-four, he replaced Samuel Hough as Superintendent Marine of the East India Company (the equivalent of Admiral)[150] as well as becoming Senior Member of the Council of Bombay.[151] He had scant time, though, to enjoy these pinnacles of Company supremacy because he was dead within two years. His cause of death is unknown, but Bombay's parish record book has a note that his burial took place on the 22nd of June 1776.[152]

A year after his father's death, twenty-three-year-old George was in Bombay, laid low with a severe illness.

His widowed mother, who'd lived in Bombay since babyhood, decided to retire to England and embarked on the six-month sea journey around the Cape of Good Hope.[153]

George, it seems, was also of a mind to relocate to England, because the bulk of his, and his mother's, valuable possessions were packed and stowed on a ship bound for Britain's distant shores.[154]

No doubt reluctant to spend further time in Broach awaiting Scindia's army, George embraced the opportunity of seeing his widowed mother safely settled in England. But, instead of sailing with her, twenty-three-year-old George decided to trace the ancient caravan trails across the Arabian peninsula from the Persian Gulf to Egypt.

The overland route was of keen interest to the East India Company, whose intelligence between India and England was constricted to the same, slow route around Africa that George's mother was taking. As a result, the Company "frequently in India had no intelligence from England for eight or nine months".[155] An incident during the Seven Years War, of 1756–1763, had made them realise that their snail-speed communication might easily cause their doom.

The Seven Years War had been sparked when Prussia wrested the province of Silesia from the Austrian Hapsburg Empire. England, who'd sided with Prussia, had been simultaneously warring France for possession of North American and Indian territories.[156] When Spain secretly allied with the French in 1760,[157] the British in India didn't "hear of the rupture with Spain for upwards of eleven months".[158]

James Capper, an East India Company army officer, noted that, during this same time, the French had "regularly transmitted advices by Suez, to and from India, by which means they frequently anticipated us in intelligence, and of course counteracted our operations".[159]

Fortunately, Spain "being slow in their deliberations, and by no means quick in their operations, took no advantage of [the Company's] want of information".

Unlike Spain, Britain was quick to take advantage of changes in allegiance and used their superior naval power to grab Spanish-owned Manila, in the Philippines, and Havana, in Cuba. However, neither party wanted to sustain hostilities and, in a treaty signed at the end of the Seven Years War, England agreed to swap Manila and Havana for Spanish-owned

Florida.[160]

Realisation that Spain could have decimated the East India Company's tally of territories was a loud wake up call. As James Capper put it, "we may find all our settlements invested before we know they are in danger of being attacked and hear of them being totally lost before we relieve them."[161]

The Company in India needed to know, as quickly as possible, of threats from Europe. If an adventurous young man, such as George Matcham, found a viable route across the Arabian peninsula, news could reach them from Europe three times more quickly than when carried around the Cape of Good Hope.[162]

According to George's contemporary, James Capper, the Red Sea "route to India was once the most frequented of any, but after the discovery of the passage around the Cape of Good Hope, it was neglected by most European nations, and almost entirely abandoned to the Mohammedans",[163] whose holy city, Mecca, lay equidistant between Aden and Suez.

Three years before, in 1774, the East India Company had attempted to procure the Red Sea route from Suez to Aden, in present-day Yemen. The Company's ambition to secure the Red Sea route had been the brainchild of Warren Hastings, the Governor General of Bengal,[164] who'd "proposed to some merchants in Calcutta to send a ship to the Red Sea, loaded with a proper assortment of goods for the Turkish markets ; and … advised their being sent directly to Suez ; by which means he expected to establish a new trade equally beneficial for [the Company] and the Turks in general, and also for opening a new channel for transmitting intelligence backwards and forwards, between India and Europe."

Unfortunately for Hastings and the East India Company, the Turkish merchants had been "apprehensive of suffering by the prices of India goods being lowered in their markets" because it would undercut their profits from their customary trade route across the Arabian peninsula between Basra and Aleppo.[165] The merchants obtained an edict from Sultan Abdülhamid I to stop British merchants using the Suez route.[166] The embargo was so effective that Company men attempting to reach Cairo from Suez were "plundered and murdered by a body of Arabs".[167]

The press circulated a letter, that had been penned in Cairo in October 1775, which revealed that the Pacha of Jedda had now blocked all Europeans from docking at Suez:

"The Pacha of [J]edda has made very strong representations to the Porte, upon the prejudice it is both to him and the Cheriff of Mecca, that

the English vessels touch at Suez. He fears that the vessels of that nation, which come now to [J]edda, may for the future take the same route, which would deprive him of a duty of ten percent, which he divides with the Cheriff, and which is the only revenue of his place... An order is likewise sent here which forbids the porte of Suez from admitting any European vessels whatever. [168]

An alternative, safe route to Egypt was certainly needed, both for transporting merchandise and transmitting intelligence as rapidly as possible.

The Company was fearful of France forming a coalition with the Dutch East India Company. Both nations coveted Britain's "extensive and valuable possessions in the East Indies" but were individually powerless to challenge Britain's dominion. The French had "no port nearer to the Peninsular of India, than the island of Mauritius". Conversely, the Dutch, whose navy was weak, possessed the Sri Lankan port of Trincomalee, which was "by far the best situated in all of India" for "annoying" the British. [169]

Although the need to reach Egypt safely was stronger than ever, when George told his friends that he was going to seek a route, they were horrified because George was severely ill with a damaged lung. His friends begged his doctor's opinion hoping he'd order George to stay safely at home, but the medic thwarted them by pronouncing, simply, that George's health was so bad that it didn't matter if he stayed or went. [170]

For good or ill, George ventured forth, no doubt itching for adventure after his pasty-faced, sun-shaded, no frills upbringing under East India Company rule.

Somewhat ironically, the first part of George's overland expedition was by sea, and may have been similar the journey a British traveller, William Francklin, took from Bombay to the Persian Gulf a decade later:

"I at length embarked on board an Arabian ship, bound for Bussora [Basra] in company with Captain Mitchell and Lieuts. James and Curry, of the Madras military establishment, who were on their way to Europe over land. We had on board an exact epitome of Asia, being a collection of Armenians, Persians, Arabians, Ethiopians, Jews, and Indians, who created much confusion of tongues as at the building of the tower of Babel."

The sea route turned into the Persian Gulf, pausing at Muscat, whose harbour entrance was "truly picturesque [having] a bold shore, with a range of high mountains extending about sixty miles in length... to form a very grand prospect ; the ruggedness of the rocks marking very characteristically the country of Arabia."[171]

Although the Turkish merchants' route ran from the Persian Gulf port of Basra to Aleppo, it's unlikely that George started his own journey there because the port had been closed to the Company since 1773, following plague and Persian occupation.[172] George may have landed in nearby Kuwait instead.

James Capper, recommended the following kit to Brits attempting to cross the desert:

"a strong second-hand post-chaise [enclosed carriage] which will cost between thirty and forty pounds : a large trunk, a small one behind, and a chaise seat will carry as much or more baggage than is necessary for two gentlemen, and one servant ; allowing each gentleman a Turkish dress, two coats, a dozen and half of shirts, two dozen pair of common, and one dozen pair of silk stockings, two pairs of shoes, and other necessaries in the same proportion. This perhaps may be thought a scanty allowance ; for generally travellers prepare for their first excursion on the continent, as if nothing could be procured out of their own country".[173]

Turkish dress was a loose, Islamic-style gown, which Europeans donned "to avoid insults from the populace".[174]

George –accompanied by unnamed friends– had no post-chaise and, likely, few pairs of silk stockings stowed in his baggage, for he travelled light, with only a small Persian rug to sleep on.

It surely must have been worrying to traverse the Middle Eastern desert in full awareness of how murderously brutal the Arabs could be to English travellers, but George pressed ever onwards, seemingly undaunted.

He noted in his journal that his party was "compelled to ride on untam'd horses at a rate of sixty or seventy miles a day, sometimes exposed to a burning sun".[175] With inland temperatures on the Arabian peninsula reaching over 40°C/105°F,[176] the near-thousand-mile crossing would have taxed anyone, let alone an inexperienced, single-lunged traveler whose doctor thought him already as good as dead.

Capper advised British explorers to provision themselves with several pounds of tea and portable soup:

"Those who are fond of tea, and are nice about the quantity of it, as many Englishmen are, will do well to take two or three pounds with them ; for that which they will find in the inns abroad or any where on the way will be rather coarse and unpalatable. It may also be proper to take a few

cakes of portable soup... to which may be added a bottle or two of essence of sellery, with which and a little vermicelli or rice, a person may prepare a good mess of soup on the Desert, with the same fire that serves the Arabs to boil their coffee. [177]

George's diet was infinitely simpler. As his destination was Egypt, not Aleppo, his south-westerly route veered far from the water-giving river Euphrates, likely heading directly for Damascus, as described in a book published in 1800:

"The shortest route [from the Persian Gulf] is that of Damascus, which crosses the interior of the desert ; but it is less followed, because the caravans are liable to perish there with thirst." [178]

George's solution was to subsist "entirely on mare's milk". [179] He then seems to have passed into mountainous Lebanon – a short hop coastwards from Damascus – because he noted in his journal that he was sometimes exposed "to the cutting air of the mountains, and often obliged "to sleep in the open air." [180]
Capper advised:

"As to medicines it is universally allowed the fewer he is obliged to take the better, still however he should consider his condition, and if he is subject to any particular disorder, he will do well to consult his physician about carrying with him a small quantity of those medicines he is most likely to require. The most healthy and robust are not exempt from accidents, therefore every person may take from England half a dozen papers of James's powders, and two pounds of bark, which are cheap, and easily carried, and besides the former is seldom to be procured so good in any foreign country". [181]

However, despite George's collapsed lung, exposure to the elements agreed with him so well that his lung healed (although it never entirely recovered). [182]
George must have felt elation when he succeeded in reaching Egypt from the north-east, thus thwarting the sultan's embargo, and the murderous Arabs patrolling Suez. What joy to have survived the desert crossing and found a way for Company men to transport merchandise to Egypt without having their throats slit, or worse!
George's first, exhilarating glimpse of Cairo may have been similar to Capper's:

"When about three miles from Cairo, from the summit of an Hill, you perceive that city situated in a fertile valley, and watered by the Nile, which meanders at the side of, and beyond its walls through a rich country as far as the eye can see."

If the weather wasn't hazy, as it had been for Capper, the vista George beheld would have included the "Pyramids in the background of this charming landscape."

Unlike the towns of Europe, Cairo could be entered without being "stopt and interrogated", though guides immediately escorted western visitors to their consul.[183] George –again like Capper– may have rushed to one of Cairo's bathhouses for his health and the pleasure of having the layers of accumulated desert grime scrubbed off, and travel-soreness massaged from his tired limbs.[184]

George's triumphant joy for reaching Egypt was, though, soon crushed. He lamented to his old school friend, Charles Warre Malet, "The wretched Egyptians are sadly oppressed by an aristocracy, and as there is no security in the Government, it is poor as to adventitious wealth, tho' rich in its native fertility".[185]

Being a mercantile East India Company man to the core, George enthusiastically sought the company of Egyptian country merchants, but was compelled to travel to their homes, ignominiously, on the back of a donkey because Christians weren't permitted to ride horses. He was saddened to learn that these Egyptian "merchants could not even raise money enough to purchase the Italian cargoes".[186]

George and his companions journeyed from Cairo "down the hill to Alexandria" where he noticed that:

"The old walls are still remaining, flanked by towers, a noble monument of antiquity. The reservoirs of water which the canal supplied occupied as much space below as the city did above... The beautiful and lofty column of Pompey, the obelisks, the many fragments of granite porphyry, and other marble with which the ground is everywhere covered, occasions a melancholy reflection of what this city once was and what it now is. We cannot sufficiently regret these despicable tyrants chacing away from this happy country the arts, sciences, and commerce ; for what it still retains of the latter may be compared to the sweeping of a great warehouse".[187]

From Alexandria, he took a ship across the Mediterranean Sea and "dawdled home through Europe", where he displayed cultural prejudice by declaring the countries he passed through "the height of civilisation in contrast to the East".[188] Having successfully traversed the overland route from Iraq to western Europe, he sailed to England and joined his mother in her new county home of Charlton Place, close to Canterbury in the south-eastern county of Kent.[189] [190]

His mother's rented country house was very grand. It had a new extension comprising a row of pillars that supported a central pediment –a triangular, ancient Greek-style gable.[191] The effect was so spectacular that the rock supergroup, Pink Floyd, staged a concert there in 1970 and, when put on the market in 2021, the house was valued at £3.5 million.[192]

George, still restless, toured England and Ireland, penning Indian-style sketches as he went "for his mother's amusement."[193]

George, like his mother, wanted to stay in England and not go back to Broach, Bombay, or any other precarious subcontinental enclave. He wrote to friends in India:

"If the bulk of our fortune should come home safe, I mean to buy an estate jointly with my mother. I shall then marry and have three principal sources of amusement ; my wife, farming and hunting. If our fortune should not be happily remitted, I must again betake myself to Bombay."[194]

Alas, "the bulk" of George and his mother's fortunes failed to reach England safely, forcing them to postpone buying a joint estate, and necessitating George returning to India to re-accumulate enough wealth for his, and his mother's, comfortable retirement.

Chapter Five: Second Overland Journey:
Scanderoon to Basra

1780 – 1783

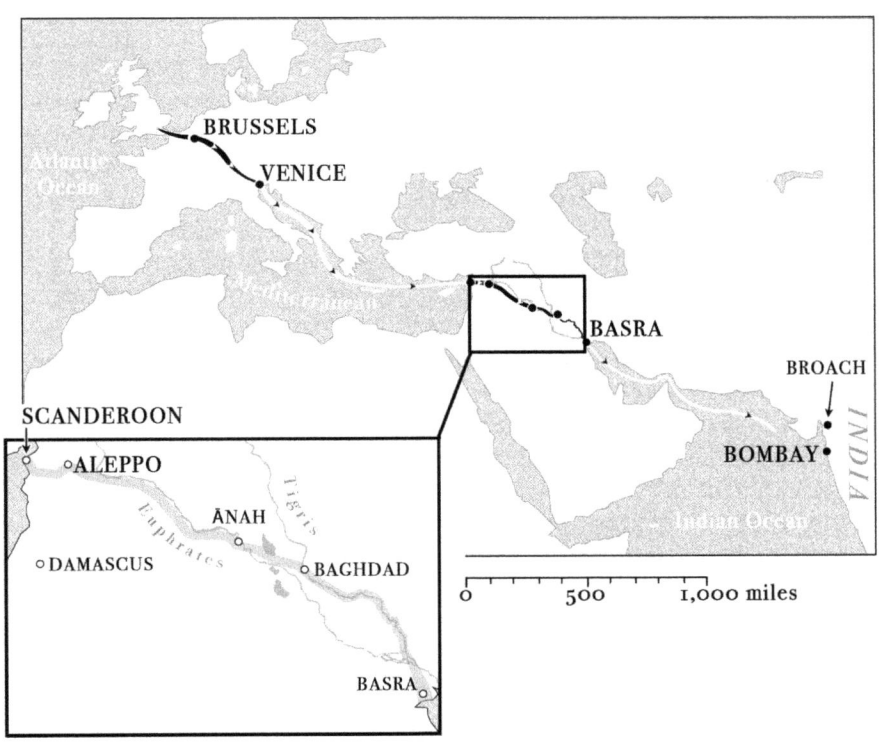

> *"O! while thy secrets I explore,*
> *And traverse all thy regions o're,*
> *The patient camel I bestride—*
> *May no ill hap his steps betide!"*
> *(Eyles Irwin, Ode to the Desart, 1777).* [195]

Despite the bad luck that his, and his mother's, fortunes had been lost at sea, George –ever positive– embraced the opportunity to scout out another overland route: this time the Turkish merchants' trail to Basra from Aleppo, which was a major Middle Eastern city which George would have been eager to visit.

The East India Company was still in need of safe passage over the Arabian peninsula. Grisly reports of merchants murdered near Suez were flooding the press. For example, in 1779, English, French and Dutch merchants were dumped in the desert, naked, to die of heat exposure. The few who survived had been forced to drink their own urine:

"Cairo, June 30. Four vessels arrived this year from Suez, two English, one Dutch, and one Danish. Mr. Vande Velden, a Dutchman, formerly in the Dutch East India Service, which he had quitted for reasons not publickly known, came to Calcutta under the protection of the English, and from thence embarked on board one of his own vessels for Suez. In going over the desert of Suez, in his way to Cairo, in company with several persons, English and French, they were unfortunately plundered by Arabs, about 25 miles from Suez. Mr Vande Velden, Capt. Barrington, and Mr. Inkers, with two Frenchmen, were killed by being exposed naked to the rays of the scorching sun ; their treasure was loaded upon 400 camels, and was valued at a million piastres ; four of their company were saved by an honest Arab, who brought them to this place, after their passing two days without any nourishment, and being obliged to drink their own water to quench their thirst. This robbery is said to have been done by the Arabs, out of revenge, because the Bey of Cairo will oblige people to use his camels to transport their merchandise instead of those belonging to the Arabs." [196]

Two months later, Saunders's News Letter printed an extract of a letter from Alexandria:

"The commerce which the English merchants had established between the Red Sea and the Mediterranean, for the supplying of Europe with the productions of India by the old way, is in the greatest danger of being destroyed by the multiplicity of dangers and impediments to which it lately has been subject." [197]

George set sail for the continent and, in September 1780, dashed a note to his mother from Brussels:

"I shall certainly not remain two years in India without some

considerable employment... I preserve my health, am perfectly reconciled to returning and feel myself quite happy. "[198]

From Belgium, he travelled south and crossed the Alps into northern Italy. He arrived in Venice, on the north shore of the Adriatic Sea, as winter was setting in, hoping to find a ship willing to carry him to Scanderoon[199] (İskenderun) in south-eastern Turkey.

The Mediterranean was choppy and unpredictable during winter months,[200] and the sea journey from Venice to Scanderoon was no small hop, being a total distance of 1,614 nautical miles,[201] traversing the entire east coast of Italy, the west coast of Greece, past Crete, then along the south coast of modern-day Turkey.

Unsurprisingly, George found no ships willing, or able, to transport him to Scanderoon. He wasn't the only British adventurer stranded there when, on the 6th November 1780, fellow explorers, Eyles Irwin and Smyth, arrived in Venice.[202] Irwin and Smyth found, "Mr. Matcham, with Messrs. Beet and Scot in his suite" all waiting for a ship to carry them to Scanderoon.[203]

John Beete was an attorney at law[204] who, like George and the other men seeking passage from Venice, wanted to reach India more quickly than sailing around the Cape of Good Hope allowed.

Irwin's party had also travelled to Venice via Brussels but, unlike George, possessed passes to speed their journey because were couriering urgent Company despatches.[205]

Irwin was two years George's senior and, like him, had been born in Company-ruled India, then educated in an English boarding school. Another similarity was the restlessness of their hearts. As well as being an intrepid explorer, Irwin was a prolific writer. He kept a detailed journal of this travels and published several volumes of poetry.[206] His portrait, painted by an upcoming artist, named George Romney, shows him with unpowdered, mouse brown hair that's styled, as per fashion, with a single line of curls flipped over his ears. His youthful face is well-proportioned with wide, flat cheeks, small brows over almond-shaped eyes, a straight nose, and the beginning of a soft smile on his lips.[207]

Venice had recently become a key tourist destination and must-see stop for wealthy young adults undertaking *the grand tour* of Europe,[208] which had established stops and has been compared to a travel-based "cultural finishing school" for those who could afford it.

The city's popularity was rooted not only in its architecture and canals, but in its pleasure-seeking, liberal culture where British visitors –even ladies– could roam unhindered by etiquette or servants. Coffee houses and bookshops satisfied the needs of intellectuals, whilst music resonated from gondolas plying the waterways, and theatres that rarely closed.[209] Irwin noted that, although he was disappointed to have little time in Venice, he and Smyth "made the best use of [their] time to gratify the curiosity, which so singular a city had excited" in their minds.[210]

The captain who'd agreed to transport Irwin and his party to Syria, refused to leave port "during the present appearance of the weather". Fortunately, the British consul, Mr. Watson, intervened on account of the urgency of their despatches, and the ship's captain, reluctantly, set sail on the 14th of November.[211]

Major Nicol, another Company man wanting to get to India from Venice, had attached himself to Irwin's party and departed with them. However, George and his friends, whose business wasn't urgent, were forced to wait out the winter in Venice.

At long last, in the early spring of 1781, they found a captain willing to carry them to Scanderoon. They may have provisioned themselves with good wine for the ten-day voyage,[212] in line with James Capper's advice to Brits sailing for the Orient.[213]

George, Beete and Scot arrived in Scanderoon in early March, when temperatures hadn't yet reached the heights which, exacerbated by heat "reflection from those mountains", drove the port's European inhabitants to spend May through to October in the cooler, high altitude town of Bylan.

In Scanderoon, they would have stayed in the house of the British consul, William Sholl, and his wife, Maria Teresa.[214] Food was plentiful during the colder months when wild fowl massed on the surrounding marshes and the sea teemed with fish. Pork was delivered, surreptitiously, to Scanderoon's European population by their Muslim neighbours, who hunted wild pigs on the mountains and sold the meat to Christians "as privately as possible, lest they should be reviled by their brethren, who hold it an abomination to have a swine touch their garments."[215]

George, Beete and Scot's next destination was the Syrian city of Aleppo. Swift-footed couriers, employed by Europeans, were able to run the eighty-mile mountain crossing in forty-eight hours to deliver salted cod to Aleppo and bring salted beef back. Otherwise, the route around the mountains, which was forty miles longer, took four days on horseback, or eight days by caravan.[216]

Their route took them along "a very stony and bad road"[217] etched across "a chalky plain".[218] From a distance of two or three miles, Aleppo emerged as "a striking object... of vast extent. The mosques, the minarets, and numerous cupolas [made] a splendid spectacle ; and the flat roofs of the houses… situated on the hills, rising one behind another [formed] a succession of hanging terraces, interspersed with cypress and poplar trees."[219] Towering above all, the castle standing "on the highest hill" made a "good figure at a distance".[220]

Parched earth had now given way to a lusher, arable vista from which "little whitened villas" peeped "from among the vineyards on either hand."[221]

Aleppo's sprawling suburbs were "inhabited by Greeks, Armenians, and others of the Christian persuasion",[222] as well as *Turkmans, Kurdeens* (Kurds), Arabs and others.[223] Here, large gardens extended outwards from the city's ancient walls, watered by "A sluggish, deep rivulet, called the Coich [Quaiq]," whose banks were crowned with poplar trees, but was "of little other use than watering the gardens of the inhabitants, and giving a pastoral appearance to the confines of the desart [sic] which stretches almost to the very walls of Aleppo".[224]

"Besides the wall, the city was fortified with a broad, deep ditch ; which [was] in most places filled up with rubbish, or converted into garden grounds", that "by gradual encroachments [had] been raised on the ruins of the old ramparts". During the spring, when the stagnant water was less pungent, "Arabs of the desert" known as *bidoweens* camped around the city walls.[225]

The ruling Ottoman Turks called Europeans *Franks*. When visiting Aleppo, or anywhere else in the Ottoman Empire, Franks needed to swiftly enlist protection from a consul. Otherwise, "should he neglect to do this, and any Turk should insult him, he would have no redress." Franks also had to wear hats at all times, "whether he use the European dress, or should find it more comfortable to assume the long dress (as the dress of the country is called), since, in case of non-compliance, should he beaten by a Turk, or otherwise insulted, his consul could not obtain any redress for him, as the Turk who abused him would say that they did not know him to be a Frank."[226]

Therefore, every European George saw wandering the environs of Aleppo would have worn a hat or wig, even if otherwise dressed "in the Eastern habit", which many French and Italian residents chose to wear.[227]

Being Brits, George and his friends would have sought the English consul, who, along with Aleppo's three other consuls –French, Venetian and Dutch– was permitted to reside within the city.

When George, dusty from his journey, passed through one of the ancient gates piercing the city's crumbled, flower-planted walls, he was delivered into a sprawl of stone buildings and lofty bazaars, between which well-maintained roads, with raised pavements, teemed with Allepo's multi-ethnic populace, whose "normal gait was slow and grave." Aromas of coffee and Persian tobacco, accompanied by strains of oriental music, wafted from myriad, gaudily painted coffee houses, whilst, five times a day, calls for prayer harmonised from the city's many mosques.[228] [229]

The English consul's domain took up the entire side of a great *khan* – former caravansary– and was accessed through iron gates, guarded by a porter.[230] Britain's custom's house occupied the ground-floor, and the consul's residence was accessed via stairs. Both floors were stone-built and "strongly arched", with no "wood in their composition, except the window frames." The floors, like the walls, were fashioned from stone, or plain brick, but softened, here and there, with rugs.[231]

The English consul, John T. Abbott,[232] was half-Greek, nearing fifty, and well-versed in diplomacy because his father had been the English consul in Istanbul.[233] John T. Abbott's Swiss wife, Marianna, was much younger[234] and a very amiable hostess.[235] George, Beete and Scot would, therefore, have been put at ease by their hosts' cordial welcomes. They were thoroughly surprised, though, to discover that Eyles Irwin and his party were there too, as they'd expected them to be far ahead, and likely already in India.

Irwin's party had been delayed through treachery. When their ship from Venice had run into a winter storm, its captain had tricked them into staying on board while he evacuated himself and his crew.[236] To cut a long story short, the captain's foul play had cost Irwin's party valuable weeks, and an unexpected Christmas spent in Greece.[237] Then, upon reaching Aleppo, on the 21st of February, with their "first care" having been to "provide a means to cross the vast desert", they couldn't find any camels. The dirth of dromedaries had been caused by the Basra caravan setting out "later than usual, and no tidings had yet been received of its motions." Irwin and Smyth had enlisted the aid of a sheik, named Abdul Azah, to fetch camels from Damascus, but the journey there and back took two or more weeks,[238] hence their presence in Aleppo when George Matcham and his friends arrived on the 11th of March 1781.

Although the consul's first-floor home was spacious enough to have its own chapel,[239] it was crowded with Brits waiting to cross the desert to Basra. In addition to George, Beete, Scot and Irwin's party –which comprised Smyth, Major Nicol and Irwin's servant, Richard Segur– there were Irwin's friends, Messrs. Burke and Churchill, who'd found their way to Aleppo following their own series of adventures and brought with them "a French cook of Mr. Burke's". Despite all these unexpected guests, the consul's wife, Marianna, treated them with cheerful politeness[240] and they enjoyed many pleasant hours "in the hospitable society of Aleppo", [241] which was uniformly European, for *Franks* had "little or no social intercourse with the Turks".

The European population of Aleppo comprised settlers from England, France, Venice, the Netherlands and Tuscany, whose lingua franca was Italian.[242] They co-existed harmoniously, and enjoyed reciprocal "card parties, weekly concerts, and sometimes, in the Carnaval, masquerades [and] Neither competition in trade nor the intervention of national ruptures in Europe, broke off sociable intercourse in Syria… the private relation of men brought together by accident in a distant country, whom choice had led to form friendly connections" wasn't sundered by European wars.[243]

"The Tables of the Europeans [were] well supplied with provisions of all kinds". Sea fish was a delicacy that could "only be procured fresh in the winter." Their cooks, and most other servants, were Armenian, but had "been taught French or English cookery, and only now and then, by way of variety" produced Armenian dishes.[244]

Aleppo homes were two-storied, with a flat roof that could be used for dining and, even, sleeping, but not between October and March when – perhaps surprisingly for a desert city– it was extremely chilly. During these months, reciprocal entertainment was held indoors, except on Saturdays, or sometimes twice weekly, when the consuls and merchants had a custom of airing their "excellent horses" and dining out, under tents "on some green spot on the banks of the river Coic." Participants took turns paying for liquor and food, which was prepared "under a small tent, called a cook's tent". As many as "five or six such tents" might be pitched, "some two or three, others four or five miles from the city."[245] [246]

Otherwise, life for the Europeans in Aleppo was "rather sedentary" with many hours "spent in the counting house, or in indolent lounging on the sopha".[247]

George would have enjoyed exploring the ancient city's streets and, more to the point, its wealth of mercantile goods, whose eye-popping plentitude would have wetted any good East India Company merchant's appetite:

"the clothiers, mercers, and venders of all kinds of silks, cottons, muslins, and embroidery, occupy more than a dozen bazars. In all there are to be seen immense quantities of the richest goods from India, Constantinople [Istanbul], Smyrna, Damascus, and other places, besides the various manufactures of Aleppo; all of which constitute an immense value… Some of those bazars are very long and broad, one of them is more than half a mile in length, occupied by confectioners, fruiterers, &c. "[248]

No matter how much the British East India Company coveted Aleppo's merchandise, they had no trading rights there, as these belonged to the Levant Company.

Like the East India Company, the Levant Company –also known as the Company of Turkey Merchants– had received its first charter from Elizabeth I. It had been established as a means of dealing directly with Ottoman merchants to bypass Dutch and Venetian middlemen and the cuts they took. The Levant Company was also responsible for appointing and maintaining English consuls, including John T. Abbott, who so cordially welcomed George and his friends to Aleppo in 1781.[249]

The Levant Company's sole rights to English trade prohibited George from setting up meetings to discuss mercantile matters –or any other subject– with the Turkish elite, who seldom interacted with Europeans, "but in the way of business". This was "usually transacted through an interpreter" even if the *Frank* in question could speak Turkish.[250]

There were said to be thirty-seven, lofty, stone-built, arched bazaars dotted around the centre of Aleppo, though few western visitors managed to find them all and, no matter how many bazaars George found, he could broker no deals.

The bazaars' interiors were lit by apertures on the sides of the enclosing arches "so situated as to give sufficient light, and at the same time exclude the sun and rain.[251] Shopkeepers could be "Turks, Jews, or Christians", but always men. The women, instead, were "frequently seen in all parts buying".[252]

"Women of every class" wore thin yellow, knee-high boots, yellow slippers[253] and body-length linen veils with which they wrapped themselves from head to foot, and "brought over the face in a manner to conceal all but one eye." Their single, exposed eye, however, was enhanced with black "Kohol" applied to "the inside of their eyelids. The veils of Christian and Jewish women were undyed, whilst Turkish women's were patterned with red or blue checks.[254] Turkish women were seen so frequently that "were a stranger to judge from the number he daily meets on the streets, he would hardly think himself in a country where the women are supposed to be prisoners for life."[255]

The only women exempt from wearing veils were "sometimes some poor women from the neighbouring villages, or Arab women from their tents" who ventured into Aleppo to sell eggs and other produce.[256] These Bedouin women were quite striking with blue-tattooed lips, and coarse, wide-sleeved blue dresses which opened "a little at the breast" to reveal patterns of blue flowers and abstract marks that were indelible "like what may be seen among sailors, and some of the common people of England."

Blue tattoos also adorned their cheeks and arms. They wore their hair "braided with beads and cowries [and] a large ring of gold or silver, pendant from the nose" some being at least an inch and a half in diameter. [257]

During the cooler months, Ottoman men wore "three furred garments, over one another". Their turbans, "commonly white, but sometimes dyed a pale, or deep green colour", were wrapped around a "stiff, quilted, round cap, flat at the top, and covered with cloth, of whatever colour" they chose. [258]

George, Beete and Scot were keen to join Irwin's expedition to Basra, but there were still no camels to be found, and Sheik Abdul Azah –who'd yet to return from Damascus– hadn't been tasked with bringing camels for three newcomers. Thankfully, Abdul Azah had been prudent:

"It was no small difficulty, however, that these gentlemen hired camels, to accommodate themselves for such a journey ; and in this they were assisted by the prudence of the shaik [sic] who returned to Aleppo on the 17th of March, with some spare camels, over and above the number contracted for." [259]

When, two days later, they were ready to depart, Irwin's ever extending party had been joined by thirty-four-year-old Dr. Adam Freer, [260] "the physician of the factory [warehouse in Aleppo] who had the company's permission to proceed to India ; and both from his professional skill, and his knowledge of the Turkish and Arabic languages," [261] was a welcome addition to the group.

On the evening of the 19th of March 1781, Irwin's party left Aleppo by the Damascus gate and went to their encampment, accompanied by Consul Abbott, his brother and other friends they'd made in the Syrian city. Three tents had been pitched for them, and two for the sheik and fifty well-armed Arabs, recruited from tribes they were likely to encounter, to serve both as guards and negotiators. The hired Arabs were in a celebratory mood and "began to fire guns as usual".

Irwin reflected:

"Had a citizen of London suddenly been transported to this place— had he seen our preparations, our horses to ride, and our mahfas, carried by camel, to travel in during the heats—the provisions made for our journey, and a gentleman above seventy years of age, among us—he would have laughed at the notion of fatigue or scarcity attending us." [262]

It's not clear who the aged gentleman was, but George and Beete's companion, Scot, may have been "George Scott Esq.ʳ", who was one of the two executors Simon Matcham appointed when he wrote his will in 1758.

When a British explorer, Abraham Parsons, embarked on a similar journey from Aleppo in March 1774, the spacious, furnished tent he described may have been similar to the one George stayed in (though nothing like the two tents the fifty Arabs were billeted in):

"at half past five we arrived at the camp of the caravan, on the banks of the River Coie, where we found our servants had pitched my tent, and got every thing ready for our reception.

We had a store of fresh mutton, bread, and fowls, for four or five days, and sufficient room in the tent to spread our mats and beds on them, besides room for our table and chairs, and for servants to walk round between them; and although it was exceedingly cold, we passed the night very comfortably." [263]

For George, in 1781, waking up in a tent would have been exciting after eight nights spent in the consul's house. Today, finally, they were going to head into the desert.

But any initial optimism for a speedy departure was soon quelled.

The city guards had been alarmed by the previous night's gunfire and, not realising it had been part of the Arabs' celebrations, had reported it to the pacha who, in turn, laid an embargo on Irwin's party leaving "on account of the disturbance of the previous night." Irwin sent an Arab for a departure order from the consul, but this didn't "arrive before ten o'clock, and the consul soon following it, we decamped at eleven, forming a caravan of eight camels, and nearly as many persons." Irwin added:

"Our stages to Baghdad are adjusted, and we are to perform the journey in sixteen days, if no obstacles prevent it." [264]

They set off in a south-easterly direction across the flat plain but, after an hour, a horseman warned them of a hostile tribe ahead. Although the Ottoman Empire's embargo was against Europeans using the Suez route, the desert tribes held little love for Christians and weren't above murdering them anyway. Irwin's party took the precaution of veering south, in a similar fashion to Parsons' excursion seven years earlier:

"In the morning we struck our tents... loaded our camels, and began our march eastward. Our sheik had previously sent two men, mounted on

dromedaries to reconnoitre, who returned, after three hours, and advised us... they had discovered a numerous tribe of men, camels, and horses, with tents pitched, covering the space of more than two miles, in the direct road where we were to pass."[265]

Irwin's caravan stopped at three in the afternoon when they reached an oasis. George, Irwin and Smyth shared frustration at the slow, two-and-a-half miles an hour pace of the camels, which, after five hours, had carried them only thirteen miles. They decided to use the horses they'd brought with them to ride "the whole stage",[266] leaving the plodding camel train behind as they galloped across the Syrian desert with the sun on their backs and the wind cooling their faces.

Their route through Syria followed the course of the river Euphrates, which provided vital drinking water and was often flanked with ruins. On the morning of the 2nd of April, exactly two weeks after departing Aleppo, they passed an abundance of ancient aqueducts as they approached the desert town of Ānah. The city transpired to be in a sorry state with "forsaken mosques and towers... a broken bridge and surrounding ruins."

The settlement of Ānah, which dated to at least 2,000 BC, had once flourished by trading crops grown in the fertile mud of the Euphrates. The ruins George encountered had been smashed into existence by sacking Persians a century before.[267]

Despite its ruinous state, the food in Ānah was sumptuous: "good mutton and fish, which were carp from the Euphrates, of a size, that, perhaps, no table in Europe could boast. The milk was excellent, and fruit was brought to us in abundance."

By Irwin's calculation, Ānah was three hundred and thirty-eight miles from Aleppo."[268]

A week, and two-hundred miles, later the party approached Bagdad; the setting of the famous *tales of the Arabian nights*.[269]

Irwin noted, in his journal, "Messers Smyth, Matcham and myself remounted our horses, and, accompanied by our servants and seven Arabs well-armed, we bid our friends adieu, and pushed on for the city, in order to hasten preparations for our journey down the [river] Tygris... What crowned our satisfaction, on having so happily finished our arduous journey by land, was to find from our host that a boat was engaged to carry us directly to Busrah.[270] But, "Rude materials and ruder workmanship marked the only vessel in Bagdad, that was to be procured for money".

This city of *the Arabian nights* had been controlled by Mamluks –a breakaway Georgian and Circassian faction of the Ottoman Empire– since 1704,[271] and had, as a result, fallen into such disrepair that Irwin's party was confronted with "dirty streets, ill-built and worse designed houses, deserted market-places, with more than half the city lying level with the ground".[272]

They languished in dilapidated Baghdad until the 21st of April 1781 when they finally secured a *bark* (boat) capable of transporting them for the nearly five hundred mile journey down the river Tigris to Basra.[273]

Their river journey was impeded by frequently attacking tribes, whom Irwin's party evaded by crouching low and pulling their boat against the river bank.

A sample day of their progress down the Tygris is provided by Irwin's journal entry for Sunday the 29th of April:

"We unmoored at eight this morning, but found our bark so fast on the mud, that all attempts to move her were fruitless... we hauled her out with some trouble into mid-stream. It was by this time ten o'clock... At 11 A. M. we were once more ashore... in order to wait for two boats which were coming up the river with a fair wind... the large bark ran by us; but the [smaller one] has been twenty-two days from Busrah, and brings advice, that no English vessels were there when she left it, but some daily expected. This was a sort of check on our satisfaction ; as no expedition could be ensured to us from Busrah to India... At one P. M. we unmoored, and fell down the stream. We had not proceeded far, when our rudder was damaged against the bank. This brought us to two o'clock, to repair our rudder, which to our surprize, has hitherto escaped the same accident. At nine o'clock at night, the damage having been repaired, we got under sail with a fair wind ; but through unskillfulness, the boat running ashore once or twice, the mariners lowered the sail, and we fell down with the current assisted by oars... At midnight we had been but five hours afloat, since we left our moorings in the morning, which, on a medium, have brought us fifteen miles. We are therefore four hundred and thirteen miles from Bagdad."[274]

Further downstream, the rivers Tigris and Euphrates merged to form the Shatt Al Arab, on whose southern bank stood George and Irwin's ultimate goal: the port city of Basra. The surrounding terrain was "low-lying and deeply intersected by creeks and small watercourses".[275]

On the 2nd of May:

"At day-break we found the banks on both sides covered with date-trees... These groves form a spacious avenue, through which vessels sail, and give a beauty to these banks, unknown to those above... When the tide

moved against us, a small breeze sprang up in our favour and carried us along the shore."[276]

Here, after eleven days journey from Bagdad, they reached Marghill, the house of William Digges Latouche, the Company's British Resident at Basra and the Persian Gulf, who lived six miles outside the city's boundary. Latouche, the son of a French Huguenot exile, was in his mid-thirties[277] and famed for his hospitality.[278]

Latouche, who'd been expecting Irwin's party, imparted the bad news that there was no English vessel moored in Basra, but had procured an Arabian *dow* to transport Irwin, and the intelligence he was couriering, to Muscat on the Arabian coast, and had written to Bombay for a "Company cruizer" to collect them from there.

Having safely delivered them to Basra, Sheik Abdul Azah bid Irwin's expedition farewell after, "in every respect" having been "an obliging attendant, and a faithful guide".

As the *cruizer* from Bombay wasn't due for a few days, Irwin and his companions amused themselves as well as they could.

Irwin thought it would be unpardonable not to describe the Gulf port:

"It is built in a quadrangular form, and is reckoned twelve miles in circumference. Its northern face looks towards the river ; and by means of a creek which divides it, the city is intersected with canals, and abounds with good water."[279]

When they rode from Marghill to Basra, they came upon evidence of the Persians' devastation, and "observed with concern the destruction of the gardens and houses, which extended between those places down to the river."[280]

Basra's Persian rule had been brief and brutal. George and Irwin's contemporary, James Capper provides a grim description of his own arrival there after trekking across the desert from Aleppo:

"The appearance of Bassora [sic] was exceedingly gloomy, having as I have before observed been almost depopulated by a plague, a siege, and a famine. In the year 1772, there was supposed to be upwards of four hundred thousand inhabitants in this place, and on the day of our arrival, there was certainly not more than six thousand, including the Persians ; the principal streets were like a burying ground, with scarcely a space of three feet between each grave."[281]

Irwin observed, "There is scarcely a house, that does not exhibit the traces of ruin". However, he saw much potential, albeit from a Company perspective:

"The creek I spoke of, is a great addition to the beauty and cleanliness of the city. The English factory is situated on it ; and were a quay to be built to confine the channel, I know not a city which could shew a more useful or pleasant canal. From the factory alone to the river, the creek is two miles in length, and rises and falls with the tides of the river. The banks are cultivated with gardens and are said to be very productive."

George's own thoughts feel bound up with Irwin's aquatic engineering speculations. It's easy to imagine the pair of them exploring the ruins of Basra, enthusiastically bouncing ideas off each other:

"Were the surrounding marshes to be drained, and the streets to be widened, a freer circulation of air, with such a command of water, as the creek affords, and such an inducement to cleanliness, there is little doubt, but as favourable an alteration might be produced in the atmosphere of Busrah, as has taken place in Calcutta within my own observation. But these ideas are more speculative, than reducible to practice, under a government like this." [282]

On Monday the 7th of May 1781, Irwin and his party joined Latouche for dinner in the English factory in Basra, after which they boarded the dow commissioned to transport them to Muscat. There was a poignancy to the event because the fellowship of explorers would break with the dow's launch. The small Arabic boat could scarce accommodate Irwin and Smyth, with their servants and baggage. Major Nicol and Dr. Freer had opted to cram themselves onboard too, preferring "to brave all inconveniences" for the benefit of the fast passage Irwin's couriered intelligence assured. However, "Messrs. Burke and Matcham, with their company, were obliged to remain at Busrah, for the opportunity of an English vessel, which was soon expected."

Irwin reflected that he'd come to esteem George's social qualities so highly that there was a comfort in leaving him "in the house of our amiable host, Mr. Latouche, from whom no one, however urgent his vocation, can part without regret." [283]

After securing his passage for the 1,847 nautical miles separating Basra from Bombay, [284] George was greeted by the news that his Company career was on the brink of collapse.

It would have come as no surprise to George that his residency at

Broach was now in jeopardy from the Marathas,[285] and that this was due to Scindia. In his bid to reclaim territory from the British, Scindia, had captured several hostages as leverage to force the British East India Company to return Broach.[286] The Company had bowed to Scindia's pressure in June 1782, and Scindia formally accepted supremacy of Broach nine-months later.[287]

Almost simultaneously, the Ottoman sultan, Abdul Hamid I, decreed that any Muslims caught aiding Christians at Suez would be deemed traitors, deserving "punishment both in this world and the other world". [288]

Despite being ousted from his Broach residency, thirty-year-old George soon accumulated enough money and assets to retire permanently. [289] In the words of his great-granddaughter, "His ideas of an ample fortune, being now quite satisfied, no offers of further employment or prospects of greater wealth could tempt him out again."[290]

George now had the freedom and finance to realise his idyll of buying an English estate jointly with his mother and sharing it with a wife he'd find somewhere along the way.

In fact, losing Broach may have been a relief to George, but another event would have brought him very low. His Venice-to-Basra companion, John Beete, had a nasty fall from his horse and died, in Bombay, in May 1783.[291] Beete's funeral took place on August the 6th.[292]

Chapter Six: Final Overland Journey,
Part One: Basra to Kurdistan

1784 – 1785

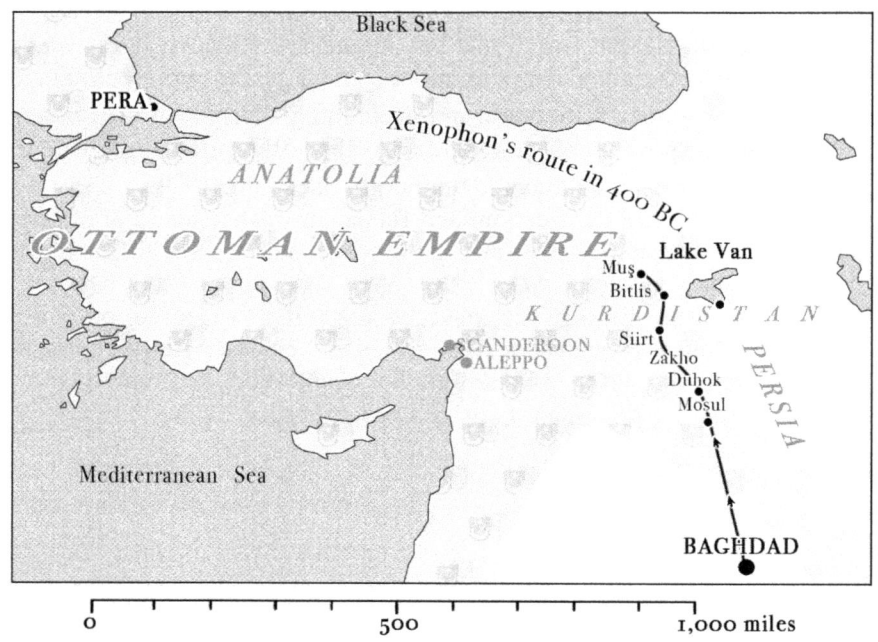

"At noontide heat, and midnight cold,
Thy vengeful stores of wrath with-hold,
Nor bid the sudden whirlwind rise,
To blend at once, hills, vales, and skies!"
(Eyles Irwin, Ode to the Desart, 1777).[293]

A year after Beete's funeral, George was in still Bombay staying with a
Mr. Nisbet.[294] This was, almost certainly, Andrew Nisbett, who had

George's father's old job of harbour master.[295] Nisbett had his own new-build residence thanks to a lease of land the Company had granted him twelve years before.[296]

According to their descendants, Andrew Nisbett's wife, Rose, was an Armenian who'd been born in Armenia and emigrated to Bombay with her family.[297] Andrew and Rose Nisbett had a fifteen-year-old son, William, and several daughters, of whom the youngest was five.

The English enclave of Bombay had been relaxing its hardline Puritanical rules. There was a committee for opening a theatre, with plans to build it on the green between the English residencies and the docks,[298] and George's landlady, Mrs. Rose Nisbett, was so uncompromising about her Armenian culture that she was openly financing the construction of a Catholic church in Bombay.[299] The Nisbett children would have been bilingual, and their home a multi-faith one, making for lively lodgings for George's stay.

George's Charterhouse chum, Charles Warre Malet, lived close to Bombay town, and visited every Monday morning with the governor, William Hornby. Malet, like George, was thirty-one and doing well within the Company. In appearance, it could be said that Malet's jaw was mallet-shaped, and that his perfectly straight nose resembled a mallet's handle. Above this, his heavy-lidded eyes and brows were dark in stark contrast to his pale hair.

When Malet introduced George, and the Nisbetts, to his friend Émïn, they hit it off instantly. Émïn, like the younger Nisbetts, was half-Armenian. George already knew him, though he'd not seen him for twelve years.

Émïn had married recently, despite being nearly sixty. He had his toddler son, Arshak, with him, but had left his wife and three other children with his in-laws in New Julfa –an Armenia settlement in Persia. How fortunate for Émïn to have Rose Nisbett to chatter with in their native tongue, and for his son, little Arshak, to have the Nisbetts' half-Armenian children to play and chatter with too.

In fact, all parties got along so well that, as Émïn recorded in his memoir, "He and his son dined with them at least three times in the week [for] nine months".[300]

Émïn was a dedicated campaigner for Armenian independence from the Ottomans. One of his close friends, and mentor of old, Edmund Burke, was a prominent Whig politician who spoke out against the East India Company's habit of appointing young boys to govern India and was also opposed to slavery and abuses of Asian people's rights.[301] [302]

Such topics would have pushed George out of his comfort zone but made for lively and thought-provoking debate.

Though outspoken, Émïn had "remarkable popularity with all classes. Royalty, workmen, nobles, rough sailors, wild savage mountaineers [and] Kurds, Governors and civilians of the E.I. Co." A British peer, Lord Teignmouth, said of him, "In Émïn we see the same man, who was a sailor, a porter, a menial servant and subsisting by charity—the companion of nobles, and patronised by princes and monarchy, ever preserving in his deepest distresses, a sense of honour, a spirit of integrity, a reliance upon Providence and a firm adherence to the principles of Christianity".[303]

Whether chatting animatedly over dinner or sipping cold drinks in the shade of the Nisbetts' verandah, Émïn's travel tales entertained George.

Both men had traced little-known paths, and traversed multiple countries, but Émïn's journeys had been through lands Europeans knew very little of: Persia, Kurdistan, Armenia and Ottoman Anatolia.

It took Émïn most of nine months to admit that he was stuck in Bombay without funds "to get his passage to Calcutta".

The non-Armenian half of Émïn was Indian and none of the captains of ships moored in Bombay harbour trusted his ability to make good on credit and demanded "to be paid on the spot in ready-money".

Charles Warre Malet intervened with Governor Hornby who, in turn, instructed one of the captains, Smith, to give Émïn free passage to Calcutta. Captain Smith, however, "was very fond of money" and demanded 300 rupees upfront, or security for it.

When Émin admitted his predicament, George "readily sat down" to write the following note:

"Mr. Matcham presents compliments to Captain Smith, and informs him that he will stand security for 300 rupees, for his friend Émin's passage-money to Bengal ; that is, if he should not be able to pay the money there, Mr. Matcham will pay it to Captain Smith."

Émïn returned to George, frowning, with Captain Smith's evasive reply:

"Captain Smith returns his compliments to Mr. Matcham, and begs leave to send back his note respecting Mr. Émïn, as he had already promised the Governor to accommodate that gentleman with a passage. Saturday 31st July 1784."

George laughed heartily and, with a mischievous flourish, scribbled a note for Émïn to take back to him:

"Mr. Émin, I congratulate you on Captain Smith's generosity.—You will observe by the above your captain means to afford you a passage

gratis: 300 rupees between your Highness and him is no mighty sum".[304]

*

A year later, in 1785, George's old chum, Malet, was granted the residency of Puna.[305]

Less joyfully, on the 2nd of December, George was summoned to the Court of Bombay. He was one of two executors Beete had named in his will.[306] The other executor, Mr. Harris, was a London merchant possessing the unusual first name of Quarles. Beet had tasked Quarles Harris with administering his English estate, and "George Matcham Esquire of Broach to be my Executor in India and to remit the Balance of my Estate here after paying my lawful Debts to Quarles Harris above named". The court in Bombay required George to attest that he "renounced his right of executing the said Will having no ways intermeddled with the Estate and without fraud or intent cheating the creditors".[307] Although the wording is peculiar, it appears to have been nothing more than legalese for ensuring that initial administration had been in Quarles's sole charge in London, where the bulk of Beete's estate was situated (the full text is provided in appendix 2).

With the court proceedings finalised, George was free to set forth on what his great-granddaughter later described as his "final and more risky return journey to Europe".[308]

As well as providing practical travel information, Émïn's tales seem to have whetted George's wanderlust. His imagination had also been fired by Xenophon's *anabasis* – a Greek mercenary leader's account of marching from Persia to Anatolia, via Kurdistan, in 400 BC. George's Charterhouse education had enabled him to read Xenophon's travelogue, and Émïn's tales of clandestinely travelling through Ottoman-ruled Armenia inspired him to see if modern Kurds differed much from Xenophon's description of their lawless Carducci ancestors.

*

When, in 1786, George arrived in Basra from Bombay ready to undertake his final overland journey, he was driven by a fascination with history and culture, as opposed to the Company's needs. In place of calculating potential trade revenues, his mind was focused on events that had taken place in 400 BC, near Baghdad, when Xenophon's contingent of Greek mercenaries found themselves on the losing side of opposing Persian armies and fled northwards hoping to reach the Black Sea and ships to take them home to Greece.[309]

It would have been easy enough for George to follow the river Tigris to Baghdad, but he ran into a problem when he arrived there. No Europeans were interested in accompanying him on his bold, arguably madcap 1,500 mile horseback journey through wild Kurdistan and the entire length of hostile, Ottoman-ruled Anatolia.

Undeterred, George set off from Baghdad with the intention of making it all the way to Pera, on the European side of Istanbul's Bosphorus, "Attended only by an Arab suite".[310]

George very likely spoke Arabic and had probably learnt rudimentary Armenian from Émïn. The British East India Company liked their employees to learn the languages of peoples with whom lucrative deals might be made. For example, when the Company established its own college in Hertfordshire in 1806, students were taught Bengali, Persian, Sanskrit and Urdu.[311]

As George was travelling light on horseback, it would have been impossible for him to carry enough provisions to last him all the way to Istanbul. He'd have eaten and drunk whatever fare could be sourced en route and would have forsaken tea for the strong black coffee the Arabs boiled on their nightly campfires.[312] After all, he was so unattached to customary English cuisine that, when travelling through the desert between the Persian Gulf and Egypt, he'd subsisted entirely on mares' milk.

During the first days of their journey, when they settled into camp each evening, saddle-stiff and sore, they were overlooked by the Zagros Mountains marking the western fringes of Persia. These mountains glowed gold in the sunset whilst the day's final *ezan* –call for prayer– sounded from as many, disparate directions as there were settlements nearby. Then, after a night under the stars, George would have woken to find those same mountains as a black block against the breaking dawn.

As George retraced the ancient Greeks' course alongside the Tigris north of Baghdad, it must surely have felt thrilling to be travelling where Xenophon himself had passed two thousand two hundred years before.

By and by, as the upstream course of the Tigris snaked closer to the lands of the Kurds, the Zagros Mountains receded and, in place, the ground buckled into the Taurus foothills, which Xenophon called the Carduchian Mountains.

The ancient city of Mosul, two hundred and fifty miles north of Bagdad, was a vibrant, cosmopolitan hub surrounded by arable fields. Sesame, fruits and vegetables were grown close to water sources and, where irrigation wasn't possible, there was enough rain to grow such a prolific quantity of wheat and barley that it was exported all the way to Basra.[313]

After Mosul, Xenophon's ancient path followed the river's north bank until they "arrived where the river Tigris is altogether impassable by reason of its depth and largeness, and there was no road along its bank, but the Carduchian mountains hung steep over the very water".

George, although travelling with minimal luggage, may have carried Xenophon's Anabasis to read, piece by piece, in situ. Even without it to hand, he'd been avidly familiar with Xenophon's explanation of the merits of attempting to cross Kurdistan's forbidding terrain:

"it seemed, as it needs must, to the generals, that it was necessary to march through the mountains. For they heard from [their prisoners] that, if they passed through the Carduchian mountains [they would evade their Persian pursuers].[314]

After veering north from the Tigris, Xenophon's route passed through Duhok: a linear settlement, squeezed between ridges.[315] In George's day, Duhok's population was predominantly Kurdish, though these didn't match the "lawless" Carducci Xenophon described. The Kurds of Duhok – and elsewhere outside the Taurus Mountains proper – had been subdued and repressed by engulfing waves of Islamic cultures.

The Kurds, George's heart was set on meeting, dwelled high in the Taurus Mountains where, as for the Basques in northern Spain, they had held on for millennia and maintained their own language, religion and culture. Even in "tame" Duhok, Kurdish men were distinctive for their particoloured striped or plaid turbans with "long strings, attached to the end of the bandage... forming a deep fringe, to hang down about and between their shoulders."[316]

The Kurds' cuisine incorporated exotic flavours to titillate George's tastebuds. Mountain-greens, whose use was unique to Kurdish cooking, were used to flavour mutton and goat-meat raised by local shepherds. Also popular was a charred fish-dish, called *masgouf,* which was served with flat breads still hot from the oven. This, and everything else, came with rice and, after dinner, hot, sweet black tea.[317]

After Duhok, the next sizeable, modern settlement intersected by Xenophon's ancient route was the city of Zakho, lying close to Iraq's border with Turkey, where the river Khabur, a source of the Euphrates, slows its course after cascading down from the Taurus Mountains.

The Kurds' mountain domain was a "region south-east of Armenia, extending about 300 miles in length by 150 in breadth, and forming a kind of descent from the high table land of Persia to the low alluvial plains of Mesopotamia [where the inhabitants are] nominally subject to Turkey, and the southern portion to Persia, yet they virtually maintain their independence".[318] The steep, scrubby landscape was punctuated, here and there, with glinting lakes[319] and paddy fields for growing rice.[320]

A Christian missionary, who visited the area in the early 1800s, observed that the Kurds "uniformly showed us great respect as European travellers. When approaching us on horseback, they often dismounted at a distance, and made their obeisance".[321]

In 400 BC, the Kurds' ancestors evacuated their villages ahead of the Greek army, leaving houses stocked with ample provisions and "furnished with a vast number of brass utensils". But they displayed no subservience.

George would have progressed through "wild" Kurdistan with trepidation, lest the Kurds of his day shared "the lawless habits of the Carducci, their ancestors".[322] He'd have recalled Xenophon's experience:

"When the last of the Greeks were descending to the villages... the Carduchians being collected together, set upon the last, and killed some, and wounded with stones and arrows, being themselves but few : for the Grecian army fell upon them unexpectedly. If, however, they had been collected in greater numbers, a great part of the army would have run the risk of being destroyed."[323]

From that point onwards, the vanquished Greeks "drawn up in order of battle" were bombarded, ceaselessly, with missiles hurled by Kurdish "barbarians", who were much nimbler than the Greeks because "they had nothing else to carry but their bows and slings" and "gave much trouble".

An intrepid American, Horatio Southgate, who visited Muş in Eastern Turkey during the early 1800s, paints a sensationally negative picture of Kurds who ventured into town to sell yoghurt and firewood:

"Their women are poorly clad, and their small children, for the most part, are quite naked. The men appear in the streets armed with a sword and the small round shield which they constantly wear about them, and followed by their women and girls bearing burdens. Nothing can present a more wretched picture than these females. They are poorly dressed and filthy. They go bending beneath their loads, and their faces, always unveiled, wear the deepest impress of misery. The countenances of the men were the most ferocious and brutal that I have ever seen. They were mostly of a middle stature, with stout and broad frames. Their faces were thin and dark, the nose hooked, and the eye black and merciless."[324]

An account from 1809 similarly defames the Kurds as an infesting "race of robbers", of whom "most of them were on foot, and had chiefly clubs and javelins".[325]

In answer to George's curiosity about the similarity between Xenophon's Carduchians and eighteenth-century Kurds, although Kurdistan was still "lawless" because not one of their powerful neighbours –Turks, Arabs and Persians– had bent them to their will, the Kurds George came across weren't as barbaric as popularly believed. They practiced their millennia-old religion of Zoroastrianism,[326] and there were also adherents of Yazīdīsm, a minority Kurdish religion which had originated in the Taurus Mountains, north of Iraq.[327]

Here, in their homeland, the Kurdish people were free to dress according to their own custom, which was very colourful, especially for the women who wore several layers of vividly dyed garments, comprising baggy trousers and a sheer petticoat of patterned or embroidered fabric.[328]

Happily, not one of them murdered George with javelins or clubs.

Chapter Seven: Final Overland Journey,
Part Two: Armenia to Anatolia,
and the South-east Mediterranean

1786

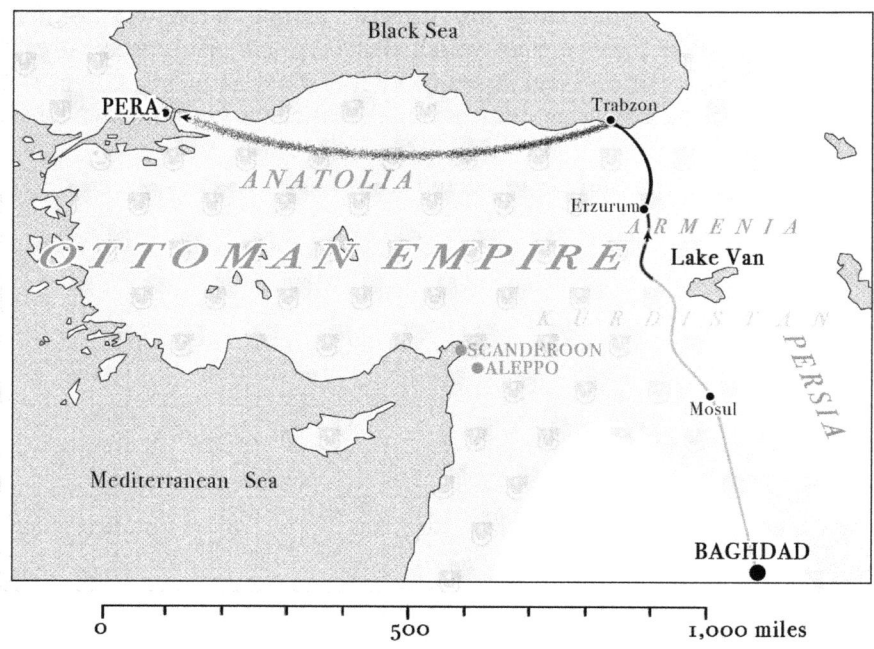

"To mark where thou first court'st the gale,
The poet's stretch of thought might fail,
Might heroes shudder to behold,
The wonders which thy depths unfold."
(Eyles Irwin, Ode to the Nile, 1777). [329]

A thousand-years before the advent of Islam, it took the Ancient Greeks seven, long days to cross the breadth of the Taurus Mountains, during which time they "suffered evils that were not equalled by even the whole of what they had endured from the king [of Persia]".[330] Even when the Greeks attempted to exit into Armenia, the Carduchians "collected together, with their arms, in great numbers" and "shot from their bows and slings".[331]

In her 1911 book, the Nelsons of Burnham Thorpe, George's great-granddaughter, Mary Eyre Matcham, says that the Kurds he met in 1786 differed little from the lawless Carducci of Xenophon's time. George, like Xenophon, may have felt massively relieved to escape Kurdistan alive.

In Xenophon's day, Armenia was "all a plain and smooth hills... there were not villages near the river on account with the wars with the Carduchi. The village to which they came was both large, and had a palace... and upon most of the houses there were towers, and provisions were abundant."[332] Historians believe this was either Bitlis or Tatvan, near the western shore of Lake Van[333] –pronounced *vwAHn*– which is a vast body of water within the present bounds of eastern Turkey. According to a recent guide, the lake is a "magical reflecting pool, shining bright blue on sunny days and fiery red at sunset. Just after dusk, the lake becomes like quicksilver. The high alkaline content of the waters renders the liquid a smooth silk".[334]

From the western shore of Van, the Greeks followed "the river Teléboas", through countryside that was "beautiful [with] many villages about the river."[335] The river is thought to have either been the Murat or the Karasu, which would have led the Greeks to the town of Muş.[336]

George would have been keen to locate a troglodyte village which Xenophon vividly described:

"The houses were under ground, with a mouth like that of a well, but wide below : the entrances for the cattle were dug, but the men descended by ladders. In the houses were goats, sheep, oxen, fowls, and their young : and all the cattle were fed within doors upon hay. There was also wheat and barley, and legumes and barley wine in jars : and the barley itself was in them on a level with the brim : and there lay in them reeds, some larger, some smaller, having no joints. It was necessary for him, when a person was thirsty, to take these into his mouth and suck; and it was very strong, unless some one poured water on it, and was a very agreeable beverage to a person taught the use of it"[337]

Horatio Southgate, in his early 1800s travelogue, came upon Armenian cave villages which he equated with the troglodyte village of Xenophon's time:

"Their villages may be described in nearly the same words which Xenophon used respecting them 2200 years ago... if it had not been summer, I might have added as he does, 'All the cattle were maintained within doors with fodder.' [These] houses, however, are not properly subterranean, in the common sense of the term. They are generally made by excavating the earth and raising a wall of loose stones to the required height. Trunks of trees are then laid across for rafters and covered with branches. Then the earth is piled on until the whole is covered and the fabric attains a semi-globular shape. Sometimes the whole is built upon the surface, but, in both cases, the external appearance is that of a bare mound of earth." [338]

According to Southgate, the Armenian population west of lake Van, whom George would have encountered a couple of decades beforehand, were "poorly clad, timid and of servile demeanour". Uncharitably, Southgate added, "The women are especially ugly and filthy". As we've seen, Southgate spoke equally harshly about the Kurds he saw in Muş.

Here, as there were no ambassadorial residences or Company factories for George to billet in, it was necessary to secure accommodation from the local populace. Southgate complained that, in Armenia, "Both men and women are generally unwilling to give lodging or food, or do so in so slow and sullen a manner as to render their hospitality hardly endurable." Their sullenness may have been provoked by Southgate's habit of requisitioning their homes while the owners were away, then being mystified that they weren't happy, because he'd intended to pay them a bit of rent money. The Armenians were also likely sullen because of Southgate's bristling contempt that the entire Armenian population was "unintelligent and spiritless [and] extremely ignorant and unclean in their persons and houses".

One of the meals Southgate cajoled Armenian villagers into serving him was, to his self-pitying disgust, "coffee and a dish of yoghourt with bread".

Southgate fared somewhat better in larger Armenian villages where his judgemental, American eyes were occasionally "cheered by the sight of domestic industry, cleanliness and thrift" and he was even, on extremely rare occasions, "cordially received".

It's worth a bet that George, who'd lodged with an Anglo-Armenian family in Bombay and spent nine-months in the close company of Émïn, had learnt enough of the Armenian language to exchange pleasantries and would have been more enthusiastically welcomed into locals' homes.

Without exception, said Southgate, the most prominent buildings in Armenian villages were churches, for they, alone, were built above ground, as "small and simple edifices constructed of square stone with a sloping roof... often venerably old and mantled with wild weeds growing from chinks [and standing] amidst moss-clad grave-stones, the last and only memorials of those who once worshipped within their walls."[339]

George would have noticed little difference between Armenian cuisine and that of the Kurds and Iraqi Arabs, but he may have noticed that the Armenian version of stuffed vine leaf *dolma* was "thick and loosely wrapped with lots of spices and olive oil".[340] The Armenians' go-to guest-food, *khorovats*, comprised sour-marinaded lamb that was barbecued with herbs, garlic and spices until it was charred on the outside but tender and flavoursome within.[341]

Just as their cuisines were close, Armenians and Kurds dressed similarly too. Armenian women wore colourful dresses with elaborately embroidered aprons of cotton or velvet, and an abundance of silver jewellery, belt buckles and baubles fixed into their braided hair. The men, who also dressed colourfully, wore wide trousers, shirts patterned with geometric red embroidery, and distinctive sash belts.[342]

Xenophon's archaic route trailed a hundred and seventy-five miles northwards to the Armenian city of Erzurum, which George, as an East India Company merchant, would have been excited to visit because it "was once the thoroughfare of most of the over-land commerce between Europe and the East, which was not destroyed by the discovery of the passage around the Cape of Good Hope."[343]

In George's day, Erzurum was "the largest city and the bulwark of the Armenian possessions of Turkey [and was] situated near the foot of a mountain on the south-eastern side of the plain to which it gives its name."[344]

A nineteenth century Scottish traveller was moved by his first sight of Erzurum:

"we had a full sight of Arzeroom, lying in the hollow of a vale beneath, and completely surrounded by mountains. It was not more than three miles from us when we saw it. The city appeared large ; and its lofty houses of stone gave it an air of magnificence, which totally vanished on more intimate acquaintance. However, the near as well as distant view of its embattled citadel revealed porcelained and glittering mosques, and cemeteries filled with monuments [After entering the suburbs] and soon after passing along part of an extensive bazar, [we] rode through the

opened double gates, which were strongly coated with iron, into the town.
[All was] bustle, both with men and animals ".[345]

Erzurum's houses were "built of dark stone, and generally of one story
[giving them] a cheerless and diminutive appearance. A green sward has
grown over the terraces of dirt, by which, instead of roofs, they are all
covered, and gives [the houses] when viewed from an eminence above,
almost as much the aspect of a meadow as a city."[346]

From Erzurum, Xenophon pressed onwards to reach the Black Sea, a
hundred-and-eighty miles to the north.

The countryside beyond Erzurum is described, poetically, by an early
nineteenth-century trio of missionaries, Smith, Harrison and Dwight:

"there is an uninhabited mountain tract of 12 hours. We made half of it
[in one day]. The ascent was difficult, but once upon the top we were
conducted through a succession of valleys, beautiful for the meadow-like
luxuriance of the grass that clothed, and the variety of flowers that
ornamented them. The declivities of many of the hills and mountain
summits too were covered with woodlands and forests... every mile or two
brought us to a khan or shop, where provender, butter and cheese, bread
and fruit, were exposed for sale. The bread was indeed coarse and black,
but it was in regular loaves, such as we had not seen for many a month".
[347] [348]

Another writer reminisced that, further north along this same route,
their party found themselves "in the midst of delightful country... before
us was seen the entrance of one of the most beautiful valleys perhaps in the
world... A small river meandered through the valley and joined the Black
Sea some leagues further north."[349]

Sir Robert Ker Porter, who, like George, attempted to retrace
Xenophon's footsteps through Armenia, declared:

"Few passages in history are more affecting than those in which
[Xenophon] describes the feelings of his Greeks on running up that
mountain, and beholding the Euxine, whence they were to embark for their
country ; their shouts, and cries of The sea ! the sea ! calling him up, to
enjoy the same grateful sight, whilst the hardiest veterans by his side,
burst into tears, embracing each other, in the fond hope of soon returning
to their wives and children."[350]

The place from which Xenophon sailed was the Greek colony of Trebizond (Trabzon), "that long celebrated port of the Black Sea".[351]

Though long-fallen to the Ottoman Turks, eighteenth-century Trebizond retained many ninth-century churches and high walls built to mimic those of Christian Constantinople, which the Turks had taken too and renamed Istanbul.[352]

George's experience in Trebizond would have been similar to that of a fellow westerner, who sailed there from Istanbul in 1796:

"Though we were dressed in the Tartar fashion, we were objects of curiosity for the small town of Trebizond, and we found ourselves surrounded with Turks and Lazes : however, being used to travel in the Levant, I had no apprehension as to the object of their visits, and I did not perceive that they viewed us with any dislike."[353]

The Lazes, or Laz, are Caucasian Muslims whose language, Lazuri, is related to Georgian.[354] A nineteenth-century account tells that their men were skilled with short rifles and, although they had no towns, they occupied most of the Black Sea coast east of Trebizond in "cottages scattered singly over the country". Laz people living close to Trebizond, were, according to the author, more civilised because, they came "frequently into contact with the townspeople".[355]

From Trebizond, Xenophon and his ten-thousand Greek compatriots procured boats to sail home to Greece as swiftly as they could, but George, in 1786, wasn't done with exploring. No record has come to light of the route George took from Trebizond across Turkey, beyond it having been on horseback with his Arab suite. He may have followed the Black Sea shore, or he may have detoured inland to visit places of interest, such as the tomb of the revered Sufi master, Rumi, in Konya. All we do know is that he travelled with his Arab companions all the way to Pera, on the European side of Istanbul, the seat of the Ottoman sultan, Abdul Hamid I.

Bearing in mind that Sultan Abdul Hamid I had recently decreed that Muslims aiding Christians were traitors, George's decision to ride the entire length of Turkey to Istanbul may have felt just as perilous as venturing across Kurdistan. The only clue to George's feelings on this matter comes from his great-granddaughter, Mary Eyre Matcham's brief note that his final overland journey was "more risky" than his first two. [356]

In Istanbul, George would have ended his months-long sojourn away from Western culture by staying with British Ambassador, Sir Robert Ainslie. Ainslie's residence was in Pera (Beyoğlu) where, in the modern-day, the fashionable İstiklal Caddesi (Republic Street) sparkles with countless high-end shops.

Sir Robert Ainslie, who was twenty-three years George's senior, was good at his job for he was a favoured companion of Sultan Abdul Hamid I. [357] Ainslie's good standing with the sultan would have made things easier for George and assuaged any fears he may have had that Abdul Hamid would persecute him for being a Christian.

George and his host would have enjoyed lively conversations, for Sir Robert Ainslie had a keen interest in Islamic culture and architecture, and was commissioning an artist, Luigi Mayer, to produce detailed etchings of Egypt, Palestine and the southern coast of Turkey.[358]

A contemporary British traveller, Thomas Watkins, who was a guest in Sir Robert Ainslie's ambassadorial residence in 1788, favourably recalled the hospitality he received, which would have been more, or less, identical to George's pampered treatment two years before:

"No man can bear higher the dignity of a British Ambassador than he can when necessary, and no man so agreeably forget that dignity in the private society of his house. This politeness is not artificial, but genuine, being the result of a good heart, and an easy intercourse with men of sense and manners... Since my arrival [other British men] have been received by Sir Robert, so that our society is increased, and indeed improved, as they are all agreeable men. We generally breakfast in our private apartments, and from that time to dinner, wander about the city and its environs, being furnished by our generous host with every necessary accommodation ; interpreters, janizaries [Ottoman guards], servants, horses, &c. He has told us to do whatever we please in his house, and to command him at all times but in the morning, as he was then employed with his dispatches, and other business.

At four we sit down to a table spread with delicacies, and after dinner a l' Angloise, have before us twenty kinds of wines —the most rich and rare of Europe, the Greek islands, Jerusalem, and the coast of Asia Minor. On retiring to a drawing-room, about seven, we are served with what I never tasted before I came here, good coffee, for you have it not in England, as it loses so much of its flavour on the sea. Afterwards, we generally accompany his Excellency on his visits to the other foreign Ministers. There being no carriages in Constantinople, we go on foot, and in great style, preceded by half a dozen janizaries, and as many livery servants with flambeaux. On our return, the evening is concluded with cards or conversation."[359]

Of Istanbul itself, Watkins tells:

"There is no city in Europe,—perhaps in world, that contains such a variety of inhabitants ; Turks, Greeks, Armenians, Franks, Jews, &c. &c. The three first of these nations are scattered over the whole, though the Greeks and Armenians have distinct places in which the body of them resides. The Franks dwell among the foreign Ministers in Pera, and the Jews in Galata."[360]

George, being mercantile, would have been sure to visit Istanbul's Grand and Spice Bazarres, which were enthusiastically described by a goggle-eyed nineteenth-century visitor:

"the vast extent of these markets at Constantinople created a still more vivid impression. To say that the covered row of shops must altogether be miles in length—that vista after vista opens upon the gaze of the astonished stranger, lined with the costliest productions of the world, each collected in its proper district—that one may walk for an hour, without going over the same ground twice, amidst diamonds, gold, and ivory ;- Cashmere shawls, and Chinese silks ; glittering arms, costly perfumes, embroidered slippers, and mirrors ; rare brocades, ermines, Morocco leathers, Persian nick-nacks; amber mouth-pieces, and jewelled pipes— that, looking along the shortest avenue, every known tint and colour meets the eye at once, in the wares and costumes, and that the noise, the motion, the novelty of this strange spectacle is at first perfectly bewildering".[361]

*

When George left Istanbul, it was probably on a boat that he'd hired, for his great-granddaughter tells us that, after Turkey, he visited, "the Greek Islands (in the examination of which he passed several months, having hired a vessel for that purpose)".[362]

Though the majority of Greece, at this time, was part of the Ottoman Empire,[363] Christianity was permitted and George would have shed his Turkish-style long, loose shirt. Mile by mile, and day by day, his extended odyssey was giving way for his home culture.

When he finished exploring the Greek islands, George visited "almost all the countries and courts included in the usual continental tour."[364]

In 1786, one of the grand tour's key destinations was Naples which – being less than a day's sail from the Greek island of Kefalonia– was plausibly amongst the "almost all" of the "usual tour" that George called into.

Naples was a popular stop off point because its recently-widowed British ambassador, Sir William Hamilton, was not only an excellent host of impeccable class –for he'd been the childhood companion of the current king, George III– but was a foremost authority on the excavations of Pompeii and neighbouring Herculaneum, as well as the volcano, Vesuvius, that had buried the Roman towns to begin with.[365] As well-educated, wealthy, young Europeans of this era were ravenous for all things classical, staying in Sir William Hamilton's ambassadorial residence was high on their agendas. Sir William's newest houseguest was a beautiful, but common born young English woman named Emma Hart.

Regardless of whether, or not, George visited Naples, his great-granddaughter tells us "he became acquainted with many persons of note, including the emperor Joseph II."[366] Joseph II, the Holy Roman Emperor, resided in Vienna and was the brother of the famous, and doomed, French queen, Marie Antoinette.[367]

Part Three:
English Country Gentleman Idyll
(1786–1816)

Chapter Eight: Love and Marriage

1786 – 1787

Thirty-two-year-old George was young, rich, good looking, approximately 5' 8" (173cm) tall and lithely fit from his exertions crossing Kurdistan, Armenia, Anatolia and Europe. Now focused on finding a wife, he commissioned a new suit[368] and a respected artist to render him in a flattering light. The painter he chose, Gilbert Stuart, was a visiting American whose portrait of President Washington adorns modern United States dollar bills.

In Gilbert Stuart's half-length portrait of George, he sports the 1780s fashion of a short, powdered wig, which –like Eyles Irwin in Romney's painting– has a single curl running over his ears, and a queue (ponytail) bound with black silk.[369] George's velvet jacket is green and has brass buttons. Beneath this, his waistcoat and shirt are pristine white. The slimness of his chest gives credence to his belief that he only had one lung. He's painted from below, as if standing on a pedestal. Although he's turned slightly away, his hazel eyes regard the viewer with a relaxed air of shrewd assessment. His thick, dark eyebrows contrast against fair, rosy skin. The bridge of his nose is bumped, and his nostrils are slightly flared. A cleft chin and indented philtrum give his lips a Cupid's bow. Here is a successful, confident young man ready to embrace life. A man who could at last realise his eight-year-delayed idyll of settling down on his own estate to enjoy a "wife, farming and hunting."[370]

According to his great-granddaughter, George's widowed mother had settled at "Enfield, near Bath".[371] However, George's later marriage settlement clarifies that Enfield was a village in the county of Middlesex, which is now a borough of north London and over 130 miles east of Bath. [372]

Mary Eyre Matcham relates:

"The winter of 1786-7 found George settled with his mother at Enfield, near Bath, and here, among the social festivities of that gay

neighbourhood, he met Catherine Nelson. Family tradition says that he was desired by mutual friends to attend a Bath ball, in order to meet Miss Scrivener". [373]

Though George's great-granddaughter implies that George made a short hop to Bath to meet the eligible Miss Scrivener, it was actually a two-day stagecoach journey along the Bath Road. [374]

An idea of the journey is provided in a 1780 newspaper advertisement for William James and Son's Flying Waggons [sic], which were "very convenient for passengers [with] a guard in and out for their safety". Their scheduled coach set out from the Three Cups in Bread Street, London on Wednesday evenings and arrived in Bath on Saturday mornings. [375]

George, who'd travelled through the wild regions of the Kurds, and from Belgium to Basra, may have considered the distance negligible and/or played down its length in later family tellings so his children and grandchildren didn't think he'd been too eager.

The date of George's arrival in Bath is unrecorded, but his wealthy mother, Mrs. Elizabeth Matcham, was noteworthy enough to have her own arrival listed in the Bath Journal on the 11th of December 1786, along with "His Grace the Archbishop of York and Family, Earl of Milltown, Lady Mary Burt [and] Sir Bellingham Graham". [376]

The town of Bath, in western England, is named for its thermal spa that had been built by the Romans in the first century. [377] Though the baths were popular with British royalty prior to the eighteenth century, [378] the spa didn't gain wider appeal until the early seventeen hundreds.

Bath's new popularity had caused a frenzy of grand, neoclassical redevelopment using local, gold-toned Bath stone. In the early eighteenth century, architect John Wood had laid out "crescents, circles and squares in Palladian [symmetrical, classical] style" and the trendsetting Beau Nash had established "the complex etiquette that governed the social and recreational life". [379]

An early nineteenth century guide for gentlemen travellers, claims the entrance to Bath:

"cannot fail in removing... frigid apathy and awaken his feelings to the numerous interesting objects which, in rapid succession, present themselves to his notice [The ancient city] rises with peculiar grandeur, and amphitheatric arrangement of crescents, splendid seats, &c. surrounded by the lofty hills... The appearance of BATH is all together nouvelle, possessing a rank exclusively its own, and from its uniformity and classic architecture, has to boast of a decided Roman character." [380]

The Royal Crescent, an elegantly curved terrace of thirty residences, had been designed by John Wood the Younger,[381] who was also responsible for Bath's new Assembly Rooms, which, after opening in 1771, had been deemed "the most noble and elegant of any in the kingdom."[382]

With England's wealthier classes flocking to Bath like moths to a flame, the spa town was one of the best places for aspiring English gentlemen, such as George, to meet eligible ladies.

In the winter of 1786/7, balls were held both in the less fashionable "Lower" Assembly Rooms[383] and in the new "Upper" Assembly Rooms, where:

"The elegance of the ball-room astonishes every spectator, it is 100 feet 8 inches long, 42 feet 8 inches wide, and 42 feet 6 inches high. The ceiling is beautiful, ornamented with pannels [sic] with open compartments, and from which are suspended five superb glass chandeliers : the windows from which the rooms receive daylight, are on a ball night covered with boards painted with ornaments on them to correspond with the uniformity of the other side of the room. The walls are also painted and decorated in the most tasteful style ; and Corinthian columns and entablature resembles statuary marble. At each end of the room are placed, in magnificent gilt frames, the most splendid looking-glasses that could be procured to give effect to the general brilliant appearance. The whole suite of rooms are furnished in the same elegant style to correspond."[384]

Mary Eyre Matcham notes, "public balls took place on Tuesdays and Fridays, opening at six o'clock",[385] and, according to Bath Magazine, the Upper Assembly Rooms' Monday's event was a dress ball, Wednesday's was a concert, and cotillions (country dances) were held on Thursdays."[386]

Cotillions were choreographed, sequential dances in which couples were expected to keep perfect time. However, instructions issued to violinists in 1768 show that timings often went awry:

"It frequently happens, in dancing the Cotillons, that Ladies & Gentlemen finish out of Time at the termination of the first part of the Tune; ending sometimes too soon, & sometimes too late. In order to avoid the Confusion which would otherwise be the consequence of such Inattention or Mistake, the first Violin ought to know the Air by Heart; and when the Dancers do not come to their Places soon enough, instead of Playing it only twice or thrice, he must repeat it till they are all properly

arrived there; and, on the contrary, when the Dancers are so quick as to get their Places too soon, he must keep pace with their Movements, and proportionally shorten the repetition. If this Rule is punctually observed, no Confusion can possibly ensue".[387]

Jane Austen describes the packed hecticness of an Upper Assembly Room ball in her 1803 *Northanger Abbey:*

"The season was full, the room crowded, and the two ladies squeezed in as well as they could. As for Mr Allen, he repaired directly to the card-room, and left them to enjoy a mob by themselves."[388]

In late December 1786, a ball in the new Assembly Rooms was attended by "650 ladies and gentlemen".[389] Possible attendees, who were among many notable arrivals listed by Bath Chronicle and Weekly Gazette on the 28th of December, were: "Prince Gallitzin, Lord Loughborough, Lady T. Bathurst... Lady and Miss Howes... Hon, Mr. Dillon, Sir Watts Horton,... Mr. Serjeant Bolton, Gen. Matthew, and Sir John Danvers".[390]

Miss Scrivener, whom, according to the family story, George had set out to meet, was twenty-five-year-old Dorothea, the only surviving child of John Freston Scrivener and Mary née Howman. When George found Dorothea in that fateful winter ball in Bath, she was with her nineteen-year-old cousin, Kitty Nelson, who shared the Scriveners' Suckling ancestry.

The ballroom would have been heavy with the "powerful and varied floral bouquet" of expensive civet, ambergris and musk, whose combined scents eased "into a very light sweet musk."[391] This sweet perfume battled to mask the reek of rotten teeth –a common problem at this time– body odour, and mutton-fat pomades.[392]

Balls were competively fashionable, and attendees dressed to impress in costly brocaded satins, silks, and ruffled lace.[393] Their Rococo fashion was led by the famous French queen, Marie Antoinette,[394] who, by the mid 1780s, had taken to dressing in a more subdued manner than her flamboyant extravagances of the decade before. Towering, powdered wigs had made way for *au natural*[557] coiffeurs of frizzed or curled hair volumised with pads, twisted into ringlets, and looped over the head.[395] Dresses had low necklines, tight half-length sleeves, and were "of delicate floral-and-foliate patterned lace and white silk bows.".[396]

Style inspiration came from mass-produced copies of portraits by fashionable artists, such as Sir Joshua Reynolds and George Romney (the artist who'd painted George's travel chum, Eyles Irwin). With the *au natural* look's popularity on the rise, there was high demand for prints of Romney's paintings of his muse, Emma Hart, who'd posed in free-flowing, ancient Greek-style robes,[397] and whom George may have met in the flesh, as it were, along with Sir William Hamilton in Naples the year before.[398]

In Bath, balls were big business. Laying on the type of fancy fare the attendees were accustomed to would have decimated profits. Alcohol wasn't served, but cheap refreshments, comprising day old "thinly sliced stale bread, dry cakes, lemonade, coffee, and tea", could be purchased at about ten in the evening, for approximately sixpence, from a side room with no tables and only a few chairs.[399]

This chaotic bustle seems to have been more similar to modern-day club parties in Ibiza than the stately ensembles reenacted in costume dramas, and very different from George's regimented upbringing in Puritanical Bombay.

It was here, amidst a sensory riot of high fashion, pressing bodies, perfume, stink, violins, haphazard dancers, and poor food, that his eyes passed over the eligible Dorothea Scrivener and were, instead, hooked by her cousin, Kitty Nelson.

A contemporary miniature shows Kitty as daintily pretty and entirely *à la mode* in a low-cut white satin or silk dress with opulent lace spilling over her shoulders and cascading over her midriff to partially conceal a loose sash of the same sky blue as the ribbon atop her bushy, *au natural* puffs of rigid, powdered hair, framing a porcelain-white face. Kitty's eyes are enormous and dark as jet, contrasting with her snowy complexion. Looking fragile as an ice sculpture, her gaze is cast demurely down to focus on a point behind the artist's easel. Her dark brows hint that her natural hair colour is a deep brunette, perhaps black, as revealed in a much-later portrait.

Born on the 19th of March 1767, Kitty Nelson was the favourite sister of the not-yet-famous Captain Horatio Nelson of the Royal Navy, who their family called Horace.

Kitty's mother had died when she was eight-months old, leaving her to be raised by her sickly father, Reverend Edmund Nelson, the vicar of Burnham Thorpe in the county of Norfolk.[400]

In 1786, Horace, moved by Kitty's passionate, teenaged pleas, had been "prepared to pay for a second season in Bath so that she would not be stuck in Norfolk Society".[401]

When George struck up conversation with nineteen-year-old Kitty Nelson in that Bath winter ball, she may have confided that her older sister, Ann had, most poignantly, perished from catching a chill after leaving a different Bath ball without a cloak, three years before.[402] As we'll see, the ill-fated Ann's reckless personality may have led her to another, earlier, misadventure which the family had hushed up.

According to the Matchams' family story, when George fell in love with her, Kitty "proved equally susceptible and two months later they were married at Bath by her father the Rev. Edmund Nelson."[403]

Sixty-four-year-old Edmund Nelson is shown in portraits in his clerical black robe and starched white tie, and shoulder-length grey hair that's swept back from a sallow face which, like Kitty's, is oval with high cheekbones and full lips. Though his eyes are deep-set and soulful.

Nuances of Edmund Nelson and Kitty's father-daughter relationship unfold in Mary Eyre Matcham's 1911 Nelsons of Burnham Thorpe, which is largely based on correspondence "Kitty kept and safeguarded [with] coloured satin ribbons, dainty as her little self [and] of which many were from her father."[404] Kitty's family circle, presided over by Edmund Nelson, is described as a cheerful one in which "their father still stayed on in the old home, with a ready welcome to any one of the wanderers, come when they would."[405] Mary Eyre Matcham, however, notes a vein of clinginess in Edmund Nelson's letters to Kitty: "He begs, a little pathetically, for correspondence to 'throw a little variety into my amusements',"[406] and "the Rector has again to remonstrate gently with Catherine [Kitty] for her neglect of her correspondence".[407]

Kitty seems to have continued staying with the Scriveners after her father came to Bath in the early months of 1787, because her and George's allegation to marry in Walcot's St Swithin's church (dated the 23rd Day of February 1787) attests that George and Reverend Edmund Nelson were residing in the central parish of St. James, but "the usual Abode of Her the said Catherine Nelson has been within the said parish of Walcot for the Space of Four Weeks immediately last past". [408] This was in accordance with a 1753 ruling that marriage by licence could be granted by a bishop providing that at least one party had been living in the parish for four weeks.[409] [410] The same ruling classed nineteen-year-old Kitty as a minor, and the marriage allegation[411] was drawn up between Edmund Nelson and George:

"KNOW all Men by these Presents, that We George Matcham Esq. & the Rev. Edmund Nelson, Clerk, both of the parish of St James in the City of Bath & County of Somerset are held and firmly bound to the Rt. Rev. Father in God Charles by Divine Permission, Lord Bishop of Bath & Wells in two hundred pounds of lawful money of Great Britain to be paid [...] by these presents sealed with our seals Dated the twenty third Day of February in the Twenty seventh year of the Reign of our Sovereign Lord

George the Third [...] in the Year of our Lord one Thousand Seven hundred and eighty seven."

With permission duly granted (and £200 having been paid to the Bishop of Bath and Wells) George and Kitty were married by licence, on the 26th of February, in St Swithin's, Walcot, by Edmund Nelson as a guest vicar.[412]

Bath Chronicle and Weekly Gazette reported:

"...was married at Walcot Church, by the Rev. Mr. Nelson, (rector of Burnham in Norfolk) Geo. Matcham esq; of Enfield, Middlesex, to Miss Nelson, daughter of the said Mr. Nelson."[413]

St. Swithin's had been consecrated ten years before, in 1777, as part of Bath's grand, neoclassical development under the architectural conductorship of John Wood the Younger, who'd masterminded the Royal Crescent and new Assembly Rooms.[414]

Despite having no tower, St Swithin's was made prominent by standing on a low rise, and was "a handsome stone building [whose interior] is extremely interesting, it might be said grand".[415]

The parish of Walcot was awash with the earthy tangs of hops and yeast from Sayce & Kelson's Northgate Brewery, which had opened in 1770.[416] Walcot's population had been continuing to grow so rapidly that the ten-year-old church of St Swithin was already in need of an extension. [417] However, space inside wasn't an issue for George and Kitty because eighteenth century marriage ceremonies were small, serious occasions that were attended only by close family and friends, of whom two were required to stand as witnesses.

In keeping with the solemnity of the occasion, the church would have been undecorated [418] though the high, columned interior would have been brightened by light streaming through St Swithin's many tall windows. A 1787 plan of the church's interior shows twenty rows of pews with three columns and six windows each side of the aisle.[419]

The couple would have stood before Reverend Edmund Nelson, with his swept-back grey hair, sallow face, and black vicar's robe. George very likely wore a beautifully tailored suit of dark brown wool, comprising knee-length breeches, matching waistcoat and close-fitting jacket that was passed down through the Matcham family and whose tailoring corresponds to the late 1780s. The coat's "bucket" cuffs and natural waistline were typical of the last two decades of the eighteenth century, and its shoulders were padded in silk. The overall tailoring was very fine —some areas having 17-20 prick stitches per inch.[420] (A detailed description of his suit is provided in appendix three).

Custom dictated that Kitty carried a small bouquet tied with ribbon or lace.[421] She may have worn a similar outfit to Miss Jane Bailey, whose 1780s wedding dress, of cream coloured silk patterned with tiny flowers, was low cut with tight, elbow-length sleeves and a long skirt rouched to accentuate the width of her hips.[422]

The marriage witnesses were John Freston Scrivener and Kitty's petite, [423] thirty-one-year-old sister, Susanna Bolton.[424] A miniature portrait shows Susanna as elfinly pretty with a porcelain complexion, large, green-grey eyes and fair hair pinned beneath a voluminous, mobcap-style bonnet. [425] Susanna had travelled to Bath all the way from Norfolk, despite being the mother of a baby, named Thomas, and six-year-old twins, named Jemima and Catherine, who may have also attended the wedding ceremony, along with the Misses Marianne and Dorothea Scrivener.

After vows, in accordance with the Book of Common Prayer, George would have placed a ring on Kitty's finger and declared:

"With this ring I thee wed, with my body I thee worship, and with all my worldly goods I thee endow. In the Name of the Father, and of the Son, and of the Holy Ghost. Amen."[426]

In addition to the vows and ring, a massive, four thousand word, four-page legal settlement was drawn up, measuring approximately four feet wide by three feet high (a full transcription is provided in appendix four). Eighteenth-century marriage settlements were legally binding prenuptial agreements for the eldest son of an estate,[427] [428] in which the executors were made the legal owners of property as financial insurance for the bride and any future children. George and Kitty's settlement was unusual because, although George planned to buy an estate, he owned no land at this time. The executors were Kitty's father, Edmund Nelson, her brother, Reverend William Nelson and her maternal uncle, William Suckling. The latter two, living in London and Norfolk respectively, didn't attend the ceremony and agreed to add their signatures and seals when the newlyweds visited them after the wedding.

According to their marriage settlement:

"the said George Matcham being possessed of thirteen thousand three hundred and thirty three pounds six shillings and eight pence three per cent consolidated Bank Annuities standing in his name did upon the Treaty for and in consideration of the said intended marriage propose and offer

to transfer to and vest in the hands of the Trustees the said sum... to make a provision for the said Catherine Nelson and the Issue of the said George Matcham by her".[429]

George's contribution –£13,333 6s 8d– is the equivalent of over a million pounds sterling in the present-day. Kitty, for her part, contributed a total of one thousand six hundred and sixty six pounds thirteen shillings and four pence (£128,000 in today's money) which had amassed from £1,000 bequeathed by her uncle, Maurice Suckling, and its accumulated interest.

The majority of their four thousand word marriage settlement dictated how George and Kitty's combined contributions were to be handled and shared between any future children. The first page, however, cited Kitty's uncle, Maurice Suckling's, will, dated "the third day of August One thousand seven hundred and seventy one" which:

"(amongst other things) Give and bequeath unto Ann Nelson spinster and the said Catherine Nelson his nieces the respective sums of one thousand pounds a piece to be paid them respectively by the Executors in the said Will... And in case any of his said Nieces should depart their Life before she or they should have attained her or their age or ages of Twenty one years leaving issue of her or their Bodies lawfully begotten then the said Testator gave the Legacy of her or them so dying to their issue in equal shares".

Essentially, the clause specified that if Ann or Kitty died before the age of twenty-one, any lawfully born children were entitled to an equal share of Maurice Suckling's £1,000 bequest to the mother. In truth, the relevant section of Maurice Suckling's will names all three of his Nelson nieces: Susanna, Ann, and Kitty. So why wasn't Susanna likewise named in this section of the marriage settlement, and why was this clause specifically cited? A compelling explanation is that Ann had borne an illegitimate child whom the Nelson family was very much aware of. Eighteenth century English society held such a low opinion of unmarried mothers that families hushed things up. As such, it's hard to find evidence of out of wedlock births. However, a family story, related by a co-lateral descendant, Dr. Tim Ridge, is that Ann Nelson was employed as an apprentice lace maker in London and bore the child of an unmarried surveyor, named William Robinson, who was based in Old Street Road, Shoreditch. Their son, also named William Robinson, was taken in by the father.[430] A detailed version of Tim Ridge's account is provided in appendix five. Available records confirm Ann's lace making apprenticeship, and Nelson biographer,

Hibbert, mentions Ann's out of wedlock child:

"The middle sister, Anne, was… apprenticed, for a premium of £100, at Capital Lace warehouse in London where she was to be seduced and, having borne a child whose father abandoned her, to return home in disgrace at the age of twenty, and, not long afterwards, to die at Bath, having caught a chill 'occasioned by coming out of the ballroom immediately after dancing.'"[431]

Knowledge that Kitty's sister had borne an illegitimate child would surely have shocked George, whose prissy East India Company upbringing had ingrained him with an unshakeable belief in the sanctity of marriage. [432]

Whatever the truth, the unfortunate Ann Nelson had been buried three years before George and Kitty's marriage and the newlyweds were ready to forge their new, shared life together.

Their honeymoon, told through the dates and places of signatures added to their marriage settlement, comprised a leisurely, three-week journey across the breadth of England, from Bath to Norfolk.

George's in-laws likely took a faster route to their Norfolk homes, leaving the happy couple to dawdle, sightsee and revel in the romantic bliss of being wedded for love.

Temperatures were several degrees warmer than usual in the spring of 1787, but it was still chilly, averaging only 6 degrees centigrade (43 Fahrenheit) in March.[433] Foot warmers would have been needed inside carriages. If they chose to ride, warm cloaks would have been a necessity.

Of the attractions George and his delicate, dark eyed bride may have stopped to enjoy were Salisbury Cathedral and Stonehenge, both of which they visited during a tour of southern England several years later.[434]

They were in London by the first week of March. The population of England's capital had swelled to nearly a million after droves of people abandoned rural lives and streamed into the city in search of employment. London's cobbled streets were loud with clattering carts and street hawkers shouting their wares under pollution thick enough to black out the sun. Rich people were carried in sedan chairs whose bearers heaved their human cargos through the mayhem of pedestrians and carriage congestion that had been known to block traffic for as long as three hours.[435]

The newlyweds' destination was the home of Kitty's fifty-six-year-old, recently remarried uncle, William Suckling, who lived in the clean aired, rural parish of St Pancras,[436] [437] close to the grand, neoclassical British Museum which had opened thirty-years before.[438]

Law dictated that marriage settlement executors' signs and seals were witnessed by two or more credible citizens. In Bath, Edmund Nelson's witnesses had been John Freston Scrivener and his daughter, the still eligible Dorothea. In London, when William Suckling signed and sealed George and Kitty's settlement on the 8th of March, one of his witnesses was a black servant named James Price.[439]

Although slavery was outlawed in mainland Britain,[440] the status of black servants was questionable as some were neither paid nor free to leave. For example, Pero, who'd been taken to Bristol from the Caribbean plantation island of Nevis, seems to have been kept as a slave in England until his death in 1798.[441] However, James Price's signature on George and Kitty's marriage settlement implies that William Suckling deemed him a worthy legal witness.

Public opinion had been swaying against slavery, following the lead of post-revolutionary America, where abolitionist ideas had been gaining momentum in northern states, such as New York. England's first anti-slavery campaign group, *the society for effecting the abolition of the slave trade,* was founded in May 1787, two months after George and Kitty's visit. [442]

Having actively sought the company of merchants in Egypt, George would have relished talking shop with his new uncle-in-law, William Suckling, who was a career clerk in London's Custom House: the fast-beating heart of England's incoming trade which merchants flocked to from across the globe.[443] Custom House was 189 feet long and flanked by Tuscan wings either side of vast ground floor warehouses and an upper storey supported by columns.[444] This behemothic structure stood proudly adjacent to the Tower of London. Robinson Crusoe's author, Daniel Defoe, wrote of it:

"The stateliness of the building, showed the greatness of the business that is transacted there: the Long Room is like an Exchange every morning and the crowd of people who appear there, and the business they do, is not to be explained by words, nothing of that kind in Europe is like it".[445]

However, Custom House's stateliness was at odds with the prevailing stench of the Thames, into which 260 tons of raw sewage was emptied on a daily basis.[446]

Half-a-mile westward, along the north bank of the stinking river, George would have met Kitty's eldest brother, Maurice Nelson, whose address was at Queenhithe harbour.[447] Described variously as having an "open frank manner"[448] and being "conscientious, kindly and rather dull",[449] Maurice Nelson was a Navy Office clerk who was frequently in debt [450] and, through George's East India Company lens, a poor model of mercantile Christianity. Despite being a vicar's son, Maurice made little secret of having a nearly blind common law-wife, named Sukey, who was already married.[451]

After, no doubt, having also visited George's mother in Enfield, he and Kitty needed one more signature to make their marriage settlement legally binding: that of Kitty's brother, Reverend William Nelson, the recently appointed vicar of Hilborough in north-west Norfolk.

The most direct route to Hilborough passed through Essex into Norfolk's scrubby heathland which bustled with fellow travellers –both poor and rich– though the roads were "little better than meandering trackways through the gorse and bracken [though, fortunately] the sandy soils and low rainfall meant there were few of the muddy 'quicksands' found elsewhere to bog-down cart wheels".[452]

Portraits show Reverend William Nelson with his back ramrod straight and lower lip drooped. He signed George and Kitty's marriage settlement on the 15th of March, a week after William Suckling's signature was witnessed by James Price. One of William Nelson's witnesses was his paternal cousin, Ellen Rolfe.

George's new grandmother-in-law, who lived in Hilborough too, had a warm disposition and would have greeted George with open arms and lavished him with everything she could provide. Her compact, little house was of local style red brick and flint walls supporting a terracotta tiled roof. Her parlour's low ceiling was strutted with exposed beams pointing towards her modest hearth.[453]

Born in 1698, and now nearly ninety, Mary Nelson was "The good grandmother, at Hilborough [who] did all in her power to promote the happiness and comfort of her son's children... [she] was a fine old lady, and possessed uncommon wisdom, with extreme good-ness of heart. Her faculties were so lasting, that she could see to read the smallest print, and execute the finest needlework, till the close of her prolonged life".[454]

Her husband, Edmund Nelson senior, had been vicar of Hilborough from 1734 until his death in 1747, forty years before George's visit. Mary's widowhood hadn't been lonely because Hilborough's vicarship was something of a family business. Her son-in-law, Robert Rolfe was made vicar after her husband's demise, and the position was now held by her droop-lipped grandson, William Nelson, who lived in the rectory next-door with his "little... pretty black-eyed"[455] wife, Sarah.

George couldn't tarry in the warm sphere of Mary Nelson's hospitality because Kitty's father was waiting for them in Burnham Thorpe.

Chapter Nine: Newlywed in Norfolk

1787 – 1790

George's plan of buying an estate with his mother was superseded by his new father-in-law, Edmund Nelson's care needs. The "young couple, in intervals between other visits, spent their first summer together [in the] snug, little deep-roofed" rectory at Burnham Thorpe with George's new father-in-law. [456]

Burnham Thorpe, thirty miles north of Hilborough, was one of seven Burnhams: villages near the north-western Norfolk coast, flanking the river Burn. The other Burnhams were Burnham Deepdale, Burnham Norton, Burnham Overy, Burnham Sutton, Burnham Ulph and Burnham Westgate;[457] the region's main commercial hub which boasted avenues of neat Queen Ann and Georgian architecture.[458] In comparison, Burnham Thorpe's cottages were of the local, north-west Norfolk style of redbrick framed flint walls surmounted with pan-tile roofs. It was "a remote and peaceful little place, with a large church nearly six hundred years old, a few farmhouses, a big village green... with a stream running through it",[459] and a pub, called The Plough. The rectory occupied a pair of red-roofed cottages, that were joined at right angles, and overlooked a lush garden. Both buildings were two-storeyed, but the upper storey of one was an attic with dormer windows set into its pitched roof [460] –a far cry from both the architectural grandeur of Bath and the smelly, metropolitan bustle of London.

The countryside around Burnham Thorpe comprised "a large-scale, arable and grassland landscape over mostly rolling terrain, providing long views over remnant heath and mixed woodland belts",[461] that was undergoing profound change instigated by Thomas William Coke, the first Earl of Leicester, whose new hall at Holkham, neighbouring Burnham Thorpe, had been completed in 1764.[462] Earl Coke had successfully increased his crop yields through his innovations of soil nurture, crop rotation and replacing traditional strip fields and common land with enormous, enclosed fields. Coke's success had ricocheted to inspire wealthy yeomen farmers to employ his methods on their own farms.[463] A popular crop was barley, which was made into malt for beer and exported from nearby Wells.[464]

Reverend Edmund Nelson employed an inside servant named Will, and a gardener, whom he described as "the Aid de Camp, Peter Black, poor, forlorn; tho' as wise as ever." Parish records reveal that Peter Black was eight years younger than his employer.

According to Mary Eyre Matcham, Edmund Nelson suffered his severance from Kitty as a long-lasting wound, but "their separation came gently upon him, while his gain in the affection and help of a son was immediate and lifelong."[465]

Ever-restless, George threw himself into reworking the rectory's garden, deeming it in need of "vast landscape gardening improvements." His enthusiastic clearing, planting, and aquatic engineering of "the stream running bright and swiftly by the Rectory grounds", prompted Edmund Nelson to quip, "Myself and Peter as under Artists in Improvements, must have another lesson from 'Capability M' before we can make a finish." [466] This being a play on the name of the famous landscape gardener, Capability Brown, with "M" signifying Matcham.

There were plenty of other new in-laws to meet. For George, whose only siblings had died in early childhood, Kitty's multitude of brothers, sisters and other close kin would have felt bountiful. The Nelson clan seem to have been pretty eccentric. His father-in-law described himself as whimsical[467] whilst few, if any, of Kitty's seven siblings adhered to contemporary norms.

Kitty's twenty-three-year-old brother, Suckling Nelson –named for their mother's family– was a wastrel. Suckling owned a shop in nearby North Elham, but neglected it "for the more entertaining pastimes of greyhound racing and drinking in the local inn".[468] Mary Eyre Matcham says of him: "Suckling, born in 1764, had tried business with no success, and was still unsettled in any profession ; constantly in money difficulties, taciturn, good-natured, fond of sport and indolent, yet ready to be influenced for good".[469]

George's thoughts on the unconventional lifestyles of his new in-laws are unrecorded. His upbringing, under Presbyterian-dominated East India Company rule in Bombay, had been rigidly strait-laced with profit-making and adherence to Christian diktat valued above all else. Suckling Nelson's lacklustre work ethic, and Maurice Nelson's disregard for the holy state of matrimony were shockingly reprobate according to East India Company morality.

A less eccentric new in-law was Kitty's sister, Mrs. Susanna Bolton, who'd witnessed their marriage and resided a five-and-a-half-mile horse trot east of Burnham Thorpe in the thriving port of Wells.

Like George, Kitty enjoyed horse riding.[470] The approach to Wells was ideal galloping ground of heath dotted with trees and fields of ripened grain that glowed pale gold under the summer sun.[471] Cantering under Norfolk's deep blue skies, with the sun on his face and the wind rushing past his ears, would have reminded George of horseback dashes across the Syrian desert when he, Irwin and Smyth procured horses to speed ahead of the excruciatingly slow camel train. [472]

The little town of Wells was an enclave of "narrow lanes near the quay, and [a] wealth of Georgian… buildings"[473] at the head of a North Sea inlet cutting through a vast swathe of tangy salt marsh.

Susanna, who was just as dainty and petite as Kitty, had twin daughters and an infant son with another baby due in November. Thankfully, her husband, Thomas Bolton, was a successful coal and corn merchant who was well able to support his growing family.[474]

At the age of twenty-six, Thomas Bolton was five years younger than his wife. His miniature portrait shows him with a cleft chin; small, neat lips and wide, slate-blue eyes surmounted by bushy, black brows. His nose has a slight "ski-jump" curve and his complexion is fair. His powdered hair is wavy, but brushed back from his forehead, where it forms a widow's peak. His jacket is dark with large buttons. His prominent white collar harmonises with his neat, white cravat.[475]

Thomas Bolton employed Kitty's twenty-four-year-old brother, Mun[476] (Edmund Nelson junior) as an accounts clerk.[477] Merchant-minded George would have been excited to discuss the accounts with Mun and curious to learn every facet of the business from Thomas himself. George, who'd filled his journals with ideas for improving cotton production in Broach, would have approved of the state-of-the-art methods for increasing local crop yields, and news that Wells was now hot on the heels of Great Yarmouth as Norfolk's biggest malt exporter[478] may have motivated him to slap Thomas Bolton on the back. He'd have been less happy though to hear that Thomas, and fellow merchants and ship owners, were pitched in an ongoing battle against criminals hellbent on stealing their goods and profits. The year before, Thomas had been one of ten subscribers to a newly formed association for bribing informants:

"We whose Names are hereunto subscribed, being Merchants, and Owners of Keels and other Craft trading to and from Yarmouth, having entered into an ASSOCIATION for the more effectually prosecuting any Person or Persons who shall at any Time hereafter steal, purloin,

embezzle, or receive any stolen Corn, Coals, Wares or Merchandizes, of or belonging to any Person or Persons who are, or may be Members of this Association, out of or from their Keels or other craft, or out of their Malting Offices, Granaries, Warehouses, Coal Yards, or other Places belonging to them : And for the better discovering and bringing to Justice any such Person or Persons, we do hereby offer a Reward of TEN GUINEAS to any Person who shall discover, or give Information of any Person or Persons so offending to be paid immediately upon Conviction, by Mr. EDWARD SQUIRE, Treasurer to the said Association.

Edward Squire	*Clement Parnell*
John Lock	*Thomas Bolton*
Henry Mountain	*Bernard Wigg*
Mrs. Dye	*Thomas Burrell*
Thomas Thompson	*Richard Wright.* "[479]

Kitty would have been disappointed that George still hadn't met her favourite brother, Horace, who was serving with the Royal Navy in the Caribbean.[480]

*

George may have been relieved when he and Kitty moved into Barton Hall, their own, private, marital home, in the autumn of 1787, but Edmund Nelson lamented that they'd abandoned him, adding, pitifully, "The wind is very cold".[481]

Barton Hall was rented from the Preston family of Beeston[482] in western Norfolk. It was located in the remote eastern Broads: close enough to Burnham Thorpe to be in easy reach of Edmund Nelson –and Kitty's other, dispersed relatives– but distant enough to enable marital seclusion.

The Broads, which were the byproduct of digging peat for fuel,[483] were a vast wetland of reed-beds and *broads* (lakes) interconnected by narrow, slow-moving waterways.

Barton Hall, which came ready furnished,[484] was grand and modern with a smart coach-house constructed from the same red brick as the main house.[485] In flashy disregard for the government's window tax,[486] Barton Hall's, two-storeyed front façade glinted with eighteen, high, Georgian-style windows. The central rooms jutted out beneath a crowning pediment. The lower of these was the main parlour, which boasted three windows facing the lawn, and one each side facing, respectively, north and south. Despite its luxuriant quantity of windows, the room remained shadily cool, even during high summer.[487]

For George and Kitty, at "Barton happy days are told of in note-books, scribbled in for a few days and left half empty"[488] and Kitty's "journal of these days is a record of contentment. Both at Burnham and Barton they read, rode, studied, and gardened to their heart's satisfaction. Relations and neighbours flowed in and out in a constant stream of genial intercourse." [489] George was generous to the poor of the parish whose aid to them was "at various times received". [490]

Barton Hall stood to the immediate south of Barton Turf village with grounds comprising a:

"pleasant park sloping gently down to Barton Broad below, with distant view of windmill and church steeple, the nearer and lowest point enlivened with chocolate sails belonging to the lazy little boats which creep about in its winding channels. Standing by the wicket which opens at the bottom of the field, it is easy to imagine the cheerful companies, full of youth and good spirits, strolling on warm evenings down the pathway and out upon the strip of bordering common, with its many domestic beasts and wild birds".[491]

Here, George's idyll of owning an estate and enjoying a "wife, farming and hunting" was partially fulfilled for –though Barton Hall wasn't his and he didn't farm the land– he was with his new wife and the Broads had plentiful wild birds to be brought down with shotguns.

A hunting and fishing journalist, writing in 1829, described George's new surrounds with enthusiasm:

"The in-land broads, as they are called in Norfolk, are wonderfully ornamental (if I may use the term) to a sporting manor in that county : they abound with line fish, admirable nurseries for domestic wild-fowl, and the skirts form excellent covert for stray pheasants."[492]

There were bitterns, *shovelards* (spoonbills), *black curlews* (glossy ibis), *shoeing horns* (avocets), migrating storks,[493] coots and young ducks for *flapper shooting* by boat.[494] For those who preferred fishing, enormous pike lurked the still waters and could be caught with a *jigger*: a "long cylindrical float, made of wood or cork, or rushes tied together at each end" from which bait dangled and painted floats of cork or wood bobbed to indicate if a pike was caught.[495]

An early Victorian guide to the fauna of the Broads deemed that the landscape of "flat and marshy borders, covered with reeds and rank vegetation have little to interest the seeker after picturesque beauty.[496]

Kitty, though, was so moved by the Broads' beauty that she waxed lyrical:

"We walkt on the broad... the water was calm and of a deep blue, corresponding to the ethereal arch. How beautiful did the scenery round present itself, the circling wood varied with steeples and mills, cattle grazing on the water's brink, the fishermen with their eel spears in pursuit of their prey ; the common spread with the various domestics of the tennants [sic], cows, pigs, geese, ducks ; the whole afforded a picture of plenty and enjoyment. "[497]

While George amused himself hunting and fishing, Kitty occupied herself with craft projects –painting tea sets, engraving copper plates, and "an immense amount of tapestry work". Her love of nature spilled into notebooks in which she jotted observations gleaned during walks and rides:

"the women weeding in the field ; the waterlilies flowering on the broad ; the laylocks fading ; birds singing concealed in trees and shrubs in the heat of noon ; the cows seeking the shade, while horses feed exposed. "[498]

Life, though, went on beyond that "ethereal arch" of George and Kitty's happy, Broadland bubble.

George's father-in-law wrote to Kitty telling her to congratulate the William Nelsons in Hilborough for the birth of their first baby, Charlotte, who was born on the 20th of September 1787.[499] Shortly after this, on the 12th of November, Thomas and Susanna Bolton's new baby was given the name George.

Kitty's attention was yanked further from their honeymoon bliss by the news that her favourite brother, Horace had returned to England after several years of service in the Caribbean.

Like George, Horace had married in the spring of 1787.[500] His bride, Fanny –a widow with a young son– hailed from the Woolward family of Nevis who, like the majority of the tiny plantation island's white populace, owned slaves.[501] Their wedding had taken place on Montpelier Plantation, which belonged to Fanny's uncle. Horace's best man had been Prince William Henry[502] (the future King William IV) who'd joined the navy when he was thirteen.[503]

George was amused by Kitty's hero-worshipping devotion to her seafaring brother. When George came across a mention of Horace in a newspaper, he read it to Kitty, playfully pretending the article referred to someone else. But Kitty, undeceived, told George, "I know that was my brother".[504]

To Kitty's immense frustration, the Admiralty delayed granting Horace leave to come home to Norfolk. However, his eight-year-old stepson, Josiah arrived in Hilborough in January 1788 accompanied by one of Horace's servants and instructions for George's brother-in-law, Reverend William Nelson, to enrol him in a good boarding school.[505] Kitty wanted to hurry to London to find Horace, and George was happy to take the opportunity to visit his mother who'd "settled there". They set off for London on the 12th of January 1788, only for Kitty to be frustrated again. She wrote to her father, "Brother Horace gone to Bath, I was very low spirited".

Edmund Nelson replied, "Your disappointment (I will not say a little one) I anticipated... Respecting Self it now hails and snows, no wonder I am as Meagre and as shivering as... a poor Highland curate". [506]

Kitty's father was terrified that his humble, drafty parsonage would offend Horace's bride, whom he thought of as a great lady. Edmund Nelson told Kitty, "I am not now anxious to see them... [Horace] for a day or two I should be glad of, but to introduce a stranger to an infirm and whimsical old man, who can neither eat nor drink, nor talk, nor see, is as well let alone". He then wrote to Horace instructing him to delay bringing his wife to Burnham Thorpe and to, instead, take her to stay with relatives, such as George and Kitty, whose homes were more fitting for a refined lady.[507] Duly diligent of Edmund Nelson's instructions, Horace and his new wife arrived at Barton Hall in the summer of 1788.[508]

Kitty likely jumped up and down with excitement when, at long last, she was reunited with her most beloved brother.

George, who'd have no doubt witnessed Kitty's bubbling joy with amused affection, would have been curious to finally get to know his wife's favourite brother, whom she'd told him so much about. In later years, he wrote that Horace was "Of a delicate structure, of a reflective mind, strongly tinged with melancholy, retired and domestic in his habits". [509]

When George first met him, twenty-nine-year-old Horace, like Kitty, was short in stature, but big in personality and adored his family completely. Few people could resist his charismatic warmth and vitality. He touted a fashionably rakish mop of disheveled white hair[510] and was remarkably scruffy for a Royal Navy officer.[511]

Horace's Nevis bride, Fanny, had been variously described by Horace's crewmen as, "pretty and sensible", "pretty and attractive" and, less flatteringly, as having "some beauty, and a freshness of countenance [but possessing] unremarkable intellect."[512] She had a birdlike gait,[513] was slim, with sloping shoulders, fair hair, large, doleful eyes under generous brows, and small, frown-prone lips.[514]

Horace told George and Kitty, fretfully, that Edmund Nelson, "though cheerful" was "more unwell then usuall [sic] by the addition of a tertian Ague". Kitty urged her father to come to Barton Hall so she could care for him, but he refused "her anxious prescription of rest and change at Barton" saying "the shaking Feind [sic] is driven off" and "the charming, open Lawns, and pure air collected from the large fields of Thorpe" were a better tonic than the "Effluvia of Barton Broad".[515]

In October, Horace stood as godparent for his brother, William Nelson's second child, who was baptised in Hilborough on the 26th of October and named Horatio in Horace's honour.[516] George's sister-in-law, Susanna Bolton already had four children, but both Kitty and Fanny were still childless after eighteen-months of marriage. Given Kitty's later, prolific fertility it may be that she'd miscarried.

Horace was keen to go back to sea, but England was at peace so the Admiralty had no need of him.[517] He instead settled down with Fanny in his father's rectory in Burnham Thorpe where Suckling had also retreated, having entirely given up as a shopkeeper.[518] Horace passed his time, as George had done, by attacking the rectory's "garden, where his father and old Peter Black had been raising a ha-ha, preparing beds for roses, lilacs and hyacinths, and creating a pond".[519]

The year of 1789 was momentous for the extended Nelson kin: Kitty's feckless brother, Suckling, decided to train for the clergy and travelled to Melton Mowbray in Leicestershire to lodge with a tutor. In London, Maurice Nelson's debts were cleared,[520] and in Barton Turf, Kitty had at last conceived. Her pregnancy was progressing well, but her and George's joy was marred when, on the 4th of July 1789, Kitty's doting grandmother, Mary Nelson, died in her Hilborough cottage. The family's distress was increased by Kitty's brother, Mun's dire health. He'd become so ill that he'd given up working for Thomas Bolton in Wells and joined Kitty's father, Horace and Fanny in the rectory at Burnham Thorpe.

In the wider world, and unknown to George and his grieving in-laws, a revolution was exploding in France that would, ultimately, change their lives forever.[521]

On the 2nd of December 1789, ten days before Mun's death, George and Kitty's first child, George Matcham junior was baptised in Norwich.

Eight days after this, *Bath Chronicle and Weekly Gazette* included George's mother in their round up of notable arrivals.[522] Bath's incoming throng was as prolific and well-to-do as ever. The spa town was shaping up for yet another packed season of partying. The French revolution was now common knowledge, but England had, so far, kept peace with its Gallic cross channel neighbours.

Back in Norfolk, Horace was still twiddling his thumbs in his father's rectory wondering if the Admiralty would ever call him back into service and, on a more personal note, if Fanny would, at long last, conceive and bear him a child of his own.

Chapter Ten: Idyll Achieved

1791 – 1798

Though Mun's demise was a huge blow for elderly Edmund Nelson, he wasn't alone in Burnham Thorpe's drafty rectory because Horace and Fanny were still staying there. In the summer of 1790, George took advantage of the situation by taking Kitty on a tour of southern England looking for suitable land for manifesting his long hoped-for idyll of owning a country estate.

Mary Eyre Matcham tells that, during their tour of southern England, after having been "delayed by the breaking down of their chaise they journeyed to Worcester, past the Malvern Hills and on through Hereford to Brecon where the good roads failed." This may have been especially hard on Kitty, who was pregnant again. Then:

"Exploring the show places on the way; they passed by Bath, Stonehenge and Salisbury with the object of seeing a property near Ringwood in Hampshire. The country near Ringwood satisfied them, but there was no house; but what could please them better than building one and planting the grounds with woods". [523]

A contemporary travel writer described this land near Ringwood as "covered with heath" and "black and dreary"[524] but George and Kitty thought it a pleasant "spott". [525] The site, named Shepherd's Spring, was in Hampshire's ancient New Forest, near the border with the Matchams' ancestral county of Dorset. It was nine-miles north of the coastal town of Christchurch; and the nearest village, Ringwood, was about three-miles to the north and large enough to have two pubs: the White Hart and The Crown.[526]

George and Kitty travelled 230 miles from Hampshire back to Norfolk in time for their second child to be born in Barton Hall on the 4th of February 1791. He was baptised, two days later, in the parish church, and named Henry Savage Matcham for George's childhood mentor.

111

Edmund Nelson wrote to Kitty on the 14th of March:

"With respect to your removing, your sentiments are quite proper... If the large glass in your present drawing room is in the catalogue of saleables, one of your acquaintances Even My Self would buy it. You kindly offered Mrs. Nelson [Fanny] to give her the marble Slab. She declined it, still I believe it would be pleasing to them Both. Still my opinion is there is neither occasion nor obligation to give away much. I dont think you are quite rich enough".[527]

On the 10th of August 1791, George obtained formal consent from the trustees of his and Kitty's marriage settlement –Edmund Nelson, William Nelson and William Suckling– to release part of the capital to purchase a mortgage on the New Forest land he'd viewed. In legalese, this was:

"the sum of Eight thousand pounds | part of the within mentioned sum of Thirteen thousand three hundred and thirty three pounds six shillings and eight pence | three per cent consolidated Bank annuities which had produced the sum of six thousand seven hundred and forty pounds in Cash and had advanced and lent to the said George Matcham [...] part thereof upon a mortgage of certain Estates in the County of Southampton".[528]

Construction of George's dream home in Hampshire –the "County of Southampton"– commenced quickly. Despite it still being a building site, George formally departed Barton Turf in September 1791 when, according to the Norfolk Chronicle, the poor of the parish returned "their sincere thanks to G. Matcham, Esq. for the many benefits they have at various times received, and particularly for a donation of 4 [pounds and] 4 [shillings] when he left the parish."[529]

Though the majority of any charitable donations will have gone unrecorded, George was a "subscriber" (financial supporter) of an English translation of a Scottish language comedy, *the gentle shepherd,* of whom the first-listed subscriber was "Her Royal Highness the duchess of Gloucester, 4 copies."[530]

Ringwood Meeting House & History Centre hold a copy of an 1801 legal document pertaining to George's purchase of Shepherd's Spring:

"Roll 87
Trinity Term 31st K Geo 3rd: 1791
C[o] of Southampton
Edmund Nelson clerk William Nelson clerk & William Sucking Esq.

Plts [plaintiffs] George Matcham Esq. & Catherine his wife Defen^s [defendants] – of one thousand two hundred acres of forage and heath [,] one hundred acres of moor [,] common of pasture for all manner of cattle [,] common of Turbary [the common right to cut turf for fuel] & common of Estovers [the right to have wood from the New Forest for fuel] with the appurts ["appurtenances" aka property assets] in Barren[?] Field otherwise Barn Field in the parish of Christchurch Twyneham & in the New Forest[.] Before S^r. Henry Gould Kn^t [Knight] one of the Justices of the Common Bench 27 Augt 31st K Geo 3

Returnable from the day of the Holy Trinity in 3 weeks

Examined with the entry of the Kings Silver Office Elm Court Temple March 11th 1801"

Although a first glance at the document may give the impression that George's inlaws were suing him for having failed to repay a debt, the writ's 1791 date coincides with the executors' consent to release marriage settlement funds for the mortgage of Shepherd's Spring and the 1801 date of the writ's examination coincides with George selling a portion of the land to William Driver 1st Earl of Malmesbury.[531] Despite the confusing legalese, it doesn't, therefore, seem that the writ's purpose was to press George to repay a debt, especially as Kitty is also named and their marriage settlement's purpose was to ensure financial provision for her and any children. And they kept having more. George and Kitty's third child, a girl, was baptised Catherine Ann Matcham in Ringwood's parish church of St Peter's & St Paul's, on the 8th of August 1792.

George wanted the house he was having built at Shepherd's Spring to be a grand home for his growing family. Edmund Nelson wrote to him of the pros and cons of investing in furniture:

"*Whether it is most prudent to buy cheap and often, or substantially good, such as Grandchildren may see and admire, is a question fit for discussion in a Schooll of Aeconomy [sic]*" [532]

As George ruminated on the merits of economising on the quality of the home he was building, his infant son, Henry Savage Matcham, fell ill and died. He was buried in Ringwood's cemetery in the autumn of 1792. The inscription on his tomb reads:

"*Here lieth the body of Henry Savage Matcham*
Son of George & Catherine Matcham
He died Sept. 30th 1792 - Aged 19 months"

The loss of George's second son –named for his childhood mentor– was a huge blow and would have dampened his enthusiasm for his New Forest idyll.

Horace sent condolences to Kitty:

"BURNHAM, Oct. 1st 1792
MY DEAR SISTER : Mrs. Nelson & myself were most truly sorry for the loss you & Mr. Matcham have sustained, but the loss of children is certainly to be expected and we are surprised that from so many complaints which the poor little things are subject to, that so many are reared to Mature age."[533]

George and Kitty weren't isolated in their grief. Shepherd's Spring, incomplete as it was, was already attracting a multitude of visitors who "flocked to them undaunted by the abominable roads which led from Bath."[534] One of these was George's cousin, Harriet Armstrong of Castle Armstrong in Ireland, who'd spent the summer with them until, as she noted in her travel diary "23rd October 1792 Left Ringwood this morning..."[535]

After Harriet Armstrong's departure, George and Kitty left their children in Ringwood and went to London where they visited Kitty's brother Maurice. Edmund Nelson opted not to travel to London too because he didn't want to encourage Kitty to spend more time away from her children.[536]

In another letter, dated the 15th of December 1792, Horace chatted about country affairs in Burnham Thorpe, including an anecdote about two ladies in a party who'd believed the Matchams were "Mitchams" living in India,[537] adding:

"Maurice tells me that you sett off from London on Wednesday last week and are I think now settled at Ringwood for the winter, which we must soon expect to make its appearance."

On the 16th of January 1793, Edmund Nelson sent news to Shepherd's Spring that the Admiralty had, at long last, reemployed Horace:

"the result of your Bro's application for a ship, which at last has been attended with all the Success He could hope, or wish. With great politeness and expressions of regard for His Character, the first Lord gave him his choice of two 64 Gun Ships now getting ready... This Event, though wished for, puts us in a little Hurry. Poor Mrs. Nelson will I hope, bear up with a degree of chearfullness at the separation from so Kind a Husband and my own loss of the constant freindly and filiall regard I have

experienced, I do feell. However He himself is in Good Spirits and Health. When He has his commission he will write. He is at Thorpe."[538]

Following this, on the 26th of January, five days after revolutionary France alienated England entirely by cutting off King Louis XVI's head with a guillotine, Horace took command of Agamemnon: a 64-gun ship of the line.[539] [540]

When news reached Shepherd's Spring of France's 1st of February 1793 declaration of war on Britain[541] they'd have been poignantly aware that Horace, in command of Agamemnon, was perilously engaged. Subsequent news that France's dainty, fashion-setting queen, Marie Antoinette was guillotined, seven-months later, on the 21st of September, shocked British hearts to the core. What level of monsters were these French revolutionaries?

Fanny resented Horace's keenness to go back to sea[542] and wished he'd stayed quietly at her side in rural Norfolk, where she and Edmund rubbed along amicably. Fanny, like Edmund, was frail and suffered dreadfully from the cold.[543] They were also both worriers. Fanny vexed Horace with her inability to correspond cheerfully. In one letter she told Horace, "This winter will be another anxious one. What I did not suffer in mind, the last one!"[544]

Edmund Nelson was worried about George and Kitty's new-build home, and wrote to them on the 27th of May 1793, "I tremble for your new house as a habitation. Our sun is not so powerfull in its exhalation as at Bombay. Only two years ago this sleeping place was a Lump of Chaotic Mud", but added "cautious congratulations that Shepherd's Spring was at last ready for habitation."[545]

George got on well with the Ringwood locals. He mused, "Foreigners complain of the incivility of our lower class of people. They are mistaken ; the common people of England are civil and even respectful, but when assailed in a high tone and abrupt manner, they feel indignant and return insult for insult. One set of Beings are proverbially rude. Hackney Coachmen... This arises from their daily dealing with various people, some of whom attempt to trick them... But from country labourers you may be assured of civil attention, provided your own conduct merits it. Affected politeness would be absurd... but gentle and orderly commands, kind enquiries of their families, of their own healths &c. will ensure their respect".[546]

A 1798 travel guide lists George's "seat" three-and-a-half miles to the left of Ringwood, along with fellow landowners, all of whom he'd have been acquainted with:

"One Mile and ½ from Ringwood, on l[eft] is Avon Cottage, Robert Drummond, Esq.
Two Miles on the r[ight] of Ringwood, is Somerly, D. Hobson, Esq.
About 2 miles from Ringwood, on l. is Barnfield, G. Jennings, Esq.
About 3 ½ Miles on l. is a Seat of George Matcham, Esq..."[547]

With Shepherd's Spring complete, George was in a position to fine-tune his idyll of owning an estate with his mother and having a "wife, farming and hunting" as his "three principal sources of amusement". [548] Although, judging by the number of children they produced, he evidently enjoyed Kitty very much. He didn't own Shepherd's Spring with his mother, and Edmund Nelson, determined to put paid to George's plan to take up farming, cautioned:

"Landed property [is] a circumstance in this country which gives weight and consequence to a man's actions, makes him respectable and a usefull member of society... Look forward to what ever your country can bestow... except Gain by Farming. Believe not every spirit that would tempt you into this snare. Use it as a pleasure, but not a Trade... All Well at Thorpe, perhaps it may be news to say Mr. and Mrs. Coke[549] *have visited there".* [550]

In another letter, Edmund Nelson opined that George was "no match for the chicanery and cunning of illiberal men. Gentlemen Farmers are for ever boasting of their Great Gain. The Real Farmer is always complaining and He has the profit".

Mary Eyre Matcham speculates: "This distrust was further increased when others of the family were bitten with farming enterprises. The Boltons were at this time planning to move from Norwich with the same intention, though still in doubt as to their destination ; but the rector continued to allure G. M.'s energies towards other pursuits : 'Farming fatigued you and very wisely in my opinion you gave it up. Let building be [your] amusement [instead]'".[551]

George duly abandoned the idea of farming and opted, instead, to develop a pine plantation.[552]

As for realising the hunting element of his idyll, he purchased an area of the New Forest, a few miles north of Ringwood[553] called Plumley Heath,[554] for which he employed a gamekeeper, named John Merryweather, in the latter months of 1793.[555]

The New Forest was home to such a fine population of red deer that King George III's master of the stag-hunt used them to top up the numbers in Windsor Forest "for his majesty's enjoyment of field-sport".[556]

New Forest villagers had a long tradition of hunting squirrels to make into pies –squirrel meat being more delicate than rabbit– but gentlemen preferred to hunt foxes (which they didn't eat).[557]

In the year that George acquired Plumley Heath, Sporting Magazine published a poem celebrating fox hunting near Ringwood:

"CHARACTER OF A FOX-HUNTER.
THE squire is proud to see his courser strain,
Or well-breath'd beagles sweep along the plain...
When thy sleek gelding nimbly leaps the mound,
And Ringwood opens on the tainted ground..."[558]

Kitty, who was heavily pregnant again, may not have relished being left home alone when George went hunting. However, the part of his idyll that involved sharing an estate with his mother may have been realised to a degree. It seems probable that George's sixty-year-old mother, Mrs. Elizabeth Matcham, stayed in Shepherd's Spring as, amongst other things, a helpmeet to pregnant Kitty and her tumble of tiny Matcham children. There are no 1790s newspaper records of "Mrs. Matcham" arriving in Bath, and none of Kitty's Nelson siblings lived nearby, so who else could have offered practical female support whilst George was merrily gallivanting around the New Forest as a gentleman hunter?

George's idyll was now happily complete. He was "pleased with the spott... their pretty property ; the house they had built ; and the precious plantations so lately put in." [559]

His fourth child was born on the 28th of November 1793: in good time for their celebration of Christmas in their now-readied house. They named him Edmund Nelson Matcham for Kitty's father. Sadly, the baby appears to have died young, the last mention of him is in 1802. The ill-fated infant's namesake, Reverend Nelson, was now in the sole care of Horace's wife, Fanny. Though both Fanny and Kitty had wed in the spring of 1787, Fanny –unlike Kitty– remained unblessed with children. With Horace away at sea, if Fanny wasn't pregnant already, she'd have no chance of conceiving unless Horace survived the war against France and sailed home.

In Shepherd's Spring, George was still in active –and profitable– correspondence with the East India Company. He received a letter from their agent in Soho, dated the 16th of September 1794, informing him:

"Sir,

I have the satisfaction to inform you that the Lords of the Treasury have made an order for payment of £100 to you as by your last memorial on your giving an Indemnity against the Certificate ever being produced by any of person — The Bond their Lordships have directed to be prepared by their solicitor Mr. Whyde of Lincolns Inn and as soon as I can procure it from him I will forward it to you in order that it may be executed." [560]

George, ever restless, had now tired of Plumley Heath and he dispensed with his gamekeeper, John Merryweather, in the latter months of 1796, in favour of renting Bourne House, which had an attached acreage of prime hunting ground and was located near to Christchurch on the sparsely populated Hampshire coast where the present-day resort of Bournemouth now stands. In the words of Bournemouth Local History:

"From 1796, Nelson's brother-in-law George Matcham had been living at Bournemouth – or more precisely Bourne House (sometimes called Decoy Cottage)... It was a property he rented from Lord of the Manor, Sir George Ivison Tapps." [561]

The lease for Bourne Lodge, drawn up on the 26th of April 1796, obliged George to pay "£2 per annum and a consideration of £170 of Decoy Pond and 25 acres." The fee was for the use of both the house and the land. "The whole property was known as the Decoy Pond Estate, and it was definitely a hunting estate – for shooting ducks. It was the remnant of Stourfield Chase, a hunting estate which extended from Bournemouth to Hengistbury Head (where there was a warren for hunting rabbits)." [562]

By early 1797, George had decided that his children's educational needs would be better met in Bath. [563] He now had three living children with a fourth on the way. George "saw no difference to be attended to the education of boys and girls except their being taught Latin and Greek." [564] Beyond this, and regardless of his children's education –after all, he could afford tutors– his country gentleman idyll was completed and it was time for the ever-restless George to apply himself to something new. He and Kitty were, nonetheless, reluctant to leave their self-build Hampshire home.

Horace, still away at sea, had been promoted to Rear Admiral of the Blue. Fanny seems to have written to him about buying Shepherd's Spring, because he replied, from HMS Theseus, on the 12th of July 1797, "I never saw Sheppards Spring nor do I fancy if it was within our purse it would suit us."

Though neither George nor Kitty had seen Horace since he went to sea four years before, he wrote home regularly. His right eye had been all but blinded during a skirmish at Corsica in 1794,[565] and a British naval disaster in Tenerife, in July 1797, had resulted in Horace losing his right arm and being sent home on sick leave. When he arrived in Bath, in early September, Fanny and his father whisked him into their rented address at No.17 New King Street.[566]

George and Kitty hastened to Bath from Shepherd's Spring but, when they set eyes on Horace, their "sorrow was mixed with rejoicings [to see him again] for he was in a miserable state of suffering". He looked "so sickly it was painful to see him",[567] but he was still plucky and hopeful that Bath's spa water "would ease the pain of the stump of his right arm. [568]

Here in Bath, well-to-do people contstantly paraded the latest fashions. For men, the use of hair powder had been dwindling since *the duty on hair powder act* was introduced in 1795 to raise funds for the war against France.[569]

The French revolution had changed female fashion for a different reason. The brutal removal of Queen Marie Antoinette from fashion prominence[570] had caused trend-seeking eyes to focus, instead, on Lady Hamilton, the wife of Sir William Hamilton, the cultured British Ambassador to Naples. Lady Hamilton was the new incarnation of the poor-born Emma Hart, whose *au natural* Romney portraits had been prized a decade before when George and Kitty first met. Emma's marriage into the British peerage had smashed through the era's rigid class and gender boundaries and elevated her further into the public eye. In the 1790s, *"muslin en chemise* dresses were finally accepted as a type of formal attire through the influence of [Emma] who wore the same revealing ensembles to perform her 'Attitudes'."[571] Emma's Attitudes were an entirely new art-form, of her own invention, in which she performed a series of tableaux depicting scenes from ancient Greek and Roman classics.[572] The poet, Goethe noted, "with a few shawls [she] gives so much variety to her poses, gestures, expressions, etc, that the spectator can barely believe his eyes." In line with dressing "à la Lady Hamilton", [573] by the latter part of the 1790s, shawls had become "the rage as fashion accessories"[574] to accompany the ancient Grecian inspired, high-waisted dresses that would have been seen all around Bath adorning ladies escorted by equally fashionable gentlemen with unpowdered hair. George and Kitty –being young and socially conscious–

would have wanted to emulate these new styles; as did Fanny, whose 1798 portrait shows her looking worried in a high-waisted, *à la Lady Hamilton* dress.

When Horace, still weak from his Tenerife wounding, departed Bath with Fanny for London,[575] George took Kitty back to rustic Shepherd's Spring, to which he was no longer attached. The last straw came in March 1798 when his youngest child, Mary Anne, died aged just one year. Enough was enough and it was time to relocate to Bath.

Chapter Eleven: Hero Horace

1798 – 1799

There was excitement in January 1798 when George and Kitty were briefly reunited with Horace, and "A happy family party gathered at Bath, it's pleasures enhanced by the Admiral [Horace]'s presence in renewed health and spirits."[576]

George was now in his mid-forties, so more than half way through the Bible's threescore years and ten. He'd done well, considering his single lung and the Bombay doctor's pronouncement that, as a youth, he was so ill that attempting to cross the Arabian peninsula would make no difference to his likelihood of survival.

The Matchams had moved into No. 19 Kensington Place in the up-and-coming parish of Walcot[577] with its shiny new, honey-gold, Bath-stone terraces and air spiced with the rich, piquant aroma of yeast from Sayce & Kelson's brewery. The population of Walcot had swelled so rapidly that St Swithin's church, where George and Kitty had married in 1787, had been extended eastward and had been embellished with a classical spire added in 1790.[578]

Three-storeyed Kensington Place was built alongside the London road and had been designed by an architect named John Palmer. Sale notices of its houses had appeared in local papers in the autumn of 1796.[579] Kensington Place had the obligatory neat Bath-stone frontage, whilst its rear was built from cut stone and rubble[580] with gardens extending as far as "grounds adjoining the river [known] as Kensington Meadows".[581]

Middle-class, late Georgian town homes had a drawing room at the front of a ground floor, in which visitors were received. Interiors were rich with classical details and Axminster carpets, featuring patterns based on Roman mosaics, were highly prized,[582] with Ancient Greek motifs being popular too.[583]

The ground-floor parlour was a plainer room in which the family could relax. The dining room –normally connected to the parlour via double doors – was a more formal space for entertaining guests. [584] On special occasions, pineapples were rented by the hour as show-off table centre-pieces.[585] After dinner, gentlemen remained in the dining room to enjoy camaraderie and cigars whilst the ladies retired to the drawing room.

The master bedrooms occupied the floor above this and, above that again, were bedrooms for children and guests. Servants were quartered in the attic and, sometimes, in the basement adjacent to the kitchen.[586]

Fashionable homes showcased exotic artefacts. George, like his mother, may have brought knick-knacks back from India, whilst others showed off objects of interest they'd acquired during their Grand Tours of Europe. Edmund Nelson's Norfolk neighbour, Thomas William Coke, installed a Roman mosaic of a lion fighting a leopard in the library of Holkham Hall, which he'd acquired in Italy during his grand tour in the early 1770s.[587]

George and Kitty's new neighbourhood was praised for its genteel grandeur, in which:

"every progressive step strengthens the impression of the respectability and importance of Bath ; the eye not being familiar with the smoothness and cream-coloured appearance of the free-stone, which gives the houses such an air of cleanliness, altogether, that the effect is unusually cheerful... Kensington-Place is also a terrace of some quality, with a carriage-way to it, the front enclosed with iron rails, and gates at each end of it. Opposite to this handsome range of dwellings are gardens; and, the houses upon the hill, rising above each other to a great height, cannot fail of interesting the attention of the passing stranger."[588]

One of the friends George made in Bath was Henry Stanyford Blanckley, alternatively known as HSB. He was British Consul to the Balearics, but considered Bath his home.[589] HSB resided in his beloved, widowed aunt, Anne Harrison's three-storey house at No. 8 Paragon Street, half-a-mile from Kensington Place.[590] [591] HSB's mother had died in Bath in January 1797,[592] and then his wife, Mrs. Mary Blanckley, had lingered in Bath hoping its celebrated spa waters would cure her illness, but she'd died the next year in the spring of 1798.[593]

HSB and George had much in common to chat about in Bath's many new coffee houses, such as St James's that had opened in 1796 behind the Royal Crescent.[595] HSB's nephew by marriage had married one of the Anglo-Armenian Nisbett girls George had lodged with in Bombay. Also, both HSB and George had been born in British overseas colonies in the early 1750s and grown up in warm climates. Both had settled in England in the late 1780s, started families, and focused their attentions on game-lands –although HSB had been employed as a gamekeeper, rather than employing one, as George had. HSB, however, was no merchant. His earlier career was military and he'd been stationed in Quebec during the American Revolutionary War.[596]

Edmund Nelson wrote to Kitty from Ipswich in September 1798 with news that Horace, leading the British fleet, had been unable to locate the French:

"My dear, I am glad to tell you that yesterday a letter arrived Here from your Good Bro : dated July 20th off Syracuse, wherein He sais 'I have little to add to my former letters, except I am in perfect Health. Have not yet seen the French fleet, after Having been at Malta; Alexandria, Asia, Syria &, But hope for better Success'."

Edmund Nelson went on to discuss the unready state of Roundwood – Fanny's new house in Ipswich– and asked Kitty to find suitable winter accommodation for them in Bath:

"Lady N. is apprehensive this place may be too cold for the winter, and Morover [sic] the House wants paint &, therfore Intends, no accident preventing, to remove to Bath about the End of Nov, or early in December. Must therfore request you to Look at your Leisure for a House, for 4 or 5 months certain, in a Good Situation; that is in Bladud's Buildings or Axford, Fountain buildings, Edgar or Belmont as far as No. 5 or 6, the field side of Gay Street. A small House abt 4 Guineas pr week. Kitty Bolton and George are at Round wood. Your Sister will spend a week or 2 with us before she removes to Cranwich. Pray God prosper Her. 3 or 4 months this winter, your Bro : Wm, His wife and daughter intend being at Bath for the improvement of Charlott."[597]

Edmund Nelson's plan to overwinter in Bath was superseded by the momentous news he wrote of to Kitty a month later:

"This Morn an Express [letter arrived] with the News of the Glorious victory your Great & Good Brother has obtained... All the rest Gazettes &c will tell you. A universall Joy is Spread. God Bless you All. Lady N. is Well."[598]

The entire Nelson family was "stirred to its depths by the victory of the Nile"[599] at Aboukir Bay on the 1st of August 1798 when Horace's bold, lateral thinking and man-of-the-people leadership had led England's navy to smash the superior French fleet.[600] England was ecstatic, and it's easy to imagine Kitty jumping up and down with excitement telling George, emphatically, that she'd always known her "Bro" was made for greatness. She was, though, distressed to hear that Horace had received a major head wound above his eye and wrote to him:

"I am all anxiety to hear, more particularly being apprehensive the wound be over the bright [uninjured] eye, and as a sister, I may be allow'd to think appearances, as all the ladies will be looking at you, for you see all the ladies are looking very brisk, when they hear you are not an old man".[601]

Horace was lauded as "Rear Admiral Horatio Lord Nelson"[602] and George's identity was completely overshadowed by his brother-in-law's sudden hero status. Letters streamed to him marvelling at his close familial relationship to the Hero of the Nile. For example, his school friend Charles Warre Malet, wrote to him from Bond Street, in London, gushing:

"MY DEAR FRIEND ; In the joy of my Heart I cannot refrain from letting out a little of its Fullness, in congratulating you, & still more than you, your amiable Lady, on that glorious Success of her Brother... "[603]
Sir Mordaunt Martin –a family friend from Burnham Thorpe– wrote:
"DEAR SIR ; Reflection that it was from the longstanding Friendship between the Family of your gallant Brother in Law & mine, that I acquired the highly valued Friendship & protection which you so kindly exhibited to my son".[604]

Mention of Horace was even scribbled into the postscript of an unrelated letter about selling Plumley Heath:

"Dear Sir,
I embrace the opportunity by W. Downes's servant by informing you that I have not at present a prospect of finding a purchaser for Plumley...
P. S. Have you lately heard from your noble and brave Brother in Law? "[605]

When Edmund Nelson made his way to Bath, in the latter months of 1798, he travelled without Fanny, who was busy finishing the renovations of Roundwood, near to Ipswich in Suffolk, in readiness for Horace's return.
George's seventy-six-year-old father-in-law, "still in the midst of

shoals of compliments and congratulations", wrote to Kitty from London in November, "Every creature Here is as full of the most exalted praise as Ever, from St. James to Tower Hill".[606]

Horace was constantly in the newspapers, but November's news that King George III had made Horace a baron would have already reached George Matcham by letter:

"His Majesty having taking into his royal consideration... has determined to give and grant the said Admiral Lord Nelson [the title of] Baron Nelson of the Nile, and Burnham Thorpe, in the county of Norfolk, and... an annuity of [£]2000".[609]

News reached England from Naples, in Italy, that Europe's favourite fashion icon, Lady Hamilton, had celebrated Nelson's Nile victory by dressing in blue with "gold anchors all over." Lady Hamilton's decision to use anchor motifs to represent Nelson's victory ricocheted across the continent, both as a must-have fashion accessory and as a way of expressing pride for Britain's naval triumph over Napoleon. In England, ladies were quick to emulate Lady Hamilton by wearing "gold anchors that celebrated their hero."[607] Princess Augusta, daughter of George III, sat for a portrait with an anchor pendant hanging prominently on her neck.[608]

The ensuing winter was the coldest for several years.[610] There was "a great Fall of Snow, in the Beginning of the Year 1799."[611] Edmund Nelson endured the frigid months in Bath where he, George and Kitty enjoyed warm, tête-à-tête discussions about Horace's comet-like ascension.

Kitty would have been highly impressed that Horace's greatness had been recognised by Lady Hamilton, whose "elegance and taste of her manners" the English press praised effusively.[612]

George's brother-in-law, Reverend William Nelson, was so greedy to gain from Horace's ascension that Kitty tutted, "I dare say the [bishop's] mitre is very near falling on his head now".[613]

Fanny thought William Nelson vile and, "the roughest mortal that ever lived," whose disposition was of "ambition, pride and selfish[ness]" and whose motto was "gain, gain".[614] For her own part, Fanny didn't engage with the prevailing mania for "Lord Nelson" and refused pressure to act as the movement's figurehead or to deck herself in anchor motifs.[615] Though Kitty might have thought Fanny's refusal mean-spirited, George – who didn't share his wife's ingrained hero-love of Horace– may have sympathised. After all, Fanny had tried to dissuade Horace from signing back up with the navy because she'd not wanted him to risk his life by playing the hero.

Newspaper obituaries, in December 1798, carried sobering news: "At Kentish Town, in the 69th year of his age, William Suckling, Esq., of the Custom House, London."[616] George would have been saddened by the death of his in-law, who'd been one of his marriage settlement trustees and an active presence in his English life.

Despite being absent, Horace drew his family's attention like a magnet. Stories of his dramatic activities in Naples flooded the press, albeit with a two-month lag. Alarming news, in January 1799, was that, "The King of Naples it appears is unable to stop the progress of the French troops, which are marching against his capital".[617]

A month later, good news followed that Horace had used Vanguard – the British warship he commanded– to evacuate the Neapolitan royals to the island of Sicily. According to the Kentish Gazette, "the Queen owed her safety very much to Lady Hamilton, who assisted in getting her away". [618]

Back in England, a second family tragedy dogged the heels of William Suckling's demise. George's feckless brother-in-law, Suckling Nelson, died during a fit in April 1799, aged just thirty-five. William Nelson, continued to alienate himself from the family by speaking uncharitably at Suckling's funeral.[619]

The family's mourning was disturbed by accusations that Horace had acted as judge and jury of the Neapolitan rebels and treated them too harshly. On the 12th of August, the Whig Morning Chronicle "accused Nelson of seizing some of the rebels 'contrary to an express engagement, on the faith of which they had acted'."[620] Horace's own description of events quickly appeared in other papers:

"ADMIRALTY-OFFICE, AUGUST 16, 1799
Extracts of letters from Rear Admiral Lord Nelson, K. B. to Evan Nepean, Esq. dated Bay of Naples, June 27, and July 14, 1799.
I am happy in being able to congratulate their Lordships on their possession of the city of Naples.—St. Elmo is yet in the hands of the French ; but the castles of Ovo and Nuovo I took possession of last evening, and his Sicilian Majesty's colours are now flying on them. All the rebels are now on board His Majesty's fleet. Capua and Gaieta will very soon be in our possession, when the Kingdom will be liberated from anarchy and misery... "[621]

George would have wondered at the truth of the matter. If Horace had come quickly home, instead of dallying in Naples, he'd not have had these allegations laid against him. Shouldn't Horace have prioritised the needs of his ageing father? And what of Fanny, who'd been nursing Edmund Nelson without complaint whilst Horace was championing strangers' needs in Naples? And what too of his own dear wife, Kitty, who so yearned to be reunited with her darling bro?

Soon after George's eighth child, Harriet, was baptised in Walcot on the 21st of September, the press filled with accounts of Horace having been hero-worshipped by the Neapolitan royals. "On the 3d September, 1799, a fete was given at their Sicilian Majesties Palace in Palermo, by their youngest son Prince Leopold, to celebrate the recovery of the kingdom of Naples". After Horace's praises had been sung, guests were ushered to a "magnificently illuminated" Grecian palace "supported by columns, and ascended by a flight of steps [where] three figures, representing Lord Nelson, Sir William and Lady Hamilton... of wax, as large as life— That of his Lordship, in the middle, dressed in his naval uniform ; on one side, Sir William in the Windsor uniform, and on the other, her Ladyship in white, with a blue shawl, on which were embroidered in letters of gold, the names of all Captains who shared honors of the memorable first of August... the young Prince ascending, placed a crown of laurel on the head of the figure representing Lord Nelson, while the music played " Rule Britannia."[622]

Whilst Kitty yearned for her beloved bro to return to English shores, there was happier news for George, whose old school chum and lifelong friend, Sir Charles Warre Malet, who'd settled in Enfield, where George's mother had lived. It was there, in Enfield's parish church, that on the 17th of September 1799 Malet married Susannah, the daughter of James Wales, who was an accomplished artist and fellow returnee from India.[623]

The ensuing winter was as bitter as the last[624] and, as the new century rang in, George had fallen so gravely ill with a bilious fever that he'd lost all use of his limbs.[625]

This could possibly have been a relapse of *barbeers,* a disease endemic in eighteenth-century India, described as "a dreadful illness of the paralytic kind, that attacks mostly Europeans, and deprives them of the use of their limbs."[626] *Barbeers* may, in fact, have been a mosquito-carried disease called chikungunya fever, which can cause limb paralysis,[627] and is believed to have been present in the eighteenth century.[628]

Though George's health recovered in January 1800, the severe recent winters had put him well and truly off living in England. Unsettled yet again, he decided to relocate to France as soon as the war against French ended.[629]

Edmund Nelson was in an even worse state. He spent the winter being nursed by Fanny in rented rooms in St. James Street, London. News reaching the Matchams in Bath was grim. Maurice Nelson voiced fear that his elderly father would "slip away 'like the snuff of a candle'" and William Nelson's teenaged daughter, Charlotte, thought her grandfather was "very much broken". Fanny believed Edmund Nelson was clinging to life in the hope of seeing Horace, adding, "It is impossible to describe how very feeble he gets."[630]

George received an offer of £5,000 –the modern equivalent of £220,000– for Shepherd's Spring but wanted Horace to have first choice. Kitty wrote to her father, who passed the question to Fanny, who, in turn, replied that it was impossible for her "to say much on the subject" because Horace had said nothing about buying property. Edmund Nelson thought it would be better for George to accept the offer and save "a great deal of trouble hereafter." [631]

Edmund wrote to Kitty saying, "From your Bro : a short letter dated Palermo, Feb. 7th, and from him I collect these two things, first that he is in good health, and further that he has at present no thoughts of coming to England. His words are 'I hope we shall one day meet, but When, or Where, God only knows.'"[632]

Being a lady living in vogue-obsessed Bath, Kitty would have donned the "fashionable bonnet that at present decorates the persons of our fair *belles... denominated the *Hamilton Hat*, being *Costume du Tete* in which Lady William Hamilton repaired to the Vanguard, when she fled from the massacres of Naples to the protection of Lord Nelson's flag ship, and so spiritedly facilitated the escape of their Sicilian Majesties."[633] To add to the effect, Kitty's naturally lustrous, wavy, dark brown hair was perfect for pruning and tweaking into the fashionable, short-cropped, *à la Lady Hamilton* coif.

Horace and the Hamiltons' press attention was unprecedented beyond the ranks of royalty. Like media superstars of the modern-day, journalists battled to record the minutest details of the famous trio's activities.

George and Kitty would have found this unlooked for stream of information both exciting and confusing, especially as reports were frequently contradictory:

8th March 1800: *"A letter from Genoa, dated the 4th ult. [preceding month] inserted in the Paris papers, states that Admirals Keith and Nelson had sailed from Leghorn, but that their destination was not known."[634]

14th March: *"Sir William and Lady Hamilton are supposed to be among the numerous travellers trapped in Hamburgh by the severity of the season."[635]

25th March: *"It is said that the Emperor Paul has distinguished Lady

Hamilton with the Great Cross of the Order of Malta."[636]

31st March: *"Malta is now closely blockaded by Lord Nelson in the Foudroyant of 80 guns".*[637]

7th April: *"It is positively said, that Admiral Lord Nelson had succeeded in coming up with the remainder of the French squadron, and that he had taken two others of the larger French vessels."*[638]

19th May: *"Sir William and Lady Hamilton, we understand, have no intention of ever revisiting this country. They have settled in Florence."*[639]

Also on the 19th May: *"Admiral Nelson is coming home, to act as second in command under Earl St. Vincent."*[640]

14th June: *"Lord Nelson is on his passage to England in a frigate, accompanied by Sir William Hamilton. He may be expected in the course of a week [Sir William has] left Lady Hamilton at a country-side house, which he has taken between Luca and Pisa."*[641]

However, days passed into weeks without Horace arriving. Edmund Nelson, now back with Fanny in Roundwood, wrote to Kitty on the 8th of July, "The hope of receiving the news of your Bro['s] arrivall in England, has been so long deferred, we know not from what cause".

Rumours started trickling into England that Horace and Lady Hamilton's relationship had gone beyond innocent friendship.[642] George likely heard these whispers, though he may have chosen to ignore them. After all, tongues were bound to wag because Horace was now as famous as Lady Hamilton and she was much younger than her husband, Sir William.

At last, in November, the Matchams received the longed-for news that Horace had alighted on British soil at Great Yarmouth in Norfolk. The good tidings first reached them in Bath via newspapers and letters Edmund Nelson sent from a hotel in the prestigious district of Mayfair:[643]

"NEROTT'S HOTEL,
LONDON.
I may now venture to say with more certainty than ever, that your Brother was in Yarmouth yesterday..."[644]

A much-circulated report was published on the 11th of November:
"LORD NELSON OF THE NILE
...At Yarmouth, the instant he landed, the mayor and corporation waited on him with the address and freedom of the town... LORD NELSON and SIR WLLIAM HAMILTON and LADY HAMILTON [went to the

church] to join in thanksgiving...
On arriving in London, on Sunday at three o'clock, they were met by his venerable father and LADY NELSON at NEROT'S HOTEL. "[645]

More news followed from Edmund Nelson:

"Nov. 15th, 1800
MY DEAR, As I have no other, nor better news to tell you, then the safe arrivall of your Good, long expected Brother, a very few lines will give you much pleasure. He looks well, is active & cannot rest Long in a place therefore I my Self can only see Him for a minute...
EDM. NELSON. "[646]

Kitty's father's next letter refers to her inability to join them in London because of her advanced pregnancy:

"MY DEAR, The Cause which at present hinders your travelling, I hope in proper time will be happily removed and we shall rejoice in each other.
Your Brother has taken [17 Dover Street] for a year... When Mr. Matcham with ease can come to London, I can answer every one will be truly glad to see him. "[647]

Although Kitty was immobilised with pregnancy, George was free to travel. He accepted an invitation to a dinner, on Wednesday the 3rd of December, [648] hosted by the Directors of the East India Company for "the "Rt. Hon. Lord Nelson, for his service to his country." [649] The Company had ample reason to celebrate Horace's Nile victory because it nullified the threat the French navy had posed to their merchant vessels.

When George was reunited with his hero brother-in-law in London, the scruffy Horace of old was long gone. In his place, strutted Horatio Lord Nelson, the hero of everyone, who was resplendent in medals and exotic jewels, including a magnificent, diamond-encrusted *chelengk* pinned to his cocked –bicorn– hat, "like a turban jewel". [650] The *chelengk* was a gift from the Sultan of Turkey and contained a clockwork mechanism that made it rotate.[651] He liked to stand out as a crowd-pleaser and likely wore his Royal Navy full dress uniform more often than he ought.[652]

Though both Horace and Lady Hamilton ignored dress convention, while Lady Hamilton's creative style had instigated a European fashion revolution, Horace's habit of covering himself with "stars, ribbons and medals" was being lampooned for making him look "more like the prince of an opera than the conqueror of the Nile."[653] In fact, Horace's flamboyance was the antithesis of the new male trend for somber neatness and meticulously knotted, starched cravats set by a socialite, named Beau Brummel, "who cheerfully eschewed the sugary flummery of satins and silks and patterns for streamlined minimalism."[654] Brummell's domination of male fashion had begun the year before. Like Lady Hamilton, Brummel had risen from common stock to become bosom friends with royalty. Lady Hamilton's royal best friend was the queen of Naples. Beau Brummel's was the heir apparent and future George IV of England. [655] If Horace's maximalist lead had been followed instead of Brummell's understated elegance, Jane Austen's world would have had a very different look.

Although Horace –at about 5' 4"– was shorter than George, half-blind and half-armless, he had the charisma of someone whose praises had been sung so often, and so loudly, that their presence felt larger than life.

The East India Company's lavish dinner was held in The London Tavern[656] which was a popular, meeting venue located in the rapidly re-developing east London area of Bishopsgate.[657] The London Tavern had reopened in 1768 after the original building was destroyed by fire. It boasted a spacious dining hall whose high roof was supported with Corinthian columns.[658]

Hampshire Chronicle reported:

"Nearly two hundred persons sat down to dinner ; among whom were the Duke of York, the Lord Chancellor, the Chancellor of the Exchequer [and] the Speaker of the House of Commons… Rule Britannia was encored with plaudits of the honourable society who had met to celebrate his lordship's victory." *[659]*

The atmosphere was of "cordiality and good humour"[660] when Horace stood to address his eager admirers. He told them, "Gentlemen, I drink your health and thank you for the distinguished honour you have done me."[661]

A week after the East India Company's dinner, George may have read The Porcupine's outraged refutal of slurs against Horace; the last straw having been The Times's claim that he'd openly-wept tears that had been dabbed "fondly" by Lady Hamilton:

"If there ever was a man, who might reasonably have hoped to receive the applauses of his grateful countrymen, unmixed with the poisonous

insinuations of envy, that man is LORD NELSON ; yet, it now appears that, if such were his Lordship's expectations, he was cruelly deceived. We have frequently observed, in several London Papers, attempts to tarnish the reputation of this matchless naval hero, to wound his feelings, and to destroy the peace of his family ; but the following article, which we extract from The Times of yesterday, certainly goes a step further than any thing we had before seen on the subject :

'The following article is said to have appeared in a Paris Journal:— Among the distinguished personages who hastened to pay their respects to Sir William and Lady Hamilton, and Lord Nelson, on their arrival at Hamburgh, was Dumourier. During their short stay in that city, the Ex-General was invited to one of their parties. After supper, Lady Hamilton sang ' God save the King,' at the request of Lord Nelson ; but when she came to the couplet reflecting on France, she was interrupted by his Lordship. Dumourier, who had listened in ecstasy to the sweet melodies of the delightful warbler, deeply affected by this act of delicacy, and filled with gratitude, burst into tears. Lady Hamilton, fancying she saw the tears of a Royalist, of a heart overflowing with love for its country, glistening in his eyes, wept in excess of softness. —Lord Nelson began to weep from sympathy, and old Sir William went to a distant corner of the room, and wept to keep the others company. Lady Hamilton, in constant activity, wiped away the tears of the Admiral with her handkerchief fondly ; then those of her husband slightly ; then those of Dumourier kindly ; then her own delicately ; and then Dumourier, falling on his knee, implored, as the greatest possible favour, that the charming Lady Hamilton would make him a present of the handkerchief. Lady Hamilton softened into compliance, the favour was granted, and Dumourier, having received the handkerchief, with a holy respect, retired to meditate on the miraculous destiny, which had deigned to unite, in his favour, in the same handkerchief, the relics of so many great personages. To see, touch, and kiss this famous handkerchief are now considered on the continent the proudest honours ; and, as such, are sought with all the enthusiasm of superstition.'

...Tell us not that the nation is innocent of what we impute to The Times. Those who print that Paper print it to sell. They well know what suits the taste of their customers, and it was to gratify that taste that the article which we censure was inserted". [662]

Chapter Twelve: Enter Emma

1800 – 1802

Precisely how much George did –or didn't– believe of rumours that Horace and Lady Hamilton were lovers, meeting both parties in the flesh – as it were– would have raised his loyal East India Company man's eyebrows.

George was probably staying in Dover Street with Horace, Fanny and Edmund Nelson. If he'd not previously met them in Naples during his final overland trek, it may well have been here that he first met Sir William Hamilton and his famous, younger wife, whose correct address was "Emma, Lady Hamilton" because the title was her husband's.

Here now stood Emma, Lady Hamilton in living, breathing reality. George would have been familiar with her appearance from myriad prints out of which her wide, glinting eyes met the viewer's, often cheekily, and with her voluptuous body draped in artful reminiscence of ancient Greece and Rome.

If Horace seemed larger than life as Lord Nelson, Lady Hamilton was gargantuan. She was naturally tall, but caricaturists and gossips thought it hilarious that she –the famous beauty– had become *embonpoint,*[663] meaning attractively fat. Despite this, Lady Hamilton was graceful with the sparkling charm of a natural performer who –unlike Fanny– was comfortable under lime-light.

Lady Hamilton would have greeted George effusively, her rich voice softened with a Cheshire lilt. As a gentleman, George would have returned her greeting warmly and, of course, also greeted elderly Sir William who, having turned seventy on the 13th of December, was only eight years younger than Edmund Nelson.

Sir William was a refined aristocrat who'd grown up as foster brother to the current king, George III.[664] He had a proud Roman nose and "such an air of intelligence blended with distraction in his countenance as powerfully attracted and conciliated all who approached him."[665] He'd authored and illustrated several books cataloguing classical art-work, with which George was likely familiar.

Horace would have leapt to embrace the Hamiltons, happily telling George that they named themselves the *tria juncta in uno* –"three joined as one"– and that they adored each other equally.

Fanny –thin-lipped, slight and pale– would have observed from the sidelines with a frozen smile and panicked eyes.

Edmund Nelson –frail and sallow with his swept-back hair– would have stood by Fanny, or, more likely, sat, for he was still infirm. She was the old rector's stalwart companion and nurse, and his loyalty to her ran deep. Yet Horace was the light of Edmund Nelson's life. Horace and Kitty had always been his favourite children,[666] and now, Horace was Europe's hero who'd only just come home. Fanny herself had said that the rector had clung to life solely to see Horace again. As loyal as he was to Fanny, and as much as he relied on her support, darling Horace could do no wrong even if he and Lady Hamilton were... well, making doe-eyes at each other and being, ahem, somewhat physical with their hands.

Yet Horace and Lady Hamilton swore that their relationship was nothing more than innocent friendship. Furthermore, Sir William seemed untroubled despite Horace and Lady Hamilton's touchy-feely behaviour, so... had George been jumping to unsavoury conclusions? Whatever the truth of the matter, it couldn't be at all easy for poor Fanny, who'd not been able to stomach England's Nelson mania, and was now confronted not only with this new, medal-dripping incarnation of her husband, but also with Lady Hamilton literally singing his praises, for she was an acclaimed singer who loved to give impromptu performances and had a growing repertoire of Nelson-themed songs. She also enjoyed drinking and gambling: activities the East India Company frowned upon.

George would have felt troubled during his return journey to Bath. Should he broach his suspicions about Horace and Lady Hamilton's affair to Kitty, or should he spare his heavily pregnant wife that awkwardness? The important thing was to get back to No. 19 Kensington Place to support her during the final stages of her pregnancy. He'd have hoped their coming baby would be born strong and healthy. Compared to other parents, they were lucky to have lost only three of the eight children born so far, but it still wasn't easy to bear the loss of any child.

Kitty, who stayed quietly at home producing plentiful babes, shone as the paradigm of female virtue, as laid out in a 1743 Lady's Companion which foretold the perils of women who, like Lady Hamilton, were bold and fond of alcoholic drink:

"such a degenerate Age do we live in, that every Thing seems inverted, even Sexes, whilst Men fall into the Effeminacy and Niceness of Women, and Women take up the Confidence, the Boldness of Men... Vices of Men

are carefully copied by some Women, who think they have not made a sufficient Escape from their Sex, 'till they can be as daringly wicked as the other… And when to this a Woman adds the Sin of Drunkenness, nothing that is human approaches so near a Beast. She who is first a Prostitute to Wine, will, soon be led to Lust also".[667]

When George returned to Bath, Kitty likely begged him to describe every detail of Lady Hamilton's attire, whilst the press, on an almost daily basis, provided constant reports of Horace and the Hamiltons' ongoing antics. News, on the 15th of December, was that "Lady Hamilton has not yet been at Court. The cause is said to be her not having received any answer from her Majesty to the letter of recommendation, of which her Ladyship was the bearer, from the Queen of Naples."[668] This was followed by reports, in multiple papers, that, on the 22nd of December, Horace visited the Wiltshire town of Salisbury with the Hamiltons and was given the keys to the city. After this, "Lord Nelson, Sir W. and Lady Hamilton, and some foreign gentlemen, are gone on a visit to Mr. Beckford at Fonthill".[669] Beckford, who was a cousin of Sir William, was a recluse in the process of squandering his inherited fortune on walling himself into a fairytale-style palace of his own design.[670]

Horace wasn't so swept away by the fairytale environs of Fonthill that he forgot his family. He wrote to George on New Year's Day 1801 with good news from the penal colony of New South Wales. George had been trying to help his widowed cousin, Mary Pitt née Matcham,[671] emigrate to Australia with her adult son and four daughters, where land grants were issued to free settlers.[672] Horace had received a reply from the governor of New South Wales, Philip Gidley King,[673] whom he'd written to requesting him to help the Pitts:

"My dear Mr Matcham, Long ago Mr King has been asked the question about your friends journey to Botany Bay. Mr K says they shall be sent free of Cost, and desires that their names ages and descriptions as to their professions shall be sent… The fleet sail for that Colony in March.
Remember me kindly to her [Mary Pitt] and Mrs Matcham and believe me Sir Your Affectionate Nelson."[674]

Another woman George helped was a resident of Ringwood, who wrote to him later in the same year:

"G. Matcham, Esqre near Bath.
SIR, I knowed your honor to be a good Gentleman, always kind to we

poor folk in Hampshire and that makes me bold to ax you to do good to a good and charitable woman. I was sick and she relieved my distress. I can never be out of her debt in my mind. Send to herself but not to her father the £12 and letter in this cover and God blessing be on you and family ever and amen. If so be as how she wont tak it, tell her as I says she must, cause your honour doan't know me, nor where to return it.
    ELIZABETH FULLER." [675]

Kitty delivered their ninth child on the 6th of January 1801. The baby was baptised six days later with the unusual name of Horatia to honour Kitty's favourite bro. It was a mercifully warmer winter than the previous two had been, so infant Horatia Matcham wouldn't have suffered too much from the elements on her way to and from St. Swithin's.

Alas, George and Kitty's family bliss was quickly shattered by news that Horace had walked out on Fanny during a dinner party and permanently moved into the Hamiltons' house in Grosvenor Square, Piccadilly.[676]

Fanny blamed herself for the break up, fearing she'd failed to convince Horace of her affection and appreciation, and that, if she'd angered him, "It was done unconsciously, and without the least intention."[677]

William Nelson, greedy to wring personal profit from Lady Hamilton's goodwill, ruthlessly shunned Horace's discarded wife. When William Nelson visited them in Bath, George and Kitty told him off for making disparaging comments about Fanny.[678]

There was a new, derogatory tone in press references to Lady Hamilton. For example, it was alluded that she was incapable of learning manners:

"Notwithstanding all the accomplishments which Lady Hamilton acquired in Italy, the Gentleman with whom she was lately on a visit to Font-Hill, is supposed to have knowledge of Italian Manners, to which this charming Lady must ever remain a stranger!" [679]

Further, it was implied that the properly behaved British queen would never receive her:

"Lady Hamilton has received no answer whatever to the recommendatory letter which the Queen of Naples gave our Queen". [680]

And that dances inspired by Lady Hamilton's Attitudes risked immorality:

"*A new dance has been introduced in the fashionable circles, under the title of the Polish Waltz. It is something in the attitudinary style of Lady Hamilton, but trenches a little too much on the confines of decorum. The morality of the dance, however, depends on the leader of the band*".[681]

Horace was called back to Royal Navy service and set sail from Yarmouth to Denmark and the Baltic on the 6th of March 1801.[682] Caricaturist James Gillray lampooned the *tria juncta in uno* with a cartoon of a grossly massive Lady Hamilton distraughtly watching the British fleet sail away whilst a cuckolded Sir William dozed obliviously behind her ample back.[683]

As Horace sailed for Denmark, Edmund Nelson was lodging in Bath when Kitty's eldest brother –forty-eight year old Maurice– wrote to her on the 4th of April:

"*MY DEAR SISTER, I thank you & My Father for your kind congratulations on my appointment to the principal seat in the Office. It is one of the things I have always been looking up too, and it has proved the more gratifying to me as there was not any Interest made for it, but devolved upon me as a matter of right... No Official accounts yet from the Baltic [where Horace was engaged], but we must have some very soon. Give my love to Our Father & best wishes to Mr. Matcham and all your family and believe*
Your truly affectionate Brother
MAURICE NELSON."[684]

George's good friend, Sir Charles Warre Malet, wrote from London, on the 19th of April, with happy news of Horace's success at the Danish capital of Copenhagen, in the Baltic:

"*MY DEAR SIR, receive if you please and Madam Matcham My Sincere compliments for the new laurels gathered by Lord Nelson, never one have seen two so great victorys obtained in the same fleet's situation, as this of Aboukir and this of Copenhagen, but this last has been More difficult by the strong batteries of the forts.*"[685]

Alas, bad news always seemed to harry the heels of good. Less than a week after Malet's letter, Horace's friend, Alexander Davison, wrote anxiously to Edmund Nelson that Maurice had suffered violent head pains.

The physician Davison recommended, Sir John Hayes, had diagnosed "brain fever." Though Maurice seemed to recover, he died during a fit on the 24th of April.[686] Edmund Nelson rushed Davison a black-sealed reply, postmarked 27th April, with instructions for Maurice to be buried in Burnham Thorpe.[687] Edmund realised that, in his hurry to reply, he'd forgotten to tell Davison that he wanted "the black servant to attend" Maurice's funeral.[688] This was James Price who'd lived with Maurice and his common law wife, Sukey, since William Suckling's demise in December 1798. Edmund Nelson sent his instruction about Price to Davison in a second letter, postmarked the same day.

Davison took care of the funeral arrangements with George's brother-in-law, Thomas Bolton. Sukey's distress during the service[689] was omitted from press reports:

"The remains of the late MAURICE NELSON, Esq. of the Navy Office, the brother of Lord Nelson, were on Sunday last conveyed to Norfolk, and interred in the family burying place."[690]

George received an anguished, unpunctuated letter from his cousin, Mary Pitt, who'd embarked on an Australia-bound vessel waiting in Portsmouth dock, only to be told horror stories about conditions in New South Wales:

"31 May. On board 'Canada', Portsmouth Docks. Good sir, We came on board yesterday. My situation here is very bad and the shocking account of the wicked country I dread I have brought up my children with fear and care God knows my heart I would rather fall into the hand of a merciful Creator or to sufer any poverty by his grace to restrain me from falling into the hand of wicked people a Gentleman who came from there informs me the whole land is a corrupted wicked people and if please God my children should live I hope they will find a friend in the Governor according to your good intentions I cannot expect to live long I am in a little hole among all sorts of people I can scarce see to write God almighty be my guide and send me a place of rest and his blessing attend you and yours for ever is the earnest wish of your obligded humble servant Mary Pitt."[691]

Mary Pitt, her five children, and a human cargo of female deportees, were, along with two sister ships, kept waiting in Portsmouth Dock for three weeks until, on the 22nd of June "sailed Minorca, Canada, and Nile transports, with female convicts, for new South Wales."[692]

On the 1st of July 1801, as Mary Pitt was sailing to the other side of the world, Horace arrived back from Denmark, jubilant to have been created Viscount Nelson of the Nile and Burnham Thorpe in his absence. [693] The title was hereditary and would pass to Horace's male heir or –if he didn't have one– to "the heirs-male severally and successively of Susanna the wife of Thomas Bolton, esq; and sister of Viscount Nelson" or –if the Boltons had no surviving male heir– "to the heirs-male of Catherine the wife of George Matcham esq; another sister of Viscount Nelson."[694]

On the 17th of July, the Morning Post announced, "Lord Nelson and Sir William and Lady Hamilton have taken up their residence at Shepperton [in Surrey] for a few days, as it is said, for the benefit of the air, and the amusement of angling."[695] Whereas –according to a Nelson biography– The Oracle was more satyrical:

"The gallant Lord Nelson, the terror of the French, the Spaniards and the Danes, is now amusing himself with Sir William and Lady Hamilton by catching gudgeons at Shepperton."[696]

Horace had only a few weeks of shore leave before being posted to the English channel,[697] though his heart remained with Lady Hamilton. He'd decided he wanted to own a farm to live in with her, [698] and tasked her with finding a suitable place to transform into a home of their own. She found an ideal property named Merton Place, in the county of Surrey –near the modern-day tennis courts at Wimbledon– that was ideally situated between London and Portsmouth. However, its asking price of £9,000 was beyond Horace's means. Alexander Davison, Horace's friend and prize agent –who administered his Royal Navy awards– offered to help him finance the property.[699]

George retained his own small plot at Plumley Heath, near Ringwood. He resumed hunting there, despite it being a long journey from Bath, and recruited Samuel Dowden as its gamekeeper for 1801's autumn hunting season.[700] [701]

France and Britain called a tentative truce on the 1st of October and Horace, granted shore leave, sped to join Lady Hamilton at Merton Place. Kitty received a letter from her father in London, posted on the 9th of November. "Yesterday I came to Lady Nelson [Fanny]'s House… where I mean to stay a fortnight and then go to your Brother at Merton, from whence it is my design to move to Bath".[702]

Family correspondence abounded. Kitty wrote to Fanny asking her to send back a "chit chat letter",[703] and Edmund Nelson wrote to Kitty again, on the 20th of November, "Your Good Bro is truly in better Health and Happier in himself then in Good truth I have in any passed Time observed Him to be... His love and affection to you and yours depend upon it is very Sincere & unshaken. God Bless you All".[704] In Edmund Nelson's next letter, sent six days later, he informed Kitty, "On Tuesday next I propose setting out for Bath and do Intend being at your House on Thursday about 4 o'clock. Whatever lodging is engaged I will be satisfied with."[705] Edmund Nelson duly departed Merton, on the 29th of November,[706] for the sumptuous lodgings George and Kitty had procured for him in Pulteney Street,[707] which was "the widest, grandest thoroughfare in Bath, flanked on either side by beautiful Georgian properties."[708]

Edmund Nelson phrased any concerns about Horace's live-in relationship with Lady Hamilton carefully. He wrote to Horace from Bath, "What you possess, my good son, take care of... what you may still want, consult your own good sense in what way it can be attained. Strive for honours and riches that will not fade, but will profit in time of need. Excuse my anxiety for what I esteem your real good."[709]

Having successfully lured his elderly father to Merton, Horace was keen for the rest of his family to spend Christmas there.

Teenaged Charlotte Nelson was already in residence, benefitting from Lady Hamilton's tutelage in language, music and deportment,[710] for Lady Hamilton –despite being common-born– had mastered all these skills, and more, to an astonishing degree.[711]

Charlotte's father, Reverend William Nelson, who'd been quick to grasp the advantage of fostering Lady Hamilton's goodwill, had steered his wife, as well as Charlotte, to befriend her as soon as Horace separated from Fanny.[712]

William Nelson's other child, Horatio, arrived in Merton from Eton College, and Susanna Bolton's daughters, Eliza and Anne, arrived from their own boarding school in Enfield.

This was a delicate situation for George to navigate for, on the one hand, he was on friendly terms with Fanny, but, on the other hand, Kitty's beloved bro was eager for them to spend Christmas with him and Lady Hamilton. George's solution was to permit some of his brood to go to Merton, whilst he and Kitty stayed in Bath with Edmund Nelson.[713]

The Matcham children returned to Kensington Place with tales of Merton's stately splendour, Uncle Horace's warmth, Lady Hamilton's kindness and grace; their hosts' sweet, little ward, Horatia –who was remarkably small for a baby of fourteen-months– and their dog, who was named Nileus in honour of Uncle Horace's victory at the Nile.[714]

Horace pressed Kitty to visit in the new year of 1802. "Can you give me an idea when you may chuse [sic] to make us a visit at Merton… any time will suit us."[715] Kitty's suggestion of the 23rd of January met with his approval. "[This] will suit us perfectly well, therfore [sic] let it rest for that day".[716]

However, illness dogged the dispersed Nelson kin as an unshiftable, black cloud. Kitty, who was six-months pregnant, became so unwell that she cancelled her January visit and Horace wrote, "I am truly sorry for the cause which has deprived us of the pleasure of seeing you… but to say truth I think a Journey the latter part of April or beginning of May will afford more pleasure to all parties, for then you will I trust be quite well and our weather much better."[717]

A peaceful future was promised when, on the 27th of March 1802, a treaty was signed at Amiens, in France, between Napoleon's forces, Britain, Spain and the Netherlands.[718] The cessation of conflict guaranteed extended home leave for Horace to enjoy with the Hamiltons in Merton.

In Bath, George found his own entertainment in seeking nautical engineering solutions for moving, and raising sunken watercraft with "great weights," leather balloons, and steam power.[720] Steam power was no new invention. It had been in use since Thomas Savery's 1698 patent for "a pump with hand-operated valves to raise water from mines by suction produced by condensing steam."[721] Shortly after George's steam power experiments began, Penydarren Ironworks, in nearby South Wales, recruited an engineer to develop the first steam train.[722] However, existing steam engines weren't designed for mobility and the machine George used would have been monstrously heavy. Add to this the "great weights" and leather balloons, and George's apparatus would have taken vast effort to move. He'd have found willing assistants from the membership of the Bath and West of England Society, which George had joined in 1801, and whose focus was "the encouragement of arts, agriculture, manufacturers & commerce".[723]

The most accessible watercourse from Kensington Place was the river Avon, which was a short hop from the end of George's back garden across Kensington Meadows. If he wished to test his apparatus at sea, a sturdy boat could have carried his equipment down the navigable river to the Bristol Chanel.[724]

His renewed enthusiasm for aquatic engineering may have been kindled by the construction of a canal between London and Bath, of which the stretch between Bath and Devizes had been completed one year before, in May 1801.[725]

George's experiments would have caught attention and attracted interest, and, though humble, George was affable and sociable enough to relish explaining his procedures to interested parties. In his own words:

"The mode I propose of raising great weights (for instance, what I had primarily in view, a barge from a lower to an upper canal,) is by inflating a leather balloon, attached by cordage to a wooden case, in which is a weight preponderating the barge to be drawn up. At the end of the upper canal, adjoining to the inclined plain or precipice where the barge is to be drawn up, a reservoir of water is to be formed, the depth of the inclined plane or precipice, in which is suspended, by inflation, a balloon, with the attached weights..."

If, at this juncture, his audience still appeared to be listening, he'd have carried on:

"A rope leads from it over a roller, and is locked to the boat in the lower canal ; the mouth of the neck of the balloon being opened, the water, pressing round it expels the air and the balloon sinks in the water..." [726]

But the precise details of his acquatic plans may not have made for the most rivetting dinner party entertainment.

Alas, in early April, poor Kitty was so ill that George sent their children to stay with Reverend Mr. Davies in Ringwood. Twelve-year-old George junior wrote home complaining about the unruliness of his sisters, seven-year-old Eliza and two-year-old Harriet, who were running around unchecked and refusing to say their prayers. Reverend Mr. Davis's house seems to have overlooked a stagecoach stop because Eliza had a habit of watching passengers through the window. George replied from Bath, on the 8th of April:

"your Mother has left you in charge & you must consider yourself the Father of the house, if you find any has been visiting the damsels of the kitchen or nursery order them not to admit them —— I see my dear George that Eliza conducts herself with due submission to Mr. Davies that she doth go to the windows to stare at the passengers – Harriet if can will be very unruly, but threaten her with my wrath when I return.

I hope you be careful and regular in your devotions, we ought to be grateful for the good things we enjoy & express ourselves so —Divine will I am certain that can it make Eliza & Harriet say not only their morning X [prayers] daily but also their noon prayers"

A second letter from George junior seems to have arrived before

George senior had posted his reply, and an extension to his letter, penned on the inside of the envelope, reveals his intent to take immediate advantage of the Treaty of Amiens by holidaying in France:

> "*My dear George,*
> *…my trip to France must be defer'd with your Mother's recovery, when if it please God I shall devote a month to a place [in] the country– some future time if you are able to converse in French you may accompany me*"

George's attention next turned to learning – for both George junior and his eight-year-old brother, Edmund, who was learning to play the violin:

> *Edmund I hope has begun to learn musick & as his time is at present of no great consequence – he may practice two hours a day — his memory seems good, I shall therefore beg of Mr. Davies to let him keep it in practice by learning by heart every day … Edmund has many tricks – he must not prick his face – & he must be careful to hold up his head – set him the example George – & recall it every one ought to be ashamed of holding his head down, unless he means to pick pockets — what a difference between the slouching souls & the upright boy with an open countenance – must I beg of you always to learn every verse of your songs – some that I have selected are good pieces of poetry – Can you make a pen well? And do you ever draw from real objects instead of from copies?– When you come home shew me some sketches of houses barns and country round you*"

George paused his torrent of fatherly advice to declare:

> "*Your Mama is better — your writing is very well – but do not flourish your Ds – the plainer with the D — flourishes generally lead to negligence, as I have explain'd*
> *Write me fully. God Bless you*
> *Your affection.*^te *father*
> *G Matcham*
> *How doth the dancing go on?*"[727]

George and Kitty's tenth child was delivered safely and baptised Susannah, on the 23rd of April, in Walcot St. Swithun's.

Kitty was finally free to visit her favourite bro's Merton home, and for she and George to take their children on a tour of France, but ill-luck again felled their plans. As George told Horace, Edmund Nelson had fallen into a "great danger" of health.[728]

Horace replied that he, too, was ill:

"My Dear Mr. Matcham from your kind letter of yesterday describing my Father's situation I have no hopes that he can recover. God's will be done. Had my Father expressed a wish to see me unwell as I am I should have flown to Bath, but I believe it would be too late ; however should it be otherwise and he wishes to see me, no consideration shall detain me a moment... With kindest affections to my Sister. Believe me Ever Your most affectionate Brother".[729]

As Horace predicted, Edmund Nelson's newest illness proved his last. George's frail father-in-law gave up his long fight against poor health on the 26th of April 1802. He died in Pulteney Street a month after his eightieth birthday.[730]

Horace forwarded George's black-edged letter to William Nelson in Hilborough, who sent George condolences and instructions for dismissing Edmund Nelson's servants:

"I had heard ye melancholly [sic] intelligence from my Brother... The suddenness of ye account shocked me much, as I had no idea of his illness till my Brother sent me your letter... God's Will be done ; he has lived to a good old age, and we must be thankful we had him so long... Probably you will discharge the coachman and horses soon, as I understand they are a job. You will do what is proper about mourning for servants, and everything belonging to my father will be kept together, 'till after the funeral, when we will consider what to do with them... we leave everything to you and my Sister, to whom I beg my love, shall be glad to hear she bears ye shock tolerably".[731]

Edmund Nelson's obituary, in an East Anglian newspaper, stated:

"Monday se'nnight died at Bath, in the 80th year of his age, the Rev. Edmund Nelson, A. M. (father of the Right Hon. Lord Viscount Nelson, Duke of Bronte), Rector of Burnham Thorpe, in this county... His death will be long and sincerely lamented, not only by his relatives and friends, but by all his parishioners, to whom he was a zealous and faithful pastor, till his age and infirmities compelled him to relinquish his ministerial duties."[732]

On the 11th of May, the rector was buried in Burnham Thorpe beside his wife, whom he'd survived for thirty-four years. [733] [734]

While his father's funeral was taking place, Horace, who'd not travelled to Norfolk, wrote to George with advice that a former Royal Navy surgeon living in Paris would assist him during his sojourn around France:

"Merton May 11th 1802
My Dear Mr Matcham,
Mr Este and his son the Banker at Paris, came down here on Sunday in hopes of meeting you [he] returns in a few days He has sent me letters for you to his House at Paris, but as it is probable this will pass you on the road I keep them here. Mr Este will be happy to afford you every assistance which you may want Kind care to my Sister and believe me ever your affectionate
Nelson & Bronte"[735]

George, though, had abandoned his plans to go to France because of Edmund Nelson's death. Fanny's life was also impacted. Edmund Nelson had been her strongest tie to Horace's family. Letters flew between Fanny, Kitty and her sister, Susanna Bolton, whilst Lady Hamilton sent the sisters condolences and invitations to Merton Place.[736] A letter from Susanna Bolton, sent to Fanny in mid May, shows that her allegiance had shifted to Lady Hamilton:

"Your going to Bath, my dear Lady Nelson, was of a piece with all your conduct to my beloved father [however] I am going to Merton in about a fortnight, but, my dear Lady N, we cannot meet as I wished, for everybody is known who visits you."[737]

Kitty –at last freed from illness and pregnancy– joined Susanna at Merton. We can assume from Horace's letter, dated the 11th of May, that George accompanied her.[738] Horace and Emma's Surrey home, dubbed "paradise Merton", was small in comparison to other county homes, but had a newly-built ancient Greek-style porch supported by columns[739] and like the rectory at Burnham Thorpe, formed from two buildings joined together. The main entrance was on the eastern façade of the conglomerated structures. Bow windows flanked the steps leading up to the grand entrance lobby where a large, marble bust of Horace was displayed. The spacious bow-windowed chambers, either side of the hall, were the dining and drawing rooms. Both boasted "Sienna, Egyptian and white marble chimney pieces" and "rich India paper hangings". The dining room's table groaned under the weight of commemorative dinner services that had been gifted to Horace, one each for the Nile and Baltic; and silver sauceboats inscribed with "Tria Juncta in Uno". An oak-panelled staircase led to five bed chambers on the floor above the main house. There was a modern water closet, but this may not have been upstairs. There were five smaller bedrooms on the upper floor of the rear building, which is where the servants were quartered.

The household was efficiently managed by Emma's mother, known to all as Mrs. Cadogan, who'd remained quietly, and faithfully at Emma's side throughout her soaring rise to fame.

The Bombay fashion of verandahs had now spread to England, including Merton Place. The trellised verandahs here, which overlooked the landscaped gardens, were accessed via mirrored, glass doors, and shady under arch-beamed roofs. There was also "a long passage with glass doors opening into the lawn behind".[805]

In every room and corridor, the walls were hung with a proliferation of prints and portraits of Emma and Horace "of all sizes and sorts and representations of his naval actions, coats of arms, pieces of plate in his honour".[806] The highlight of the extensive gardens was an ornamental canal dubbed "the Nile".[740]

Horace and the Hamiltons departed Merton soon after the Matchams left. The excited press was, as ever, filled with news of their movements. In the second week of July, for example, "LORD NELSON appeared... at Covent-garden [in London] and was greatly applauded by the populace."[741]

Horace wrote to George, "On Wednesday we fix to dine at Oxford. I wish you to fix the Inn, we have yet seen nobody who can tell us anything about it."[742]

Chapter Thirteen: Moving Times

1802 – 1803

It was an unseasonably cool summer[743] when, at five in the evening on the 21st of July 1802, a party of eight assembled in a private room in a prestigious Oxford hotel. The elegant diners wouldn't have looked out of place in a modern Jane Austen film –perhaps an adaptation of Pride and Prejudice. The ladies, being fashionable, would have worn long-sleeved, high-waisted frocks and short hair-dos from which curls tickled their graceful necks. Coloured silks with metallic trimmings were very much in vogue.[744] The gentlemen would have dressed more sombrely, in line with Beau Brummel's understated elegance,[745] unless, that is, Horace had donned his rotating *chelengk*. But, when he'd written to George asking him to reserve their table, he'd advised, "Need not say for who."[746] When with family, Horace tended to switch his hero outfit for civilian attire. This was usually a black suit, although he sometimes donned a coat of bottle-green or, perhaps, a knitted jumper under his frock coat.[747]

In a contemporary miniature, George wears a dark jacket with a Beau Brummell-style knotted, white cravat. His slightly wavy, greying hair is cut short and brushed back from his forehead. He's still slim, with no sign of jowliness or double chins. His eyebrows are dark and neat and there's the hint of merriment tickling the edges of his closed lips.[748]

This is a cosy, private, family get-together, and the diners are Horace, George Matcham, Kitty, George junior[749] –perhaps to reward his good behaviour in Ringwood–, Reverend William and Sarah Nelson, and Sir William and Lady Hamilton[750] whose singular style Kitty, Sarah, and the rest of fashionable female Europe copies. Kitty will be hoping Lady Hamilton approves of her apparel.

The venue is the Angel Inn, which boasts "a frontage to the High-street of 102 feet [31 meters] forming altogether one of the largest and most commodious Hotels in the kingdom".[751] Early nineteenth century inns were "superior to pubs and alehouses",[752] and The Angel Inn was grand enough for King Christian II of Denmark to have stayed in it in 1768.[753] The inn's front had been replaced in 1783 with rows of tall Georgian windows –some with arched pediments– and iron-railed balconies along the entire course of the first floor.[754] The interior would have reflected the refined, formal aesthetics of the exterior, with low-relief, classical motifs painted in delicate hues.[755]

Sir William, with his beak-like Roman nose, was seventy-one, infirm, [756] and cared "not a fig" what the world thought of his wife and Horace's obvious relationship.[757] Lady Hamilton, at thirty-six, was almost half his age and celebrated for her "rounded arms" and "lovely girlish face on a full woman's body".[758] Unlike William Nelson –who had a gluttonous lack of table manners–,[759] Lady Hamilton was graceful and slimmer than when George had met her eighteen-months before. But she still dwarfed Horace, especially without his trademark bicorn hat.

Though five years George's junior, Horace was wizened with battle scars and had turned prematurely grey. Unmasked, the hero of the Nile was frail, 5' 4", one-armed, half-blind and with poor dental health accrued from scurvy and "yellow Jack" (the Georgian era name for malaria or typhus). [760] Horace self-consciously combed his mop of hair over his forehead to conceal a dent in his skull.[761] [762] His spirit, though, remained undaunted and his lips –so much like his father's– were full and generous. He'd have shone with sheer joy to be reunited with his family.

The party had assembled in Oxford because Horace, and the two Williams, had been cordially summoned to receive honorary degrees of Doctors of Civil Law,[763] and Horace was to be granted freedom of the city too. William Nelson had received similar honours in Cambridge twelve-days before,[764] which would have broken his long journey from Norfolk.

Early Regency custom dictated that every dish, for every course, was placed on the table ahead of the meal. A popular starter was artichoke soup. Later courses would have comprised roasted meats, game and fish. Vegetables were served half-drowned in butter, which was expensive and, therefore, a status symbol. Desserts often comprised pyramids of stacked marzipan and fruit.[765] Sweet and savoury aromas, emanating from the combined courses, would have mingled with ladies' perfumes of sandalwood, musk, orange blossom, Madagascar jasmine and lily of the valley.[766]

George junior later reflected that his famous uncle had a sarcastic sense of humour, but was quiet and unassuming during dinners:

"Lord Nelson in private life was remarkable for a demeanour quiet, sedate and unobtrusive, anxious to give pleasure to everyone about him...

he delighted in quiet conversation, through which ran an undercurrent of pleasantry not unmixed with caustic wit. At his table he was the least heard among the company, and so far from being the hero of his own tale, I never heard him voluntarily refer to any of the great actions of his life". [767]

Lady Hamilton, chestnut hair agleam in the candlelight, was skilled at putting people at ease, and would have pressed George to call her Emma. Sir William was also expert at putting people at ease, having served as British Ambassador in Naples for half of his long life. Part of that duty had been hosting dinners for visiting Brits in his ambassadorial residence of Palazzo Sessa.

The Hamiltons had a trove of terrific tales to tell. They'd nursed the English prince, Augustus Frederick, Duke of Sussex and, in the darkest days of the French revolution, procured passes to visit the deposed queen Marie Antoinette, in her dismal Paris gaol.[768] And –oh!– their grand progress home from Naples across Europe had been glorious with vast crowds gathered wherever they passed, cheering and throwing flowers at their feet. Queen Maria Carolina, several royal children, and fifty of her retainers had accompanied them as far as Vienna –where her daughter was living with her exiled husband, Ferdinand III, Grand Duke of Tuscany.[769]

George, whose travel-itch was flaring, would have been keen to hear descriptions of the cities Horace and the Hamiltons had explored, and was particularly taken with their descriptions of Vienna –which was cramped within its city walls, but neat, with well-built houses, "chiefly plastered and white-washed", and "regular, well-paved" streets, lit at night–[770] and Dresden, the capital of Saxony, that had been contemporarily described as the "amiable asylum of the graces and arts of the North", with "so many fine promenades, that no other capital has so many in proportion to its size, and no other place is so rich in natural and artificial beauties of this kind." In Dresden, Horace and the Hamiltons had stayed in Hotel de Polgne and been entertained by the resident British minister, Hugh Elliot, who – unfortunately– had transpired to be a snob who'd treated them with less admiration than they'd grown accustomed to.[771] Thankfully, their welcome to Hamburg had been more enthusiastic. Among the many who'd come to meet them was an elderly pastor who'd begged Horace to sign his Bible because he'd believed him to be the saviour of the Christian world. [772]

Horace, though reluctant to sing his own praises, repeatedly told any and all who'd listen that he couldn't have "saved the Christian world" without Emma's intervention with the Naples queen to release the supplies he'd needed for his fleet to reach the Nile in the first place.

Twelve-year-old George junior would have listened raptly. He had his mother's dark, wavy hair, an imprint of his father in his eyes and jaw, and a long-lasting admiration for Emma's elegance.[773] [774] [775]

Kitty had few, if any, qualms about accepting Horace and Emma's relationship. After all, two of her siblings –Ann and Maurice– had been in unwedded relationships without their family disowning them or, indeed, having loved them any less.

William Nelson, and his wife, Sarah, had been described as "very strange-looking people".[776] William, who was always hungry to gain as much as possible from Horace and Emma's celebrity, had taken his family to Merton so often that they'd been allocated their own rooms.[777]

George, though, was less comfortable with Horace's split from Fanny. For him, marriage was a sacred, unbreakable state. Horace's separation from Fanny was the antithesis of George's core, Christian beliefs and contrary to the fabric of his universe. In a later reflection, he revealed a belief that he held Emma responsible for Horace and Fanny's split, because Horace was too open-hearted and family-loving to be culpable and Emma's "disposition was satirical not… from malignity… but from an affectation of point and wit" and that "Her letters and even casual notes were never free from this despicable propensity."[778]

Though mentions of Fanny were likely avoided, mutual grief would have been shared for Edmund Nelson's recent passing. Another safe –but maybe dull– topic was George's aquatic engineering experiments. Although the technical details of leather balloons and steam power may not have interested all present, George subsequently gained patenting assistance from Horace's elderly assistant, Francis Oliver,[779] who was nicknamed "the Jackal".[780] Oliver had once been Sir William Hamilton's secretary in Naples, and had later moved to Austria,[781] where Horace and the Hamiltons had ran into him in Vienna. Oliver had been quick to attach himself to Horace, and was now living in Merton.[782] [783]

Horace and Emma would most certainly have talked about their two-year-old "ward", Horatia, who lived with a nurse, named Mrs. Gibson, but visited Merton frequently.

There's no record of when –or even if– Horace told his family that Horatia was his and Emma's biological daughter –just as there's no record of the Nelson family having known about Ann's illegitimate son– but the likelihood is that everyone present that evening, in the Angel Inn's private room –bar maybe twelve-year-old George junior– knew exactly who Horatia was.

Horace and Emma were painfully aware of the need to hide Horatia's illegitimacy from public knowledge, not just because society scorned bastard-born girls, but because the mothers of bastards were ostracised too.

In an effort to conceal Horatia's parentage, Horace and Emma pretended she'd been born in October 1800 –three months before her true birthdate– during their very public journey across Europe (meaning it would have been impossible for Emma to have given birth without it being noticed). They attributed Horatia's parentage to a non-existent sailor's wife, named Mrs. Thompson, whose equally non-existent husband was a crewman on Horace's ship.

How likely would it have been for George not to have noticed Emma's heavy pregnancy when he first met her in December 1800? After all, he'd witnessed Kitty carrying nine babies full-term, so was well-versed with the signs. And, although Emma's signature high-waisted gowns had worked wonders in covering her telltale curves, her great size had been spotted by all and sundry. There was even a spoof version of the national anthem that had gained enough popularity to be set in print:

> *"Also huge Emma's name,*
> *First on the roll of fame,*
> *Now let us sing*
> *Loud as her voice, let's sound*
> *Her faded charms around,*
> *Which in the sheets were found,*
> *God save the King.*
> *Nelson, thy flag haul down,*
> *Hang up thy laurel crown,*
> *While her we sing.*
> *No more in triumph swell,*
> *Since that with her you dwell,*
> *But don't her William tell –*
> *Nor George your King."*[784]

In truth, Horace was markedly inept at concealing his paternity of Horatia.[785] His ongoing stream of honours, and the jubilant cheering he received wherever he went, bolstered his belief that he could break conventions without rebuff. It, therefore, seems improbable that Horace could have hidden Horatia's identity from George and Kitty, though –of course– there's no certain evidence that he told them (just as there's none for Ann's son).

To maintain the charade that two-year-old Horatia was the daughter of Mr and Mrs Thompson, they'd christened her, on the 13th of May, in St Marylebone, London, with the subterfuge name of Horatia Nelson Thompson, and supplied her concocted, earlier birthdate for inclusion in her baptismal record.[786] Interestingly, Horatia's baptism took place a very swift two days after Edmund Nelson's funeral, suggesting that the old rector had known exactly who Horatia's parents were, and that he'd have objected to Horace giving false testimony to the Church.

Another telltale sign that Horace's close kin knew Emma was Horatia's mother, is the fervency with which they embraced her into their family.[787] Kitty and George had held back for longer than the Boltons and William Nelsons, suggesting, perhaps, that the truth about Horatia had been slower to reach them. In fact, George and Kitty may not have learnt of Horatia's secret until their first visit to Merton, less than two-months before the Oxford meal.

After dinner, Horace may have begged George for a quiet, private word on a subject he'd already broached by letter: this being his hope that George would loan him £4,000 from his and Kitty's marriage settlement to buy land adjoining Merton Place.[788]

On the following day –Thursday the 22nd of July – George and Kitty accompanied Horace to Oxford Town Hall for his award of freedom of the city. The frail, 5' 4", one-armed, half-blind, almost toothless Horace they'd dined with the night before had transformed himself into the Right Honorable Lord Viscount Nelson Duke of Bronte.

The high street outside the Angel Inn was always busy with milling students and masters, whose picturesque "collegiate costume" of cloaks and tasselled, square caps –"graceful, but inconvenient, being of no use against sun, wind, or rain"– inspired a Spanish visitor to remark, "there is a total want of drapery in the dress of Englishmen, every where, except in the universities."[789]

Horace, however, out-dazzled every person on the high street. His vice admiral's full-dress uniform comprised a "Blue Coat, with Blue Lapels and round Cuffs, White Lining; the Lapels to have One Row of Gold Lace, and the Pockets Two ; laced Button-Holes :— Two Gold Epaulettes :—Gold-laced Hat. —White Waistcoat and Breeches. Two Silver Stars on each Epaulette, and Three Rows of Lace on the Cuffs."[790] All of which was, of course, bedazzled with his medals, ribbons and clockwork *chelengk*. If this wasn't eye-catching enough, both he and Sir William were Knights of the Order of Bath and would have donned their tasseled, floor-sweeping, crimson, silk robes.[791]

The town hall was only a few hundred metres from the Angel Inn, but the high street's whole couldn't "be seen at once, because it is not sufficiently straight."[792] The distance would have thronged with an excited crowd, eager to glimpse the Hero of the Nile. The lower classes would have cheered for Emma too. Unlike the Tory press, they weren't bothered about her lowly birth which, in fact, made her rise to glory all the more appealing.[793]

Oxford Town Hall, which had been purpose-built in the 1740s,[794] had a "neat and commodious edifice".[795] A corn-exchange, with arched vaults, occupied the ground-floor and the hall, situated upstairs[796] was spacious enough to hold seven hundred people.[797] Here, George and Kitty witnessed the "elaborate ceremony" in which "the Right Honorable Lord Viscount Nelson Duke of Bronte", was presented with honorary freedom of the city "as a proof of the high veneration and respect which this City entertain for a Nobleman who has upon so many occasions rendered the most important services to his King and Country". Horace's freedom of the city was "engraved on Vellum under the seal of [the] City and presented to his Lordship in a gold box by Richard Weston Esq. Mayor."[798]

The pomp continued. On the morning of Friday the 23rd of July, another large assembly gathered to witness "the honorary degree of Doctor in Civil Law [being] conferred on his Lordship and Sir William Hamilton… and at the same time the Rev. William Nelson… was admitted to the same degree".[799]

Horace, Emma and elderly Sir William –who didn't give a fig– were happily engaged in travelling from town to town, being cheered by the public and –for the men, at least– receiving multiple honours. The Matchams accompanied their merry company as far as Gloucester, forty-seven miles to the west of Oxford. A contemporary guidebook describes the Cotswolds city as "situated on the banks of the Severn, nearly in the centre of a fertile and extensive tract of country [but] like most other towns of antiquity was formerly much disfigured by the irregularity of its buildings… the inhabitants are hospitable and attentive to strangers…"[800] Sure enough, their arrival was met with, "a hearty welcome from crowds and the cathedral's bells", then "another tour of a city, including the gaol.[801] From here, George, Kitty and George junior returned to Bath, while Horace and the Hamiltons headed to Wales to inspect estates Sir William had inherited from his first wife.

George's knowledge of his brother-in-law's activities once again flipped from first-hand to enthusiastic press mentions, the first of which relegated George, Kitty and their son to a single, anonymous "&c":

"The party of Welsh tourists, consisting of Lord Nelson, Sir William and Lady Hamilton, &c. arrived on Saturday at Gloucester ; and on Sunday morning they reached the Swan Inn, Ross. After breakfasting there,

they walked through the botanical garden, belonging to Mr. Hill, to the banks of the Wye, and embarked on a pleasure boat for Monmouth, where their equipages were directed to meet them, in order to proceed in their route through South Wales. The progress of the party having been announced previously to their arrival at Ross, his Lordship was ushered into the town by the ringing of bells and the acclamation of the inhabitants."[802]

Simultaneously, a Merton neighbour, Abraham Goldsmid, had hosted a lavish fête "at his delightful villa" in which an an effigy stood in for Horace's real-life presence:

"The [fashionable] company assembled in the hall, and proceeded through the bow parlour into a spacious and elegant saloon... tastefully illuminated with festoons of variegated lamps, interwoven with leaves of laurel; the bridges over the canal and different parts of the garden were also decorated with appropriate devices. At each quarter of the saloon, were placed transparencies of Their Majesties, Lord Nelson, Sir Sydney Smith, etc, etc. Opposite the entrance was a circular orchestra, in which a military band performed during tea..."[803]

It's not clear if the Hamiltons were omitted from the report because Goldsmid hadn't included them in his "who's who" of transparencies, or if their omission had been down to the journalist adhering to the growing anti-Emma trend and, like the Matchams in Gloucester, relegating them to the anonymity of "etc." The latter seems probable, because Goldsmid proved a staunch ally to Emma in later years.

George and Kitty appear to have visited Merton again in August 1802, as Horace wrote to him and Kitty in July, saying, "we may have you both for a fortnight at Merton when we return from Wales, which will be in August certainly".[804]

Emma wrote to Kitty, on the 13th of September, with news of a property near Merton she hoped to tempt her and George to move to:

"We have just been to see the place at Epsom for you & of which I enclose you the particulars... if it would be worth Mr Matchams while to come to see it we shall be most happy to see him... Oh how our Hero has been received I wish pass Cou'd Come to hear all our story most interesting Coud you not come for 2 or 3 days"[807]

Home in Bath, and in no hurry to relocate to Surrey, George resumed his humbler routine. In late September, the newest member of his brood, Susanna, was five-months old; unruly Harriet had turned three —was she now dutifully saying her prayers?– and he was in the mood to indulge in his love of hunting. He took a leisure trip to the New Forest and confirmed Samuel Dowden's ongoing employment as his gamekeeper for Plumley Heath.[808]

Horace wrote to "My Dear Mr. Matcham", on the 23rd of December 1802, politely pressing George to loan him £4,000 to purchase land adjoining Merton.[809] Emma added a note to Kitty, "We have 3 Boltons, 2 Nelsons, & only want 2 or 3 Little Matchams to be quite en famille."[810] George agreed to lend Horace the money from his and Kitty's marriage settlement[811] –which would have necessitated formal approval from William Nelson as the only surviving trustee– on condition that Horace paid twice yearly interest.[812]

A flurry of correspondence reveals that George –ever restless– had set aside his plans to holiday in France in favour of Dresden or Vienna. On New Year's Day 1803, Merton's live in secretary, Francis Oliver, told George he considered Vienna preferable, and that Horace would agree: "His Lordship will tell you the same that you would soon be tired of Dresden".[813]

On the 4th of January, Horace wrote:

"I have directed 4000 to be the Specific Mortgage. I agree with you it is so best, but (every) Lawyer thinks his own mode the best ; they never allow anybody else to know anything...

Lady Hamilton gave a little Ball last night to the children ; they danced till 3 this morning and are not yet up.

Remember my kind love to my Sister & your family & Believe me ever your much obliged & affectionate Brother Nelson & Bronte."[814]

In reply, George queried both the mortgage and the comparative merits of Vienna and Dresden. Horace said, on the 11th of January, he couldn't immediately visit his London agents about the mortgage because it was so stormy that tiles were being blown off roofs:

"I should have gone to London today to have settled with my agents... I shall go tomorrow or Thursday, for our friends will not let me go this tile falling day"

As for the best holiday destination:

"The Environs of both Dresden & Vienna are beautiful I believe. Dresden much the cheapest place".[815]

In the same month that George loaned Horace £4,000 to extend Merton, Fanny left her calling card at No. 19 Kensington Place without knocking.[816] In one account, Kitty regretted having been out when Fanny called, saying, "We should have told her, as we have always declared it is our maxim if possible to be at peace with all the world."[817] Conversely, a letter from Kitty to Emma suggests she'd callously observed Fanny from the window. "I have seen Tom Tit once. She called her carriage at Lady Charlotte Drummond's, who lives next door. The lady was not at home, but she got out of her carriage, walked stiff as a poker about half a dozen steps, turned around, and got in again. What this Manoeuvre was for I cannot tell, unless to show herself. She need not have taken so much pains if nobody wanted to see her [any] more than I do. She was stiffer than ever."[818] Emma replied that Fanny was "a nasty vulgar bad-hearted wretch".[819]

The sad, likely reality is that Fanny had frozen in panicked uncertainty about the Matchams' welcome. George seems to have spurned her too, because Horace commented, "the Matchams should have returned her card."

Kitty's use of her siblings' "Tom Tit" nickname to ridicule Fanny's fast-step, birdlike waddle,[820] shows she was no longer of the mindset that had once driven her to upbraid the William Nelsons for mocking Fanny. As previously speculated, her change of attitude may have come about from having learned of Horatia's true parentage during her first visit to Merton in June 1802, six months before the Kensington Place calling card incident.

Rightly or wrongly, the Nelson family's irritability with Fanny might be explained by her ongoing refusal to accept Horace's relationship with Emma,[821] as this scraped against the convention for wives to accept husbands' mistresses without fuss.[822] Divorce was effectively impossible,[823] but Horace –who wasn't rich– was voluntarily paying half his income to his estranged wife.[824]

Fanny, though genuinely shy and anxious, was also clingy and possessed of a steely will. She refused, pointblank, to let Horace go and had no qualms about playing the injured damsel so as to manipulate heartstrings and win people to her side, thus turning them against Emma.

The simple fact is that, though Fanny would have made an ideal second wife for Edmund Nelson,[825] she and Horace were totally incompatible. At the time of their marriage, Horace had been hellbent on living up to others' expectations so as to get ahead and this had included having a well-bred wife. His patrons at the time of his reaching his captaincy had suggested he marry, as society viewed it only proper for an officer of a certain rank to be respectably wed. In marrying Fanny, Horace wed the woman he sensed his father wanted for him: a quiet, conservative recluse who was made miserable by cold drafts and was panicked by the idea of her husband facing any danger, ever. In total contrast, Emma was a liberal and creative soul who flourished under limelight and revelled in Horace's risk-taking courage. Where Fanny mourned Horace's war wounds, Emma's exultation in his derring-do made him aware of who he was and what he actually wanted.[826]

Tellingly, when one-armed Horace arrived in Naples, fresh from the Nile, he'd written guilelessly to Fanny about Emma's welcome:

"Up flew her ladyship and exclaiming: 'Oh God is it possible' fell into my arms more dead than alive.'"[827]

So, Emma made one-armed Horace feel whole (in possession of both arms). They clearly adored each other and had a child together. Horace had dealt with Fanny in as kind, and as generous a manner, as he could. But she wouldn't back away gracefully.

Is it any wonder that Horace's kin were annoyed with her?

George preferred to focus on his science projects. On Francis Oliver's advice, he applied to patent his system for moving and raising boats,[828] and his application was approved on the 29th of January 1803. A summary of his patent was recorded in the Repertory of Patent Inventions:

"GEORGE MATCHAM, of the City of Bath, Esquire ; for a principal or mechanical power for raising great weights, in preventing ships which are disproportioned to shall-water capable of entering rivers, passing bars, or shoals, or otherwise moving in shallow water ; and for a variety of other useful purposes."[829]

George's friend, HSB, had returned to his consular posting in Minorca, but his widowed aunt, Anne Harrison, remained living at 8 Paragon Street and was a good friend of George's much-loved mother. The companionable old ladies attended church together in nearby Bathford.

Now aged seventy-four, Mrs. Elizabeth Matcham was at the end of her long life. Her "miniature, together with her beautiful collection of Oriental embroideries, china, &c. [gave the impression of] a comfortable old lady, of good taste and liberal expenditure."[830] She passed away on the 3rd of April 1803.[831]

Three days later, Horace wrote to George, distraught. "Our dear Sir William died at 10 minutes past Ten this morning in Lady Hamilton's and my arms without a sigh or struggle."[832] On receipt of George's letter, he wrote to Kitty, on the 8th of April:

"My Dear Sister. In a house full of affliction I can readily conceive feelings so nearly similar to what we are feeling.

I shall almost hate April ; look at the last three years. Good Mr. Matcham has seen our Parent go out of the World and now his own. I now trust that the Work of Death will cease for many years. Lady Hamilton suffers very much, but desires her kind love to you and Mr. Matcham."[833]

Sir William Hamilton was buried in Wales beside his first wife, and George's mother was buried in Bathford beside Kitty's sister, Ann, not far from the tomb of HSB's mother.[834] Both ladies had been called Elizabeth.

George decreed for his mother's grave to be marked with a tall sarcophagus sumounted by a fluted cupola, like a flattened Indian dome, and an inscription informing posterity that she was the "relict of Simon Matcham, esq., of the Island of Bombay".

Elizabeth Matcham's hand-written will bequeathed sums of £10 and £20 to various sisters, nieces and nephews for the purpose of buying memorial rings, but she left the remainder of her estate to George, whom she named her sole executor.[835]

Chapter Fourteen: Peace Collapsed

1803 – 1805

The Peace of Amiens lasted for just fourteen short months. Unresolved bickering over Malta culminated in Britain declaring war on France in May 1803.[836] The ensuing collapse of peace jettisoned Horace from the comfort of Lady Hamilton's arms into being Commander-in-Chief of the Mediterranean fleet.[837] He was ordered to Portsmouth to assume command of a warship with the inspiring name of Victory.[838]

A month later, George and Kitty had the joy of baptising their thirteenth child, Horatio Nelson Matcham, in Walcot St. Swithin's, but George's personal peace was then shattered by a catastrophic discovery.

One of the aquatic engineering solutions he'd included in his patent had been previously described in a pamphlet published by Dr. Fothergill.[839] Dr. Anthony Fothergill was a fellow member of Bath and West England Society.[840] Had he stolen George's idea after assisting with his experiments?

Muddying the waters further, Francis Oliver –the man who'd urged George to pursue the patent– was considered a fool by Horace and despised by Sir William Hamilton, who thought him a "most ungrateful and impertinent rascal",[841] begging the question of why they'd employed Oliver to begin with.

Whilst Horace settled himself aboard Victory, in Portsmouth, George went to London to admit his error to the Court of Chancery. He confessed that, although the bulk of the methods described in his patent were unique, with regard to his method:

"of floating vessels in shoals by buoyancy I have found has some time since been communicated to the public by Dr. Fothergill, of Bath. The ideas suggested in his pamphlet so closely accord with my own, that I can lay no claim to priority as to the buoyancy of vessels, &c. by inflated bags, thereby expelling the grosser element of water."

George's inheritance from his mother enabled him to buy a respectable property close to Bath's genteel Royal Crescent. No. 2 Portland Place was an "elegant house, 34 feet 3 inches in front, and proportionally deep, with a third room on each floor, convenient offices, and all necessary fixtures... substantially built... and from the size of the principal rooms, well adapted for a large family."[842]

The weather having been exceptionally hot and dry[843] George let off steam by taking a vacation to Plumley Heath, where he reconfirmed Samuel Dowden as his gamekeeper for the hunting season of 1803–4.[844]

George and Kitty had kept up correspondence with their friend, HSB – Henry Stanyford Blanckley– in his consular posting at Minorca. HSB, as British consul to the Spanish-ruled Balearic islands, had been under duress since Spain allied with France in 1796.[845] Kitty wrote to Horace, on Victory, asking him to help. Horace replied, on the 12th of December 1803:

"MY DEAR SISTER : ... if it is in my power to be useful to Mr. Blankley in the way he wishes I shall be very glad. Mr. Blankley wrote me word that he knew our dear father very well & you & Mr. Matcham, but our dear friends the Spaniards will not suffer us to use Minorca, and if they would, I would not trust them with the British fleet".

Horace then urged Kitty to relocate to Merton, praised her kindness for having written "large" for the ease of his failing vision, and commented, wryly, about the good condition of the French fleet, which his own fleet was blockading in Toulon:

"I hope by the time I get back that you will have found a house near Merton.
You did well to write large I can read it very well.
I suppose Buonaparte have not taken you yet nor have I much fears that he will, but I wish it was all over for I can't help being anxious. My friends in Toulon are very well and look very gay, compared to our weather beaten Ships, but should they come out, I dare say they will wish themselves in again. I beg my kind remembrances to Mr. Matcham... and be assured I ever am My Dear Sister
Your most affectionate Brother NELSON & BRONTE."[846]

Horace's next letter to 19 Kensington Place was addressed to George:

"VICTORY feby 14th 1804
I have so much to write, that I neglect, I fear My friends think, those I ought to be attentive to, but be assured my Dear Mr. Mm, that whether I

write or not, my heart always stands in the right place to you, My Dear Sister & your family.

I am momentarily expecting the french fleet to put to sea. We have been long anxiously looking for them. With my kindest Love to my Dear Sister and to all your family. Believe me

Ever your most affectionate Brother

NELSON & BRONTE. "[847]

Kitty added each and every one of her beloved bro's letters to her collection of correspondence, which she daintily tied into separate packets with coloured satin ribbons.[848]

However, treasured as Horace's letters were, the Matchams "remained on at Bath, which they had no wish to exchange for the proposed establishment near Merton."

In fact, George's wanderlust had been roaming so much further afield than Merton, that he purchased "a considerable estate in Schleswig".

Schleswig was a duchy of Denmark occupying the broad neck of land between the German port of Hamburg, in the south, and Denmark, in the north. George's investment there was, alas, an unlucky one. The collapse of the Treaty of Amiens thumped him with the double whammy that, on the one hand, the renewed continental war made emigrating to Denmark too risky to consider and, on the other hand, the value of his Schleswig estate plummeted. On top of this was worry that Kitty's health was suffering because the strain of it all.

George wrote to his agent, in February 1804:

"My apprehensions have been extreme, from the dread that it might have made my wife miserable, who, with her usual goodness, has been comforting and encouraging me at the expence [sic] of her own health"[849]

In March, news filtered to England from the war-torn Mediterranean that, in addition to aiding HSB in Minorca, Horace had aided another British consul. John Falcon in Algiers had got into trouble with the Dey – the Ottoman governor– after the French had, very sneakily, planted Muslim women in his ambassadorial residence while he was out, and then alerted the Dey's guards:

"the British Consul (John Falcon, Esq) and the Dey were not on very friendly terms. The misunderstanding had long subsisted, but the breach was much widened by a charge being falsely made against the Consul that he harboured Moorish women in his house, a usage not allowed by the

laws of Mahomet. By French intrigue the women were introduced into the Consul's house during his absence, and therein found by the guards who were sent in search. In consequence of this circumstance, Mr. Falcon was ordered away, and otherwise treated with much indignity... Lord Nelson then said, that if the Dey would not consent to do justice to the British Consul, he must be under the necessity of compelling him by force.—The Dey's answer was, that if Lord Nelson fired a single gun, he would consider it as a declaration of hostilities, and immediately open the batteries against his ships.—Lord Nelson not having instructions to proceed to extremities, has sent the particulars of the affair to Government, and waits their answer to govern his conduct in this curious affair."

Meanwhile, in Minorca, the Spanish governor, Felipe Ramirez,[850] was growing increasingly hostile towards HSB and his family, which comprised his wife, Mary, their baby daughters, Elizabeth and Henrietta; and HSB's fourteen-year-old son from his first marriage, Edward Blanckley. HSB was put under house-arrest and, when his butler attempted to go out, Ramirez's Spanish guards mistook him for HSB and stabbed him with a bayonet.[851]

Although the *tria juncta in uno* was no more —with Horace leading the British fleet in the Mediterranean and Sir William having passed away— when George flicked through the papers, there was ample mention of Emma, not all of which was bad. Despite the rising tide of disdain since her return to England three-and-a-half years before, esteem for her singing and musical prowess was untarnished. She also had many friends amongst the aristocracy and knew how to put on a good show.

In April 1804, the Daily Advertiser and Oracle noted "The Countess of ALDBOROUGH'S ensuing Musical Parties, it is said, will have the powerful aid of LADY HAMILTON."[852]

In the same month, news reached George, and his fellow English readers, that the Admiralty had received dispatches from Horace that a French fleet had sailed from Toulon which he believed was heading to Sicily.[853]

In May 1804, George would have read that Emma hosted a music party and ball in Chesterfield Street, London, "which was attended by a numerous party of fashionables."[854]

Sir George Shee, a fellow East India Company man whom George knew from Bombay,[855] offered to help him iron out problems with the estate he was coming to regret having bought in Schleswig:

"If you wish to be presented to [Prime Minister] Mr. Pitt before you set out I will with great pleasure go with you to him this morning, or if you would prefer postponing your visit until a time of less hurry, after your return from the Continent, I shall then be at your Command."[1856]

The papers now told George that Horace was urging the French and Spanish fleets to face him for a fight,[1857] whilst, in London, it was noted (with triple exclamation marks) that "Lady Hamilton has retired from Clarges-street to Lord Nelson's villa at Merton, in Surrey, where she intends to spend the summer in rural seclusion ! ! !"[1858]

On the 30th of July, George confessed to Sir George Shee that he no longer wanted to go to Schleswig. Shee replied:

"Your Reasons for thinking of relinquishing your Plan of settling on the Shelswick [sic] Estate are very strong. I thought as you did on the Subject, before you went to the Continent, but certainly as you observe Inducements ought to be very strong indeed where our habitual comforts are to be relinquished".[1859]

On the 10th of August 1804, closer to home, Emma changed her mind about staying in Merton alone: "Lady HAMILTON, and the Rev. Mr. NELSON and Family have taken a house in Albion Place."[1860]

Emma was part of the "beauty and fashion" attending a ball in Ramsgate.[1861] But, in other news, "Meanwhile Lord Nelson confines attention principally to Toulon".[1862]

Whilst George and his in-laws worried for Horace's well-being, life went on and they tried, individually, to retain their morale and George returned to his little haven at Plumley Heath.[1863]

December newspapers told of Emma's attendance at a Drury Lane theatre production in the company of the Duke of Bedford and the Duchess of Devonshire.[1864] The London Morning Herald noted that, for Christmas 1804, "Lady Hamilton has taken an elegant house in Upper Grosvenor Street for the season."[1865]

In January 1805, the press remarked upon Lady Hamilton's handsome, new "Chariot, body painted yellow, lined with red morocco leather, fancy lace, with seat cloth fully trimmed."[1866] And Horace, "the gallant Admiral", was rumoured to have captured the island of Minorca from the Spanish.[1867]

Kitty remained at home, in Kensington Place, heavily pregnant, yet again.

In February, Emma, who'd not sung publicly for two seasons, performed in the Marchioness of Abercorn's concert, where the supposition that "on her reappearance in the fashionable circles she would astonish her hearers [was] fully answered by [the] uncommon powers gained with her voice".[868]

In March, the Marchioness hosted another concert in which Emma sang and performed her celebrated Attitudes.[869]

George and Kitty's twelfth child was baptised, in Walcot St. Swithin on the 23rd of April 1805, with the name William Alexander, perhaps in honour of Kitty's eldest surviving brother, Reverend William Nelson, and Horace's prize agent, Alexander Davison.[870]

News of Horace, as ever, filtered to them via the press. Intelligence, reported in May 1805, was that the combined fleets of France and Spain had entered Cadiz on the 22nd of April –the day before William Alexander's baptism– "and LORD NELSON left the coast of Sardinia on the 19th in pursuit of them".[871]

In the latter days of May, "Lady Hamilton added her vocal charms to the happy scene of an amateur concert organised by Colonel Greville and the Honourable William Spencer.[872]

Just as Emma hadn't shaken off the performer-persona of her past, George's youthful spirit of adventure still shaped his life. However, he may have wished his irrepressible wanderlust hadn't lured him into buying that estate in Schleswig, because he was now under pressure to visit it, war or not.

Colonel Coehoon, a Schleswig resident, wrote to him on the 11th of May 1805:

"My dear friend hesitate not a moment... The season is favourable... Your presence is absolutely necessary... I hope Mrs. Matcham will appreciate the necessity of your coming over to this country, and I am sure that the sister of Lord Nelson will have resolution and be reasonable enough to feel the urgency of the circumstance, and I promise her that your absence will not be above a month... M. O. Coehoon.'"[873]

Sailing to mainland Europe during the war was risky, even though Denmark was a neutral country. However, George had invested a lot of money in the Schleswig estate, and Colonel Coehoon believed his personal attendance there was urgent. No details have emerged about George's solo trip to Denmark –which would have been an overnight sail each way– beyond his great-granddaughter's comment that "A visit to the place was undertaken by G. M. in May 1805".[874]

In June, the press excitedly reported month-old intelligence that Horace had crossed the Atlantic Ocean to the Caribbean,[875] whilst, in real time, Emma was sighted near Windsor, looking "gay, blooming and roseate, as the Goddess of Health."[876]

Mary Eyre Matcham tells that, during the summer of 1805, the Matchams' life in Bath comprised:

"Plays, musical parties, fetes, dinners, breakfasts, dances, long rides and walks, fishing-parties and antiquarian excursions filled up the round of life at Bath. Friends flocked round them. The Bowens, Mrs. Warden, the authoress, Mr. Barry, with his brother Lord Barrymore, well known for their eccentricities in the fashionable world, the Malets from Wilbury, Pieles, of Spye Park, and the Days at Hinton, where much happy time was passed."[877]

The "Malets from Wilbury" were George's old school friend, Charles Warre Malet, his wife, their eight children and, somewhat controversially, three children Malet had fathered with a Punjabi princess, named Amber Bibi, during his East India Company residency at Puna.[878]

Exciting news reached George, in mid July, that Horace had tracked the combined French and Spanish fleets to Antigua.[879] Then, on the 10th of August, Saint James's Chronicle published new intelligence that Horace had called into Gibraltar, a month before, "for refreshments" during his dogged chase of the combined fleets.[880]

To the Matchams' relief, Horace's flagship, Victory, arrived safely in Portsmouth on the 18th of August 1805.[881] The warship was held in quarantine for two days, after which, "Lord Nelson came on shore, and immediately set off for London."

As a downer to the Matchams' joy, the report continued, "The Victory is ordered into harbour to be got ready for his Lordship's flag again with all possible dispatch." So, Horace's home-leave would be a brief one. Happily, though, "When the populace understood that his Lordship was coming on shore, they assembled in great numbers at the sally-port, and huzzaed him repeatedly, and would have taken the horses from the carriage that conveyed him to town, but his Lordship begged that they would not, as it was his earnest wish to lose no time in proceeding on his journey."[882]

George and Kitty would have exchanged knowing smiles. Dear Horace had sped to Emma and Horatia in Merton as swiftly as he could.

Two days after disembarking from Victory, Horace and Emma wrote to Kitty jointly from Merton. Horace told her, "I need not my dear sister say how happy I shall be to see you & Mr Matcham". Emma added a note in her fluid, cursive script: "Come as soon as you Can we shall be happy most happy".

A few days later, Emma wrote to George, this time from her London address of Clarges Street:

"My dear Mr Matcham our Nelson begs his love to you – Mr Matcham I shall be most happy to see you at Merton & I need not say how pleased I will be to see you in Clarges Street"

Then, on the 22nd of August, Emma, back at Merton, wrote again:

"We have Room for you all, so Come as soon as you can. We shall be happy, most happy. Here are Sir Peter Parker and God knows who, so Nelson has not time to say more then that he Loves you and shall rejoice to see you Ever your affectionate
EMMA."

But, keen as they were to be reunited with Horace, George and Kitty were bound by a fraught family matter which immobilised them in Bath. Emma's letters had coincided the swift decline of their newest family member, baby William Alexander, who was a "well formed child, with fair complexion and fine blue eyes." Tragically, the baby'd had a bad reaction to a formative vaccine inoculation that caused him dysentery which "shortened his days".[883]

Four-month-old William Alexander Matcham died on the 27th of August 1805. This was a bitter blow for George and Kitty to come to terms with whilst Horace waited eagerly for them at Merton, with scant days of shore-leave.

Susanna Bolton, who'd arrived in Merton promptly, wrote to Kitty in Bath:

"We all feel for your situation, but I write now in the name of Both my Lord & Lady to say they think the sooner you leave such a melancholy scene the better. Therefore let me beg of you to come Imediately [sic] lest you should not be in time to see our Dear Brother. It is very uncertain. He looks remarkably well & you will find him such a kind & affectionate Relation and Friend as seldom is to be met with. Seeing and hearing him will soothe your Griefs. Mr. Bolton too will I fear be gone if you do not come Immediately & he will be much vexed if he does not see you Both."[884]

Emma penned an emotive postscript:

"I took the pen from Mrs. Bolton... My dearest friend pray sett off & Come immediately. Lord Nelson begs his Love to you & Mr. Matcham. I can only say you will meet with affectionate Hearts. Ever ever your most affectionate
EMMA HAMILTON."

Horace, though, would just have to wait because baby William Alexander needed a proper, Christian burial. His funeral took place on the 31st of August, five days after his death. He was buried at Bathford,[885] where George's mother and Kitty's sister, Ann, were interred side by side. Then, regardless of grief, George and Kitty packed their bags and sped to Merton. They arrived on the 3rd of September 1805.[886]

Merton Place had been extended since George's first visit, thanks, in part, to the £4,000 he'd loaned Horace for the purchase of adjoining land. A new entranceway on the north-east corner of the grounds had a lodge and gravel drive that led visitors to the house via ornamental pleasure gardens.[887]

Horace and Emma's child, Horatia, was now a robust little girl of four, whom Horace doted on completely, and called his angel. A porcelain artist, Thomas Baxter, sketched Horatia in one of Merton Place's trellised balconies, standing beside a bridled rocking horse that was taller than her, despite a top hat perching on her curls.

Emma's capable and calm mother, Mrs. Cadogan, was a familiar fixture at Merton, whom George would have known well. She'd acted as Merton's housekeeper from the get go, and continued to run the estate with admirable competency, despite now being in her sixties.

The only-known portrait of Mrs. Cadogan depicts her with a homely, broad-nosed face that's neatly framed beneath heavy-brows and a utilterian mobcap surmounted with a generously big black satin bow. Her hair, peeking beneath the white fringes of her cap, is curly and greyish brown. Her neck is wrapped with a pristine white scarf, and there's a hint of a double chin, suggesting that she's enjoyed a plentiful supply of wholesome meals.

George and Kitty summoned their eldest child, George junior, to join them as quickly as he could.[888] When he arrived at Merton, late at night, it was raining and everyone was in bed. Emma appeared "en chemise" and directed him to his cousin, Thomas Bolton's room, where he was billeted to sleep.

George junior's diary describes Horace's home-leave at Merton from a teenager's perspective. For example, on the 4th of September, the day after George junior's arrival, he dutifully paid his respects to his uncles Horace and William Nelson, William's wife Sarah and his aunt Susanna Bolton.

George junior then went hunting with William Nelsons' son, Horatio, before joining a "Large Company at dinner" after which he lost 11 shillings and 6 pence playing cards. Happily, "Lady H[amilton]" presented him "with £2 2s from Lord N[elson]."

This was the second time George junior had met his famous uncle (the first time having been in the Angel Inn, in Oxford). He later reminisced that his uncle Horace was a man of temperate habits who spent quiet, family time "in his plain suit of black".[889]

On Friday the 6th of September, George junior was bored. Having tried, and failed, to catch a fish in Merton's pond, he wandered aimlessly around the grounds. Dinner that day was more interesting to him because the Duke of Clarence joined them. This was the future King William IV, who'd been Horace's best man when he married Fanny. George junior noted that the royal prince deferred to Horace's opinions.[890]

Another visitor was John Whichelo, a young artist who rendered Horace's profile in coloured chalk.[891] Although Horace preferred to wear plain clothes when relaxing with his family, he sat for Whichelo in his Royal Navy coat festooned with medals and a bulky gold epaulet weighing down his shoulder. In Whichelo's sketch, Horace's hair is grey, straight and cropped short enough to expose the tip of his ear, though brushed over his brow to hide his damaged to his left eye and skull. His closed lips have a determined set, and the eye we can see –his working one– is blue irised and unfocused, as if he's caught in troubled thoughts.

George (senior) later recalled that Horace was "Of a delicate structure, of a reflective mind, strongly tinged with melancholy, retired and domestic in his habits".[892]

The Admiralty called Horace to London to receive orders to sail from Portsmouth three days later, on the 12th of September. George seems to have taken Kitty to London at this time because there's a record of her having been shocked by Horace's glum demeanour when she met him after he received the Admiralty's order.

When Kitty asked why he seemed so down, he told her, "Ah! Katty, Katty, that gipsy."

Kitty had instantly known he was referring to the fortune teller who, many years before, and most dramatically, had halted a reading she was giving Horace at the year 1805, declaring, "I can see no further."[893]

Horace was aware that his naval career, which had already cost him an arm and an eye, would likely cost him his life. He wanted to save his young nephews from his precarious fate and pressed George to promise to bar his sons from joining the military, either as "Sailors or Soldiers".[894]

The Admiralty's schedule permitted him only one more day in Merton.

He informed Emma and his family of their order and booked a chaise to take him to Portsmouth at half-past-ten on the following evening: the night of Friday the 13th of September 1805.

Horace wished for his final day in his beloved Paradise Merton to be spent quietly in the company of his close family and friends, these being Emma, Horatia, George, Kitty, George junior, Susannah Bolton, Lord Minto, Horace's forty-nine year old neighbour, James Perry –owner of the Morning Chronicle– and his wife, Ann.

Lord Minto rushed from London to reach Merton in time for Horace's last dinner at half-past-three in the afternoon, only to find Horace absent with Lady Hamilton. Dinner was postponed until the couple returned two hours later.

An uninvited guest gatecrashed into Horace's last evening. William Beckford –the late Sir William Hamilton's reclusive cousin– had ventured out of his Wiltshire estate of Fonthill. George junior disliked Beckford and thought him too full of his own praises and that he played the harpsichord atrociously.[895] Turning away from Beckford's clamour, Horace slipped upstairs to bid farewell to his and Emma's sleeping four-year-old child, Horatia.[896]

When the Portsmouth-bound chaise arrived at half-past-ten, Emma sobbed, too distraught to watch Horace leave. George, alone, accompanied Horace through Merton Place's grand front door and down its elegant steps to the chaise waiting on the night-dark, sweeping drive.

Still raw with grief for baby William Alexander, who'd perished only seventeen-days beforehand, George was the last person Horace spoke to at Merton.

According to Emma biographer Sylvia K Robinson, "in their final conversation Nelson expressed regret that he had not yet been able to repay the £4,000 George had lent him." But George had replied, "My dear Lord, I have no other wish than to see you return home in safety. As to myself, I am not in want of anything." [897]

Horatia biographer, Winifred Gérin, suggests, "it is not improbable that in these last moments [George Matcham] was asked to protect [Horatia] if [Horace]" didn't make it home alive.[898] If this was true, Horace would have begged George to protect Emma also.

When George returned, having bid Horace goodbye, Emma was sobbing uncontrollably beside an uncomfortable looking Lord Minto.[899]

Though such things are never committed to text, or even voiced, Emma's heartbroken refusal to accompany Horace to the waiting chaise combines with the prophetic tale of the fortune teller to hint that Horace had resigned himself to death in battle. He may, perhaps, have had his mind set on sparing Emma the burden of nursing him through his steadily collapsing health.

*

On the 6th of November 1805, the ring of church bells, near and far, grew and grew like a storm that must soon break. Then did.

The broadsheets bore news that rocked his whole family to the core. Britain's navy had annihilated the French and Spanish fleets at Cape Trafalgar, off the southern tip of Spain, but Horace's resounding victory had cost him his life.[900]

Kitty collapsed and, after this, George junior noted that the news of Horace's death had made his mama very ill.

Details of Horace's last moments flew around England with great gusto. Brave Lord Nelson had ignored the tradition by which naval officers saved their skins by leading from behind. He'd instead insisted on wearing his full Royal Navy admiral's uniform on HMS Victory's open deck, complete with his array of medals and sun-catching gewgaws. Bold and bright, leading from the front, Horace's uniform had made him an easy mark for a sniper perched on a French tall ship's mast.

George reflected that, from Horace's physical frailty and proneness to melancholy, "it might have been imagined that he was ill-fitted for war & hardship. But ... He went a willing victim to his country's safety and renown".[901]

George, Kitty and Susanna Bolton, distraught themselves, sped to Merton to support the heart-broken Emma.

Part Four:
Life After Horace
(1806–1833)

Chapter Fifteen: Standing with Emma

1805 – 1806

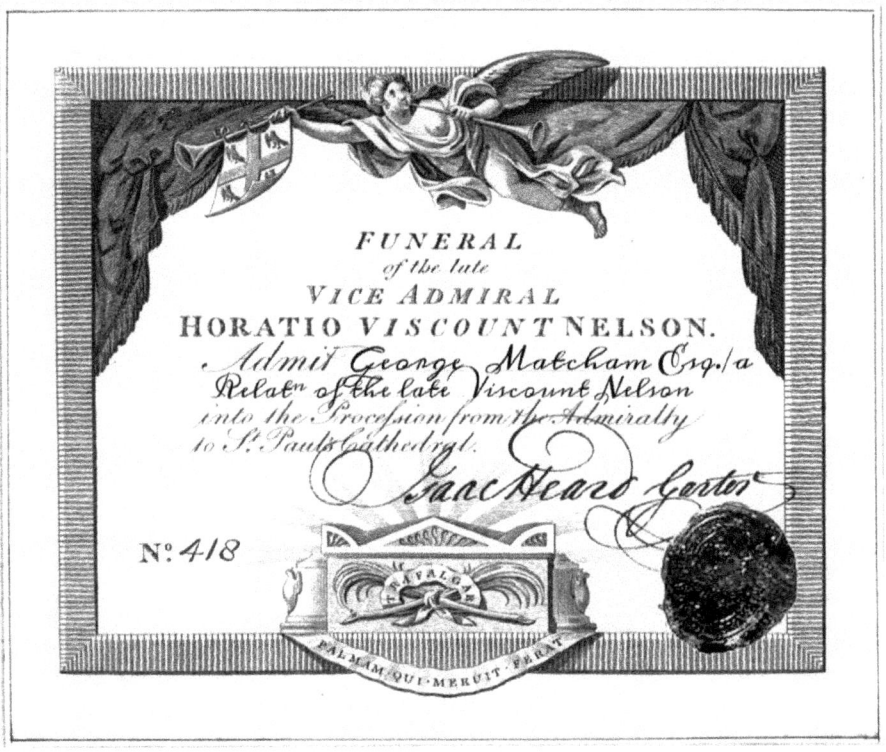

"For the rest of her life, Lady Hamilton's affairs were a source of worry to those who, for the Admiral's sake, would have wished her to live in comfort and quietness. But this was beyond her powers." Mary Eyre Matcham, 1911.[902]

George and Kitty couldn't mourn Horace as other beloved brothers were mourned. The State and Admiralty curated every detail of how Lord Nelson was to be mourned, which was as a saint in all but name (Protestant England canonised no one). Emma was permitted nowhere near Horace's body, whilst George, Kitty and the rest of their family were allowed to view him with the thousands of others who flocked to sob for the nation's fallen hero. Fanny was resurrected as Lady Nelson, the sanctified widow upon whom honours were bestowed, but William Nelson took the lion's share of largess and was exceedingly happy to do so.

George's married life had long been overshadowed by his brother-in-law's fame. At the time of Horace's death, George's precise thoughts regarding Emma and Fanny are unrecorded. The Matchams had been slower to switch allegiance to Emma than the Boltons and William Nelsons but seem to have done so in the summer of 1802 after learning the true identity of Horace and Emam's "ward" Horatia. The decision to support Horace's extramarital relationship would have stretched George's ingrained East India Company moral compass, but Fanny had failed to provide the child Horace so craved and he and Emma had clearly adored each other. Society, for its part, hadn't cared what their hero did in his spare time, but things were different now he was dead.

Patriarchal Georgian society had started turning against common-born Emma several years before because she'd dared to be great in her own right. In society's misogynist worldview, only men had the right to greatness. This suited William Nelson very well for, as Horace's only surviving male sibling, the Government treated him as a proxy recipient for Lord Nelson's largess.

While George and Kitty comforted grief-stricken Emma, William Nelson's hallmark selfishness propelled him to abandon her with callous brutality.

George found himself under duress to abandon Emma and Horatia too, despite anything he'd promised to Horace. Most of this pressure came from William Nelson who required George to publicly endorse him as Lord Nelson's surrogate.

William Nelson and his wife, those "very strange-looking people", [903] had been immediately created Earl and Countess Nelson of Trafalgar and Merton, [904] and their teenage children, Horatio and Charlotte, were now Viscount Merton of Trafalgar and Lady Charlotte. William Nelson was overheard bragging that Trafalgar had been a great day because it had granted him an earldom.

As the autumn leaves fell, the press's pages filled with William Nelson's ascendency, broadcasting it far and wide, not least to Merton where Emma would "never now read a paper". [905] Though past forty,

Emma was still beautiful,[906] but now her renowned charm was cut through with grief.

Kitty wrote to George junior in mid November:

"in a few days we shall think of returning home, for here we feel our loss more every day, but it is cruel to mention our going to [Emma] at Present. Merton is very dull; quite the reverse to what you knew it".[907]

George and Kitty accompanied Emma to her London home at 11 Clarges Street, from which Emma wrote to the politician, George Rose, at the end of the month:

"I write from my bed, where I have been ever since the fatal sixth of the month, and only rose to be removed from Merton here… My dear Sir, my heart is broken. Life to me now is not worth having; I lived for him. His glory I gloried in; it was my pride that he should go forth; and this fatal and last time he went I persuaded him to it. But I cannot go on – my heart and head are gone… I am very ill… All the family are with me and very kind."

HMS Victory arrived back in England, on the 6th of December 1805, and Captain Blackwood delivered Horace's effects to Emma in Clarges Street, where William Nelson was waiting.

Emma later recalled:

"When Capt. BLACKWOOD brought it (the will) home, he gave it to the present Earl Nelson, who, with his wife and family, were then with me".[908]

Emma was given Horace's coat, which was stiff with dried blood around the hole of the fatal bullet that pierced his left shoulder.[909]

Shortly after Blackwood's visit, George Rose relayed news to Emma from Horace's captain, Hardy:

"You will learn from the Captain that Lord Nelson within the hour preceding the commencement of action, in which he immortalized his name, made an entry in his Pocket Book strongly recommending a remuneration to you for your service to the country… I will take the earliest opportunity of a personal communication with [Prime Minister] Pitt, to enforce that solemn request upon him".[910]

In mid-December, a committee at Lloyds decided that the most appropriate way to commemorate Lord Nelson was to issue vases, worth £500 a piece, to William Nelson, Vice-Admiral Lord Collingwood (Horace's second-in-command at Trafalgar) and Fanny, whose effective divorce from Horace was ignored.[911]

Horace's will was proved on Christmas Eve, in the presence of William Nelson. A stipend of £1,000 a year was bequeathed to Fanny "Viscountess NELSON: widow of the deceased". Gifts Horace had "received from distinguished persons, and from public bodies [were to be] distributed among his brother, Earl NELSON, and his two sisters, Mrs. BOLTON, and Mrs. MATCHAM". Horace had bequeathed Emma "The house and furniture at Merton, and seventy acres of the adjoining land, are given to Lady HAMILTON, together with a legacy of £2000 and a rent-charge, on the Bronte estate, of £500 a year during her life." However, it was decided that William Nelson's newly-invented title of "Earl Nelson and Bronte" corresponded with "The Estate and Dukedom of BRONTE" enabling the entire Bronte dukedom to pass to him instead.[912]

William Nelson was excited by plans to make Horace's funeral "the grandest state occasion of the era",[913] at which he would preside as the venerated family figurehead.

Horace had wanted Emma to sing at his funeral, but the organising committee wanted her nowhere near the event. In a news report, printed on Christmas Day 1805, Emma is not named, but it would have been obvious to readers that the music referred to had been sung by her in Naples. William Nelson's effort to bring the piece to the committee's attention suggests pressure from the Matchams and Boltons. The opera singer, Mrs. Billington was a close friend of Emma's:

"Earl NELSON reported, that some music was in his late brother's possession, which was performed to the Royal Family at Naples, at which [Lord Nelson] was present, and was so much pleased with it, that he obtained a copy of it, and had been heard to say, it should be performed at his funeral. Mrs. BILLINGTON had seen the music and had very kindly offered to put appropriate English words to it, and, if necessary, to give her vocal aid [After the music was examined] it was deemed of too light a nature to be performed on the solemn occasion."[914]

William Nelson's next move was to pull his teenaged daughter, Lady Charlotte, from Merton,[915] where she'd been lodging for several years to benefit from Emma's unpaid tutelage in languages, music and deportment. [916]

George and Kitty seem to have objected to Horace's funeral wishes being vetoed because they let it be known that they didn't want to attend.

When, on the 6th of January 1806, Horace's body was laid out in Greenwich's Painted Hall, George, Kitty and the Boltons confounded William Nelson by going to Emma in Clarges Street.[917] Although William Nelson had betrayed Horace's explicit wish for Emma to be protected and supported, the Matchams and Boltons stood by her, loyal and firm.

Eighteen-year-old Lady Charlotte Nelson imperiously commanded George to attend Horace's funeral, and the College of Arms, which was responsible for organising it, decreed that George and George junior had no choice in the matter.

The brown-wool suit George likely wore to his marriage to Kitty in 1787 seems to have been re-tailored for sixteen-year-old George junior to wear to Horace's funeral.[918]

On the morning of the 9th of January, inner London was chaotic with "Carriages... driving in all directions",[919] as the reluctant Georges – father and son– made their way to Hyde Park, where coaches were assembling for Horace's funeral procession.

Horace's coffin was transferred to a funeral car that had been modified to look like HMS Victory, and the procession set off at eleven in the morning, led by the venerable Admiral Sir Peter Parker, who was now in his eighties.

Carriages bearing dukes and earls took precedence behind Admiral Parker's leading coach, preceding the Royal dukes, of whom the "Prince of Wales had two Carriages in the procession".[920] Last listed were "Relations of the deceased, in mourning coaches."[921]

The crowded pavements had been fitted with seating, which carpenters and upholsterers had whipped up in a frenzy. Every window along the nearly two-mile route had been washed clean. The streets had been scraped free of their usual build up of horse dung and mire, then covered with neat gravel. Within this spick and span arena, "The business of the day was so extremely well arranged that every Corps was able to station itself [leaving] no vacancy to its right or left."[922]

The presence of the male Matchams and Boltons endorsed William Nelson and the State's veto of Emma singing. Their presence also legitimised broader wranglings to write Emma from history and resurrect Fanny as Horace's beloved life-long spouse.

George may have preferred not to take part in the funeral spectacle, but there were thousands of people who'd have given their eye teeth to take his place. The sparkling first-floor windows along the route were packed with spectators, who'd paid 100 guineas a piece for the view.[923] And

"Groups of men, women and children, in a more humble situation of life [were jostling for] places where there was a more friendly or a less costly accommodation to be found ; and even the poorest classes of the people [feeling] themselves so much interested in the scene, that they flocked together from every quarter, endeavouring to get a place where they might have good standing room in the street, and hoping that they might have even a glance of the procession as it passed."[924]

The crowd cried, "The conquering hero comes. Dead! Dead!"[925] And cheered loudly when they saw crewmen from Victory, "those seven gallant Tars" marching in the parade, bearing the ship's flag.[926] [927]

George and his kin didn't arrive at St. Paul's until well after one o'clock.[928] They were accorded their own, exalted section amidst the many dignitaries granted entry to St. Paul's:

RELATIONS OF THE DECEASED.

Earl Nelson	*George Matcham, jun. Esq.,*
Viscount Nelson	*Thomas French Berney, Esq.*
Thomas Bolton, Esq.	*Rev. Robert Rolfe*
George Matcham, Esq.	*Hon. George Walpole, M. P.*
Thomas Bolton, jun. Esq.	*Hon. Horatio Walpole, M. P.*

The royal princes, who'd been allocated places on a platform at the front, "stood during the whole service [then] the coffin was uncovered and the coronet placed upon it [with the moment] fast approaching that was to consign to his last home the mortal remains of a consummate hero... Every bosom heaved with unfeigned emotions of sorrow and gratitude... Oh ! Immortal Nelson !"[929]

Horace's coffin was now borne up the steps, accompanied by herald-trumpets, flutes and bursts of kettle drums. The Highland Regiment lined the circle beneath St. Paul's great dome, and a combined choir of over a hundred singers "all in surplices and black silk scarfs" rendered an appropriately sombre dirge which "none but those who had the mournful pleasure of hearing it can possibly conceive". The coffin, with its procession of dignitaries, including the Prince of Wales, now "entered the choir, close to which followed, in deep sables, the Rev. Earl Nelson [and] his eldest son, Lord Merton". Then came the Royal Navy dignitaries, Greenwich pensioners "in mourning loose coats" and the Duchess of York, attended by her ladies[930] –demonstrating that Emma's sex wasn't the reason for her exclusion.

When the service was completed, George and George junior went straight to Emma.[931]

The Boltons also remained staunch allies of Emma and she spent the spring in Norfolk with them in Cranwich.

With Horace dead, George and Kitty, as "The Admiral's family", where "often a subject of gossip among the Bath neighbours". When Mr. Tyson visited them he talked about Charlotte Nelson quitting Emma to "go home."

A happier social call was made by Charles Warre Malet who brought his Anglo-Indian family with him.[932]

On the 12th of May, five months after Horace's spectacular funeral, the king nudged Parliament to issue generous grants to Horace's kin (but not to Emma):

"Lord H PETTY brought down a message from his Majesty respecting the provision to be made for the family of Earl Nelson. The Message requested the House to take into consideration the best means of enabling his Majesty to settle an annuity of [£]5,000 on Earl Nelson during his life, and also for enabling his Majesty to issue [£]120,000 for the purchase of a house and lands, to be annexed to the dignity of the family of Nelson. Independently of these sums, it was proposed to allow [£]10,000 to the two sisters of the late Lord Nelson".[933]

The Matcham and Boltons' share was worth nearly half a million pounds sterling a piece in today's currency, whereas William Nelson's grant of £120,000 is the modern equivalent of five and a half million pounds, with his additional annual income of £5,000 corresponding to a 2024 UK salary of £235,000.

It's no surprise that William Nelson, who was penny grabbing at the best of times, was perfectly delighted by this. Surprisingly, however, he went straight to Emma in her Clarges Street home where, having tucked into her food, he pulled out Horace's last codicil and threw it on her dining table with a triumphant sneer. It transpired that he'd appropriated it from Captain Blackwood in December to prevent her using it as leverage to divert any Government's funds from him to her.

Kitty, now thirty nine, was pregnant with her thirteenth child. Their new baby was born on the 30th of July. It was a boy who may have been sickly because she and George delayed christening him until the 23rd of August. They named him Charles Horatio Nelson Matcham.

Chapter Sixteen: Ashfold Lodge

1807 – 1816

Now aged fifty three, and barred from foreign travel by the continuing war, George chose to escape the busy-ness of Bath by reclaiming his country gentleman idyll. He needed space to breathe and recharge after the circus of Horace's hyped up funeral and William Nelson's relentless, shameless clamour to profit whilst, with one hand, pushing Emma down and, with his other hand, forcing his extended family to stand mutely at his side affirming his worthiness as Horace's surrogate.

George used his and Kitty's £10,000 Government grant to buy a Jacobean manor, named Ashfold Lodge, in the mid Sussex parish of Slaugham (pronounced "slaffam").[934] [935] They seem to have heard about the property from Horace's former lawyer, William Haslewood, because his home was next door to Ashfold Lodge,[936] and the Matchams had kept in contact with him after Horace's demise.[937] Haslewood was a young man of thirty-three years who'd married four years previously in Mayfair, at St. George Hannover Square, to a Hampstead lady named Charlotte Maria and their first child, who'd been born on the 7th of January that year, had been chirstened Horatia.[938] [939]

The Matchams' journey to Slaugham from Bath, in the early summer of 1807, was a jolting two hundred miles requiring three post-chaises to accommodate George, Kitty and their nine children.

A late eighteenth century watercolour depicts Ashfold Lodge as a substantial two-storey construction of pale stone with a protruding right wing. The frontage is dominated by a bay window jutting out above a central entranceway. There are two rectangular windows per floor either side of the central bay. The roof, which looks to be slate, is surmounted by a tall chimney with a dormer window on each side. A twentieth century analysis surmises that, in George's day, Ashfold Lodge "had been refaced in the 18th Century when plain rectangular sash windows of many panes were put in. A pair of dormers in the hipped roof is partly concealed by a parapet and the only surviving feature of interest is a battlemented oriel above the front door."[940]

The estate's vast extent is revealed by a newspaper advertisement for its sale fifteen years after George bought it:

"To be SOLD, by PRIVATE CONTRACT, with immediate possession, a valuable and desirable FREEHOLD ESTATE, called ASHFOLD LODGE, in the parish of Slaugham, in the county of Sussex, consisting of a modern and convenient Family House… with porter's lodge, barns, stables, coach-houses, detached dairy, laundry, and other commodious out-buildings, extensive and well-cultivated garden and pleasure grounds, and about 170 acres of arable, meadow, pasture, and wood land. The House comprises well-proported [sic] breakfast parlour, dining and drawing rooms, library, butler's pantry, servant's hall, housekeeper's room, kitchen, scullery, wine and beer cellars, and 13 bed rooms, and is in every respect well calculated for the residence of a genteel family. The premises are situate in a highly-desirable part of the County of Sussex, being within one mile of Handcross, on the much-frequented road from London to Brighton, and adjoining the turnpike road from Handcross to Horsham, and are distant thirty-three miles from London, eighteen from Brighton, six from Crawley, six from Cuckfield, and six from Horsham. The House stands on an elevated and well-sheltered spot, and commands fine and extensive views of the South Downs, and the intervening picturesque country."[941]

Ashfold Lodge's thirteen bedrooms amply hosted guests on top of George's multifarious offspring, and the 170 acres of land gave him plenty of scope for any farming projects he dreamt up.

According to a mid-Victorian history of Sussex:

"This Wealden parish [of Slaugham]… though somewhat sterile, is undulating and picturesque, and well suited for country houses and villas. A tributary of the lower Ouse—or perhaps the Ouse itself—rises at upper Beeding, close by, and here, at Slaugham mill, expands into a lake of 25 acres."[942]

Handcross, the nearest village,[943] was two miles to the north-east, with the forest of Tilgate and the wonderfully named Pease Pottage Gate fringing the northern side of the way.[944] Handcross, with its houses of weathered red brick and thatched or slated roofs, perched on a hill high enough to give "the horses a breathing".[945]

Merton was only thirty miles distant. It's ironic that Horace's wish for the Matchams to relocate near to Merton was realised with a Government grant for his death.

Emma first visited Ashfold Lodge in August 1807. She arrived with a large contingent of family and friends: these being her mother, her maternal cousin, Cecilia Connor; her six-year-old daughter, Horatia; Susanna Bolton and her children; and the acclaimed opera singer, Jane Bianchi.

Emma may, or may not, have admitted that her holiday funds had been raised by pledging Merton to a money lender on the 24th of July.[946]

Their combined parties wanted to move on from the long, grim months following Horace's death by taking a vacation by the sea. They set out, en masse, for the resort of Worthing, twenty miles due south of Slaugham, and "were fortunate in finding a good house."[947]

The William Nelsons, notably absent from the fun-seeking extended family group, stayed with the Archbishop of Canterbury in his official palace instead.[948]

Meanwhile, in Worthing, George and his fellow merrymakers wiled away their evenings with visits to the theatre.[949] Worthing's Theatre Royal was on Ann Street,[950] a block or two behind the town's celebrated promenade and pebbled beach.

Whilst breakfasting one morning, the party was imposed upon by Reverend Fusilique, who was excited for them to know that he'd been a chaplain present at the Battle of the Nile. The cleric was so talkative that "nothing could stop his tongue, not even a reproof from his wife."[951]

George junior tells that "the younger half" of their large group, including Emma's daughter Horatia, twenty-four year old Cecilia Connor and eighteen-year-old Ann Bolton, had fun "driving themselves in little vehicles drawn by asses". The five Matcham girls –Catherine, Elizabeth, Harriet, Horatia and Susanna– were now aged between fifteen and five, and likely joined in with the donkey cart fun.

1807 Worthing was one of England's most fashionable resorts. The Prince of Wales's eleven year old daughter, Princess Charlotte, was holidaying there for the summer. It's unlikely though that the young, etiquette-bound princess was permitted anywhere near ass-drawn carts. [952]

The press reported that that Prince of Wales visited his daughter in Worthing on the 9th of August.[953] He may have passed a moment with Emma too, for he, and two of his princely brothers, stayed with her in Merton three months after this, in November.[954]

The extended family were still in Worthing in September when George junior recorded that they dined "en famille" before going to a ball where they danced until half past three in the morning. Little sleep was had after this because "the party resolved to dine at Ashfold next day" and wanted to set off in the early morning.[955]

Back in Ashfold Lodge, George and Kitty became good friends with the Sergison family of neighbouring Slaugham Park, a long, low, end-gabled house whose estate possessed a much-written about fourteenth-century ruined mansion.[956] As this was an age in which ruins were valued so highly that landowners built fake ones, known as follies,[957] the existence of genuine ruins was a boon.

Keen for his own gardens to be well-maintained, George employed a gardener, Mr. Marsh, who lived with his wife in a little stand of cottages known as Truckers Hatch Place, on the Horsham Road that formed the northern perimeter of Ashfold Lodge's grounds.

The hot topic shortly after the Matchams' move to Slaugham was the mysterious case of "Sleeping Beauty" Sarah Smith, a maid employed by a widow in nearby Cuckfield, who'd slept solidly for seven days. Many doctors had "bled and blistered her to no avail", and hundreds of curious locals invaded her bedchamber to gawp. Upon waking, the "Cuckfield nymph" left her mistress's service to go to "London, to consult the Sooth-sayers of Warwick-lane, respecting the propensity to which she is subjected."[958] [959]

This would have been a favoured topic for George to discuss with another of his new friends, Dr. James Lawrence, who was Ashfold Lodge's former owner.[960] Lawrence and George were kindred spirits who shared the propensity for inventing things that other people took credit for. Lawrence wrote to George, from his new home in Watford, seeking advice for gaining recognition for remedies of his invention that the royal physicians had used to treat King George III's madness. The cure Lawrence outlined sounded decidedly unsafe for a monarch or, in fact, for anyone:

"About 15 or 16 years since I made use of a preparation in vivid lunacy in four cases, it cured three and one died..."[961]

George hadn't lost his wanderlust. However, despite Horace's Trafalgar victory annhilating the French and Spanish fleets, Napoleon's land armies were still a power to be reckoned with, thus compelling George to stay in England.

Colonel Coehoon wrote from Hamburg, on the 5th of September 1807, with bad news about the Schleswig estate George was trying to sell:

"I have tried to dispose of your mortgage, but without any success whatever... Money is scarce here beyond conception ; those who have any

keep it disposable".[962]

Thankfully, the Government's grant for Horace's death saved George from dependency on selling Schleswig, and he was in a position to loan his new friend, Dr, Lawrence, £400.[963]

Christmas at Ashfold Lodge would have been a merry affair, but for a gruesome event that took place on an unspecified date a few days before the 29th of December, and with which George was directly involved. His gardener's wife, Mrs. Marsh, had been sitting by her fire in her Tuckers Hatch cottage when she had a fit and fell into the blaze. George, who'd been passing by, "rendered the poor woman every assistance in his power, but too late ; she having been so dreadfully burnt, that she expired in a few hours, in greatest agony."[964] This wouldn't have been something that George could easily put from his mind.

With Christmas having been ruined, the new year proved no better. The nineteen year old Viscount Horatio of Trafalgar, William Nelson's only male heir, died of typhoid fever on the night of Sunday the 17th of January 1808.

The press couldn't resist post-scripting his obituary with speculation:

"By the death of Lord Trafalgar it is probable that the title so gloriously acquired by the immortal NELSON, will go into the female line. The two sisters, Mrs. Bolton and Mrs. Matcham, have each numerous family, and failing issue male of the present Earl, the next in remainder is Thomas Bolton, a minor, son of Thomas Bolton, Esq. of Cranwich".[965]

George junior commented, "Poor fellow I am truly sorry for him and his loss is irretrievable to his family." His journal then reveals that, on the 22nd of January, "My Father who went to town on Wednesday returned, having seen Lady H. and the Earl [William Nelson]."

William Nelson revealed to George (senior) that "Poor Ld T[rafalgar] had been for some time indisposed, but was not supposed in a dangerous state, till a few days before his death."[966]

It's not known what George discussed with William Nelson or, in fact, with Emma, on the 22nd of January 1808, but there's no mention of Matchams or Boltons attending the stately funeral William Nelson commandeered for his son in St. Paul's Cathedral three days after this. Bizarrely, however, the Matchams' Slaugham neighbour, Haslewood, was a chief mourner:

"Chief Mourners attending the coach carrying Mr. Archdeacon Young (Uncle to the Deceased) Alexander Davison, Esq. William Haslewood, Esq. Rev. Dr. Outraim.
Mourning Coach with four horses (with two Pages attendant), carrying two servants of the deceased.
Earl Nelson's Chariot.
Mr. Davison's Chariot.
Mr. Haslewood's Carriage." [967]

A full transcription of the London Chronicle's report is provided in Appendix 8.

Could it have been that the Matchams and Boltons, who'd been coerced into attending Horace's state funeral a year before, had refused to participate in this second state affair? We can't know for certain, but George junior's diary note that his father (sans Kitty) had met with both Emma and William Nelson three days beforehand implies that pertinent discussions were held.

Mary Eyre Matcham comments, in the Nelsons of Burnham Thorpe:

"William, Earl Nelson [had] some estrangement with his sisters [following] his own sudden elevation in rank is obvious but unexplained. So many difficulties are traceable throughout in connection with Lady Hamilton." [968]

As George and Kitty's first winter at Ashfold Lodge dragged on, an even worse tragedy befell them. Their eleven year old son, Francis, became suddenly ill and died, on the 15th of February.

In stark contrast to the pompous funeral William Nelson had arranged for his son in St Paul's, the Matchams chose for Francis to have a simple burial in Slaugham's parish church:

"February... 21 Mast.[r] Francis Matcham. Age 11. Nephew to the Great L.[d] Nelson" [969]

The press was so excited to have the death of another of Lord Nelson's nephews to report that they didn't bother to get Francis's age, or George's name, right:

"Lately, of an internal inflammation, Francis, second son of T. Matcham, Esq. by the sister of the deceased Lord Nelson, a very promising youth of twelve years of age." [970]

Life, as always, went on, careless of personal pain. Spring sprang and, on the 19th of April, the annual Easter Tuesday pedlar's fair was held on a stretch of the parish's open ground.[971]

Emma remained close to the Matchams' hearts and her visits to Ashfold Lodge were treated as red letter days.[972] But, in the world beyond Slaugham's sleepy borders, Emma's worth was forgotten. Society no longer named the female fashion she'd instigated "à la Emma" and, instead, referred to it as "Empire" for Napoleon's wife, Joséphine.[973]

Horace's only dying wish –that Emma and Horatia received state pensions– was still denied. Perhaps worse, although Horace had bequeathed Emma a jointure of £800 a year, the fund was administered by William Nelson, and he'd paid her none of it before this year, and was still so consistently tardy with the stipends due to her that Emma was forced to humiliate herself by begging him for every penny.[974] [975]

Emma's Merton neighbour, Abraham Goldsmid –who hosted a fête with an effigy of Horace while the Tria Juncta in Uno toured Wales in 1802– gathered a group of trustees to provide Emma with financial aid, but her debts rose faster than Goldsmid's group could allay and she was forced to face the unthinkable of giving up Horace's paradise of Merton.[976] [977]

In June 1808, George junior was "going over Westminster bridge [when he] met Lady Hamilton, who was low on account of ye house at Merton not being sold when put up to auction the day before."

After George (senior) visited Emma in London, on the 8th of October of the same year, he wrote to his eldest in dismay:

"I went to Ly. H – s' & was offered a bed, there were some citizens at dinner, but alas how different was that table now to what I had before been accustomed, where formerly Eloquence presided Vulgarity, & Crassity was now introduced. I could have almost wept at the change [A] plan of accounting has been most laudibly [sic] laid down for her L[adyshi]p but I [could] have wished that the Crowd of obsequious attendance had been entirely dismissed".[978]

A month later, George junior received a second letter of lamentation from his father:

"Lady Hamilton has been harassed and grievously insulted by her creditors... Two maids and a foot boy are all her household servants. I hope she will contrive to be prudent and feel the comforts of it".[979]

George's childhood friend, Sir Charles Warre Malet, was unaffected by the public's growing animosity toward Emma. He wrote to George, in 1810, "I envy you the entertainment and information of Lady Hamilton's company. She has I think been very ungratefully treated for her publick services."[980]

In rural Sussex, George's idyllic country life was comfortably slow and insular. The local gentry, among whom he was numbered, took turns hosting impromptu balls and parties.[981]

Eschewing the wider world's busy-ness, George set his focus on securing a substantial family pew in Slaugham's parish church of St. Mary's, which required ecclesiastic approval, termed a "faculty", from the Diocese of Chichester. [982]

It's evident that George had been adhering to his original country gentleman dream of enjoying his "wife, farming and hunting" because Kitty fell pregnant again, despite being in her forties. She delivered a baby boy on the 11th of February 1811. They named him Nelson.

The congratulations William Nelson sent to George carried a heavy dollop of self-pity:

"*I most sincerely congratulate you on the birth of another Son, and that my Sister and the Infant are likely to do well. You are indeed fortunate to have more supports added to your family, whilst I who had but One, should have had the irretrievable misfortune to have that One snatched from me. But perhaps it is wrong to complain. God's will be done. He alone knows what upon the whole is best for us, so I will drop the subject, tho' it is never absent from my thoughts either sleeping or waking*".[983]

In May, Emma asked George to lend her £100. He loaned it to her from his and Kitty's marriage settlement, but asked her not to tell anyone he'd done so.[984] After this, she politely declined both the Matchams and Boltons' invitations for her and Horatia to spend the summer with them. [985]

When, in January the following year, Emma told them that Horatia had contacted whooping cough, Kitty's worried reply reveals that George too was incapacitated with a cough and that Ashfold Lodge was snowbound:

"*God grant she is still doing well ; this is very severe weather, and we have nothing but coughing all over the house, My good man is far from well ; his cough is very bad. Do give our best love to our dear girl, and tell her we hope, as soon as the doctors allow her to change the air, her uncle will go in the coach as far as Reigate take a postchaise from thence,*

*which will give our horses time to rest, and she will be at Ashfold Lodge
before dark, I need not say, my dear Lady, what happiness it would be to
us to see you with her, but if you cannot manage to come, we will
endeavour to supply your place. You know she is one of our children, and
while we have a loaf for them she shall have it & with it our best
affections. We have a fine snow scene and not able to stir out of the house
either in the carriage or on foot."*[986]

After recovering his health, George donated £1 and 1 shilling to the
British and Foreign Bible Society.[987]

Alas, the budding spring of 1812 brought more ill news. George
learned that breakwater plans he'd designed had been copied by an
engineering duo, Rennie and Whidby, who'd been tasked with creating a
calm harbour for the south-west England naval port of Plymouth.[988] Dr.
Lawrence wrote to George on the 27th of March:

*"Your son & myself went to the House of Commons on Monday to get
a view of the plan that is to be adopted in the break-water at Plymouth, we
did not succeed; I suppose calling again as soon as the house opens. I
think 120 thousand pounds is more than would be required to accomplish
the harbour in your plan. Very truly yours J Lawrence"*[989]

As we know, people had a habit of pilfering George's ideas. The only
invention he'd sought to patent –his system for moving and raising
vessels– had been compromised by Dr. Fothergill. Apparently, George's
design for reworking wetlands into "the pleasure grounds of St James'
Park [were] officially recognised",[990] but there's no trace of this having
happened, and sole credit is now given to James Nash.[991]

The evolution of George's feelings towards Emma is uncharted beyond
a diatribe, circa 1822, in which he accused Emma of having artfully
inveigled Horace's affection and tainting him with her "despicable
propensity" for satire.[992] However, in February 1812, George and Dr.
Lawrence believed Emma was the best person to approach the MP, George
Rose, about his plagiarised breakwater plans.[993] Sadly, Dr. Lawrence
died shortly after this.[994]

Parliament had continued to treat Emma with so much disdain that she
sent an attention-grabbing letter to the press:

*"This Lady has published a narrative of the services she rendered to
her Country, by her influence with the Queen of Naples while resident with
her husband, the late Sir William Hamilton at that Court, the cost of*

which, and the losses sustained by her in the accomplishment of these services she states at [£]20,000... The following anecdote relative to the codicil of Lord Nelson's will, in which he bequeathed her Ladyship to the protection of the country, we believe is new:—

'When Capt. Blackwood brought it (the will) home, he gave it to the present Earl Nelson, who, with his wife and family, were then with me, and had indeed been living with me many months.—To their son I was a mother and their daughter Lady Charlotte, had been exclusively under my care for six years.—The Earl, afraid I should be provided for in the sum that Parliament was expected to grant, to uphold the hero's name and family, kept the codicil in his pocket, until the day [£]200,000... was voted for that purpose : on that day he dined with me in Clarges-street. Hearing at table what was done, he took the codicil threw it at me, and said, with a very coarse expression, "that I might do as I pleased with it." I had it registered the next day at Doctors' Commons, where it now rests for the national redemption. '"[995]

More happily, in October 1812, The Globe reported Consul General Blanckley's arrival in Bath.[996] This was George and Kitty's good friend, HSB, who'd brought his family to England following six years residence in Algiers as British Consul there. The Blanckleys settled into HSB's maternal aunt's home at No. 8 Paragon Buildings.

In May 1813, dire news reached at Ashfold Lodge that Kitty's sister, Susannah Bolton, was gravely ill. Kitty and George made all haste to the Norfolk town of Bradenham, where Susannah was staying. Kitty wrote from there to George junior:

"We compleated [sic] our journey within twenty four hours, which delighted your poor Aunt, to think I could be with her in that time… she feels no pain, is perfectly cheerful and the happiest creature you ever saw. When they think she will exert herself too much to talk to me, she smiles and says 'then if you will let me look at her I shall be content. '"[997]

Susannah Bolton died on the 19th of July. Haslewood sent condolences to Kitty, "Though your mind has been prepared for the blow, I know the reflection that you will not again embrace on this side the grave a sister whom you loved so affectionately, will give you many a pang."[998]

The Matchams were deeply concerned for Emma's welfare as her situation had deteriorated further, and she and Horatia had been confined to debtor's prison. Emma may have confided to George and Kitty that their imprisonment coincided with William Nelson entirely stopping thre payments of the stipends due to her from Horace's will.[999]

George assured Emma:

"We will supply you with potatoes all the winter, and send you a turkey by the first opportunity. If you find it impossible to pay us a visit, Mrs M. and I shall be tempted to go to Temple Place [the debtor's prison] before the close of winter and pass a day with you. We have always been sensible of the ingratitude you have met with... write as soon as ever you can, and give directions for anything our farm can supply, etc."[1000]

One of his daughters added:

"Mama has not been at all well for some time but we hope in a short time to see her regain her usual spirits and strength."[1001]

After a bitterly cold winter, during which the Thames froze over, things started to look better. In April 1814, George junior's qualified as a lawyer at St. John's College, Cambridge,[1002] and news came that Napoleon had abdicated:

"FOREIGN-OFFICE, APRIL 9, eight p.m.

Dispatches have this day been received at this office from Gen. Lord Viscount Catchart, K. T. announcing the abdication of the Crowns of France and Italy by Napoleon Bonaparte, in terms of which the following is a translation :—

'The Allied Powers having proclaimed that the Emperor Napoleon was the only obstacle to the re-establishment of the peace of Europe, faithful to his oath, declares that he renounces for himself and his heirs, the Thrones of France and Italy, and that there is no personal sacrifice, even that of life, which he is not ready to make to the interest of France.'"[1003]

While England celebrated,[1004] George was especially elated that the decade-long freeze on foreign travel was over so he could take his family overseas. He wrote promptly to Emma, who'd been reinterred in debtor's jail:

"We are all anxious, my dear Lady Hamilton, to see you at Ashfold. The summons to Mrs. M. and myself to escort you and dear Horatia to this place would be most grateful to us. You have heard of the Earl [William Nelson]'s conduct; he has been as inimical to the whole family as his present means allowed. But, I have no doubt, the principal train of his thoughts are directed to injure as much as possible those who were loved by his brother, the good & noble Lord. When our house is free of visitors,

Mr. [George junior] M. & myself purpose going as far as your house, and staying with you a few hours. We shall not go into London, our only object will be to see you & talk over our future destination. The dear beautiful Ashfold is offered for sale… You will… infer that we seek another country. We do; but where, I cannot determine till I have some conversation with my travelled friends. Write us frequently. I offer a joint wish that we may all settle abroad in some city, town, or village, etc."[1005]

For a brief moment, all their futures looked bright. That is until, on the 21st of April, a bombshell landed in the form of two volumes of Horace's private letters to Emma. The letters included damning and defamatory words about the Prince Regent which Horace had jotted during a fit of jealous fear that the prince would seduce Emma. She swore the letters had been copied and published without her knowledge, but the damage couldn't be undone. There was no way now that the Prince Regent would support Emma's ongoing petitions for the British Government to honour Horace's last codicil.

The Matchams learnt, belatedly, that, in early July 1814, Emma had taken advantage of being released from debtor's jail to quietly slip herself and Horatia onto a boat moored on the Thames that was due to sail to Calais in north-east France.[1006]

Six months later, in January 1815, devastating news came that Emma had died in Calais and that thirteen-year-old Horatia was stranded there with her mother's creditors closing in like circling sharks.

George wasted no time in sailing for Calais to rescue Horace and Emma's daughter. This was the first time he'd left English shores since the summer of 1805, and it would have felt wonderful to feel the sea spray on his face, but for the graveness of the circumstances.

When George found Horatia in Calais she was, understandably, not looking well.[1007] Her dead mother's creditors were determined to wring her unpaid debts from Horatia, but she and George hatched a plan to sneak her onto an England-bound boat disguised as a boy.[1008]

According to biographer, Gérin, Horatia arrived just before her fourteenth birthday, on the 29th of January 1815.[1009] George junior's brief journal entry tells, "Friday January — , The Squire arrived with Horatia from Dover",[1010] making the date of Horatia's arrival January the 27th.

Within days of bringing Horatia safely to Ashfold Lodge, George received news that his lifelong friend, Charles Warre Malet, had died in his Wiltshire home.[1011]

Grief was pushed aside and, according to Gérin:

"At Ashfold Horatia found her five girl cousins (ranging in ages from twenty-three to eleven) and none of them as yet engaged, and the four boys whose education was mostly given at home. Tolerance, good-breeding and kindness were the family's characteristics. The Matcham's world, like the world of their contemporary Jane Austen, was conditioned by rural surroundings and limited society; its occupations and interests derived from the country pursuits and its pleasures were dependent on good neighbourliness... Their balls and parties were mostly impromptu affairs, organized between neighbours". [1012]

George's aching desire to travel to Europe was postponed, yet again, by Napoleon's escape from exile on the island of Elba. Napoleon was quick to rally an army of loyal followers. Thankfully, not least for George, Napoleon's last dash was quickly quashed by the British, led by the Duke of Wellington, at Waterloo in Belgium, on the 18th of June 1815. [1013]

The heart-rending task of fetching Horatia home after Emma's death, five months before, had reassured George that crossing the channel was safe for young ladies despite the war. Nothing now would stop him from taking his family overseas.

Chapter Seventeen: Continental Life

1815 – 1822

George Matcham, "the most unsettled man alive", rushed his family to the French capital within weeks of England's victory at Waterloo. Wellington's symbolic march into Paris at the head of the allied troops was a moment of history he didn't want to miss and, besides, it was a good excuse to travel abroad without delay.

He was assisted by a Mr. Grenside, who also wanted to witness Wellington's triumphal parade and knew how to obtain the necessary papers. Grenside wrote to George at Ashfold Lodge on the 15th of July 1815:

"If you take the early Coach on Thursday, I mean the Dart, which drives into the City, I should be obliged by your calling on me at No. 26 Mark Lane which is only five minutes walk from the Inn. We can then take a Coach and after leaving your Port Manteau at my House in Henrietta Street, proceed to the French Ambassadors House where Passports are obtained and can immediately take places for Saturday morning so that we may hope to reach Paris before the Duke of Wellington has marched Southward—which appears probable—I am told we shall most likely be detained one day, after applying for Passports". [1014]

If Grenside's plan worked, George, Kitty and their large brood would have set sail for Paris on Saturday the 22nd of July. Horatia's thoughts on the matter are unrecorded, but she may not have been keen to return to the proximity of her mother's recent death.

George was in a jollier mood. This time, upon setting sail for France, he could enjoy the sea spray and wind on his face as he crossed the channel free at long last to travel for leisure. Then, upon setting foot on Continental soil, there was the excitement of hearing French spoken as he guided his wife, children and Horatia through Paris with the giddy exhilaration of not knowing what lay around the next bend.

Intrepid as he was, George needed to travel with care. Though France was well-charted and had a much friendlier climate than the Arabian deserts of his youth, post-war Paris remained militarised,[1015] and George was now sixty four with fragile females in his charge.

There's every possibility that the Matchams reached Paris in time to witness the pageantry on the 25th of July, when, in his polished boots and gold trimmed scarlet coat, "The Duke of Wellington, with the Allied Sovereigns [proceeded] through the Champs Elysees, to the Place de Louis XV where they halted for the purpose of seeing the troops file off, in their presence, back to their quarters." An eye witness gushed:

"The appearance of the British cavalry was truly magnificent. The regiments of British guards and hussars were particularly admired for the unostentatiously martial air of the men, the infinite superiority of their horses to those of the Continental cavalry, and the complete manner in which they were had in hand by the men".[1016]

It would have felt somewhat poignant to the Matchams that the hero England now cheered was the Duke of Wellington, not Horace, and that he'd survived his moment of greatest victory. But it may have felt liberating too, for the pitiless spotlight they'd been under as Horace's closest kin had, at last, swivelled elsewhere.

There's a small possibility that they met up with HSB's eldest son, Henry Stanyford Blanckley junior who, having been at Waterloo with Wellington, had hastened to reach Paris on the 25th of July, only to learn that Wellington had already departed for Vienna.[1017]

It was at about this time that a full-length portrait of Horatia was produced which purposefully echoed a 1792 portrait of her mother merrily posing in front of dark mountains with a tambourine held high. In Horatia's portrait, she has a cameo of Horace bouncing on her bosom and –in true teen fashion– an expression of non-jubilant nonchalance.[1018] The origin of this portrait is unknown, but the people best positioned to have commissioned it were George and Kitty. Who else, at this time, would have paid an artist to make Horatia look like Emma in her glory days?

Beyond restlessness, George's original determination that, "whenever we have peace, to go to France"[1019] had been because he wanted to escape Britain's cold months after contracting limb paralysis during the icy winter of 1799/1800. However, despite this, George took his family back across the Channel to overwinter in England.

His travel plans for 1816 were delayed by an important event he was invited to attend in May, for he was numbered among the select few of "ancient nobility and families of distinction" that were to be presented to the Prince Regent at his royal levee in Carlton House, London, on the 15th of May.[1020]

The date of the Matchams' second departure is revealed by Horatia who said, in a letter dated the 16th of May 1816, "we purpose quitting England in a fortnight".[1021] Hauntingly, on this precise same day, Beau Brummell –Emma's male fashion-setting counterpart– fled England to Calais to escape his creditors and never returned.[1022]

George's chosen destination this time was the Atlantic city of Lisbon, the capital of Portugal, which had staunchly remained England's ally throughout the Napoleonic wars.[1023] The Matchams likely sailed there because overland travel across mainland Europe would have been arduous and slow.

George junior remained in England, so there were only three Matcham boys in comparison to eight girls. The eldest daughter, Catherine, was twenty-three whilst fourteen year old Susannah was nine months younger than their adopted sister, Horatia.

Their sum total of oestrogen would have been enough to sink the most manly of men to his knees.

The girls enjoyed fashion, which now favoured vertical, willowy silhouettes enhanced by the highest dress waistbands ever known. *À la mode* hairdos sported centre partings and ringlets dangling over the ears. [1024]

George, who was still a mercantile East India Company man at heart, negotiated export agreements with Lisbon merchants of wine, fruits and vegetables, all of which would have been in high demand in England after decades of war. His dealings were unhurried and there was plentiful time for his party to forge friendships with Lisbon's British residents, who included civilians and garrisoned officers.

The gaggle of young ladies "walked, danced, dined and made up picnic parties into the surrounding countryside, the beauty of which together with the climate gave the summer an atmosphere of enchantment." Horatia described herself as a "giddy girl" and was wooed by a Mr. Newcomb, while one of the Matcham girls took a shine to a Colonel Browne.

George and Kitty were of a liberal mindset and made no effort "to prevent the girls corresponding with their recent escorts" after leaving Lisbon in October 1816.

The Matchams' winter address was No. 64 Baker Street, London, which George rented for the season. The Baker Street house had room enough for George junior to stay in too, and the young lawyer arrived in a happy buzz of young love. William Nelson, in an uncharacteristic fit of avuncular bonhomie, had proved adept at matchmaking whilst the other Matchams were in Lisbon. The damsel William Nelson had selected for George junior was Harriet Eyre, who was the sole heiress of a large Wiltshire property, named Newhouse, which adjoined his Trafalgar estate. [1025]

George junior married Harriet Eyre in her local church of Whiteparish, on the 20th of February 1817. William Nelson officiated and George Matcham (senior) stood as a witness.[1026] George's wedding gift to the happy couple was an estate, called Hoadlands, whose grounds lay next-door to Ashfold Lodge.

The Matchams' good friends, the Blanckleys, had settled in Versailles, near Paris. HSB had ushered his family there from England the previous year citing similar purposes to George of escaping cold winters and having no fixed destination.[1027] HSB, however, seemed perfectly content to remain in Versailles and had enrolled one of his teenaged daughters in a weekly boarding school. George liked the idea of sending the younger members of his own brood to school with the Blanckley girl and asked HSB to find him a suitable home to rent.

Horatia didn't share George's ongoing wanderlust and opted to stay with the Boltons in northern Norfolk instead of accompanying the Matchams overseas for a third time.[1028]

After bidding Horatia farewell, George and his family found the Blanckleys living comfortably in Paris's stately suburb of Versailles, which clustered neatly in front of the baroque gates of the famous palace. Louis XIV, France's Sun King, had commissioned both the palace and town to be built from scratch in the late seventeenth century. The resulting residential district was meticulously laid out in a neat grid of broad streets with well-proportioned houses of honey-coloured stone.

HSB, who was a year George's senior, was a seasoned diplomat and no pushover. When, in September 1806, he'd first met the Dey of Algiers, HSB had good reason to be terrified because the Dey, who kept Christian slaves, had a reputation for executing anyone who displeased him.[1029] [1030] HSB, however, had refused to submit himself and his audacity paid off by earning him a place in the bloodthirsty dey's heart.[1031]

In Versailles, HSB's family comprised his much younger, second wife, Mary; their teenaged daughters, Elizabeth and Henrietta, and the girls' half-brother, Edward Blanckley, who was the youngest child from HSB's first marriage. Twenty-seven year old Edward was a comely, dark-haired naval lieutenant who'd driven his step-mother crazy before their emigration to Versailles by staying up all night, every night, partying and being, in his more indulgent father's words, "the gayest man in Bath".

[1032] There's no record of Edward's lifestyle in Versailles, but he hit it off particularly well with George's middle daughter, Harriet, who'd rebelled against saying her prayers as a small girl.

Also coming and going from Versailles was HSB's older son, Henry Stanyford Blanckley junior, who'd married in Nova Scotia seven years before and whose wife, Elizabeth Diana, bore him a son –HSB junior junior– in Calais on the 11th of August that year.

Versailles, elegant and sedate, was only eleven miles from central Paris, which was recovering quickly from the deprivations of war and hosting a plethora of operas, such as the Barber of Seville and Spontini's Fernand Cortez.[1033]

The Matchams and Blanckleys weren't the only people who moved to Paris at this time. The restoration of the French monarchy had inspired an influx of re-settlement into the French capital where there was bountiful vacant property thanks to the long war it had endured.[1034]

The house HSB found for George and his family was in Boulogne-sur-Seine (Boulogne-Billancourt) and had an annual rent of £116. George's twenty two year old daughter, Eliza, was amazed by the scale of their new Parisian home, which felt to her like it belonged in one of the popular Gothic novels by Ann Radcliffe. It had an "immense Coach House and Stabling", which was very useful because a carriage could be hired for £5 a week to transport them the eight miles to and from central Paris's all important entertainments of theatre, opera, an art gallery, parks, palaces and the site of the Bastille. Evenings at home were relished in their grand, rented, Gothic mansion in which comfortable dinners and quietude were enjoyed.[1035]

George wiled away his luxuriantly leisurely hours composing a light-hearted fiction, entitled *anecdotes of a Croat*,[1036] to entertain his family on cosy evenings. His manuscript was compiled from a haphazard collection of scrawled notes, many, no doubt, scribbled during journeys by sea or road. He can be imagined rising from his chair to address his gathered family, and maybe a few Blanckleys, as they relax in the Gothic splendour of the house in Boulogne-sur-Seine, and, with a flourish, producing his latest instalment of *anecdotes of a Croat*:

"CHAPTER XXVIII.
ONE little contrivance I cannot help mentioning. In a lower room in the palace, adjoining the castle, he fixed a seat on springs, that would hold six persons, to which there was a crank which, leading out of the room into the open air, was attached to a wheel which was turned by a sluice of water: it could be accelerated or retarded at option by admitting more or less water so that you might ride at the rate of four, six, or ten miles an

hour. This was a delightful recreation for the children in rainy weather,
nor did the adults of the family despise it, but often took a ride when the
weather was so bad as not to admit of out door exercise: an hour or two's
ride gave them, they said, an appetite for, or assisted the digestion after
dinner". [1037]

George sent his youngest daughters, Susannah and Horatia Matcham,
to the weekly boarding school that one of HSB's girls attended. [1038] This
may have been Elizabeth who, at fifteen, was the same age as George's
youngest. The other Blanckley girl, Henrietta, was younger still.

Whether they liked school or not, Susannah and Horatia Matcham
weren't obliged to attend it for many weeks. George was too restless at
heart to stay in the same place for long when there was nothing to hold
him immobile. The world was his oyster and, in the summer of 1818, he
steered his family southwards to Italy. Edward Blanckley appears to have
travelled with them for, on the 24th of April 1819, he married Harriet
Matcham in Naples. [1039] Their wedding venue would likely have been the
ambassadorial residence of Sir William à Court, who was the current
British Envoy Extraordinaire[1040] and with whom they'd have lodged.
Poignantly, à Court was the successor to Sir William Hamilton and it was
here, in Naples, that Emma had enjoyed the peak of her fame and success.

George drew up a miniature marriage settlement for Harriet and
Edward Blanckley in which he agreed to pay them £200 per annum on
condition that one quarter would be put aside for purchasing property:

"On the marriage of my daughter Harriet with Edward Blanckley I
hold myself bound by bond to make over to him the amount of two hundred
pounds per annum (French Funds) with the reservation of one fourth to be
laid up in the purchase of land as agreed between him and me. This land
to be settled on my daughter Harriet and her children in the event of
having any, in case of her dying without issue to be at his (Edward
Blanckley's) disposal by will.

Signed   G. Matcham (seal)
Witnesses: G. Reilly   Henry Dobnee" [1041]

Fond farewells were hugged and waved in Naples when Harriet stayed
with her new husband and George and the rest of the travelling Matchams
set sail for Marseilles, in the South of France, where they'd arranged for
their mail to be sent.

Kitty wrote to George junior from Marseilles, in May 1819, with
heartfelt congratulations in response to his news that his first child, a boy,

had been born in mid April. Somewhat predictably, the infant had been baptised Horatio Nelson Eyre Matcham, but George and Kitty nicknamed him "Petman".

The Matchams didn't spend long in Marseilles, preferring to return to Paris and the company of the Blanckleys. George junior's letters seem to have been filled with gushing praise for his tiny son's prowess because Kitty replied to him, from Paris, on the 22nd of June:

"As for Petman, you would suppose we all expect to hear he is nothing like any other child, quite a superior being. We tell Nelson [George and Kitty's youngest child] his nephew will teach him to read, but he says No, the Child can only Squawl."[1042]

In November, Kitty told George junior:

"Paris is so full we think England must be quite deserted… We have been to the play to see the famous Talma, who I think is remarkable for his quietude of acting, the French in general being too furious both in speaking and action".

By 1820, still in Paris, Kitty talked about visiting George junior in England, saying it meant everything to her, and adding:

"Charles is grown very much. The Boy [her and George's youngest child, Nelson] is the Master of the house, so like the Earl you would be quite surprised. The Girls are all in high feather, as you would say, no particular Beaux."

Then, in July, Kitty excitedly informed George junior that the eldest of his sisters, Catherine, had become engaged:

"Our dear Kate is going to be married to a young man who appears worthy of her, which is saying a great deal for him. He made his bow only yesterday. He is the son of Mr. Bendyshe, who has good estates in Cambridgeshire… Mr. and Mrs. Blanckley have known him for years and say a better creature never lived. Thank God, our dear Girl has the prospect of being as happy as she deserves to be."[1043]

Sadder tidings found their way from India to the Blanckleys in Versailles. HSB's eldest son, Henry Stanyford Blanckley junior, having survived the Napoleonic wars, died of "complications of the liver" in Arcot, Madras, on the 1st of November 1819.[1044] The calamitous news may have been personally delivered by his grieving, pregnant widow, Elizabeth Diana, who'd been in Madras with her husband and their three children.[1045] Elizabeth Diana threw herself on the mercy of HSB and his wife, who took her, and her children, in as permanent houseguests. HSB junior's last child, Henriette, was baptised in London in June 1820, but the fatherless family spent most of their time in the Blanckleys' French enclave. It was at around this time that HSB bought a coastal property in Dieppe. His daughters loved it there but, after a year or two, he decided to abandon it in favour of returning to Versailles.[1046]

Death was always stalking. In 1821, George and Kitty were in England when their eighteen-year-old son, Horatio Nelson Matcham, fell direly ill. Their best efforts to nurse him back to health were in vain and he died in Ashfold Lodge on the 11th of October 1821. He was buried with his brother, Francis, in the parish church's graveyard.[1047]

Kitty, heartbroken, declared that she couldn't bear to visit Ashfold Lodge again. Their neighbour, Haslewood, was grieved in turn:

"I deeply lament the resolution you mention, to be so firmly fixed not to revisit Ashfold Lodge... looking back to the days when you were there so beloved and respected and, as I thought, so happy."

George, who had pressing business in Europe, wrote to George junior in July 1822:

"Never did I leave England with a heavier heart, but it is necessary that we should go. My French and Spanish concerns call for my attention... perhaps we may return in the autumn."[1048]

George junior, seemingly unaware of his father's innate restlessness, took his father's words with bad grace. He complained to his wife that his father would have stayed in England if his mother and sisters hadn't manipulated him to take them back overseas:

"I consider them as completely domiciled [in Paris] and that my Mother and sisters have succeeded in finally driving my Father from this country. I lament his facility, and they must take upon their own responsibility the consequences, good, bad, and indifferent, which proceed from it. If he had been left alone he would have still been a respectable country gentleman with an income of near £3000 a year and universally beloved and respected by all the neighbourhood... I can tell you nothing more of the Paris party... They have wandered so much about, and have so completely lost the English habits of society, &c., that what is best for them I cannot tell."[1049]

Fanny was in Paris too and "not sorry to renew old acquaintanceships." The Matchams visited her "almost every day". One of the girls commented, "We have drunk tea with her once, and are going again this evening."[1050]

Later life portraits show Fanny looking somewhat tired with her thin lips firmly closed, eyes with heavy lids and her now-jowly face swamped within a mane of white ruffles and lace that mushrooms around her head and cascades over her shoulders and halfway down her chest. In one portrait, she wears what appears to be a wig of golden ringlets and has a cameo of Horace attached to a splendid golden bracelet.[1051] [1052]

Fanny ingratiated herself with the Matchams by using her influence with the Duke of Clarence to arrange a promotion for Harriet's naval husband, Lieutenant Edward Blanckley.[1053] Duly, in 1825, Edward was awarded the rank of commander. Fanny's intervention may have caused Horace to turn in his elaborate grave, for he'd begged George to keep his sons out of the military. Edward and Harriet, however, showed their gratitude to Fanny by naming their next baby Frances Nelson Blanckley. Sadly, Fanny's namesake only lived for five days.[1054]

Chapter Eighteen: Doting Grandfather

1823 – 1833

George and Kitty moved back to England in about 1823. Part of their hearts had always remained in Norfolk,[1055] but, in the words of their great-granddaughter, Mary Eyre-Matcham:

"At last, Paris abandoned and Ashfold Lodge sold, a house in Holland Street, Kensington, became their final home."[1056]

Holland Street was a spacious, suburban, residential road of terraced, three storeyed houses constructed in the early to mid eighteenth century with facades of brown and red brick.[1057]

George's mindset of this time is revealed in his humbly wry introduction to his *anecdotes of a Croat*, the light-hearted, four-hundred-and-twenty-six page fiction he'd scribbled, piece by piece, whilst roving Europe:[1058]

"THIS feeble work was sent from the Continent ; on the writer's return he remarked several mistakes in the printing ; not to be wondered at , the original manuscript being written in so cramp a hand : having at the time no intention of returning to England , he had not an opportunity of engaging a good writer to recast the whole .

It may be asked why such a work was published ? The answer is that some suggestions occurred to the Author, but in so imperfect a form , he was fearful of communicating them in a separate treatise , and therefore ushered them in a trifling Novel ; if of any value , he imagines , by passing through abler hands , they might be of future benefit to society . A few remarks are not new , these are duly ascribed to the respective proposers . There was another inducement - he conceives too many books of harmless tendency cannot be published , there being no obligation to purchase , and often no solicitation . Should this trifle cheer an evening fire-side in the country , the purpose will be fulfilled ; should it suggest one useful hint , the Author will feel highly gratified ."

George had posted his haphazard manuscript bundle to Sherwood, Neely, and Jones for anonymous publication ahead of his return.[1059] *Anecdotes of a Croat,* was published in January 1821.

It was at about this time that George and Kitty sat for an artist who didn't sign their name. He or she rendered them in matching sombre black on black, with their pale faces as islands of muted colour. George's hair is as white as his neat starched collar and the modest, ruffled lacework clumped atop Kitty's head and gathered round her neck. Kitty's hair still holds the dark lustre of her youth, but neither she nor George are smiling and their eyes are painted dark as jet without a single gleam.[1060]

Despite the melancholy impression given by their portraits, George and Kitty still made merry and found much joy in their children and grandchildren.

Of their five daughters Catherine, Harriet and Horatia were married with children of their own, whilst Susanna, and their second eldest, Eliza – the one time dreamy youngster who'd gazed at coach passengers outside– remained unwed and at home, as was teenaged Charles and the baby of the family, Nelson, who celebrated turning twelve in February 1823. Meanwhile, in Newhouse, Wiltshire, George junior's wife was pregnant with their fourth child.

In rural northern Norfolk, Horace and Emma's orphaned daughter, Horatia, had fallen in love and married a young curate, named Philip Ward, in the church opposite the Boltons' Burnham Westgate home.

In Kensington, there were happy tidings when twenty nine year old Eliza finally found a gentleman she deemed fit enough to wed. The Royal Navy lieutenant who'd captured her heart was a decade her senior, but still handsome with a generous mop of neat fair hair, seductive eyes and Cupid's bow top lips.[1061] Eliza and Lieutenant Arthur Davis married in St. Pancras parish church in early May 1824. Their witnesses were George Matcham; his former Slaugham neighbour, Elizabeth Haslewood; Samuel Hood, 2nd Baron Bridport (who'd married William Nelson's daughter, Charlotte) and William Nelson's wife, Sarah.[1062] Press coverage of the wedding, though brief, reveals that William Nelson's bid to commandeer Horace's hero status had paid off, for the clipping names Eliza as William Nelson's niece, not Horace's:

"Yesterday, at St. Pancras New Church, Lieutenant Arthur Davies, R.N., to Elizabeth, second daughter of George Matcham, Esq. and niece of the Right Hon. Earl Nelson."[1063]

George, for his part, still had no interest in gaining glory or fame. He was content to live quietly as an English gentleman enjoying his wife –

who was perhaps relieved to now be past childbearing age– children, grandchildren and the simple, social pleasures of taking turns hosting dinners with interesting, creative-minded people and, without Kitty, visiting his gentleman's club and less-fancy taverns.

Standard fare at their weekly dinner parties comprised "soup, plain roast and boiled, ham, vegetables, pie or tarts, sherry and port".[1064]

One of the Matchams' dinner guests was an esteemed Scottish literary critic, author and moral philosopher named John Wilson,[1065] who arrived on their doorstep on the same day that, using his pseudonym of Christopher North, he'd penned a critical diatribe about the British in India, in which his final comment was:

"By the by, we dine this very day with our friend G. M., one of the cleverest and best-hearted Indians we have ever known, and entirely free from all the peculiarities which generally mark his tribe. C. N."[1066]

George self-published a second book, *parental chit-chat*, at the ripe old age of seventy two. Whereas his first book, *anecdotes of a Croat,* had been created to entertain his adolescent charges during their escapades around Europe, the purpose of his second tome was to impart his accumulated paternal wisdom to his descendants. When he "unpublished" *parental chit-chat* on the 26th of December 1826, its introduction was pitched to his future progeny:

"I please myself with the idea, that my advice may make deeper impression on your minds than that of an eloquent moralist.
Should it please God to grant life, some of you hereafter may occasionally take up the little volume, and say, ' Let us look again at the well meant cogitations of our old grandfather.'"[1067]

In 1828, George became so gravely ill that he wrote a will naming Kitty as his sole beneficiary and executrix:

"The Last Will & Testament of me George Matcham now in London relying on my dear wife Catherine Matcham to do the best for our dear children. I give & bequeath to her all my personal estate & effects whatsoever & wheresoever to and for her own absolute use and benefit for ever & also the sum that may devolve on the State of the Viscountess Nelson or any other & all the Lands that may be purchase'd for me in New South Wales In Witness whereof I have hereunto set my hand & seal this 8th day of September 1828..."

George's reference to Viscountess Nelson shows that his and Kitty's relationship with Fanny had continued to flourish. His mention of New South Wales regarded his second youngest son, Charles Horatio Nelson Matcham. George's Matcham Pitt cousins had been doing so well as landowning settlers in that part of Australia that he'd paid for his twenty-two year old son, Charles, to emigrate there also. Charles had duly waved his family a fond goodbye, in August 1828, and set sail from Plymouth for Australia, passing the breakwater of George's design as the English coast receded behind him.[1068]

In September 1828, a month after Charles's departure, George's travel partner and long-term friend, HSB, died in Versailles.

George remained in Kensington, his travel days behind him. As a septuagenarian, he no longer had enough stamina to foray into uncharted, or even charted lands. He took pleasure instead in his second youngest son's letters from New South Wales. Charles was doing so well that, in December 1830, George added a codicil to his will instructing Kitty to make all his capital over to George junior to invest in more Australian property:

"… on my death I wish my dear wife to make over to George whatever land may be purchas'd in New South Wales & whatever money may be there for further purchase on condition that the whole of the money if not already invested might be invested in further purchase of land in New S. Wales [,] my son George to reserve the greater portion of Land for himself for his own family and to distribute such portions of it as he may think proper to his brothers & sisters or to his nephews & nieces".[1069]

The furthest George (senior) now travelled was to Wiltshire where he and Kitty made "long yearly visits" to George junior, his wife Harriet née Eyre and their growing family of tiny children. Their Jacobean mansion, Newhouse, stood amidst nearly three hundred acres of park and New Forest woods dotted here and there with sparkling lakes. Newhouse itself, the Eyre family's ancestral home, was surrounded by lawns, walled gardens and outbuildings constructed from the same soft-toned red bricks as the main house, whose central three storeyed facade was flanked by wings with castle-like turrets.[1070]

Writing in 1911, Mary Eyre Matcham tells that, at Newhouse, "George (Jr.) and his wife [were] each equally devoted to the old couple" and their grandchildren adored them.[1071] She had a good source for this information because one of George's doting grandchildren was Mary Eyre Matcham's father-to-be, William Eyre Matcham.

George idled away long, merry months at Newhouse. His mobility was now impaired, but this didn't stop him, and he requisitioned a long-tailed pony to carry him around the estate's gardens and parklands, followed always by "a stream of little grandchildren running or riding after him, to whom he was a perpetual delight and playfellow."

"Full as ever of his hobbies", George junior and his wife gave him free rein to "improve" their estate, and he employed his own team of workmen for the purpose. Unsurprisingly, given George's lifelong passion for aquatic engineering, "A large pond was dug one year." On other occasions, "Planting and cottage building absorbed him."

His go to handyman was a local fellow named Noyce who spoke in a thick Wiltshire drawl and, though tolerant of George's madcap commands, wasn't above skiving off work when he thought he could get away with it. Mary Eyre Matcham's childhood was filled with fond stories of George and Noyce's antics. This is one:

"A cottage was built by Noyce, two miles away from the house; but visible upon a distant ridge of hill. To him; in the afternoon, would appear G. M., pony and grandsons.

'Noyce, where were you at eleven this morning ? '

'At worrk Sur. '

'Ah ! and where at twelve Noyce ? '

'At work Sur !'

'And didn't you step across to the Bat and Ball between whiles Noyce ?'

'No Sur,' with great asseveration; accompanied by a distracted aside to one of the small boys of 'Can't thenk how the old genelman knows on it !'

Nor was he likely to discover that the old gentleman had spent the morning, two miles off indeed, but in company with a large and strong telescope; raking the cottage and revealing the slackness of operations there. "

George made Noyce "the subject of many experiments and is reported to have once been persuaded into eating a rat."

Additionally:

"He certainly submitted on another occasion to be locked into a room; as the victim of his master's latest invented form of steam baths, and to console his discomfort was liberally supplied with a compound (possibly also of G. M.'s invention) called 'treacle-beer.'

G. M. himself awaited progress outside.

'How are you getting on; Noyce ?' he asked anxiously at intervals, always receiving the answer, 'very hot, sur, very hot,' and responding

thereto, 'Well, drink some more treacle-beer, Noyce'."[1072]

It was thus, with his elderly days filled happily with his doting wife, children and grandchildren and, when at Newhouse, Heath Robinson-style inventions and projects enough to content his ever restless heart, that, at the age of seventy-nine, George Matcham passed away in his Kensington home.[1073]

His latent curiosity, however, was so great that it outlived him. When, as per his advance instructions, a post mortem was carried out on his body, it was revealed that he'd been correct in his belief that he only had one lung. The youthful illness he'd suffered in India, maybe during his Residency at Broach, must have been severe indeed. Small wonder that his doctor had thought him so likely to die that it made no difference if he attempted to cross the waterless Arabian desert or not. George's tenacity in having survived the crossing, subsisting on mare's milk, and then undertaking two more overland treks through often hostile lands, is a mark of his dauntless courage and passion to explore less travelled roads.

His kindness to others, regardless of class, colour and creed, is revealed again and again when charting his life and is remarkable for its rarity in those less enlightened times, especially considering his East India Company upbringing.

When his travel bug subsided, his only desire had been to live the quiet life of a country gentleman. As a family man he was loyal and liberal, educating his daughters as well as his sons.

His wander-lusting soul wasn't happy for long in one place but his hankering to take his young family to Europe was curtailed by the ongoing French revolutionary wars.

It was this same drawn-out conflict that ricocheted George's charismatic brother-in-law, Horace, into international superstardom, and forced George into the spotlight with him. When, after Horace's death, William Nelson was hungrily lapping every possible drop of wealth and prestige from his brother's status as national hero, George and Horace's other kin attempted to boycott the pomp to stand with Emma instead.

Buried in Slaugham, beside his sons Francis and Horatio Nelson Matcham, the inscription on his tomb reveals George's core values:

"He died at Kensington 3 Feb 1833 in the 79th year of his age. Leaving to his numerous issue the invaluable example of a well educated, enlightened independent English gentleman, a good neighbour, an affectionate husband, a tender father and a sincere Christian."[1074]

Chapter Nineteen: George Matcham's Legacy

It's unusual to find a detailed, historical account of any person who was neither notorious nor hungry for fame, but George Matcham fits this rare niche. His desire to live quietly as a country gentleman was smashed apart by the stupendous, sudden fame of his brother-in-law, Lord Nelson. Had it not been for society's fixation on Nelson's every doing, the details of George's inner world would have been lost to the mists of time, just as other's stories are.

Much of George's wife, Kitty's inspiration for collecting family correspondence was from her love for her charismatic "bro", and her collection would have likely crumbled to dust if the public hadn't remained excited enough about Nelson for Mary Eyre Matcham to transcribe and publish them a hundred years after Nelson' death. Because of this, we know of the family's inherited affection for George Matcham and of his epic overland treks and plagiarised inventions.

George was so integral to the lives of both Lord Nelson and Emma Hamilton that he crops up in all their biographies. Examination of George's experience bounces back to further illuminate Nelson and Emma's realities. These revelations, however, might not suit all because they challenge preconceived ideas. For example, many people are attached to the sanctity of Nelson and Fanny's marriage and actively resist evidence that Nelson, in his own mind, had permanently divorced himself from her. Instead, the misogynistic Georgian and Victorian view that women could only be saints or sluts distorts Emma into an evil-doer who lured the helpless, but otherwise saintly Nelson from his equally saintly wife.

George Matcham voiced this view in one of the privately printed books he wrote in his latter years, quite likely after patrching things up with Nelson's widow in early 1820s Paris:

"[Nelson's] warm heart eagerly strove to attach itself to some object of primary affection : if Lady Hamilton had not artfully endeavoured to inveigle it, some other female would. Long before Lady H. came to

England, he had made up his mind not to remain in this country. Better would (it) have been for him, to have adopted his resolution of retiring alone to the Continent ; years might have softened mutual seeming asperities, and he and his wife might have lived at the close of life, peacefully and comfortably."[1075]

George's sentiment, however, failed to factor in Nelsons' Nile victory. In other words, if Nelson had acqueisced to Fanny's wish for them to quietly retire to the Continent, his Nile victory wouldn't have happened and, in likelihood, Napoleon's forces would have defeated England's. George's close family weren't swayed by the anti-Emma lens. His youngest son, Nelson Matcham, added a handwritten footnote to George's diatribe:

"When we reflect that that hand led him on to glory, that that head planned and devised means of intelligence which paved the way to his boldest enterprizes, that the flattering distinction of a crowned head, and the praises of an admiring world, followed those valorous achievements, and that the unfortunate lady, now no more, possessed a devotion to his glory, to his welfare, and to his interest, which knew no bounds, and hesitated at no means to promote these ends. She was moreover the depositary of every secret of his life, as well as the frequent adviser, or rather approver, of his laudibly ambitious projects ; and lastly, she was of that cheerful turn which beguiled many a tedious hour, smoothed many a rough moment of melancholy musing, and banished many an unwelcome intrusion of painful remembrance."[1076]

However, Emma's defenders were few and far between. Nelson's early biographies called her a "wicked siren" and entirely omitted his love letters to her.[1077] Chamber's 1864 Encycloepadia's entry for NELSON Horatio, states, as fact, that "The only flaw in his private character was his infatuated attachment to Lady Hamilton... a woman of questionable antecedents, but perilous fascination, with whom he was here thrown into contact. The influence which she now attained over him, she continued to the end to exercise. Early in life he had married, and married happily. If to the charms of an impure adventuress he had sacrificed, on his return to England, the wife to whom before he had been tenderly devoted, it is not necessary to divulge in comment. Let us compassionate the one cruel frailty of a man in all else and in his proper nature, as gentle and generous as he was brave."[1078]

The misogynist fantasy of Emma's shadowy evil surfaces again in Winifred Gérin's 1970 biography of Horatia.

In more recent years, George himself has been tarred as an evildoer in supposedly factual histories. His alleged crime is to have been a penniless scrounger who leached off Emma. The source of this warped view seems to be Kate Williams's 2006 *England's mistress*. One of the exciting elements that made Williams's Emma biography a best seller is her portrayal of the Matchams and Boltons as greedy paupers who were partly responsible for Emma's ruin. An example of Williams's dramatisations appears on page 281 where she describes George Matcham and Thomas Bolton, as "men of energy, but not much money... always looking for help with their packs of children."[1079] Then, on page 381, she claims that, when "Kitty gave birth to another girl in 1801, she named her Horatia as a tribute to Emma's daughter",[1080] despite the reality that Horatia Matcham was baptised before Emma and Nelson's daughter was born. Later still, Williams informs readers that the Matchams "inundated her with begging letters. Emma handed over more cash she did not have."[1081]

England's mistress has convinced others that George Matcham was a penny-pinching bad guy. Ringwood Meeting House & History Centre, interprets a 1791 legal document as a court order for George and Kitty to promptly repay a debt to her father, brother and uncle (see chapter ten). This interpretation was made by an amateur historian, named John Hawkin, who admitted to having been informed by Kate Williams's portrayal of George Matcham in *England's mistress*.[1082]

In 2017, New Forest Magazine published an article states repeating Hawkin's assessment of George pretty much verbatim.

Clearly, there has been a need for a well-researched and undramatised biography of George Matcham, which this book hopes to have satisfied. George's true story, as revealed by meticulous research, is far more interesting than the two dimensional fantasy of him as a pantomime baddie.

Not all of George's positive contributions to the world are lost. Despite having been credited to others, Plymouth Breakwater and St James's Park Lake, close to Buckingham Palace, are still going strong two hundred years on. The breakwater has been so efficient at keeping Plymouth's harbour safe that its dockyard has grown into the largest in Europe.[1083] As for St James's Park, whose most celebrated feature is its lake, nearly 20,000 TripAdvisor reviews have given it an average ranking of 4.5 stars.

In the modernday New Forest the road around the picturesque village of Ringwood bears a sign pointing to "Matchams", where the pine plantation George laid down in the 1790s still exists. A speedway circuit, established in that vicinity after World War Two, has adopted the Matchams' name, as did a nudist camp that was shut down in the year 2,000.

On the other side of the world, a semi-rural coastal area of New South Wales, Australia, is named Matcham for George's second youngest son who emigrated there in 1828. Also in New South Wales, the descendants of George Matcham's cousin, Mary Pitt, honoured their kinship to George by adopting the midde name "Matcham". One of the Matcham Pitts' many descendants, Patsy Trench, features George Matcham in her account of the Pitt's emigration in her 2012 book, *The Worst Country in the World*.

All being said, it can be hoped, that if having read this biography, or otherwise imbibed its intent, George's spirit will smile in that warm, wry, self-depreciating way of his and be happy that his extended progeny –this book's author– has harkened to his well-meant words.

Timeline

Year	Age	Life events	Historical events
1753	0	Birth in Bombay Fort	
1756	2		Black hole of Calcutta (massacre of British EI Co people by Bengalis)
1757	4		EI Co defeat Bengalis at Plassey
1758	5	Only sibling, Simon, dies	
1761	7	Birth of brother, Charles	
1763	9	Death of brother, Charles	
c. 1763	9	Sails to England with Henry Savage	
c. 1754	10	Enrolls at Charterhouse School, London	
1756			Seven Years War puts British and French EI Co.s on opposing sides
1769	16	Graduates from Charterhouse	
1769	17	Enrolls with a tutor in Bromley-by-Bow	
1770	18	Graduates from tutor and applies to enter EI Co	
1771	18	EI Co writer living with his parents in Bombay Fort	
1771	19	EI Co senior merchant in Bombay Fort	Scindia leads Marathas to take

Year	Age	Life events	Historical events
			Delhi from the Afghans
1772	19	Apointed resident of Broach in Gujarat	EI Co takes Broach in Gujarat from the Marathas
1774	21	George's father made Superintendent Marine of the EI Co	
1775	22		Start of American War of Independence. Treaty of Surat between EI Co and Marathas
1776	23	George's father dies	Treaty of Surat overruled by EI Co in Bengal
1777	24	First overland trek (Persian Gulf to Egypt)	
1780	27	Second overland trek (Scanderoon to Basra via Aleppo)	
1783	30		End of American War of Independence
1784	30		EI Co cedes Broach to Scindia
1785	32	Testifies to Court of Bombay in December	
1786	32	Final overland trek (Iraq to Istanbul)	
1786	32	Stays with mother in Enfield, near London	
1786/ 7	33	Painted by Gilbert Stuart (who later paints George	

Year	Age	Life events	Historical events
		Washington). Love at first sight with Kitty Nelson in a Bath winter ball	
1787	33	Marries Kitty Nelson in Bath	
1787	33	Moves to Barton Hall, Norfolk	
1788	34	First meeting with Nelson and Fanny	
1789	35	Birth of first child, George junior	
1791	37	Ringwood home bought. 2nd child, Henry Savage Matcham, born	French revolution
1792	38	Moves to Ringwood. 3rd child, Catherine Ann Matcham, born. 2nd child dies	
1793	39	4th child, Edmund Nelson Matcham, born, but dies soon afterwards. Nelson recalled to naval service.	Louis XVI is guillotined in Paris. England at war with France
1795	42	5th child, Elizabeth Matcham, born	
1796	42-43	6th child, Francis Griffith Matcham born. Rents Bourne Lodge as a hunting retreat	Gilbert Stuart paints George Washington
1797	44	7th child, Mary Anne Matcham born. Nelson wounded in Tenerife	
1798	44-45	7th child, Mary Anne Matcham, dies. Moves to Kensington Place, Bath	Nelson's Nile victory makes him a hero

Year	Age	Life events	Historical events
1799	45	Winter illness causes loss of limb use. 8th child, Harriet Matcham, born	
1800	46	Meets Emma and Sir William Hamilton	
1801	47	9th child, Horatia Matcham, born. Nelson and Emma's daughter is born. Also named Horatia. Nelson separates from Fanny and lives openly with Emma	
1802	48	10th child, Susannah Matcham, born. Death of father-in-law, Edmund Nelson. Sides with Emma over Fanny	
1803	49	Patents system for raising vessels. Death of mother. Death of Sir William Hamilton. Birth of 11th child Horatio Nelson Matcham. Moves to Portland Place, Bath	
1805	51	Birth of 12th child, William Alexander Matcham. Nelson on shore leave. Death of 12th child. Nelson dies at Trafalgar	Britain annihilates France and Spain's navies at Trafalgar
1806	52	Awarded £10,000 as kin of Nelson. Birth of 13th child, Charles Horatio Nelson Matcham.	
1807	53	Buys and moves to Ashfold Lodge, Sussex	The save trade is criminalised by Britain and the

Year	Age	Life events	Historical events
			United States
1808	54	Death of nephew (William Nelson's son) Horatio Nelson. Death of 6th child, Francis Griffith Matcham. Emma sells Merton	
1811	57	Birth of 14th child, Nelson Matcham	
1812	58	Learns his plans for Plymouth's Breakwater are being copied	
1813	59	Susanna Bolton dies	
1814	60	1st child, George junior, qualifies as a lawyer	Napoleon abdicates
1815	61	Emma dies in Calais in January. George brings Horatia home. Takes his family to Paris in July to witness Wellington's triumphal procession	Napoleon escapes exile. Wellington defeats him at Waterloo
1816	62	Presented to the Prince Regent. The Blanckleys settle in Versailles. George takes family to Lisbon	
1817	63	1st child, George junior, marries Harriet Eyre of Newhouse. Horatia Nelson goes to the Boltons in Norfolk. Moves the rest of his family to Paris	
1818	64	Takes his family south from Paris towards Italy	Mary Shelley publishes Frankenstein
1819	65	8th child, Harriet, marries Edward Blanckley in Naples. 1st grandchild, Horatio Nelson	

Year	Age	Life events	Historical events
		Eyre Matcham, is born in Wiltshire	
1821	67	*Anecdotes of a Croat* published anonymously by Sherwood, Neely, and Jones	
1826	72	*Parental chit-chat* "unpublished"	
1828	74	Writes will	
1833	79	Dies in Kensington and buried in Slaugham with his sons Francis Griffith and Horatio Nelson	

APPENDIX

Appendix 1: Simon Matcham's Will

In the Name of God Amen, I Simon Matcham now of Bombay being bound on a ship Hardwick to Bengal &c, knowing death is a debt all must pay sooner or later, do for the better security of my small Fortune to my Family make and ordain this my last Will and Testament viz. First after all just debts being paid I give and bequeath unto my Hon.[d] Mother, Mary Matcham of Fiddleford in the County of Dorset and her Heirs forever the sum of one hundred Pounds lawful mony of England to be paid out of my Estate. Next I will that all my slaves without Exception are free and at liberty to go where they please to provide for themselves in one Twelve Months after my Decease, lastly the small fortune which it hath please God to endue me with, after paying out of it the Legacie of one hundred pounds to my mother, I give equally divided between them one half of to my dearly beloved Wife Elizabeth Matcham and one half to my son George Matcham but should it please God to bless us with another child, as we may expect, I will that it will have an equal proportion of my fortune as to my wife Elizabeth, and son George Matcham, and I constitute make and ordain George Scott Esq[r] and my Dear Wife Elizabeth Matcham Executrixs and Trustees of this my last Will and Testament, revoke all other Wills &c made by me whatever, in Witness whereof I now set my hand, the second day of January one thousand seven hundred and fifty eight, on board the Ship Hardwick at sea.

Sworn to, before me, James Stevens and Samuel Patterson that they believe it to be the hand of Simon Matcham.[1084]

Appendix 2: Examination of John Beete's Will

In the Name of God Amen

I John Beete Inhabitant of Bombay being weak in Body but sound in Mind and Memory do make this my last Will and Testament in manner and form following...

I give and bequeath whatsoever I may died possessed of which may come upon the denomination of real and personal estate to my worthy friend Quarles Harris of London Merchant whom I appoint executor to this my last will and testament in trust that it divide the same after paying all my lawful Debts amongst my children one Son and six Daughters share and share alike when they each of them shall attain the age of twenty one years or at the days of marriage of either of my Daughters and I appoint my friend George Matcham Esquire of Broach to be my Executor in India and to remit the Balance of my Estate here after paying my lawful Debts to Quarles Harris above named and I hereby evoke all former wills made by me and declare this to be my last will and Testament Dated in Bombay the ninth day of May in year of our Lord one thousand seven hundred and eighty three signed John Beete (seal) signed sealed and declared by the Testator to be his last Will and Testament in the presence of us who in his present and the presence of each other and by his desire have set our hands as witnesses on the day and year above written (signed) W Paddock (signed) D Christie (signed) John Atkins

Bombay Town Hall 2nd Dec.r 1783

Sworn before the court whilst sitting in judgement George Matcham the Executor within named who renounced his right of executing the said Will having no ways intermeddled with the Estate and without fraud or intent cheating the creditors (signed) P. J. Maister Register

A true copy P.J Master Register

These are to rectify all whom it doth concern that the Court of Directors of the United Company of Merchants of England trading to the East Indies did in the Month of June in the year of our Lord one thousand seven hundred and eighty five —— by the Ship Restoration from the Presidency of Bombay in the East Indies aforesaid a paper Book entitled "Copy of the Register of Wills Probates and Letters of Administration granted by the Hon'ble the Mayors Court of Bombay from the 8th

December 1783 to the 6th September 1784" attested by P. J. Maister the register of the said Mayors Court "wherein I find an entry is made of the Letters of Administration and Last Will and Testament the Transcript contained ====first sides of this sheet of paper is a true copy as by examination thereof appears in writings whereof I have —— set my hand this twenty first day of December in the year of our Lord one thousand seven hundred and eighty five Tho's Morton Sec'ry

This Will was proved at London the twenty fourth day of December in the year of our Lord one thousand seven hundred and eighty five before the worshipful William Marshall Doctor of Laws Master Keeper or Commissary of the Prerogative Court of Canterbury lawfully nominated by the oath of Quarles Harris one of the Executors named in the said Will to whom administration was granted of all and similar the goods chattels and credits of the deceased having even first sworn only to administer power resolved of making their life Grant to George Matcham Esquire the other executor named in the said Will which he shall apply for the same.

Appendix 3: Technical Description of George Matcham's Wedding Suit

The following information was kindly supplied by Abel Land, curatorial assistant of the Fashion History Museum in Cambridge, Ontario, and tailor of historical menswear, via email correspondence in August 2023.

The distinctive style of how the coat and the waistcoat are styled is very indicative of the last quarter of the 18th century. However, that being said, the last two decades of the 18th century is a major transitional period in the cut and silhouette of men's clothes. Earlier in the century men's coats are very full in the skirts, and generally have a narrow collar, the coat in our collection has the shape of the earlier full skirt, but has transitioned to a tall standing notched collar. The waist coat's cut exhibiting a longer front is again a feature linked to the 1770s, however, the skirt is not long enough for the earlier dates. The waist measure is at the natural high waist, which as the 1780s and 90s progressed, so too does the height of the waist increases. The original collar notch on the waistcoat matches the coat perfectly, again a sign that the collars have not been altered. Hinting at the later years of the 1780s.

The coat and waistcoat front lines are still original for the late 1780s, allowing for the hypothesized theory of this suit being worn by George Sr. at his wedding in 1787. Regarding the use for George Jr. for Nelson's funeral, by the 1806 date, there are very strong tells within men's tailoring primarily by the shaping of the backs in men's coats that can help date the re-use. The reduction in the tail vent plackets, significantly decreasing the fullness of the skirt. And the narrowing of the center back panels. The reduction of the coat size brings it into the size range of a young man approximately aged 16, taking into effect the build of an English man of that period.

The most re-working of the suit is in the breeches. Which historically were the closest fitting to the body shape. The knee garters have been taken in, and the same reduction can be seen in the very narrow almost spindly side of the thighs. Throughout the 18th century the back panels of men's breeches were kept very fill for ease of motion and fit, however, very early in the 1800s that fullness is removed in favor of a tight-fitting rear, and all the fullness would be eased or stretched into the back of the waist band, with the addition of a closed in gusset.

As for an approximation of George's height ranges between, 5'8" to 5'10". He may be on the shorter side of things, his suit is on a 5'9" mannequin, however, his waist is not perfect on the body.

Further notes from Fashion History Museum's collection file:

Coat: two-piece back construction with a cutaway front and long back seam, the lower back panels are only 2 in / 5 cm wide each, and at the nape, they are 1 7/8th in wide. The standing collar has a ¾ inch notch at the front; the collar height is 3 in / 7.5 cm. with a center back seam. Sleeves are set into a narrow armscye, and shoulder; shoulder seam is only 5 in. / 11.5 cm. With a slight curve. There is slight ease in the sleeve cap. The sleeve is two pieces with a typical 18th to late regency bend at the elbow. The cuff is a typical 1780s-90s bucket, attached ¾ the way around and left open at the back seam for the flare. Lined in an ivory silk surge (twill). The fold was originally very finely prick stitched in place. 3 cut steel buttons set into the top cuff. The tails have a full placket from the center back to the hem, formed by pleats in the front body. The plackets have 2 cut steel buttons on each. The vent is not open to the inside of the coat, with no top stitching on the folded edge. The back panels have a ½ in / 1.3 cm notch at the top of the tails. On the hem where the side seam meets the center back panel, it is uneven in the bluff cut. Front panels: The pockets are set in even with the center back placket. The flap is scalloped with three points and lined in an ivory silk serge, and the pocket slash is left bluff (raw edge); the pocket bags are worked on the inner side of the body in fine white linen. Each pocket has three cut steel buttons set into the coat body. The left center front starting 1 2/8 in / 3 cm from the collar seam, are 8 silk hand-worked extended buttonholes, and the 3-5 buttonholes are opened 1.5 in / 3.5 cm. The right center front is mirrored with cut steel buttons x 8. Interior: lined in a silk surge (twill) on the front and back-tail panels, with no lining on the center back. On the edges, the silk is rolled and very finely prick stitched, 17-20 stitches per inch. The curtain lining at the shoulders is padded with an ivory surge and covered with silk surge (twill), decorative quilting stitches to hold the silk in place and give stability. Sleeves are lined in white cotton to the wrists (a different hand sewing this into the coat), then the silk surge to the cuff edge, one salvage edge remains. The interfacing on the front right comprises strips of coarse linen and fine linen on the outside, only where the buttons are; a line of prick stitches is seen when the linen is attached to the body on the outside. Typical late 18th-century construction. There is a small linen tape running the whole length of the front to stabilize the raw edge. The front left interfacing is a fine French linen, which has been pieced, running to the last buttonhole. Again, a linen stay tape runs the front edge. Across the top of the back vents, there is the same fine linen used to structure the seams and back split. 20th-century label saying "Eyre-Matcham" sewn into the collar.

Appendix 4: Transcription of George and Kitty's Marriage Settlement

The transcriptions are taken from a copy of George Matcham and Catherine Nelson's marriage settlement held by Wiltshire and Swindon History Centre and photographed by the author on 8th August 2023

SHEET ONE

This indenture made the Twenty third day of February in the twenty seventh year of the Reign of our Sovereign Lord George the third by the Grace of God of Great Britain France and Ireland King Defender of the faith and soforth and in the year of our Lord one thousand seven hundred and eighty seven Between George Matcham of Enfield in the County of Middlesex Esquire of the first part Edmund Nelson of Burnham Thorpe in the county of Norfolk clerk and Catherine Nelson an infant of the age of twenty on years or thereabouts one of the daughters of the said Edmund Nelson of the second part and the said Edmund Nelson William Nelson of Hilborough in the s[d] County Norfolk clerk and William Suckling of the Custom House London Esquire of the third part Whereas a Marriage is intended to be shortly had and solemnised between the said George Matcham and the said Catherine Nelson by and with the consent and appobrobatrion of the said Edmund Nelson the Father And Whereas Maurice Suckling late of the Parish of St George Hanover Square in the County of Middlesex Esquire did in and by his last Will bearing date the thirds day of August One thousand seven hundred and seventy one (amongst other things) Give and bequeath unto Ann Nelson spinster and the said Catherine Nelson his nieces the respective sums of one thousand pounds a piece to be paid them respectively by the Executors in the said Will named within Twelve Months aft his decease or when and as soon as they should severally attain their ages of twenty one years And in case any of his said Nieces should be under the Age of Twenty one years at his decease then the said Testator directed that the Legacy or Legacies of her or them being so under age should be employed and disposed of at Interest by his said Executors at their discretion during such as their Minorities and that the interest arising from the same during that time should be at the judgement of at the discretion of the said executors in the maintenance and education of the said nieces during their respective minorities or be kept in hand and be paid to them together with their said principal sums at their said ages of Twenty one years And in case any of his said Nieces should depart their Life before she or they should have attained her or their age or ages of Twenty one years leaving issue of her or their Bodies lawfully begotten then the said Testator gave the Legacy of her or them so dying to their issue in equal shares to be paid them at their ages of Twenty one years together with such Interest as should be made of the same in the mean time But in case his said nieces died without issue then he gave the said Legacy to his Brother the said William Suckling party to these [pursuits?] his Executors Administrators and assigned and the said Testator appoints the Right Honorable Lord Walpole and the said William Suckling Executors of his said Will who have duly proved the same in the Prerogative Court of the Archbishop of Canterbury And whereas by Deed Poll under the hands and seals of the said William Suckling and Edmund Nelson bearing date the Eleventh day of August one thousand seven hundred and seventy nine Reciting to the purpose or effort Hereinbefore writed And that the said Maurice Suckling the Testator was their Deed leaving the said Ann Nelson and Catherine Nelson his nieces and also having Edmund Nelson and Suckling Nelson his nephews whereby they were become intitled to their respective legacies by the said Testator's said Will bequeathed to them And Reciting that the said sums of one thousand pounds and one thousand pounds which were given to the said Ann and Catherine Nelson and also the sums of five hundred pounds and five hundred pounds therein mentioned to have been given to the said Edmund Nelson and Suckling Nelson had that duly been laid out and invested by the said William Suckling in the purchase of five thousand pounds three per cent consolidated Bank Annuities and that the same then stood in the names of the said William Suckling and Edmund Nelson They the said William Suckling and Edmund Nelson did thereby declare that the said sum so invested in the purchase of Bank three per cent Annuities then stood in their Names In Trust as to one thousand six hundred and sixty six pounds thirteen shillings and four pence three per cent consolidated Bank Annuities for the said Ann and Catherine Nelson according to their respective shares as therein and hereinbefore mentioned But subject to the contingencies therein and hereinbefore also mentioned And whereas the said Catherine Nelson was intitled under the will of her late Grandmother Ann Suckling widow deceased to the principal sum of one hundred pounds being one third part of the sum of three hundred pounds which with interest and circulation thereof this day amounted to and produced the sum of two hundred and thirty four pounds seven shillings and three pence and the said Catherine Nelson also became intitled to the sum of two hundred and seven five pounds the interest that accrued on the said one thousand six hundred and sixty six pounds thirteen shillings and four pence to the fifth day of January last Three hundred and sixty three pounds of which hath been paid and applied by the said William Suckling and Edmund Nelson in and towards the maintenance and education of the said Catherine Nelson so that there remains due to the said Catherine Nelson in respect of the said three hundred and seventy five pounds the sum of twelve pounds which being added to the said two hundred and thirty four pounds seven shillings and three pence they make together two hundred and forty six pounds seven shillings and three pence And whereas the said George Matcham being possessed of thirteen thousand three hundred and thirty three pounds six shillings and eight pence three per cent consolidated Bank Annuities standing in his name did upon the Treaty for and in consideration of the said intended marriage propose and offer to transfer to and vest in the hands of the Trustees the said sum of

SHEET TWO

Thirteen thousand three hundred and thirty three pounds six shillings and eight pence three per cent consolidated Bank Annuities upon the trusts hereafter mentioned in order to make a provision for the said Catherine Nelson and the Issue of the said George Matcham by her And it hath been also proposed and agreed between the said parties that the said one thousand six hundred and sixty six pounds thirteen shillings and four pence three per cent Bank Annuities to which the said Catherine Nelson is intitled under the will of the said Maurice Suckling in manner aforesaid shall also be transferred to the said trustees upon the Trust's Certificate also mentioned And with respect to the said sum of two hundred and forty six pounds seven shillings and three pence it hath been likewise agreed that the same and also any other Personal Estate which the said Catherine Nelson now is or shall hereafter be intitled to seal immediately upon the solemnization of the said intended marriage vest in and become the absolute property of the said George Matcham And the said sum of two hundred and forty six pounds seven shillings and three pence hath been accordingly this day paid to the said George Matcham he doth hereby acknowledge And whereas the said George Matcham in conformity to the said proposal and agreement on his part hath this day transferred to and in the names of the said Edmund Nelson William Nelson and William Suckling the said thirteen thousand three hundred and thirty three pounds six shillings and eight pence three per cent consolidated Bank Annuities and they the said William Suckling and Edmund Nelson (at the request of the said George Matcham signified by his being a party to and executing these presents) have transferred to and in the hands of the said Edmund Nelson William Nelson and William Suckling the said one thousand six hundred and sixty six pounds thirteen shillings and four pence life annuities as by the Books kept at the Bank for the transfer of that paid sum may appear Now this indenture witnesseth and it is hereby declared and agreed by and between all parties to these presents and it is the true intent and meaning of them and of these presents that the said Edmund Nelson William Nelson and William Suckling and the Survivor and Survivors of them his Executors and Administrators shall stand possessed of and invested in the said thirteen thousand three hundred and thirty pounds six shillings and eight pence and one thousand six hundred and sixty six pounds thirteen shillings and four pence three per cent consolidated Bank Annuities so transferred and vested in them as aforesaid upon the Trusts and to and for the intents and purposes and subject to the provisions declarations and agreements hereafter maintained expressed and declared of and concerning (that is to say) untill the said intended Marriage as to the said thirteen thousand three hundred and three pounds six shillings and eight pence three per cent consolidated Bank Annuities In Trust for the said George Matcham his Executors and Administrators And as to the said one thousand six hundred and sixty six pounds thirteen shillings and eight pence life annuities in trust for the same intents and purposes as the said William Suckling and Edmund Nelson stood posessed of the said one thousand six hundred and sixty six pounds thirteen shillings and four pence Bank Annuities immediately before such transfer thereof as herebefore is mentioned And from and after the solemnization of the said intended Marriage then upon Trust to permit and suffer the said George Matcham and his assigned to have write and take the Interest or Dividends of all the said Bank Annuities for and during the term of his natural Life And from and after his decease (in case the said Catherine Nelson his intended Wife shall still survive) then In Trust to permit the said Catherine Nelson and her assigned to retrieve and take the Interest or Dividends thereof for and during the term of her natural Life And from and after the several deceases of the said George Matcham and Catherine Nelson the intended Wife then as to the said thirteen thousand three hundred and thirty three pounds six shillings and eight pence Bank Annuities Upon Trust that the said Edmund Nelson William Nelson and William Suckling and the Survivors and Survivor of them and the Executors and Administrators of such survivor do and shall transfer pay and apply the Principal or Capital of the same and the Interest or Dividends thereof unto and amongst such child and children of the said George Matcham and Catherine Nelson his intended Wife at such time or times in such shares and proportions and subject to such Conditions and Restrictions and in such manner and form as the said George Matcham by any Deed or Deeds with or without power of revocation to be by him duly sealed and delivered in the presence of two or more credible Witnesses or by his last Will and Testament in Writing to be by him signed and published in the presence of the like number of Witnesses shall direct or appoint And for want of such direction or appointment then upon trust to transfer pay and apply the said Principal or Capital of the said thirteen thousand three hundred and thirty three pounds six shillings and eight pence Bank Annuities and the Interest or Dividends thereof unto and amongst all and every the child and children of the said George Matcham and Catherine Nelson his intended Wife equally to be divided between them (if more than one) share and share alike And if there shall be but one such child then wholly to such one child the parts and shares of such of them as shall be a daughter or daughters to be paid or payable to her or them at her or their age of twenty one years or day or days of Marriage respectively which shall first happen and the parts or shares of them as shall be a son or sons to be paid or payable to him or them at his

SHEET THREE

Or their age or ages of twenty one years or to be sooner employed for his or their benefit or advancement in the wo—— as the said Edmund Nelson William Nelson and William Suckling their Executors or Administrators shall think fit (and said George Matcham and Catherine Nelson being both then dead) And in the case any such daughter or daughters shall have attained her or their ages of twenty one years or be married or any such son or sons shall have attained his or their age or ages of twenty one years in the life time of the said George Matcham and Catherine Nelson then the part or share of such daughter or daughters so attaining such age or marrying and of such son and sons so attaining the said age or ages or so much thereof as shall not have been sooner employed as aforesaid shall be paid immediately after the decease of the survivor of them the said George Matcham and Catherine Nelson And if any such child or children being a daughter or daughters shall happen to depart this Life under the age of twenty one years and unmarried or being a son or sons under the age of twenty one years the part or share of his her or their so dying shall go and be paid to the survivors or survivor of them at such time or times as his or her original part or share shall by virtue of these presents become payable And it is the intent and meaning of these presents and the parties hereunto that all and every the parts and shares therein before diverted to survive shall from time to time survive with the original parts and shares untill such original parts and shares shall by virtue of these presents become payable And upon further Trust that that the said Edmund Nelson William Nelson and William Suckling their Executors and Administrators shall and do from and after the decease of the said George Matcham and Catherine Nelson his intended Wife pay and apply the Interest or Dividends of the said last mentioned BankAnnuities in the mean time to the maintenance and education of such child or children untill their respective shares therein shall become payable and in proportion to their respective shares and interests therein and as to the said one thousand six hundred and sixty six pounds thirteen shillings and four pence Bank Annuities from and after the several deceased of the said George Matcham and Catherine Nelson

Upon Trust that the said Trustees so and shall transfer pay and apply the principal or capital of the same and the Interest or Dividends thereof unto and amongst such child and children of the said George Matcham and Catherine Nelson his intended Wife at such time or times and in such shares and proportions and subject to such conditions and restrictions and such manner and form as the said Catherine Nelson by herself alone and without the said George Matcham her intended husband shall from time to time (not withstanding her coverture) by any deed or deeds writing or writings (with or without power of revocation) to be by her sealed and delivered published in the presence of two or more credible witnesses or by her last will and testament to be by her signed and in the presence of the like number of witnesses direct or appoint and for want of such direction or appointment then upon trust to transfer pay and apply the said Principal or Capital of the said one thousand six hundred and sixty six pounds thirteen shillings and four pence Bank Annuities and the Interest or Dividends thereof unto and amongst the child and children of the said George Matcham and Catherine Nelson at such time and times shares proportions manner and form and with sure benefit of survivorship as hereinbefore directed expressed and declared of and concerning the said thirteen thousand three hundred and thirty three pounds six shillings and eight pence Bank Annuities from and after the several deceased of the said George Matcham and Catherine Nelson in case of default of sure appointment by him the said George Matcham as hereinbefore is mentioned And upon further trust in case there should not be any such issue of the said intended Marriage as aforesaid or being such all of them shall happen to die before any of them being a daughter or daughters shall attain the age of twenty one years or be Married or being a son or sons shall attain the said age of twenty one years then that they the said Edmund Nelson William Nelson and William Suckling and the Survivors and Survivor of them his Executors or Advisors do and shall stand possessed of and interested in the said thirteen thousand three hundred and thirty three pounds six shillings and eight pence and one thousand six hundred and sixty six pounds thirteen shillings and four pence three per cent consolidated Bank Annuities respectively Upon Trust as to the said thousand three hundred and thirty three pounds six shillings and eight pence Bank Annuities for the said George Matcham his Executors and Advisors and to be transferred and paid to him or them accordingly And as to the said one thousand six hundred and sixty six pounds thirteen shillings and four pence Bank Annuities In Trust to assign and transfer the Principal or Capital of the said one thousand six hundred and sixty six pounds thirteen shillings and four pence Bank Annuities unto such person and persons and upon such trusts and to and for such intents and purposes and in such shares and proportions and in such manner and form and with or without power or revocation as the said Catherine Nelson by herself

Alone and as if she was a force solo without the said George Matcham her intended Husband from time to time (notwithstanding her coverture by any deed or deeds writing or writings to be by her sealed and delivered in the presence of two or more credible Witnesses or by her last Will and Testament to be by her signed and published in the presence of the like number of Witnesses give dispose or appoint the same and for want of such disposition or appointment then to assign and transfer the principal or capital of the said one thousand six hundred and sixty six pounds thirteen shillings and four pence Bank Annuities unto the Executors or Administrators of the said George Matcham Provided always And it is hereby declared and agreed by and between the said parties to these presents that it shall and may be lawful to and for the said Edmund Nelson William Nelson and William Suckling and the Survivors and Survivor of them and the Executors and Administrators of such Survivor by and with the consent and appointment of the said George Matcham and Catherine Nelson the intended Wife or the Survivor of them testified by any writing under their hands or the hand of the Survivor and after the Death of the Survivor then of the proper authority of the said Trustees to make sale of the said thirteen thousand three hundred and thirty three pounds six shillings and eight pence and one thousand six hundred and sixty six pounds thirteen shillings and four pence Bank Annuities And all the Monies arising thereby and also all Money that shall happen to be paid off by Government on the same Bank Annuities to place out at interest in the names of the said Edmund Nelson

William Nelson and William Suckling or the Survivors or Survivor of them his Executors or Administrators or Government or Real Securities and from time to time with the like consent in like manner testified to through such sureties or funds and that all new securities or funds so taken and the Monies placed out therein shall be and remain vested in the same Trustees upon the same trusts for the same purposes as all hereinbefore declared continuing the said Stocks so to be sold Provided Always And it is herebyfurther stated and agreed by and between all the said parties to these presents that in case they the said Edmund Nelson William Nelson and William Suckling or any of them shall die or be desirous to quit and be discharged of and from the trust hereby in them imposed and aforesaid at any time or times before the said trusts shall be fully executed and performed then and in such case and when and so often as the same shall happen it shall and may be lawful to and for the said George Matcham and Catherine Nelson his intended Wife and the survivor of them by any writing under their his or her hands and seals or hand and seal attested by two or more credible witnesses to nominate substitute or appoint any other power or powers to be Trustee or Trustees for the purposes aforesaid in the place or stead of them the said Edmund Nelson William Nelson and

William Suckling or such of them who shall so die or be desirous to quit and be discharged of and from the aforesaid Trust and that when and so often as any new Trustee or Trustees shall be nominated or appointed as aforesaid the said Bank Annuities and Trust promised and all stocks or funds in which the same or any part thereof may stand be effectually shall thereupon with all continuous speed be assigned and transferred so as that the same may stand and be effectually vested in the surviving or continuing or former Trustees or Trustee and such new Trustees or Trustee upon the Trusts aforesaid and that every such new Trustee or Trustees shall and may in all things out in the Trusts aforesaid every or any of them in conjunction with the others or other of them who shall survive or continue as fully and effectually in all respects and to all intents and purposes as if he or they had been originally in and by these presents nominated or appointed a trustee or trustees for the purposes aforesaid any thing hereinbefore continue to the contrary notwithstanding And it is hereby declared and agreed that the said Edmund Nelson William Nelson and William Suckling their Executors and Administrators respectively shall be charged or chargeable only each of them for his own acts and trusts payments and wilful servants and not otherwise and shall not be charged or chargeable with any sum or sums of Money other than such as shall actually come to his or their hands respectively by virtue of these presents nor with any loss or damage which may happen in placing out all or any of the Monies aforesaid on Government or Bank Annuities in manner aforesaid nor with any loss or damage which may happen by reason of the execution of any of the Trusts hereby in them reposed without his or their respective wilfull defaults and shall also be at liberty to reimburse themselves all costs and damages they shall be put to or sustain on account of the Trust hereby in them reposed And Lastly the said William Suckling out of the Love and affection which he hath and beareth for the said Catherine Nelson his niece and in consideration of the said intended Marriage Doth hereby relinquish release and give up all rights title interest property realm and demand which he now hath or which he his Executors or Administrators can or may have or claim to have in upon or in respect of the said one thousand six hundred and sixty six pounds thirteen shillings and four pence Bank Annuities or any part thereof under or by virtue of the said will of the said Maurice Suckling his late Brother deceased In Witness whereof the said parties to these presents have hereunto set their hands and seals the day and year first above written.

Appendix 5: Dr Tim Ridge's Family Story of Descent from Ann Nelson

Dr Tim Ridge's account, as given below, was relayed to the author via Messenger and email in December 2019 and July 2023.

"I inherited our tree research from a 1st cousin x1 removed who spent most of her life researching the family tree. She told me of the rumour that there was a connection with Nelson via Ann, but she did not have the benefit of online databases like we have. This is what I have: Ann Nelson born 20 Sep 1760 Burnham Thorpe to Edmund and Catherine. On 15 Apr 1775 at the age of 14 Ann was apprenticed to Alice Lilly, citizen and goldsmith of London - 7 year apprenticeship in millinery. Lived at Capital Lace Warehouse, 9 Ludgate Street. 18 Jan 1777 alleged birth of son William Robinson - who was taken in by his father, also called William Robinson. William junior went to St Paul's School, entered as the son of James Robinson, his uncle. Baptism took place 10 Nov 1789 at St Luke, Old Street, and mother named as "Anne". (This was after Ann Nelson had died 15 Nov 1783 in Bath, I think from pneumonia). William went on to do well in life, becoming a solicitor and Fellow of the Society of Antiquaries, J.P. He married Mary Ridge 28th January 1803, who was my 4th great aunt, so not direct descent, but I am in touch with present day Robinson's, so a Gedmatch comparison might be possible. The Robinsons have Horatio cropping up as a first name, and one of their houses was called Trafalgar House if I remember correctly.

The lore was passed down to me by my first cousin once removed Dr Jessie Ridge, who was single, and researched the family tree most of her life - but did not have the benefit of the internet to find information. Our impression was that the illegitimate birth had been thoroughly hushed up, owing to the position of her father and brother.

I'm a 6th generation GP, and Jessie was also a doctor - our interest has been getting to the truth rather than "claiming" a connection to Horatio

Nelson - a genealogical challenge only - and far from verified. DNA might cast some light when more people have been tested in UK - although it's now too distant for present day descendants to have much chance of shared DNA."

Appendix 6: Amendment to George Matcham's 1803 Patent

A.D. 1803 . . . . . . N° 2676.

Raising Weights, Preventing Ships Sinking, &c

MATCHAM'S SPECIFICATION.

TO ALL TO WHOM THESE PRESENTS SHALL COME, I GEORGE MATCHAM, of Bath, in the County of Somerset, Esquire, send greeting. WHEREAS His most Excellent Majesty King George the Third did, by His Letters Patent under the Great Seal of the United Kingdom of Great Britain and Ireland, bearing date at Westminster, the Twenty-ninth day of January, in the forty-third year of His reign, give and grant unto me, the said George Matcham, His especial licence that I, the said George Matcham; during the term of years therein mentioned, should and lawfully might use, exercise, and vend, within England & Wales and the Town of Berwick-upon-Tweed, my Invention of " RAISING GREAT WEIGHTS, IN PREVENTING SHIPS FROM SINKING, IN RAISING SHIPS WHEN SUNK, IN RENDERING SHIPS WHICH ARE DISPROPORTIONED TO SHALLOW WATERS CAPABLE OF ENTERING RIVERS, OF PASSING BARS OR SHOALS, OR OTHERWISE MOVING IN SHOAL WATER, IN WORKING PUMPS OF GREAT POWER, IN SUPPLYING THE PLACE OF LOCKS ON CANALS, AND IN 15 VARIOUS OTHER OPERATIONS IN WHICH A POWERFUL ENGINE FOR SUSTAINING HEAVY BURDENS OR RAISING GREAT BODIES IN WATER MAY BE NECESSARY " in which said Letters Patent there is contained a proviso obliging me, the said George Matcham, by an instrument in writing under my hand and seal, to cause a particular description of the nature of my said Invention, and in what manner the same is to be performed, to be inrolled in His Majesty's High Court of Chancery within six calendar months after the date of the said recited Letters Patent, as in and by the same, relation being thereunto had, may more fully and at large appear.

NOW KNOW YE, that in compliance of the said proviso, I, the said George Matcham, do hereby declare that my said Invention is described in the manner herein-after mentioned, viz:—

Matcham's Method of Raising Weights, Preventing Ships Sinking, &c

---

The mode I propose of raising great weights (for instance, what I had primarily in view, a barge from a lower to an upper canal) is by inflating a leather balloon, attached by cordage to a wooden case, in which is a weight preponderating the barge to be drawn up. At the end of the upper canal, adjoining to the inclined plain or precipice where the barge is to be drawn up, a reservoir of water is to be formed, the depth of the inclined plane or precipice, in which is suspended, by inflation, a balloon, with the attached weights. A rope leads from it over a roller, and is locked to the boat in the lower canal ; the mouth of the neck of the balloon being opened, the water, pressing round it expels the air and the balloon sinks in the water ; when it is at the bottom the barge will, by the rope, be drawn up into the upper canal. When again required to work, the balloon must be inflated through the leather pipe or neck, which is of the length of the depth of the reservoir. The inflation is effected by a bellows, worked by a horse or lever. There are situations in which a small steam engine will be advantageously applied as an air pump. The same application will effect the different purposes specified in the Patent ; but that of floating vessels in shoals by buoyancy I have found has some time since been communicated to the public by Dr. Fothergill, of Bath. The ideas suggested in his pamphlet so closely accord with my own, that I can lay no claim to priority as to the buoyancy of vessels, &c. by inflated bags, thereby expelling the grosser element of water. In witness whereof, I, the-said George Matcham, have hereunto set my hand and seal, this Twentieth day of May, in the year of our Lord One thousand eight hundred and three.

G. MATCHAM. (L.S.)*

AND BE IT REMEMBERED, that on the same Twentieth day of May, in the year above mentioned, the aforesaid George Matcham came before our Lord the King in His Chancery,** and acknowledged the Specification aforesaid, and all and every thing therein contained, in form above written. And also the Specification aforesaid was stamped according to the tenor of the Statute in that case made and provided.

Inrolled the same Twentieth day of May, in the year above written.[1085]

    *   L.S. stands for Locus Sigilli, meaning "place of the seal", denoting where the signatory's seal should be placed.[1086]

** "Came before our Lord the King in His Chancery" was a long-established phrase used in patents, referring to the Chancery's representation of the King's will.[1087]

Appendix 7: Evidence for George Matcham's Cousin Relationship to Mary Pitt

In her 2012 book The Worst Country in the World, Mary Pitt's descendant Patsy Trench details family lore that George Matcham was Mary Pitt's first cousin.[1088] Patsy Trench transcribes an 1885 letter written by her great-grandfather, George Matcham Pitt, who was Mary Pitt's grandson:

"According to all I know of my ancestors, and that is not much – The Pitt family, that is the Mother and Daughters and one son came to this Colony in the early part of the Century, in the good ship Canada, under the Command of Captain Jenkinson. My Grandmother's Maiden name was Matcham. She originally came from Ireland… My Grandfather died young, and he left his widow not in good circumstances. She was of an high cast of character, and she sold what she had, and finished her life here. I believe she was a good Mother, and truly religious. I know very little of my family connections in England. My Grandmother's first cousin George Matcham, married Lord Nelson's sister Catherine…"[1089]

Patsy Trench comments:

"To what extent [her great-grandfather's] *letter is accurate is anyone's guess, but it's all we have to go on. And without knowing where in Ireland she was born it is impossible to find a record of Mary's birth, so we have to take that on trust. There was a Mary Matcham who was born in Dorset in 1755 of Joseph and Martha Matcham, but for a number of reasons* [her genealogist aunt] *Barbara was convinced this is not 'our' Mary. First, the ages do not tally. On the original mill lease in 1779 Mary was recorded as 'around thirty years old', and her burial certificate in 1815 stated she was 67, both of which indicate she was born in or around 1748. And there was no mention of her being under age on her marriage certificate in 1770, when the 'other' Mary would have been fifteen. Secondly, according to GM Pitt Mary was born in Ireland. Thirdly, there is no indication of the practice of continuous given names within the family: there are no Josephs or Marthas, while there are continuous Thomases and Williams.*

This according to Barbara Lamble makes Mary's father Thomas Matcham, eldest son of Thomas and Mary (née Ford), who came from a family of weavers and quite possibly went to Ireland for the work opportunities, as other weavers were known to do at that time. As for Mary's mother, again all we have is what GM tells us: that on the death of her husband she remarried and went to America, leaving Mary in the care of two maiden aunts in Dorset. We have no idea (yet) what her name was or whether or not Mary had siblings. Accepting Barbara's theory makes Mary's and George Matcham's respective fathers Thomas and Simon brothers, and Mary and George first cousins."[1090]

Patsy Trench's tip that "Robert Pitt, Batchelor, married on the 27th day of December 1770 to Mary Matcham, Spinster of this parish"[1091] of Childe Okeford, near Fittleford in Dorset, checked out, but, confusingly, a handwritten family-tree, in Wiltshire and Swindon History Centre's Eyre Matcham collection, gives George Matcham's paternal grandmother as "Mary dau Rob.[t] Pitt died Oct 1748". This Mary was married to of "Thomas Matcham of Fittleford [Dorset] bapt Dec.[r] 28th 1662".[1092] As per every previous attempt to make sense of early Matcham genealogy, subsequent searching has so far returned nothing concrete to corroborate... well, anything.

In the Nelsons of Burnham Thorpe, Mary Eyre Matcham mentions George and Nelson assisting people to emigrate to Australia but doesn't name the people being helped to emigrate, nor does she describe them as George's family:

"A keen believer in the future of our colonies, G. M. was then helping some emigrants to Australia, for whom Government grants of land were procured, and through the Admiral's interest an introduction to Mr. King, Governor of New South Wales, was also obtained. To this day, so successful were their endeavours, the descendants of these families, and of others sent later on to join them, still remember those through whose help their future prosperity was as far as possible ensured.

'Long ago Mr. King has asked the question about your friend's journey to Botany Bay,' writes the Admiral to G. M. in January 1801. 'Mr. K. says they shall be sent free of cost, and desires their names, ages, professions may be sent. Mr. Davison has kindly undertaken to go between you and Mr. King, therefore send him the necessary answers to the questions. The fleet sails for that Colony in March...'

Nor did the Admiral's interest in the scheme end there. He kept the matter in mind all through the rest of his life. Three years later, in forwarding a letter from Governor King, he wrote : 'I hope your other friends arrived at last, if not there is an end long ago of all their cares.' The emigrants themselves, Mr. King tells him, 'are comfortably settled and will be as they have been, the peculiar object of my care, which they have rendered themselves highly deserving of, and are the best examples as settlers of any sent here. My feeble suffrages of gratulation,' adds the Governor, 'on the Brilliant achievements of your Lordship, altho past the usual date of Merit, yet I hope you will consider me as one that prides himself on being personally known to the Nation's Champion'."[1093]

Patsy Trench, who used The Nelsons of Burnham Thorpe as a reference source,[1094] transcribed the above letters in The Worst Country in the World.[1095]

However, with no alternative source to verify George Matcham Pitt's 1885 assertion that Mary Pitt was George Matcham's first cousin or, in fact, related at all, the case is somewhat shaky.

In fact, a number of Trench's assertions fall apart under scrutiny. For example, regarding the Pitt's 1801 voyage to Australia, Trench says, on page 52, "Finally, on 21 June, the ship sailed from Spithead, by Portsmouth", then, on page 53, that "There were 106 male convicts on board Canada".[1096] However, both statements are belied by a report in the Hampshire Chronicle:

"PORTSMOUTH
SATURDAY, JUNE 27.
…Monday sailed the Minorca, Canada, and Nile transports, with female convicts for New South Wales."[1097]

Trench says they sailed on the 21st of June, but the Monday before the 27th of June was the 22nd; and the convicts on board were female, not male. However, these are minor details and who knows if the newspaper itself was accurate?

This is why multiple sources are preferable. And this is why, in the absence of any secondary source, the Pitt family's passed-down belief of blood relationship to George Matcham is tenuous.

Thankfully, a much-needed secondary source turned up, unexpectedly, during a visit to Wiltshire and Swindon History Centre in August 2023.

When, in 1986, George Matcham junior's great-grandson, George Jeffreys, inherited the Eyre Matcham's Wiltshire estate of Newhouse,[1098] a vast hoard of family correspondence and other documents came with it. This was the stash of papers Kitty Nelson had daintily bound with satin ribbons, and which George Jeffreys' great-aunt, Mary Eyre Matcham, had delved through to compose her 1911 book, The Nelsons of Burnham Thorpe. George Jeffreys donated the entire collection to Wiltshire and Swindon History Centre for safer keeping. The collection is searchable online, from anywhere in the world, at:

However, the "smoking gun" letter referring to George Matcham's relationship to the Australian emigrants is hidden –like a needle in a haystack– in bundle 1369/7/2/4, whose catalogue description makes no mention of Australia, Sydney, or anything else to signify the letter's content:

"Various family letters: contemporary copy of two letters from Horatio Lord Nelson to his daughter Horatia 1803, 1805; letter to Lord Nelson 1803; letters to Countess Nelson 1839; to Mary from Edmund ? Walker in Halifax, Nova Scotia, 1848; to Catherine from Laura Bendyshe c1840; to Susanna Matcham from her solicitor on legacy matters 1828-1851."

Thankfully, researching George Matcham's biography necessitated sifting through multiple papers in the Eyre Matcham collection and –lo!– one of letters was headed "Sydney May 1803". It turned out to be the letter from Governor King to Nelson which Mary Eyre Matcham had transcribed in the Nelsons of Burnham Thorpe[1099]… except she'd omitted the crucial first words of the first of the content:

"Sydney May 1803
My Lord
I received yours of the 18th last July
The relations of Mr Matcham who you kindly interest yourself about, are comfortably settled and will be as they have been the peculiar object of my care, which they have rendered them selves highly deserving of, and are the best example as settlers, of any ever sent here.
My feeble suffrages of gratulation in the brilliant achievements of your lordship, although past the usual date of merit, yet I hope you will consider me as one that prides himself on being personally known to the Nations champion.
Mrs King and myself beg our Respectful best wishes to Lady Nelson & your Lordship…
With best wishes for your Lordships health I am very respectfully… Philip Gidley King"[1100]

Although King doesn't name the Pitts, nor their precise relationship to "Mr Matcham", both King and Nelson believed they were George's family.

Appendix 8: Press Description of William Nelson's Son, Horatio's Funeral

LORD TRAFALGAR'S FUNERAL.

"Yesterday afternoon, at one o'clock precisely, the remains of the late Lord Trafalgar were removed, in Grand Funeral Procession, from Waine's Hotel, in Conduit-street, to St. Paul's Cathedral, the burial place of his renowned Uncle, the immortal Nelson, in the following order:–

Funeral Conductor on Horseback.

Four Mutes on Horseback, two and twos with silk hat-bands and scarfs, with white favours.

His Charger, led by two Grooms, with a Servant on Horseback, uncovered, carrying the Coronet on a crimson velvet cushion with gold tassels, and a Page on each side.

THE BODY

In a Hearse drawn by six beautiful black horses, covered with black velvet, and ornamented with plumes of black Ostrich feathers—There were no escutcheons.

Chief Mourners attending the coach carrying Mr. Archdeacon Young (Uncle to the Deceased) Alexander Davison, Esq. William Haslewood, Esq. Rev. Dr. Outraim.

Mourning Coach with four horses (with two Pages attendant), carrying two servants of the deceased.

Earl Nelson's Chariot.

Mr. Davison's Chariot.

Mr. Haslewood's Carriage.

The Bishop of Chester performed the service and ceremony.

DESCRIPTION OF THE COFFIN.

(Oak covered with crimson velvet. with white furniture, inclosing a lead ditto.—Plate of inscription, 16 inches by 12.)

DEPOSITUM.

The Honourable

HORATIO NELSON,

Commonly called Viscount Trafalgar, Knight, Grand Commander of the Order of St. Joachim, only son of the Right Hon. and Rev. William Nelson, D. D. Baron Nelson of the Nile, and Hilborough, in the County of Norfolk, Viscount Merton and Earl Nelson of Trafalgar and of Merton in the County of Surrey, Duke of Bronte in the Kingdom of Farther Sicily, &c. &c. &c.; and sole Nephew in the male line of the late ever-to-be-lamented Hero, Horatio Viscount and Baron Nelson, Vice Admiral of the White, &c. &c. &c.—Born 26th October 1788.—Died 17th January, 1808.

The procession advanced from Conduit-street, down Swallow-street, into Piccadilly, down the Haymarket, through the Strand and Fleet-street, to St. Paul's Cathedral. It reached the latter place a quarter before three o'clock, when the Body was taken out of the hearse, and was met at the top of the steps by the Dean and Chapter, who conducted it into the centre of the Cathedral, when the Funeral Service ws performed under the great Dome, and immediately over the vault where the Uncle of the deceased lies. The body was taken down into the vault, the company remaining above. After the usual ceremony, the company separated."

From the London Chronicle, 27th January 1808.

Appendix 9: Photograph of Handwritten Corrections in the Matcham's Copy of

Sichel's 1805 Emma Lady Hamilton

or the eucharist, as the seal of her pardon, be administered.

Thus did one of the most extraordinary women of modern times terminate, on the 16th of January, 1815, her course of uncommon vicissitudes, in a foreign land, surrounded by strangers, and so oppressed by poverty, that her remains were nearly consigned to a spot of ground appropriated to the lowest description of the poor, for the want of means to defray the expenses of a decent funeral ; when an English merchant at Calais, shocked at the circumstance, undertook the charge ; and all the respectable gentlemen of this nation, amounting to about fifty, attended as mourners at the interment, which was duly performed in the principal cemetery of that place. The same generous person, who so humanely provided a decent sepulture for the dead, extended also his protecting hand to the child that she had left, and who was now in danger of suffering for her mother's folly and extravagance. But the liberal merchant rescued the orphan from the machinations of those creditors in France, who, according to the laws of that country, would have detained her for the debts of her parent.[1]

[1] Most of these statements are entirely incorrect. Lady Hamilton was interred in a piece of ground just

[handwritten:] Quite true. Horatia came to England in boys clothes.

248

On her arrival in England she was entrusted to the guardianship of Mr. Matcham, the brother-in-law of Lord Nelson, and who, there can be no doubt, will watch over her interests with that concern, which he would have felt it his duty to discharge, had she been committed to him by the special request of his departed friend.

Thus did the last "scene of all" in the "strange eventful history" of the once enchanting Emma comport with the rest of her

outside the town of Calais, which was used as a public cemetery till 1816. The ground was shortly after this time used as a timber yard, and all vestiges of the graves it contained were swept gradually away. On the news of the decease of Lady Hamilton reaching England, a Mr. H. Cadogan and Earl Nelson went over to Calais, where the *Not so* former paid the funeral expenses of the deceased, which amounted to £28 10s., and on his return brought her daughter Horatia back to her native land with him. Earl Nelson, as one of the trustees of Horatia, also probably thought it incumbent on him to see her safely back in England after the decease of her mother. On her arrival with Mr. Cadogan she was transferred to the care of Mrs. Matcham (Lord Nelson's sister) in accordance with the last wishes of Lady Hamilton. With Mrs. Matcham she remained for two years, and afterwards resided with Mr. Bolton (Lord Nelson's brother-in-law) until February, 1822, when she became the wife of the Rev. Philip Ward, sometime Vicar of Tenterden in Kent. By him she had a large family, and died in the 81st year of her age, March 6, 1881.

Mr. Matcham, not Earl Nelson, went over to Calais, & brought back Horatia to England, dressed in Boy's Clothes

The photographs taken by the author in Newhouse, Wiltshire, in October 2017 after the book was shown to her by George Matcham's third great-grandson, George Jeffreys.

The notes were written by George junior's son,

William Eyre Matcham.

Appendix 10: April 1816 Letter from HSB to His Daughter, Maria

Bath 23rd April 1816

My dear Maria,

As I now answer your little girls pretty letter, I would not miss the occasion of giving you a few lines, to tell you of my intention of quitting Bath principally on account of my health, as assuredly it does not agree with me; a third winter each of which I have been laid up in my bed; a proof of it is that when I am out of Bath I am quite well; last spring I went from this to London was absent four months, during that period I enjoyed perfect health. I had not returned here three days when I was taken and indeed more or less have continued down to this; the difficulty of getting rid of the lease has so long detained me, but have now surmounted it, by giving up the remaining two years to Mrs Bignall; the furniture I dispose or rather say give away to a broker, rather than be troubled with an auction.

Whither we proceed on leaving this [house] we have not determined, but for change of air towards the sea coast I fancy we shall ramble, most of the summer, and please God I mean to cheat an English winter by going somewhere to the southward on the Continent; in short no fix'd plan have we thought of. Ten or twelve days I fancy will finish our present residence

Edward is still with us he has passed a gay winter, every night (Sunday excepted) has he been dancing, the gayest fellow in Bath. I hardly see him but at dinner as he keeps such late hours, that he does not rise early, & our breakfast is generally over before he comes down. This seems to agree with him, and after his long fag as a MIdshipman he ought to be indulged in recreation. I know not at present how he intends to dispose of himself when we leave this [house]. I shall leave it to himself, it will be well if he can get employed.

I suppose you have heard of your cousins Mr & Mrs Graham and Isabella Rogers having been here most of the winter; they left this [house] about a month ago, but where they are I know not, as they never wrote to me since their departure

Elizabeth & Henrietta are with us the latter last week came to us from Corsham, where she was principally on account of health, although her education was attended to, but the person who had been her music mistress previous to her becoming a partner in a school there, quitted it in consequence of not agreeing with the other lady and therefore I would not have her left behind

They are both in perfect health and unite with me in best love to you and am

Your affect.te Father

H. S. Blanckley

References

[1] Gérin W., Horatia Nelson Oxford University Press (1970), p. 220.

[2] Howarth, D.A. and Howarth, S., Nelson: the immortal memory. London: Conway Maritime. (2004), p. 205.

[3] British India Office Births & Baptisms, writers' petitions, © copyright brightsolid online publishing ltd. Available at: https://search.findmypast.co.uk/record?id=BL%2FBIND%2FJ-1-8-PART1%2F00103&parentid=BL%2FBIND%2F393 (accessed 29 November 2023).

[4] Francklin W., observations made on a tour from Bengal to Persia, in the Years 1786-7 (1790) p. 27. Available at: https://www.google.co.uk/books/edition/Observations_Made_on_a_Tour_from_Bengal/-Kk2AAAAMAAJ?hl=en&gbpv=1&dq=persia&pg=PA137&printsec=frontcover (accessed 5 December 2023).

[5] Grose J. H., A Voyage to the East-Indies, with Observations on Various Parts There (1757) p. 46. Available at: https://www.google.co.uk/books/edition/A_Voyage_to_the_East_Indies_with_Observa/CotCAAAAcAAJ?hl=en&gbpv=1&dq=bombay+fort&pg=PA57&printsec=frontcover (accessed 14 November 2023).

[6] Burke B., A Genealogical and Heraldic Dictionary of the Peerage and Baronetage of the British Empire, Harrison, (1865). Available at: https://play.google.com/store/books/details?id=8phVTmV9ChIC&rdid=book-8phVTmV9ChIC&rdot=1&pli=1 (Accessed 07 July 2023).

[7] Hill B., the language of dissent: the defense of eighteenth-century English dissent in the works and sermons of James Peirce, p. 372, PhD thesis, Baylor University, (2010). Available at: https://baylor-ir.tdl.org/handle/2104/8083 (accessed 28 July 2023)

[8] Pincus S. C. A., Protestantism and Patriotism: Ideologies and the Making of English Foreign Policy, 1650-1668, Cambridge University Press, (2002), p. 327.

[9] Selections from the letters, despatches, and other state papers preserved in Bombay Secretariat: home series, Forrest, George, Sir, 1846-1926; Bombay (presidency) Secretariat (1887) available at: https://archive.org/details/p1selectionsfrom01forruoft (accessed 27 October 2023).

[10] Whan R., The Presbyterians of Ulster, 1680-1730, Boydell & Brewer Ltd, (2013), p. 103

[11] Hill B. (2010) The Language of Dissent: The Defense of Eighteenth-Century English Dissent in the Works and Sermons of James Peirce, p. 357, PhD thesis, Baylor University. Available at: https://baylor-ir.tdl.org/handle/2104/8083 (accessed 28 July 2023)

[12] Church of St Andrew and St Columba (2022) Wikipedia. Available at: https://en.m.wikipedia.org/wiki/Church_of_St_Andrew_and_St_Columba (Accessed: 06 July 2023).

[13] Rayburn R. S., the Presbyterian doctrines of covenant children, covenant nurture and covenant succession, reformed perspective magazine (2016). Available at: https://thirdmill.org/magazine/article.asp/link/rob_rayburn%5Erob_rayburn.CovtChildren.html/at/The%20Presbyterian%20Doctrines%20of%20Covenant%20Children,%20Covenant%20Nurture%20and%20Covenant%20Succession (accessed 1 December 2023).

[14] Grose J. H., A Voyage to the East-Indies, with Observations on Various Parts There (1757) p. 81. Available at: https://www.google.co.uk/books/edition/A_Voyage_to_the_East_Indies_with_Observa/CotCAAAAcAAJ?hl=en&gbpv=1&dq=bombay+fort&pg=PA57&printsec=frontcover (accessed 14 November 2023).

[15] Ames Library pamphlet collection, Volume 46, Issues 1–10 (1765) p. 8. Available at: https://www.google.co.uk/books/edition/Ames_Library_Pamphlet_Collection/Qr3m_Ij31noC?hl=en&gbpv=1&dq=bombay+dock&pg=RA3-PA42&printsec=frontcover (accessed 18 November 2023).

[16] CHOPRA, P. (2012). Free to move, forced to flee: the formation and dissolution of suburbs in colonial Bombay, 1750–1918. Urban History, 39(1), 83–107. Available at: http://www.jstor.org/stable/26398118 (accessed 29 June 2023)

[17] Grose J. H., A Voyage to the East-Indies, with Observations on Various Parts There (1757) pp. 73-76. Available at: https://www.google.co.uk/books/edition/A_Voyage_to_the_East_Indies_with_Observa/CotCAAAAcAAJ?hl=en&gbpv=1&dq=bombay+fort&pg=PA57&printsec=frontcover (accessed 28 November 2023).

[18] Moses H., Sketches of India (1850) p. 54. Available at: https://www.google.co.uk/books/edition/Sketches_of_India/H4cIAAAAQAAJ?hl=en&gbpv=1&dq=bombay+dock&pg=PA76&printsec=frontcover (accessed 20 November 2023).

[19] Grose J. H., A Voyage to the East-Indies, with Observations on Various Parts There (1757) pp. 81–82, 83–84. Available at: https://www.google.co.uk/books/edition/A_Voyage_to_the_East_Indies_with_Observa/CotCAAAAcAAJ?hl=en&gbpv=1&dq=bombay+fort&pg=PA57&printsec=frontcover (accessed 14 November 2023).

[20] (Presidency), B. (1893) in Materials towards a statistical account of the town and island of Bombay. Bombay: Printed at the Government Central Press, p. 530.

[21] Grose J. H., A Voyage to the East-Indies, with Observations on Various Parts There (1757) p. 61. Available at: https://www.google.co.uk/books/edition/A_Voyage_to_the_East_Indies_with_Observa/CotCAAAAcAAJ?hl=en&gbpv=1&dq=bombay+fort&pg=PA57&printsec=frontcover (accessed 14 November 2023).

[22] Moor, E. (1801) A compilation of all the ... orders ... 1750 to ... 1801 ... of the Bombay Army, by E. Moor. P. 52. Available at: https://books.google.com/books/about/A_compilation_of_all_the_orders_1750_to.html?id=QpQNAAAAQAAJ (Accessed: 29 June 2023).

[23] Moor, E. (1801) A compilation of all the ... orders ... 1750 to ... 1801 ... of the Bombay Army, by E. Moor. P. 52. Available at: https://books.google.com/books/about/A_compilation_of_all_the_orders_1750_to.html?id=QpQNAAAAQAAJ (Accessed: 29 June 2023).

[24] Brannan J., childhood in the eighteenth century (2021). Available at: https://juliabrannan.com/historical-articles/childhood-in-the-18th-century/ (accessed 1 December 2023).

[25] Hodges R., list of 18th century toys and games, National Park Service (2018). Available at: https://www.nps.gov/articles/000/list-of-18th-century-toys-games.htm (accessed 2 December 2023).

[26] How the Parsis Shaped Theatre in Colonial Bombay (no date) The Wire. Available at: https://thewire.in/culture/bombay-theatre-cinema-parsis (Accessed: 29 June 2023).

[27] Wright, C. (2008) 'view of Bombay Harbour, taken from the island of Colaba'. uncoloured lithograph by W. Watson from C. Head's Eastern and Egyptian Scenery London, 1833. printed by C. Hullmandel., The British Library - The British Library. Available at: https://www.bl.uk/onlinegallery/onlineex/apac/other/019pzz000002438u00 000000.html (Accessed: 29 June 2023).

[28] Scott and Gibson, Calcutta Gazette, 26th July 1787, p. 2. Copyright British Library Board. Find My Past: https://search.findmypast.co.uk/bna/viewarticle? id=BL/0002676/17870726/011&stringtohighlight=cricket%20bombay (viewed 7th July 2023).

[29] History of cricket (no date) International Cricket Council. Available at: https://www.icc-cricket.com/about/cricket/history-of-cricket/early-cricket (Accessed: 07 July 2023).

[30] InfoMoni (2014) The Parsi team--the first Indian cricket team to tour England in 1886, Facebook. Available at: https://www.facebook.com/Infomoni.Simplified/photos/a.1621775938368 10/717912841596613/?type=3 (Accessed: 07 July 2023).

[31] Edpope (no date) Ed Pope History. Available at: https://edpopehistory.co.uk/entries/hodges-thomas-hallett/1000-01-01-000000 (Accessed: 06 July 2023).

[32] Bombay European Regiment (no date) Bombay European Regiment - Project Seven Years War. Available at: https://www.kronoskaf.com/syw/index.php? title=Bombay_European_Regiment (Accessed: 06 July 2023).

[33] Samuel Hough (no date) My Jacob Family. Available at: https://www.myjacobfamily.com/favershamjacobs/samuelhough.htm (Accessed: 06 July 2023).

[34] Grose J. H., A Voyage to the East-Indies, with Observations on Various Parts There (1757) p. 67. Available at: https://www.google.co.uk/books/edition/A_Voyage_to_the_East_Indies_w ith_Observa/CotCAAAAcAAJ? hl=en&gbpv=1&dq=bombay+fort&pg=PA57&printsec=frontcover (accessed 14 November 2023).

[35] Physics Wallah (1969) The city in colonial India class 10: PW, Physics Wallah. Available at: https://www.pw.live/chapter-work-life-and-

leisure/the-city-in-colonial-india (Accessed: 29 June 2023).

[36] Grose J. H., A Voyage to the East-Indies, with Observations on Various Parts There (1757) p. 72. Available at: https://www.google.co.uk/books/edition/A_Voyage_to_the_East_Indies_with_Observa/CotCAAAAcAAJ?hl=en&gbpv=1&dq=bombay+fort&pg=PA57&printsec=frontcover (accessed 14 November 2023).

[37] How the Parsis Shaped Theatre in Colonial Bombay (no date) The Wire. Available at: https://thewire.in/culture/bombay-theatre-cinema-parsis (Accessed: 29 June 2023).

[38] Matcham, M.E. (1911) The Nelsons of Burnham Thorpe: a record of a Norfolk family compiled from unpublished letters and notebooks, 1787-1842, pp. 31–32

[39] Stadtler F., and Visram R., our migration story, A home for the ayahs: from India to Britain and back again (no date). Available at: https://www.ourmigrationstory.org.uk/oms/a-home-for-the-ayahs- (accessed 20 November 2023).

[40] Wiltshire and Swindon History Centre: Eyre-Matcham family of Newhouse, Whiteparish and Downton; 3 - deeds etc. Matcham family: not main estate, 1369/3/1, Probate of the will of Simon Matcham of Bombay, India (proved in Bombay) 1776; will made 1758.

[41] In colonial Bombay, slavery practiced by both Indians and the British administration (no date). Available at: https://thewire.in/history/bombay-slavery-africa (accessed 28 July 2023).

[42] Matcham, M.E. (1911) The Nelsons of Burnham Thorpe: a record of a Norfolk family compiled from unpublished letters and notebooks, 1787-1842, pp. 31–32

[43] CHOPRA, P. (2012). Free to move, forced to flee: the formation and dissolution of suburbs in colonial Bombay, 1750–1918. Urban History, 39(1), 83–107. Available at: http://www.jstor.org/stable/26398118 (viewed 29 June 2023)

[44] Pollard A. E. (1885–1900) Dictionary of National Biography: Matcham, George. Available online: https://en.wikisource.org/wiki/Dictionary_of_National_Biography,_1885-1900/Matcham,_George (viewed 29 June 2023)

[45] Francklin W., observations made on a tour from Bengal to Persia, in the Years 1786-7 (1790) pp. 27-28. Available at: https://www.google.co.uk/books/edition/Observations_Made_on_a_Tour_from_Bengal/-Kk2AAAAMAAJ?

hl=en&gbpv=1&dq=persia&pg=PA137&printsec=frontcover (accessed 5 December 2023).

[46] British Library (online), 'Bombay: History of a City' Accessed online, May 2018:
http://www.bl.uk/learning/histcitizen/trading/bombay/history.html

[47] Rodrigues, D.C. (1994) Bombay fort in the Eighteenth Century. Bombay: Himalaya Pub. House.

[48] Physics Wallah (1969) The city in colonial India class 10: PW, Physics Wallah. Available at: https://www.pw.live/chapter-work-life-and-leisure/the-city-in-colonial-india (Accessed: 29 June 2023).

[49] Matcham, M.E. (1911) The Nelsons of Burnham Thorpe: a record of a Norfolk family compiled from unpublished letters and notebooks, 1787-1842, pp. 30–31.

[50] Forbes J., oriental memoirs: a narrative of seventeen years residence in India, volume 1, pp. 420 – 421. Available at:
https://books.google.co.uk/books?id=r2IOAAAAQAAJ&pg=PA420&lpg=PA420&dq=matcham+bombay+mermaids&source=bl&ots=cBDdp7OsH2&sig=V3mPtkeUwKFFYbHQdHja-RgjNos&hl=en&sa=X&ved=0ahUKEwjL8uG0zojPAhWpD8AKHY73CIoQ6AEINjAF#v=onepage&q=matcham%20bombay%20mermaids&f=false (accessed 27 January 2024).

[51] Good, P. (2022) An 18th-century letter to Bombay shows what it was like to be in service of the East India Company, Scroll.in. Available at: https://scroll.in/article/1027201/a-letter-from-yemen-to-bombay-gives-insight-into-the-lived-experience-of-east-india-company-service (Accessed: 08 July 2023).

[52] Encyclopaedia Britannica, battle of Plassey (2023). Available at: https://www.britannica.com/event/Battle-of-Plassey (accessed 21 November 2023).

[53] Encyclopaedia Britannica, Black Hole of Calcutta | Mughal Empire, Nawab of Bengal, Massacre (2023). Available at: https://www.britannica.com/topic/Black-Hole-of-Calcutta (accessed 21 November 2023).

[54] Aris's Birmingham Gazette, 13th June 1757, p. 1. © Birmingham City Council. All rights reserved. Find My Past: https://www.findmypast.co.uk/image-viewer?issue=BL%2F0000196%2F17570613&page=1&article=002&stringtohighlight=calcutta

(accessed 22 November 2023).

[55] Derby Mercury, 10th June 1757, p. 3. Copyright British Library Board. Find My Past: https://www.findmypast.co.uk/image-viewer?issue=BL%2F0000189%2F17570610&page=3&article=010&stringtohighlight=calcutta

(accessed 22 November 2023).

[56] Derby Mercury, 3rd June 1757, p. 3. Copyright British Library Board. Find My Past: https://www.findmypast.co.uk/image-viewer?issue=BL%2F0000189%2F17570603&page=3&article=010&stringtohighlight=bombay+bengal

(accessed 22 November 2023).

[57] Newcastle Courant, 25th June 1757, p. 1. Copyright British Library Board. Find My Past: https://www.findmypast.co.uk/image-viewer?issue=BL%2F0000189%2F17570603&page=3&article=010&stringtohighlight=bombay+bengal

(accessed 22 November 2023).

[58] Wiltshire and Swindon History Centre: Eyre-Matcham family of Newhouse, Whiteparish and Downton; 3 - deeds etc. Matcham family: not main estate, 1369/3/1, Probate of the will of Simon Matcham of Bombay, India (proved in Bombay) 1776; will made 1758.

[59] Wiltshire and Swindon History Centre: Eyre-Matcham family of Newhouse, Whiteparish and Downton; 3 - deeds etc. Matcham family: not main estate, 1369/3/1, Probate of the will of Simon Matcham of Bombay, India (proved in Bombay) 1776; will made 1758.

[60] Aris's Birmingham Gazette, 11th June 1759, p. 3. Copyright Birmingham City Council. All rights reserved. Available at: https://www.findmypast.co.uk/image-viewer?issue=BL%2F0000196%2F17590611&page=3&article=007&stringtohighlight=hardwick

(accessed 23 November 2023).

[61] Oxford Journal, 14th October 1758, p. 2. Copyright British Library Board. Find My Past: https://www.findmypast.co.uk/image-viewer?issue=BL%2F0000189%2F17570603&page=3&article=010&stringtohighlight=bombay+bengal

(accessed 23 November 2023).

Markley, Robert. "'A PUTRIDNESS IN THE AIR': Monsoons and [62]

Mortality in Seventeenth-Century Bombay." *Journal for Early Modern Cultural Studies*, vol. 10, no. 2, [Indiana University Press, University of Pennsylvania Press], 2010, pp. 105–25, .http://www.jstor.org/stable/23242143

[63] Poona (no date) Poona - FIBIwiki. Available at: https://wiki.fibis.org/w/Poona (Accessed: 30 June 2023).

[64] Kosambi, M. and Brush, J.E. (1988) 'Three colonial port cities in India', Geographical Review, 78(1), p. 32. doi:10.2307/214304

Markley, Robert. "'A PUTRIDNESS IN THE AIR': Monsoons and [65] Mortality in Seventeenth-Century Bombay." *Journal for Early Modern Cultural Studies*, vol. 10, no. 2, [Indiana University Press, University of Pennsylvania Press], 2010, pp. 105–25. Available at .(http://www.jstor.org/stable/23242143 (accessed January 2022

[66] Grose J. H., A Voyage to the East-Indies, with Observations on Various Parts There (1757) pp. 48, 51-52. Available at: https://www.google.co.uk/books/edition/A_Voyage_to_the_East_Indies_with_Observa/CotCAAAAcAAJ? hl=en&gbpv=1&dq=bombay+fort&pg=PA57&printsec=frontcover (accessed 14 November 2023).

[67] Richardson A., et al, modern part of an universal history from the earliest time, (1759) p. 289. Available at: https://www.google.co.uk/books/edition/The_Modern_Part_of_an_Universal_History/t9gGAAAAcAAJ?hl=en&gbpv=1&dq=Barbeers&pg=RA1-PA289&printsec=frontcover (accessed 16 November 2023).

[68] Markley, R., a putridness in the air, monsoons and mortality in seventeenth-century Bombay, journal for early modern cultural studies, vol. 10, no. 2, Indiana University Press, University of Pennsylvania Press (2010) pp. 105–25. Available at http://www.jstor.org/stable/23242143 (accessed January 2022).

[69] Manchester Mercury, 6th March 1764, p. 2. Copyright British Library Board. Find My Past: https://www.findmypast.co.uk/image-viewer? issue=BL %2F0000239%2F17640306&page=2&article=008&stringtohighlight=ship +bombay

(accessed 19 November 2023).

[70] Hamilton, W., Nelson, H. N., Hamilton, E., Pettigrew, T. J. (1894). The Hamilton & Nelson Papers ... 1756-[1815]: 1798-1815. United Kingdom: private circulation, p. 81. Available at: https://www.google.co.uk/books/edition/The_Hamilton_Nelson_Papers_1

756_1815_179/qDeIqic5uwAC?hl=en&gbpv=1&dq=matcham+shepherd%27s+spring&pg=PA81&printsec=frontcover (accessed 8 September 2023).

[71] Marshall I., Passage East (1997). Available at: https://archive.nytimes.com/www.nytimes.com/books/first/m/marshall-east.html?_r=1&oref=slogin (accessed 18 November 2023).

[72] Diary, Consultations, and Accounts of Nathaniel Whitwell and Henry Savage, Agents of the East India Company at Gambroon [Bandar-e 'Abbās] in the Persian Gulf, commencing 1 August 1746 and ending 31 July 1752 [11v] (29/802), British Library: India Office Records and Private Papers, IOR/G/29/7, in Qatar Digital Library <https://www.qdl.qa/archive/81055/vdc_100127021648.0x00001e> [accessed 3 July 2023]

[73] Find My Past: record transcription. Ref: N-3-1. Folio: 351. Catalogue descriptions: Parish register transcripts from the Presidency of Bombay, 1709-1948. Record set: British India Office births & baptisms ecclesiastical returns. Copyright bright solid online publishing LTD. Find My Past: https://www.findmypast.co.uk/transcript?id=BL%2FBIND%2FB%2F378924 [accessed 3 July 2023].

[74] Matcham, M.E. (1911) The Nelsons of Burnham Thorpe: a record of a Norfolk family compiled from unpublished letters and notebooks, 1787-1842, p. 32.

[75] Jackson's Oxford Journal, 14th April 1764, p. 3. Copyright British Library Board. Find My Past: https://www.findmypast.co.uk/image-viewer?issue=BL%2F0000073%2F17640414&page=3&article=014&stringtohighlight=henry+savage

(accessed 19 November 2023).

[76] Matcham, M.E. (1911) The Nelsons of Burnham Thorpe: a record of a Norfolk family compiled from unpublished letters and notebooks, 1787-1842, p. 32.

[77] Newcastle Courant, 13th August 1763, p. 1. Copyright British Library Board. Find My Past: https://www.findmypast.co.uk/image-viewer?issue=BL%2F0000085%2F17630813&page=1&article=001&stringtohighlight=ship+bombay

(accessed 20 November 2023).

[78] Shipping wonders of the world, life in the East Indiamen (no date).Available at:

https://www.shippingwondersoftheworld.com/east_indiamen.html (accessed 21 November 2023).

[79] National archives, Currency converter: 1270–2017 (no date). Available at: https://www.nationalarchives.gov.uk/currency-converter/#currency-result (accessed 21 November 2023).

[80] Shipping wonders of the world, life in the East Indiamen (no date). Available at: https://www.shippingwondersoftheworld.com/east_indiamen.html (accessed 21 November 2023).

[81] British Library, Sobriety and decorum - Passengers on East India Company ships (2021). Available at:https://blogs.bl.uk/untoldlives/2021/06/sobriety-and-decorum-passengers-on-east-india-company-ships.html (accessed 25 November 2023).

[82] Portland Museum, Life on board the Earl of Abergavenny (no date). Available at: https://portlandmuseum.co.uk/life-on-board-the-earl-of-abergavenny/ (accessed 25 November 2023).

[83] Bath Chronicle and Weekly Gazette, 7th July 1763, p. 1. Copyright British Library Board. Find My Past: https://www.findmypast.co.uk/image-viewer?issue=BL%2F0000211%2F17630707&page=1&article=006&stringtohighlight=bombay

 (accessed 19 November 2023).

[84] Charterhouse, about us, (no date). Available at: https://www.charterhouse.org.uk/about-us/charterhouse/history-archives (accessed 26 November 2023).

[85] Charterhouse archivist correspondence with author by email, 2016.

[86] The Charterhouse (no date) British History Online. Available at: https://www.british-history.ac.uk/old-new-london/vol2/pp380-404 (Accessed: 02 July 2023).

[87] Marshall I. (1997) "Passage East', Howell Press. Accessed via New York Times website, 14th January 2021, http://www.nytimes.com/books/first/m/marshall-east.html

[88] Thornbury W., 'The Charterhouse', in Old and New London: Volume 2 (London, 1878), pp. 380-404. British History Online http://www.british-history.ac.uk/old-new-london/vol2/pp380-404 [accessed 2 July 2023].

[89] Ibid.

[90] Ibid.

[91] Brannan B., Education in the 18th century – boys (2021). Available at https://juliabrannan.com/historical-articles/education-in-the-18th-century-boys/#:~:text=The%20heart%20of%20an%20education,learn%20logic%2C%20history%20and%20geograpy (accessed 14 November 2023)

[92] Ibid.

[93] Goodman, R. (2015) in How to be a victorian: A dawn-to-dusk guide to victorian life. New York: Liveright Publishing Corporation, a division of W.W. Norton & Company, p. 325.

[94] Online http://www.british-history.ac.uk/old-new-london/vol2/pp380-404 [accessed 2 July 2023].

[95] Bertlatsky J., British Imperial Attitudes in the Early Modern Era: The Case of Charles Ware Malet in India, Albion: A Quarterly Journal Concerned with British Studies, Vol. 14, No. 2 (1982) p. 140. Available at: https://www.jstor.org/stable/4049188?read-now=1&seq=2#page_scan_tab_contents (accessed 8 February 2024).

[96] Charterhouse archivist correspondence with author by email, 2016.

[97] Matcham, M.E. (1911) The Nelsons of Burnham Thorpe: a record of a Norfolk family compiled from unpublished letters and notebooks, 1787-1842, p. 35.

[98] Matcham, M.E. (1911) The Nelsons of Burnham Thorpe: a record of a Norfolk family compiled from unpublished letters and notebooks, 1787-1842, p. 32.

[99] Charterhouse archivist correspondence with author by email, 2016.

[100] Hidden London, Bromley-by-Bow, Tower Hamlets: a historic East End district situated between Bow and Poplar (no date). Available at: https://hidden-london.com/gazetteer/bromley-by-bow/ (accessed 27 November 2023).

[101] British India Office Writers' Petitions Image, Find My Past archive record. Available at: https://search.findmypast.co.uk/record?id=BL%2FBIND%2FJ-1-8-PART1%2F00103&parentid=BL%2FBIND%2F393 (accessed 26 November 2032).

[102] FIBI, Lists of Free Merchants, Seafaring Men and other Inhabitants of Bombay and surrounds from 1720-1780 (2012). Available at: https://fibis.ourarchives.online/bin/aps_detail.php?id=1122935 (accessed 21 November 2023).

[103] FIBIwiki, Maritime Service (no date). Available at:

https://wiki.fibis.org/w/Maritime_Service (accessed 21 November 2023).

[104] Francklin W., observations made on a tour from Bengal to Persia, in the Years 1786-7 (1790) p. 27. Available at: https://www.google.co.uk/books/edition/Observations_Made_on_a_Tour_from_Bengal/-Kk2AAAAMAAJ?hl=en&gbpv=1&dq=persia&pg=PA137&printsec=frontcover (accessed 5 December 2023).

[105] Sugden, J. (2012) Nelson: A Dream of Glory. Random House. Kindle Edition. P. 377.

[106] East India Company, The Bengal Calendar for the Year 1787 (1788); Including a List of the ... East India Company's Civil and Military Servants on the Bengal Establishment, Etc

Volume 2, p. 61. Available at: https://www.google.co.uk/books/edition/The_Bengal_Calendar_for_the_Year_1787_17/w0EV4C6IJs4C?hl=en&gbpv=1&dq=matcham&pg=PA61&printsec=frontcover (accessed 23 November 2023).

[107] Wikipedia contributors, Joseph Émïn (2023). Available at: https://en.wikipedia.org/wiki/Joseph_Emin (accessed 27 November 2023).

[108] Émïn J., (1792) Life and adventures of Émïn, 1726-1809. Baptist Mission Press. Pp. 473-474. Available at: https://books.google.co.uk/books?id=7qY0AQAAMAAJ&pg=PA474&lpg=PA474&dq=bombay+marine+superintendent+matcham&source=bl&ots=bRidUo3QOj&sig=ACfU3U3RmY-8heB8L9BomIRFvAaHnJS33Q&hl=en&sa=X&ved=2ahUKEwis6LKRx6j1AhUsREEAHTjDAJkQ6AF6BAgQEAM#v=onepage&q&f=false. (Accessed 14 July 2023)

[109] Ancestry.com. UK, Registers of Employees of the East India Company and the India Office, 1746-1939. Available at: https://www.ancestry.co.uk/discoveryui-content/view/102675:61468?_phsrc=ECs2350&_phstart=successSource&gsfn=george&gsln=matcham&ml_rpos=1&queryId=1715966b814bce7640e7b4721263e032 (accessed 23 November 2023)

[110] https://wiki.fibis.org/w/Senior_Merchant

[111] Editors of Wikipedia, East India Company (2023). Available at:https://en.wikipedia.org/wiki/East_India_Company (accessed 11 December 2023).

[112] Chambers Encyclopaedia (1862) Vol. III. P. 743

[113] Editors of Wikipedia, battle of Plassey (2023). Available at: https://en.wikipedia.org/wiki/Battle_of_Plassey#Battle (accessed 11 December 2023).

[114] Dalrymple W., The East India Company: The original corporate raiders, The Guardian (2015). Available at: https://www.theguardian.com/world/2015/mar/04/east-india-company-original-corporate-raiders (accessed 29 November 2023).

[115] https://scroll.in/magazine/855386/glimpses-from-the-life-of-an-18th-century-english-merchant-who-made-a-fortune-selling-salt-in-bengal

[116] Editors of Wikipedia, Maratha Empire (2023). Available at: https://en.wikipedia.org/wiki/Maratha_Empire (accessed 11 December 2023).

[117] New world encyclopaedia, Maratha empire (no date). Available at: https://www.newworldencyclopedia.org/entry/Maratha_Empire (accessed 11 December 2023).

[118] BYJU, Mahadji Shinde (no date). Available at: https://byjus.com/free-ias-prep/mahadji-shinde-1730-1794/ (accessed 11 December 2023).

[119] Bombay Presidency, gazetteer of the Bombay Presidency, volume 18, issue 2

(1885) p. 284. Available at: https://www.google.co.uk/books/edition/Gazetteer_of_the_Bombay_Presidency/E4tIAQAAMAAJ?hl=en&gbpv=1&dq=Maratha+War-Camps&pg=PA284&printsec=frontcover (accessed 10 December 2023).

[120] Rajadhyaksha A., the history files, early modern India, Maratha Aristocracy: the Scindias of Gwalior (2010). Available at: https://www.historyfiles.co.uk/FeaturesFarEast/India_EarlyModern_Marathas11.htm (accessed 11 December 2023).

[121] Editors of Wikipedia, Madhavrao I (2023). Available at: https://en.wikipedia.org/wiki/Madhavrao_I (accessed 11 December 2023).

[122] Google arts and culture, Narayan Rao (no date). Available at: https://artsandculture.google.com/entity/narayan-rao/m04k3sf?hl=en (accessed 11 December 2023).

[123] Universal Magazine of Knowledge and Pleasure, Volumes 52–53 (1773) pp. 50-51. Available at: https://www.google.co.uk/books/edition/Universal_Magazine_of_Knowle

dge_and_Plea/Ki02AAAAMAAJ?
hl=en&gbpv=1&dq=broach+india&pg=RA1-PA50&printsec=frontcover
(accessed 8 December 2023).

[124] Fisher M. H., Indirect Rule in the British Empire: the foundations of
the residency

system in India (1764-1858), Cambridge University Press (1984).
Available at: https://www.jstor.org/stable/312261?read-
now=1&seq=1#page_scan_tab_contents (accessed 9 December 2023).

[125]

https://en.wikisource.org/wiki/Dictionary_of_National_Biography,_1885-
1900/Matcham,_George

[126] The European magazine, and London review, volume 5 (1784) p. 132.
Available at:
https://www.google.co.uk/books/edition/The_European_Magazine_and_L
ondon_Review/4VE3AAAAMAAJ?
hl=en&gbpv=1&dq=burke+bombay&pg=PA132&printsec=frontcover
(accessed 2 December 2023).

[127] Grose J. H., A Voyage to the East-Indies, with Observations on
Various Parts There (1757) p. 63. Available at:
https://www.google.co.uk/books/edition/A_Voyage_to_the_East_Indies_w
ith_Observa/CotCAAAAcAAJ?
hl=en&gbpv=1&dq=bombay+fort&pg=PA57&printsec=frontcover
(accessed 14 November 2023).

[128] Shah, A. (2019) Bharuch - Gujarat's ancient port city, PeepulTree.
Available at:
https://www.peepultree.world/livehistoryindia/story/places/bharuch-indias-
second-oldest-city (Accessed: 02 July 2023).

[129] Tickoo M. L. and Bhaskaran M. P., and Shanta R. R. (2005) 'Gul
Mohar', India: Orient BlackSwan.

[130] https://www.jstor.org/stable/44147197

[131] Thévenot, J. d., Lovell, A. (1687). The Travels Of Monsieur De
Thevenot Into The Levant: In Three Parts. United Kingdom: Faithorne. Pp.
7–8.

[132] Batchu, R.R. (2009) Socio-political structure of Gujarat in the
eighteenth century. Available at:
https://ia800804.us.archive.org/30/items/LandRevenueAdministrationUnd
erTheMughals_201710/SocioPoliticalStructureOfGujaratInTheEighteenth
Century.pdf (viewed 2 July2023)

[133] https://en.wikipedia.org/wiki/Bafta_cloth

[134] Thévenot, J. d., Lovell, A. (1687). The Travels Of Monsieur De Thevenot Into The Levant: In Three Parts. United Kingdom: Faithorne. P. 8.

[135] Core, The Residents of the British East India Company at Indian royal courts, c. 1798-1818 (2017). Available at: https://core.ac.uk/download/pdf/131382643.pdf (accessed 8 December 2023).

[136] The Cambridge Economic History of India: Volume 2, C.1757-c.1970, 1983. P. 347 Accessed online 14 January 2022. https://www.google.co.uk/books/edition/The_Cambridge_Economic_History_of_India/9ew8AAAAIAAJ?hl=en&gbpv=1&dq=broach+gujarat&pg=PA347&printsec=frontcover

[137] Matcham, M.E. (1911) The Nelsons of Burnham Thorpe: a record of a Norfolk family compiled from unpublished letters and notebooks, 1787-1842, p. 32

[138] Gérin W., Horatia Nelson Oxford University Press (1970), p. 220.

[139] GK Today, Treaty of Surat (2013). Available at: https://www.gktoday.in/treaty-of-surat/ (accessed 11 December 2023).

[140] Sulivan R. J., an analysis of the political history of India (1779) p. 81. Available at: https://www.google.co.uk/books/edition/An_Analysis_of_the_Political_History_of/_IbsXsKpIrkC?hl=en&gbpv=1&dq=treaty+bombay&pg=PA81&printsec=frontcover (accessed 11 December 2023).

[141] Duff J. G., A History of the Mahrattas (1826) p. 283. Available at: https://www.ibiblio.org/britishraj/Duff2/chapter09.html (accessed 11 December 2023).

[142] Gross J. H., A Voyage to the East Indies (1772) p. 98. Available at: https://www.google.co.uk/books/edition/A_Voyage_to_the_East_Indies/RrA2AAAAMAAJ?hl=en&gbpv=1&dq=surat+castle&pg=PA98-IA1&printsec=frontcover (accessed 11 December 2023).

[143] Sen N. S., the origins of the first Anglo-Maratha war, proceedings of the Indian History Congress, 22, 400–402. Available at: http://www.jstor.org/stable/44304328 (accessed 11 December 2023).

[144] History Flame, Treaty of Surat – terms, conflicts and war (no date). Available at: https://historyflame.com/treaty-of-surat/ (accessed 11 December 2023).

[145] Hunter W. W., the Indian Empire (2005) p. 391. Available at: https://books.google.co.uk/books?id=yUhvfR1S_UEC&dq=treaty+of+surat&pg=PA391&redir_esc=y#v=onepage&q&f=false (accessed 11 December 2023).

[146] Derby Mercury, 25th June 1773, p. 1. Copyright British Library Board. Find My Past: https://www.findmypast.co.uk/image-viewer?issue=BL%2F0000189%2F17730625&page=1&article=004&stringtohighlight=broach

(accessed 13 December 2023).

[147] Sulivan R. J., an analysis of the political history of India (1779) pp. 81-82. Available at: https://www.google.co.uk/books/edition/An_Analysis_of_the_Political_History_of/_IbsXsKpIrkC?hl=en&gbpv=1&dq=treaty+bombay&pg=PA81&printsec=frontcover (accessed 12 December 2023).

[148] Sen N. S., the origins of the first Anglo-Maratha war, proceedings of the Indian History Congress, 22, 400–402. Available at: http://www.jstor.org/stable/44304328 (accessed 12 December 2023).

[149] Irwin, E. (1787) A Series of Adventures in the Course of a Voyage Up the Red-Sea.... P. 142. Available at: https://www.google.co.uk/books/edition/A_Series_of_Adventures_in_the_Course_of/_VVWAAAAYAAJ?hl=en&gbpv=0 (accessed January 2022).

[150] https://www.navalhistoryarchive.org/index.php/Bombay_Marine

[151] Pp 474–475 Life and Adventures of Joseph Émïn, 1726-1809, Volume 2. P. 474 URL https://books.google.co.uk/books?id=7qY0AQAAMAAJ&pg=PA474&lpg=PA474&dq=bombay+marine+superintendent+matcham&source=bl&ots=bRidUo3QOj&sig=ACfU3U3RmY-8heB8L9BomIRFvAaHnJS33Q&hl=en&sa=X&ved=2ahUKEwis6LKRx6j1AhUsREEAHTjDAJkQ6AF6BAgQEAM#v=onepage&q&f=false

[152] https://search.findmypast.co.uk/record?id=BL%2FBIND%2F005137654%2F00023&parentid=BL%2FBIND%2FD%2F368260

[153] Matcham, M.E. (1911) The Nelsons of Burnham Thorpe: a record of a Norfolk family compiled from unpublished letters and notebooks, 1787-1842, p. 32

[154] Matcham, M.E. (1911) The Nelsons of Burnham Thorpe: a record of a Norfolk family compiled from unpublished letters and notebooks, 1787-1842, p. 35.

[155] Capper, J., Observations on the passage to India, through Egypt... (1785) p. v. Available at: https://www.google.co.uk/books/edition/Observations_on_the_Passage_to_India_Thr/HMMRAAAAYAAJ?hl=en&gbpv=1&dq=capper+red+sea&printsec=frontcover (accessed 29 October 2023).

[156] Encyclopaedia Britannica, Seven Years' War | Definition, Summary, Timeline, Causes, Effects, maps, significance, & Facts, (2023). Available at: https://www.britannica.com/event/Seven-Years-War (accessed 29 October 2023).

[157] Defence in depth, Co-dependent empires during the seven years war: strategy, Spanish neutrality, and law, King's College, London, (2017). Available at: https://defenceindepth.co/2017/09/11/co-dependent-empires-during-the-seven-years-war-strategy-spanish-neutrality-and-law/ (accessed 29 October 2023).

[158] Capper, J., Observations on the passage to India, through Egypt... (1785) p. v. Available at: https://www.google.co.uk/books/edition/Observations_on_the_Passage_to_India_Thr/HMMRAAAAYAAJ?hl=en&gbpv=1&dq=capper+red+sea&printsec=frontcover (accessed 29 October 2023).

[159] Capper, J., Observations on the passage to India, through Egypt... (1785) p. xxiv. Available at: https://www.google.co.uk/books/edition/Observations_on_the_Passage_to_India_Thr/HMMRAAAAYAAJ?hl=en&gbpv=1&dq=capper+red+sea&printsec=frontcover (accessed 29 October 2023).

[160] Defence in depth, Co-dependent empires during the seven years war: strategy, Spanish neutrality, and law, King's College, London, (2017). Available at: https://defenceindepth.co/2017/09/11/co-dependent-empires-during-the-seven-years-war-strategy-spanish-neutrality-and-law/ (accessed 30 October 2023).

[161] Capper, J., Observations on the passage to India, through Egypt... (1785) p. v. Available at: https://www.google.co.uk/books/edition/Observations_on_the_Passage_to_India_Thr/HMMRAAAAYAAJ?hl=en&gbpv=1&dq=capper+red+sea&printsec=frontcover (accessed 29 October 2023).

[162] Capper, J., Observations on the passage to India, through Egypt... (1785) p. xxvi. Available at:

https://www.google.co.uk/books/edition/Observations_on_the_Passage_to _India_Thr/HMMRAAAAYAAJ? hl=en&gbpv=1&dq=capper+red+sea&printsec=frontcover (accessed 30 October 2023).

[163] Capper, J., Observations on the passage to India, through Egypt... (1785) p. xiv. Available at: https://www.google.co.uk/books/edition/Observations_on_the_Passage_to _India_Thr/HMMRAAAAYAAJ? hl=en&gbpv=1&dq=capper+red+sea&printsec=frontcover (accessed 30 October 2023).

[164] Byju, List of Governors-General of India | UPSC Notes (2023). Available at: https://byjus.com/free-ias-prep/governers-generals-of-bengal-and-india (accessed 30 November 2023).

[165] Capper, J., Observations on the passage to India, through Egypt... (1785) pp. xvi-xvii. Available at: https://www.google.co.uk/books/edition/Observations_on_the_Passage_to _India_Thr/HMMRAAAAYAAJ? hl=en&gbpv=1&dq=capper+red+sea&printsec=frontcover (accessed 1 November 2023).

[166] Encyclopaedia Britannica, Ottoman Empire | Facts, History, & Map (2023). Available t: https://www.britannica.com/place/Ottoman-Empire/Sultans-of-the-Ottoman-Empire (accessed 2 November 2023).

[167] Capper, J., Observations on the passage to India, through Egypt... (1785) p. xxii. Available at: https://www.google.co.uk/books/edition/Observations_on_the_Passage_to _India_Thr/HMMRAAAAYAAJ? hl=en&gbpv=1&dq=capper+red+sea&printsec=frontcover (accessed 30 October 2023).

[168] Stamford Mercury, 15th October 1776, p. 2. Copyright British Library Board. Find My Past: https://www.findmypast.co.uk/image-viewer? issue=BL %2F0000254%2F17760215&page=2&article=002&stringtohighlight=sue z

 (accessed 13 November 2023).

[169] Capper, J., Observations on the passage to India, through Egypt... (1785) p. vi. Available at: https://www.google.co.uk/books/edition/Observations_on_the_Passage_to _India_Thr/HMMRAAAAYAAJ? hl=en&gbpv=1&dq=capper+red+sea&printsec=frontcover (accessed 30 October 2023).

[170] Matcham, M.E. (1911) The Nelsons of Burnham Thorpe: a record of a Norfolk family compiled from unpublished letters and notebooks, 1787-1842, p. 32.

[171] Francklin W., observations made on a tour from Bengal to Persia, in the Years 1786-7 (1790) pp. 33-34. Available at: https://www.google.co.uk/books/edition/Observations_Made_on_a_Tour_from_Bengal/-Kk2AAAAMAAJ?hl=en&gbpv=1&dq=persia&pg=PA137&printsec=frontcover (accessed 5 December 2023).

[172] Indian shipping at Basra the incident of 1820 on JSTOR (no date). Available at: https://www.jstor.org/stable/44143063?read-now=1#page_scan_tab_contents (accessed January 2022)

[173] Capper, J., Observations on the passage to India, through Egypt... (1785) pp. xxvii–xxix. Available at: https://www.google.co.uk/books/edition/Observations_on_the_Passage_to_India_Thr/HMMRAAAAYAAJ?hl=en&gbpv=1&dq=capper+red+sea&printsec=frontcover (accessed 29 October 2023).

[174] Eton, W., A survey of the Turkish Empire..., (1799), p. 105. (Available at: https://www.google.co.uk/books/edition/A_survey_of_the_Turkish_Empire_In_which/zKlXAAAAcAAJ?hl=en&gbpv=1&dq=turkish+dreff&pg=PA105&printsec=frontcover (accessed 2 November 2023).

[175] Matcham, M.E. (1911) The Nelsons of Burnham Thorpe: a record of a Norfolk family compiled from unpublished letters and notebooks, 1787-1842, pp. 32–33.

[176] World Bank Climate Change Knowledge Portal (no date) Climatology | Climate Change Knowledge Portal. Available at: https://climateknowledgeportal.worldbank.org/country/saudi-arabia/climate-data-historical (Accessed: 10 July 2023).

[177] Capper, J., Observations on the passage to India, through Egypt... (1785) pp. xxvii–xxix. Available at: https://www.google.co.uk/books/edition/Observations_on_the_Passage_to_India_Thr/HMMRAAAAYAAJ?hl=en&gbpv=1&dq=capper+red+sea&printsec=frontcover (accessed 29 October 2023).

[178] Horne T. H., A View of the Commerce of Greece, formed after an annual average, from 1787 to 1797, (1800), p. 256. Available at: https://www.google.co.uk/books/edition/A_View_of_the_Commerce_of_

Greece_formed/C5ddAAAAcAAJ?
hl=en&gbpv=1&dq=bassora&pg=PA255&printsec=frontcover (accessed 15 November 2023).

[179] Matcham, M.E. (1911) The Nelsons of Burnham Thorpe: a record of a Norfolk family compiled from unpublished letters and notebooks, 1787-1842, pp. 32–33.

[180] Matcham, M.E. (1911) The Nelsons of Burnham Thorpe: a record of a Norfolk family compiled from unpublished letters and notebooks, 1787-1842, p. 33.

[181] Capper, J., Observations on the passage to India, through Egypt... (1785) p. xxix. Available at: https://www.google.co.uk/books/edition/Observations_on_the_Passage_to_India_Thr/HMMRAAAAYAAJ? hl=en&gbpv=1&dq=capper+red+sea&printsec=frontcover (accessed 29 October 2023).

[182] Matcham, M.E. (1911) The Nelsons of Burnham Thorpe: a record of a Norfolk family compiled from unpublished letters and notebooks, 1787-1842, p. 33.

[183] Capper, J., Observations on the passage to India, through Egypt... (1785) p. 21. Available at: https://www.google.co.uk/books/edition/Observations_on_the_Passage_to_India_Thr/HMMRAAAAYAAJ? hl=en&gbpv=1&dq=capper+red+sea&printsec=frontcover (accessed 14 November 2023).

[184] Capper, J., Observations on the passage to India, through Egypt... (1785) p. 21. Available at: https://www.google.co.uk/books/edition/Observations_on_the_Passage_to_India_Thr/HMMRAAAAYAAJ? hl=en&gbpv=1&dq=capper+red+sea&printsec=frontcover (accessed 14 November 2023).

[185] Matcham, M.E. (1911) The Nelsons of Burnham Thorpe: a record of a Norfolk family compiled from unpublished letters and notebooks, 1787-1842, p. 33.

[186] Matcham, M.E. (1911) The Nelsons of Burnham Thorpe: a record of a Norfolk family compiled from unpublished letters and notebooks, 1787-1842, p. 34.

[187] Matcham, M.E. (1911) The Nelsons of Burnham Thorpe: a record of a Norfolk family compiled from unpublished letters and notebooks, 1787-1842, p. 34.

[188] Matcham, M.E. (1911) The Nelsons of Burnham Thorpe: a record of a Norfolk family compiled from unpublished letters and notebooks, 1787-1842, p. 34.

[189] Matcham, M.E. (1911) The Nelsons of Burnham Thorpe: a record of a Norfolk family compiled from unpublished letters and notebooks, 1787-1842,.pp. 33–34.

[190] Matcham, M.E. (1911) The Nelsons of Burnham Thorpe: a record of a Norfolk family compiled from unpublished letters and notebooks, 1787-1842, p. 31

[191] Historic England (no date) Charlton Park, Bishopsbourne - 1350018 | Historic England. Available at: https://historicengland.org.uk/listing/the-list/list-entry/1350018?section=official-listing. (Accessed January 2022)

[192] https://www.kentonline.co.uk/canterbury/news/mansion-where-pink-floyd-performed-for-sale-for-3-5m-256318/

[193] Matcham, M.E. (1911) The Nelsons of Burnham Thorpe: a record of a Norfolk family compiled from unpublished letters and notebooks, 1787-1842, p. 34.

[194] Matcham, M.E. (1911) The Nelsons of Burnham Thorpe: a record of a Norfolk family compiled from unpublished letters and notebooks, 1787-1842, p. 35.

[195] Irwin, E. (1787) A Series of Adventures in the Course of a Voyage Up the Red-Sea.... P. 143. Available at: https://www.google.co.uk/books/edition/A_Series_of_Adventures_in_the_Course_of/_VVWAAAAYAAJ?hl=en&gbpv=0 (accessed January 2022).

[196] Stamford Mercury, 7th October 1779, p. 1. Copyright British Library Board. Find My Past: https://www.findmypast.co.uk/image-viewer?issue=BL%2F0000254%2F17791007&page=1&article=001&stringtohighlight=suez

(accessed 13 November 2023).

[197] Saunders's News Letter, 7th December 1779, p. 1. Copyright British Library Board. Find My Past: https://https://www.findmypast.co.uk/image-viewer?issue=BL%2F0001057%2F17791207&page=1&article=005&stringtohighlight=suez

(accessed 13 November 2023).

[198] Matcham, M.E. (1911) The Nelsons of Burnham Thorpe: a record of a Norfolk family compiled from unpublished letters and notebooks, 1787-

1842, p. 34.

[199] p. 283
https://www.google.co.uk/books/edition/A_Series_of_Adventures_in_the_Course_of/_VVWAAAAYAAJ?hl=en&gbpv=0

[200] Bozic, M. (no date) Winter sailing in the Mediterranean: How to enjoy the sea during the low-season. Available at: https://www.green-sail.com/blog/winter-sailing-in-the-mediterranean (accessed 2 August 2023).

[201] Porto di Venezia (Venice), Italy to Port of Iskenderun (Isdemir), Turkey sea route and distance (no date). Available at: http://ports.com/sea-route/porto-di-venezia-venice,italy/port-of-iskenderun-isdemir,turkey/ (accessed 2 August 2023).

[202] Irwin, E. (1787) A Series of Adventures in the Course of a Voyage Up the Red-Sea.... P. 154. Available at: https://www.google.co.uk/books/edition/A_Series_of_Adventures_in_the_Course_of/_VVWAAAAYAAJ?hl=en&gbpv=0 (accessed 5 November 2023).

[203] Irwin, E. (1787) A Series of Adventures in the Course of a Voyage Up the Red-Sea.... Pp. 154 and 156. Available at: https://www.google.co.uk/books/edition/A_Series_of_Adventures_in_the_Course_of/_VVWAAAAYAAJ?hl=en&gbpv=0 (accessed January 2022).

[204] British India Office Ecclesiastical Returns - Deaths & Burials, copyright brightsolid online publishing ltd.. Available at: https://search.findmypast.co.uk/record? (accessed 30 November 2023).id=BL%2FBIND%2F005137654%2F00057&parentid=BL%2FBIND%2FD%2F369487

[205] Irwin, E. (1787) A Series of Adventures in the Course of a Voyage Up the Red-Sea.... P. 283. Available at: https://www.google.co.uk/books/edition/A_Series_of_Adventures_in_the_Course_of/_VVWAAAAYAAJ?hl=en&gbpv=0 (accessed January 2022).

[206] Wikipedia contributors (2023) "Eyles Irwin," Wikipedia [Preprint]. Available at: https://en.wikipedia.org/wiki/Eyles_Irwin (accessed 2 August 2023).

[207] Wikipedia contributors (2023) "Eyles Irwin," Wikipedia [Preprint]. Available at: https://en.wikipedia.org/wiki/Eyles_Irwin#/media/File:Eyles_Irwin_of_Slieve_Russell_Co_Fermanagh_Ireland_b_1748_d_1817.jpg (accessed 2 August 2023).

[208] Baetjer K. (2003)) Venice in the eighteenth century. Available at:

https://www.metmuseum.org/toah/hd/venc/hd_venc.htm (accessed 2 August 2023).

[209] Piranesi in Rome (no date) 18th-Century urban life in Italy: Urban life in Venice. Available at: http://omeka.wellesley.edu/piranesi-rome/exhibits/show/18th-century-urban-life/life-in-venice (accessed 2 August 2023).

[210] Irwin, E. (1787) A Series of Adventures in the Course of a Voyage Up the Red-Sea.... P. 156. Available at: https://www.google.co.uk/books/edition/A_Series_of_Adventures_in_the_Course_of/_VVWAAAAYAAJ?hl=en&gbpv=0 (accessed 5 November 2023).

[211] Irwin, E. (1787) A Series of Adventures in the Course of a Voyage Up the Red-Sea.... Pp. 156-157. Available at: https://www.google.co.uk/books/edition/A_Series_of_Adventures_in_the_Course_of/_VVWAAAAYAAJ?hl=en&gbpv=0 (accessed 5 November 2023).

[212] Porto di Venezia (Venice), Italy to Port of Iskenderun (Isdemir), Turkey sea route and distance (no date). Available at: http://ports.com/sea-route/porto-di-venezia-venice,italy/port-of-iskenderun-isdemir,turkey/ (accessed 2 August 2023).

[213] Capper, J., Observations on the passage to India, through Egypt... (1785) p. xxix. Available at: https://www.google.co.uk/books/edition/Observations_on_the_Passage_to_India_Thr/HMMRAAAAYAAJ?hl=en&gbpv=1&dq=capper+red+sea&printsec=frontcover (accessed 29 October 2023).

[214] Levantine Heritage, list of British Consular Officials in the Ottoman Empire and its former territories, from the sixteenth century to about 1860 (2011), p. 40. Available at: http://www.levantineheritage.com/pdf/List_of_British_Consular_Officials_Turkey(1581-1860)-D_Wilson.pdf (accessed 7 November 2023).

[215] Parsons, A., Travels in Asia and Africa: Including a Journey from Scanderoon to Aleppo... (1808) pp. 1-2. (Available at: https://www.google.co.uk/books/edition/Travels_in_Asia_and_Africa/stITAAAAYAAJ?hl=en&gbpv=1&dq=Scanderoon&printsec=frontcover (accessed 4 November 2023).

[216] Parsons, A., Travels in Asia and Africa: Including a Journey from Scanderoon to Aleppo... (1808) pp. 2-3. (Available at: https://www.google.co.uk/books/edition/Travels_in_Asia_and_Africa/stITAAAAYAAJ?hl=en&gbpv=1&dq=Scanderoon&printsec=frontcover

(accessed 4 November 2023).

[217] Irwin, E. (1787) A Series of Adventures in the Course of a Voyage Up the Red-Sea.... P. 280. Available at: https://www.google.co.uk/books/edition/A_Series_of_Adventures_in_the_Course_of/_VVWAAAAYAAJ?hl=en&gbpv=0 (accessed 7 November 2023).

[218] Irwin, E. (1787) A Series of Adventures in the Course of a Voyage Up the Red-Sea.... P. 282. Available at: https://www.google.co.uk/books/edition/A_Series_of_Adventures_in_the_Course_of/_VVWAAAAYAAJ?hl=en&gbpv=0 (accessed 7 November 2023).

[219] Russell, A., The natural history of Aleppo, Volume 1, (1794), pp. 13-14. Available at: https://www.google.co.uk/books/edition/The_Natural_History_of_Aleppo/7PfaAAAAMAAJ?hl=en&gbpv=1&dq=aleppo+russell&printsec=frontcover (accessed 7 November 2023).

[220] Irwin, E. (1787) A Series of Adventures in the Course of a Voyage Up the Red-Sea.... P. 282. Available at: https://www.google.co.uk/books/edition/A_Series_of_Adventures_in_the_Course_of/_VVWAAAAYAAJ?hl=en&gbpv=0 (accessed 7 November 2023).

[221] Irwin, E. (1787) A Series of Adventures in the Course of a Voyage Up the Red-Sea.... P. 285. Available at: https://www.google.co.uk/books/edition/A_Series_of_Adventures_in_the_Course_of/_VVWAAAAYAAJ?hl=en&gbpv=0 (accessed 7 November 2023).

[222] Irwin, E. (1787) A Series of Adventures in the Course of a Voyage Up the Red-Sea.... P. 285. Available at: https://www.google.co.uk/books/edition/A_Series_of_Adventures_in_the_Course_of/_VVWAAAAYAAJ?hl=en&gbpv=0 (accessed 7 November 2023).

[223] Russell, A., The natural history of Aleppo, Volume 1, (1794), p. 11. Available at: https://www.google.co.uk/books/edition/The_Natural_History_of_Aleppo/7PfaAAAAMAAJ?hl=en&gbpv=1&dq=aleppo+russell&printsec=frontcover (accessed 7 November 2023).

[224] Irwin, E. (1787) A Series of Adventures in the Course of a Voyage Up the Red-Sea.... P. 284. Available at:

https://www.google.co.uk/books/edition/A_Series_of_Adventures_in_the_Course_of/_VVWAAAAYAAJ?hl=en&gbpv=0 (accessed 7 November 2023).

[225] Russell, A., The natural history of Aleppo, Volume 1, (1794), pp. 8, 163. Available at: https://www.google.co.uk/books/edition/The_Natural_History_of_Aleppo/7PfaAAAAMAAJ? hl=en&gbpv=1&dq=aleppo+russell&printsec=frontcover (accessed 7 November 2023).

[226] Parsons, A., Travels in Asia and Africa: Including a Journey from Scanderoon to Aleppo... (1808) p. 57. (Available at: https://www.google.co.uk/books/edition/Travels_in_Asia_and_Africa/stITAAAAYAAJ?hl=en&gbpv=1&dq=Scanderoon&printsec=frontcover (accessed 12 November 2023).

[227] Russell, A., The natural history of Aleppo, Volume 2, (1794), p. 2. Available at: https://www.google.co.uk/books/edition/The_Natural_History_of_Aleppo_Containing/g7P357Nc1JMC? hl=en&gbpv=1&dq=natural+history+of+aleppo+russell&printsec=frontcover (accessed 11 November 2023).

[228] Irwin, E. (1787) A Series of Adventures in the Course of a Voyage Up the Red-Sea.... P. 285. Available at: https://www.google.co.uk/books/edition/A_Series_of_Adventures_in_the_Course_of/_VVWAAAAYAAJ?hl=en&gbpv=0 (accessed 7 November 2023).

[229] Russell, A., The natural history of Aleppo, Volume 1, (1794), pp. 15, 20-21, 23, 123, 140. Available at: https://www.google.co.uk/books/edition/The_Natural_History_of_Aleppo/7PfaAAAAMAAJ? hl=en&gbpv=1&dq=aleppo+russell&printsec=frontcover (accessed 7 November 2023).

[230] Parsons, A., Travels in Asia and Africa: Including a Journey from Scanderoon to Aleppo... (1808) p. 62. (Available at: https://www.google.co.uk/books/edition/Travels_in_Asia_and_Africa/stITAAAAYAAJ?hl=en&gbpv=1&dq=Scanderoon&printsec=frontcover (accessed 12 November 2023).

[231] Parsons, A., Travels in Asia and Africa: Including a Journey from Scanderoon to Aleppo... (1808) pp. 62-63. (Available at: https://www.google.co.uk/books/edition/Travels_in_Asia_and_Africa/stITAAAAYAAJ?hl=en&gbpv=1&dq=Scanderoon&printsec=frontcover (accessed 12 November 2023).

[232] Levantine Heritage, list of British Consular Officials in the Ottoman Empire and its former territories, from the sixteenth century to about 1860 (2011), p. 37. Available at: http://www.levantineheritage.com/pdf/List_of_British_Consular_Officials_Turkey(1581-1860)-D_Wilson.pdf (accessed 7 November 2023).

[233] Clark M. S., genealogy and history of the Abbott family of England and the Levant (2023). Available at http://www.mikesclark.com/genealogy/abbott.html (accessed 8 November 2023).

[234] Clark M. S., genealogy and history of the Abbott family of England and the Levant (2023). Available at http://www.mikesclark.com/genealogy/abbott.html (accessed 8 November 2023).

[235] Irwin, E. (1787) A Series of Adventures in the Course of a Voyage Up the Red-Sea.... P. 290. Available at: https://www.google.co.uk/books/edition/A_Series_of_Adventures_in_the_Course_of/_VVWAAAAYAAJ?hl=en&gbpv=0 (accessed 7 November 2022).

[236] Irwin, E. (1787) A Series of Adventures in the Course of a Voyage Up the Red-Sea.... Pp. 157-160. Available at: https://www.google.co.uk/books/edition/A_Series_of_Adventures_in_the_Course_of/_VVWAAAAYAAJ?hl=en&gbpv=0 (accessed January 2022).

[237] Irwin, E. (1787) A Series of Adventures in the Course of a Voyage Up the Red-Sea.... P. 203. Available at: https://www.google.co.uk/books/edition/A_Series_of_Adventures_in_the_Course_of/_VVWAAAAYAAJ?hl=en&gbpv=0 (accessed January 2022).

[238] Irwin, E. (1787) A Series of Adventures in the Course of a Voyage Up the Red-Sea.... Pp. 280-281. Available at: https://www.google.co.uk/books/edition/A_Series_of_Adventures_in_the_Course_of/_VVWAAAAYAAJ?hl=en&gbpv=0 (accessed 7 November 2022).

[239] Capper, J., Observations on the passage to India, through Egypt... (1785) p. 145. Available at: https://www.google.co.uk/books/edition/Observations_on_the_Passage_to_India_Thr/HMMRAAAAYAAJ?hl=en&gbpv=1&dq=capper+red+sea&printsec=frontcover (accessed 29 October 2023).

[240] Irwin, E. (1787) A Series of Adventures in the Course of a Voyage Up the Red-Sea.... P. 290. Available at: https://www.google.co.uk/books/edition/A_Series_of_Adventures_in_the_

Course_of/_VVWAAAAYAAJ?hl=en&gbpv=0 (accessed 7 November 2022).

[241] Irwin, E. (1787) A Series of Adventures in the Course of a Voyage Up the Red-Sea.... P. 282. Available at: https://www.google.co.uk/books/edition/A_Series_of_Adventures_in_the_Course_of/_VVWAAAAYAAJ?hl=en&gbpv=0 (accessed 7 November 2022).

[242] Russell, A., The natural history of Aleppo, Volume 2, (1794), p. 2. Available at: https://www.google.co.uk/books/edition/The_Natural_History_of_Aleppo_Containing/g7P357Nc1JMC?hl=en&gbpv=1&dq=natural+history+of+aleppo+russell&printsec=frontcover (accessed 11 November 2023).

[243] Russell, A., The natural history of Aleppo, Volume 2, (1794), pp. 12-13. Available at: https://www.google.co.uk/books/edition/The_Natural_History_of_Aleppo_Containing/g7P357Nc1JMC?hl=en&gbpv=1&dq=natural+history+of+aleppo+russell&printsec=frontcover (accessed 11 November 2023).

[244] Russell, A., The natural history of Aleppo, Volume 2, (1794), p. 10. Available at: https://www.google.co.uk/books/edition/The_Natural_History_of_Aleppo_Containing/g7P357Nc1JMC?hl=en&gbpv=1&dq=natural+history+of+aleppo+russell&printsec=frontcover (accessed 11 November 2023).

[245] Parsons, A., Travels in Asia and Africa: Including a Journey from Scanderoon to Aleppo... (1808) p. 65. (Available at: https://www.google.co.uk/books/edition/Travels_in_Asia_and_Africa/stITAAAAYAAJ?hl=en&gbpv=1&dq=Scanderoon&printsec=frontcover (accessed 12 November 2023).

[246] Russell, A., The natural history of Aleppo, Volume 2, (1794), p. 15. Available at: https://www.google.co.uk/books/edition/The_Natural_History_of_Aleppo_Containing/g7P357Nc1JMC?hl=en&gbpv=1&dq=natural+history+of+aleppo+russell&printsec=frontcover (accessed 11 November 2023).

[247] Russell, A., The natural history of Aleppo, Volume 2, (1794), p. 18. Available at: https://www.google.co.uk/books/edition/The_Natural_History_of_Aleppo_Containing/g7P357Nc1JMC?hl=en&gbpv=1&dq=natural+history+of+aleppo+russell&printsec=frontco

ver (accessed 11 November 2023).

[248] Parsons, A., Travels in Asia and Africa: Including a Journey from Scanderoon to Aleppo... (1808) p. 60. (Available at: https://www.google.co.uk/books/edition/Travels_in_Asia_and_Africa/stIT AAAAYAAJ?hl=en&gbpv=1&dq=Scanderoon&printsec=frontcover (accessed 13 November 2023).

[249] History today, The Turkey Merchants: Life in the Levant Company (1966). Available at https://www.historytoday.com/archive/turkey-merchants-life-levant-company (accessed 13 November 2023).

[250] Russell, A., The natural history of Aleppo, Volume 2, (1794), p. 11. Available at: https://www.google.co.uk/books/edition/The_Natural_History_of_Aleppo _Containing/g7P357Nc1JMC? hl=en&gbpv=1&dq=natural+history+of+aleppo+russell&printsec=frontco ver (accessed 11 November 2023).

[251] Parsons, A., Travels in Asia and Africa: Including a Journey from Scanderoon to Aleppo... (1808) p. 60. (Available at: https://www.google.co.uk/books/edition/Travels_in_Asia_and_Africa/stIT AAAAYAAJ?hl=en&gbpv=1&dq=Scanderoon&printsec=frontcover (accessed 13 November 2023).

[252] Parsons, A., Travels in Asia and Africa: Including a Journey from Scanderoon to Aleppo... (1808) p. 61. (Available at: https://www.google.co.uk/books/edition/Travels_in_Asia_and_Africa/stIT AAAAYAAJ?hl=en&gbpv=1&dq=Scanderoon&printsec=frontcover (accessed 13 November 2023).

[253] Russell, A., The natural history of Aleppo, Volume 1, (1794), p. 113. Available at: https://www.google.co.uk/books/edition/The_Natural_History_of_Aleppo/ 7PfaAAAAMAAJ? hl=en&gbpv=1&dq=aleppo+russell&printsec=frontcover (accessed 7 November 2023).

[254] Russell, A., The natural history of Aleppo, Volume 1, (1794), p. 114. Available at: https://www.google.co.uk/books/edition/The_Natural_History_of_Aleppo/ 7PfaAAAAMAAJ? hl=en&gbpv=1&dq=aleppo+russell&printsec=frontcover (accessed 7 November 2023).

[255] Russell, A., The natural history of Aleppo, Volume 1, (1794), p. 141. Available at: https://www.google.co.uk/books/edition/The_Natural_History_of_Aleppo/

7PfaAAAAMAAJ?
hl=en&gbpv=1&dq=aleppo+russell&printsec=frontcover (accessed 7
November 2023).

[256] Parsons, A., Travels in Asia and Africa: Including a Journey from
Scanderoon to Aleppo... (1808) p. 61. (Available at:
https://www.google.co.uk/books/edition/Travels_in_Asia_and_Africa/stIT
AAAAYAAJ?hl=en&gbpv=1&dq=Scanderoon&printsec=frontcover
(accessed 13 November 2023).

[257] Russell, A., The natural history of Aleppo, Volume 1, (1794), pp. 163-
165. Available at:
https://www.google.co.uk/books/edition/The_Natural_History_of_Aleppo/
7PfaAAAAMAAJ?
hl=en&gbpv=1&dq=aleppo+russell&printsec=frontcover (accessed 7
November 2023).

[258] Russell, A., The natural history of Aleppo, Volume 1, (1794), pp. 100-
104. Available at:
https://www.google.co.uk/books/edition/The_Natural_History_of_Aleppo/
7PfaAAAAMAAJ?
hl=en&gbpv=1&dq=aleppo+russell&printsec=frontcover (accessed 7
November 2023).

[259] Irwin, E. (1787) A Series of Adventures in the Course of a Voyage Up
the Red-Sea.... P. 283. Available at:
https://www.google.co.uk/books/edition/A_Series_of_Adventures_in_the_
Course_of/_VVWAAAAYAAJ?hl=en&gbpv=0 (accessed 8 November
2022).

[260] Starkey, J., Adam Freer, MD (1747–1811), (2017). Available at
https://s3-eu-west-
1.amazonaws.com/s3.spanglefish.com/s/37872/documents/the-russells-
and-friends/adam-freer-md01.pdf (accessed 9 November 2023).

[261] Irwin, E. (1787) A Series of Adventures in the Course of a Voyage Up
the Red-Sea.... P. 290. Available at:
https://www.google.co.uk/books/edition/A_Series_of_Adventures_in_the_
Course_of/_VVWAAAAYAAJ?hl=en&gbpv=0 (accessed 8 November
2022).

[262] Irwin, E. (1787) A Series of Adventures in the Course of a Voyage Up
the Red-Sea.... P. 291. Available at:
https://www.google.co.uk/books/edition/A_Series_of_Adventures_in_the_
Course_of/_VVWAAAAYAAJ?hl=en&gbpv=0 (accessed 8 November
2022).

[263] Parsons, A., Travels in Asia and Africa: Including a Journey from

Scanderoon to Aleppo... (1808) pp. 75-76. (Available at: https://www.google.co.uk/books/edition/Travels_in_Asia_and_Africa/stITAAAAYAAJ?hl=en&gbpv=1&dq=Scanderoon&printsec=frontcover (accessed 12 November 2023).

[264] Irwin, E. (1787) A Series of Adventures in the Course of a Voyage Up the Red-Sea.... P. 292. Available at: https://www.google.co.uk/books/edition/A_Series_of_Adventures_in_the_Course_of/_VVWAAAAYAAJ?hl=en&gbpv=0 (accessed 8 November 2022).

[265] Parsons, A., Travels in Asia and Africa: Including a Journey from Scanderoon to Aleppo... (1808) p. 76. (Available at: https://www.google.co.uk/books/edition/Travels_in_Asia_and_Africa/stITAAAAYAAJ?hl=en&gbpv=1&dq=Scanderoon&printsec=frontcover (accessed 12 November 2023).

[266] Irwin, E. (1787) A Series of Adventures in the Course of a Voyage Up the Red-Sea.... p. 293. Available at: https://www.google.co.uk/books/edition/A_Series_of_Adventures_in_the_Course_of/_VVWAAAAYAAJ?hl=en&gbpv=0 (accessed January 2022).

[267] Ānah (no date) Encyclopædia Britannica. Available at: https://www.britannica.com/place/Anah (Accessed: 01 July 2023).

[268] Irwin, E. (1787) A Series of Adventures in the Course of a Voyage Up the Red-Sea.... p. 315. Available at: https://www.google.co.uk/books/edition/A_Series_of_Adventures_in_the_Course_of/_VVWAAAAYAAJ?hl=en&gbpv=0 (accessed January 2022).

[269] McAllester, M. (2019) Baghdad - City of the Arabian Nights, Uae – Gulf News. Available at: https://gulfnews.com/uae/baghdad---city-of-the-arabian-nights-1.350921 (Accessed: 01 July 2023).

[270] The Tigris is navigable for shallow vessels downstream of Baghdad https://www.cs.mcgill.ca/~rwest/wikispeedia/wpcd/wp/t/Tigris.htm

[271] Mamluk rule in Iraq (no date) Academic Dictionaries and Encyclopedias. Available at: https://en-academic.com/dic.nsf/enwiki/7629889 (Accessed: 01 July 2023).

[272] Irwin, E. (1787) A Series of Adventures in the Course of a Voyage Up the Red-Sea.... p. 331. Available at: https://www.google.co.uk/books/edition/A_Series_of_Adventures_in_the_Course_of/_VVWAAAAYAAJ?hl=en&gbpv=0 (accessed January 2022).

[273] Capper, J., Observations on the passage to India, through Egypt... (1785) supplement. Available at: https://www.google.co.uk/books/edition/Observations_on_the_Passage_to

_India_Thr/HMMRAAAAYAAJ?
hl=en&gbpv=1&dq=capper+red+sea&printsec=frontcover (accessed 14 November 2023).

[274] Irwin, E. (1787) A Series of Adventures in the Course of a Voyage Up the Red-Sea.... pp. 367-368. Available at:
https://www.google.co.uk/books/edition/A_Series_of_Adventures_in_the_Course_of/_VVWAAAAYAAJ?hl=en&gbpv=0 (accessed 27 November 2023).

[275] The Editors of Encyclopaedia Britannica, Basra | History, Economy & Culture, (2023) Available at: https://www.britannica.com/place/Basra (accessed 15 November 2023).

[276] Irwin, E. (1787) A Series of Adventures in the Course of a Voyage Up the Red-Sea.... p. 377. Available at:
https://www.google.co.uk/books/edition/A_Series_of_Adventures_in_the_Course_of/_VVWAAAAYAAJ?hl=en&gbpv=0 (accessed 27 November 2023).

[277] Wikisource, the free online library, Protestant exiles from France, Volume 2 - Book Third - Chapter 20 - La Touche - (no date). Available at: https://en.wikisource.org/wiki/Protestant_Exiles_from_France/Volume_2_-_Book_Third_-_Chapter_20_-_La_Touche (accessed 27 November 2023).

[278] Irwin, E. (1787) A Series of Adventures in the Course of a Voyage Up the Red-Sea.... p. 376. Available at:
https://www.google.co.uk/books/edition/A_Series_of_Adventures_in_the_Course_of/_VVWAAAAYAAJ?hl=en&gbpv=0 (accessed 27 November 2023).

[279] Irwin, E. (1787) A Series of Adventures in the Course of a Voyage Up the Red-Sea.... p. 377. Available at:
https://www.google.co.uk/books/edition/A_Series_of_Adventures_in_the_Course_of/_VVWAAAAYAAJ?hl=en&gbpv=0 (accessed 27 November 2023).

[280] Irwin, E. (1787) A Series of Adventures in the Course of a Voyage Up the Red-Sea.... p. 379. Available at:
https://www.google.co.uk/books/edition/A_Series_of_Adventures_in_the_Course_of/_VVWAAAAYAAJ?hl=en&gbpv=0 (accessed 27 November 2023).

[281] Capper, J., Observations on the passage to India, through Egypt... (1785) p. 228. Available at:
https://www.google.co.uk/books/edition/Observations_on_the_Passage_to_India_Thr/HMMRAAAAYAAJ?

hl=en&gbpv=1&dq=capper+red+sea&printsec=frontcover (accessed 14 November 2023).

[282] Irwin, E. (1787) A Series of Adventures in the Course of a Voyage Up the Red-Sea.... pp. 380-381. Available at: https://www.google.co.uk/books/edition/A_Series_of_Adventures_in_the_Course_of/_VVWAAAAYAAJ?hl=en&gbpv=0 (accessed 27 November 2023).

[283] Irwin, E. (1787) A Series of Adventures in the Course of a Voyage Up the Red-Sea.... pp. 381-382. Available at: https://www.google.co.uk/books/edition/A_Series_of_Adventures_in_the_Course_of/_VVWAAAAYAAJ?hl=en&gbpv=0 (accessed 27 November 2023).

[284] Port of Mumbai , India to Port of Basrah, Iraq (no date). Available at: http://ports.com/sea-route/port-of-mumbai,india/port-of-basrah,iraq/ (accessed 27 November 2023).

[285] Contributors to Wikimedia projects, Dictionary of National Biography,1885-1900/Matcham, George(2020). Available at: https://en.wikisource.org/wiki/Dictionary_of_National_Biography,_1885-1900/Matcham,_George (accessed 27 October 2023).

[286] The Times of India, Delhi's Scindia age (2023). Available at: https://timesofindia.indiatimes.com/blogs/weltanschauung/delhis-scindia-age-1771-1803/ (accessed 7 December 2023).

[287] Thomas, R.H. (1851) Treaties, Agreements, and Engagements, Between the Honorable East India Company and the Native Princes, Chiefs, and States, in Western India, the Red Sea, the Persian Gulf, &c: Also Between Her Britannic Majesty's Government, and Persia, Portugal, and Turkey. Pp. 707-708. Available at:

https://books.google.co.uk/books?id=updeAAAAcAAJ&pg=PR4&lpg=PR4&dq=Broach+east+india+1783&source=bl&ots=9afOSJccCT&sig=ACfU3U3WpSNANvp5KFMYytpSl5BGiFp5sw&hl=en&sa=X&ved=2ahUKEwj4lofsm8n1AhWYilwKHdoACMsQ6AF6BAgXEAM#v=snippet&q=1782&f=false (accessed January 2022).

[288] Hereford Journal, 18th December 1783, p. 4. Copyright British Library Board. Find My Past: https://www.findmypast.co.uk/image-viewer?issue=BL%2F0000397%2F17830918&page=4&article=011&stringtohighlight=suez

(accessed 14 November 2023).

[289] Contributors to Wikimedia projects, Dictionary of National

Biography,1885-1900/Matcham, George(2020). Available at: https://en.wikisource.org/wiki/Dictionary_of_National_Biography,_1885-1900/Matcham,_George (accessed 27 October 2023).

[290] Matcham, M.E. (1911) The Nelsons of Burnham Thorpe: a record of a Norfolk family compiled from unpublished letters and notebooks, 1787-1842, p. 34.

[291] British In India, © Society of Genealogists. Available at: https://search.findmypast.co.uk/record?id=S2%2FGBOR%2FPERCY%2FB%2F08229&parentid=GBOR%2FPERCY-SMITH%2F005764 (accessed 30 November 2023).

[292] British India Office deaths & burials ecclesiastical returns, copyright brightsolid online publishing ltd. Available at: https://www.findmypast.co.uk/transcript?id=BL/BIND/D/369487 (accessed 30 November 2023).

[293] Irwin, E. (1787) A Series of Adventures in the Course of a Voyage Up the Red-Sea.... P. 143. Available at: https://www.google.co.uk/books/edition/A_Series_of_Adventures_in_the_Course_of/_VVWAAAAYAAJ?hl=en&gbpv=0 (accessed January 2022).

[294] Émïn J., Life and Adventures of Joseph Émïn, 1726-1809, Volume 2, p. 474. Available at: https://archive.org/details/JosephEmin/page/n11/mode/2up (accessed 29 November 2023).

[295] British India Office deaths & burials ecclesiastical returns, © copyright brightsolid online publishing ltd. Available at: https://search.findmypast.co.uk/record?id=BL%2FBIND%2F005137654%2F00104&parentid=BL%2FBIND%2FD%2F370906 (accessed 29 November 2023).

[296] Gazetteer of the Bombay Presidency, volume 26, part 3 (1894) p. 429. Available at: https://www.google.co.uk/books/edition/Gazetteer_of_the_Bombay_Presidency/67YBAAAAYAAJ?hl=en&gbpv=1&dq=Andrew+NESBITT+bombay&pg=PA429&printsec=frontcover (accessed 30 November 2023).

[297] Armenian Weekly, the Armenians of Singapore: an historical perspective (2015). Available at: https://armenianweekly.com/2015/01/06/armenians-of-singapore/ (accessed 30 November 2023).

[298] Wald, E., Reading Social Spaces: the life of the Bombay Theatre, 1770-1843, London: Hurst Publishers (2019) pp. 99-116. Available at:

https://research.gold.ac.uk/id/eprint/25123/7/EW%20comments%20-%20Bombay%20Theatre%20Masselos%20Volume%20%20(1).pdf (accessed 1 December 2023).

[299] Chater genealogy, Armenians in India - Behind the Scenes Forgotten History (2015). Available at: http://chater-genealogy.blogspot.com/2015/02/catholic-armenians-lets-build-church.html (accessed 1 December 2023).

[300] Émïn J., (1792) Life and adventures of Émïn, 1726-1809. Baptist Mission Press. Pp. 474, 467, 523. Available at: https://books.google.co.uk/books?id=7qY0AQAAMAAJ&pg=PA474&lpg=PA474&dq=bombay+marine+superintendent+matcham&source=bl&ots=bRidUo3QOj&sig=ACfU3U3RmY-8heB8L9BomIRFvAaHnJS33Q&hl=en&sa=X&ved=2ahUKEwis6LKRx6j1AhUsREEAHTjDAJkQ6AF6BAgQEAM#v=onepage&q&f=false (accessed 30 November 2023)

[301] Royal Museums Greenwich, review of Marshall P. J., Edmund Burke and the British Empire in the West Indies : wealth, power, and slavery (2019). Available at: https://www.rmg.co.uk/collections/library/rmgl-156695 (accessed 28 November 2023).

[302] Wilson K., A New Imperial History: Culture, Identity and Modernity in Britain and... Cambridge University Press (2004) p. 104. Available at: https://books.google.co.uk/books?id=hLZNdK7aIk4C&pg=PA104&dq=edmund+burke+aleppo&hl=en&newbks=1&newbks_redir=0&source=gb_mobile_search&sa=X&ved=2ahUKEwjaos3A8-aCAxVGXUEAHV1ZDFcQuwV6BAgNEAY#v=onepage&q=edmund%20burke%20aleppo&f=false (accessed 28 November 2023).

[303] Émïn J., Life and Adventures of Émïn, 1726-1809, Volume 2, foreword, p. viii. Available at: https://archive.org/details/JosephEmin/page/n11/mode/2up (accessed 29 November 2023).

[304] Émïn J., (1792) Life and adventures of Émïn, 1726-1809. Baptist Mission Press. Pp. 473-476. Available at: https://books.google.co.uk/books?id=7qY0AQAAMAAJ&pg=PA474&lpg=PA474&dq=bombay+marine+superintendent+matcham&source=bl&ots=bRidUo3QOj&sig=ACfU3U3RmY-8heB8L9BomIRFvAaHnJS33Q&hl=en&sa=X&ved=2ahUKEwis6LKRx6j1AhUsREEAHTjDAJkQ6AF6BAgQEAM#v=onepage&q&f=false. (Accessed 14 July 2023)

[305] Ritchie C. A., Sir Charles Warre Malet, Concluding a Treaty in 1790 in Durbar with the Peshwa of the Maratha Empire, Thomas Daniell, 1805, Tate (2022). Available at: https://www.tate.org.uk/art/artworks/daniell-sir-charles-warre-malet-concluding-a-treaty-in-1790-in-durbar-with-the-peshwa-of-t12511 (accessed 4 November 2023).

[306] British in India, © Society of Genealogists. Available at: https://search.findmypast.co.uk/record?id=S2%2FGBOR%2FPERCY%2FB%2F08229&parentid=GBOR%2FPERCY-SMITH%2F005767 (accessed 2 December 2023).

[307] John Beete, in the England & Wales, Prerogative Court of Canterbury Wills, 1384-1858. © 2002-2023 Ancestry. Available at: https://www.ancestry.co.uk/discoveryui-content/view/533791:5111?tid=&pid=&queryId=a5084b96b26321d131d90f50e5e90c0c&_phsrc=ECs2318&_phstart=successSource (accessed 4 December 2023).

[308] Matcham, M.E. (1911) The Nelsons of Burnham Thorpe: a record of a Norfolk family compiled from unpublished letters and notebooks, 1787-1842, p. 35.

[309] Wikipedia contributors, Battle of Cunaxa (2023). Available at: https://en.wikipedia.org/wiki/Battle_of_Cunaxa (accessed 7 December 2023).

[310] Matcham, M.E. (1911) in Nelsons of Burnham Thorpe: A record of a Norfolk family ... J. Lane, pp. 35–37.

[311] Wikipedia contributors, East India Company College (2023). Available at: https://en.wikipedia.org/wiki/East_India_Company_College (accessed 18 December 2023).

[312] Capper, J., Observations on the passage to India, through Egypt... (1785) pp. xxvii–xxix. Available at: https://www.google.co.uk/books/edition/Observations_on_the_Passage_to_India_Thr/HMMRAAAAYAAJ?hl=en&gbpv=1&dq=capper+red+sea&printsec=frontcover (accessed 29 October 2023).

[313] Shields S. D., regional trade and 19th-century Mosul: revising the role of Europe in the Middle East economy, International Journal of Middle East Studies, vol. 23, no. 1 (1991), p. 20. Available at: https://www.jstor.org/stable/163930?read-now=1&seq=2#page_scan_tab_contents (accessed 20 December 2023).

[314] Xenophon's Anabasis, newly translated into English... (1822) p. 97. Available at: https://www.google.co.uk/books/edition/Xenophon_s_Anabasis_Newly_Tr

anslated_Int/imG0ydRoFR0C?
hl=en&gbpv=1&dq=xenophon+anabasis&printsec=frontcover (accessed
16 December 2023).

[315] Duhok Private Technical Institute, about us (no date). Available at:
https://dhk-pti.com/website/DuhokCity.php (accessed 21 December 2023).

[316] Kitto J. the pictorial Bible (1856) p. 509. Available at:
https://www.google.co.uk/books/edition/The_Pictorial_Bible_Psalms_Mal
achi/BzoXAAAAYAAJ?
hl=en&gbpv=1&dq=dress+of+the+kurdish&pg=PA509&printsec=frontcove
r (accessed 24 December 2023).

[317] Duhok Province, food of Kurdish (no date). Available at:
http://duhokprovince.com/food-of-kurdish/ (accessed 23 December 2023).

[318] Bagster, The Bible of Every Land (1848) p. 68. Available at:
https://www.google.co.uk/books/edition/The_Bible_of_Every_Land/Wbu
KdoaGaG0C?hl=en&gbpv=1&dq=kurds&pg=PA68&printsec=frontcover
(accessed 24 December 2023).

[319] Wikipedia contributors, Iraqi Kurdistan (2023). Available at:
https://en.wikipedia.org/wiki/Iraqi_Kurdistan (accessed 7 December
2023).

[320] Shields S. D., regional trade and 19th-century Mosul: revising the
role of Europe in the Middle East economy, International Journal of
Middle East Studies, vol. 23, no. 1 (1991), p. 20. Available at:
https://www.jstor.org/stable/163930?read-
now=1&seq=2#page_scan_tab_contents (accessed 20 December 2023).

[321] American Board of Commissioners for foreign missions, Panoplist,
and Missionary Magazine, volumes 31–32 (1835) p. 167. Available at:
https://www.google.co.uk/books/edition/Panoplist_and_Missionary_Maga
zine/OsBhc4Do4yEC?
hl=en&gbpv=1&dq=kurds&pg=PA167&printsec=frontcover (accessed 17
December 2023).

[322] Matcham, M.E. (1911) in Nelsons of Burnham Thorpe: A record of a
Norfolk family ... J. Lane, p. 36.

[323] Xenophon's Anabasis, newly translated into English... (1822) p. 98.
Available at:
https://www.google.co.uk/books/edition/Xenophon_s_Anabasis_Newly_Tr
anslated_Int/imG0ydRoFR0C?
hl=en&gbpv=1&dq=xenophon+anabasis&printsec=frontcover (accessed
17 December 2023).

[324] Southgate H., Narrative of a Tour Through Armenia, Kurdistan,

Persia and Mesopotamia (1840) pp. 205-206. Available at:
https://www.google.co.uk/books/edition/Narrative_of_a_Tour_Through_A
rmenia_Kurd/5hAOAAAAYAAJ?
hl=en&gbpv=1&dq=dress+of+the+kurds&pg=PA206&printsec=frontcove
r (accessed 24 December 2023).

[325] Brown. W., the history of Christian missions of the sixteenth,
seventeenth, eighteenth, & nineteenth centuries… (1804) p. 377. Available
at:
https://www.google.co.uk/books/edition/The_History_of_Christian_Missio
ns_of_the/Wg5wb9q0slMC?
hl=en&gbpv=1&dq=kurds&pg=PA377&printsec=frontcover (accessed 24
December 2023).

[326] Kurdish people, Zoroastrianism. Available at:
https://kurdishpeople.org/zoroastrianism/ (accessed 17 December 2023).

[327] The editors of Encyclopaedia Britannica, Yazīdī, religious sect
(2023). Available at: https://www.britannica.com/topic/Yazidi (accessed 25
December 2023).

[328] Kurdistan Government Iraq representation in Austria, traditional
Kurdish clothing (no date). Available at:
http://austria.gov.krd/en/traditionelle-kurdische-kleidung/ (accessed 26
December 2023).

[329] Irwin, E. (1787) A Series of Adventures in the Course of a Voyage Up
the Red-Sea.... P. 146. Available at:
https://www.google.co.uk/books/edition/A_Series_of_Adventures_in_the_
Course_of/_VVWAAAAYAAJ?hl=en&gbpv=0 (accessed January 2022).

[330] Xenophon's Anabasis, newly translated into English... (1822) pp. 105-
106. Available at:
https://www.google.co.uk/books/edition/Xenophon_s_Anabasis_Newly_Tr
anslated_Int/imG0ydRoFR0C?
hl=en&gbpv=1&dq=xenophon+anabasis&printsec=frontcover (accessed
17 December 2023).

[331] Xenophon's Anabasis, newly translated into English... (1822) pp. 102-
106. Available at:
https://www.google.co.uk/books/edition/Xenophon_s_Anabasis_Newly_Tr
anslated_Int/imG0ydRoFR0C?
hl=en&gbpv=1&dq=xenophon+anabasis&printsec=frontcover (accessed
21 December 2023).

[332] Xenophon's Anabasis, newly translated into English... (1822) pp. 110-
111. Available at:
https://www.google.co.uk/books/edition/Xenophon_s_Anabasis_Newly_Tr

anslated_Int/imG0ydRoFR0C?
hl=en&gbpv=1&dq=xenophon+anabasis&printsec=frontcover (accessed
21 December 2023).

[333] Wikipedia contributors, map of the expedition of the ten thousand (no
date). Available at:
https://en.wikipedia.org/wiki/Ten_Thousand#/media/File:Expedition_of_th
e_Ten_Thousand.jpg (accessed 21 December 2023).

[334] Let's Go Turkey (2000) P. 435.

[335] Xenophon's Anabasis, newly translated into English... (1822) pp. 110-
111. Available at:
https://www.google.co.uk/books/edition/Xenophon_s_Anabasis_Newly_Tr
anslated_Int/imG0ydRoFR0C?
hl=en&gbpv=1&dq=xenophon+anabasis&printsec=frontcover (accessed
21 December 2023).

[336] Paradeisopoulos I. H., Route and Parasangs in Xenophon's Anabasis,
Greek, Roman, and Byzantine Studies 54 (2014) pp. 220–254. Available
at: https://www.google.com/url?
sa=t&rct=j&q=&esrc=s&source=web&cd=&ved=2ahUKEwjKk4rXm7iD
AxVdQUEAHQ7KBXAQFnoECBcQAQ&url=https%3A%2F
%2Fgrbs.library.duke.edu%2Findex.php%2Fgrbs%2Farticle%2Fdownload
%2F14993%2F6839%2F18127&usg=AOvVaw0SnR99FXNALl9nH6dIe-
m-&opi=89978449 (accessed 30 December 2023).

[337] Xenophon's Anabasis, newly translated into English... (1822) p. 117.
Available at:
https://www.google.co.uk/books/edition/Xenophon_s_Anabasis_Newly_Tr
anslated_Int/imG0ydRoFR0C?
hl=en&gbpv=1&dq=xenophon+anabasis&printsec=frontcover (accessed
27 December 2023).

[338] Southgate H., Narrative of a Tour Through Armenia, Kurdistan,
Persia and Mesopotamia (1840) p. 211. Available at:
https://www.google.co.uk/books/edition/Narrative_of_a_Tour_Through_A
rmenia_Kurd/5hAOAAAAYAAJ?
hl=en&gbpv=1&dq=dress+of+the+kurds&pg=PA206&printsec=frontcove
r (accessed 27 December 2023).

[339] Southgate H., Narrative of a Tour Through Armenia, Kurdistan,
Persia and Mesopotamia (1840) pp. 211-213. Available at:
https://www.google.co.uk/books/edition/Narrative_of_a_Tour_Through_A
rmenia_Kurd/5hAOAAAAYAAJ?
hl=en&gbpv=1&dq=dress+of+the+kurds&pg=PA206&printsec=frontcove
r (accessed 27 December 2023).

[340] Life & thyme, cuisine connects Turkish Armenians to ancient roots (2021). Available at: https://lifeandthyme.com/travel/cuisine-connects-turkish-armenians-to-ancient-roots/ (accessed 29 December 2023).

[341] Folkways, the roots and influence of modern cultures, what to eat in Armenia: traditional Armenian foods to treat yourself (no date). Available at: https://folkways.today/armenia-food/ (accessed 28 December 2023).

[342] Wikipedia contributors, Armenian dress. Available at: https://en.wikipedia.org/wiki/Armenian_dress (accessed 2 January 2024).

[343] Smith E., Dwight H. G. O., and Conder J., Missionary Researches in Armenia (1834) p. 66. Available at: https://www.google.co.uk/books/edition/Missionary_Researches_in_Armenia/-c0NAAAAIAAJ? hl=en&gbpv=1&dq=kars+armenia&pg=PA81&printsec=frontcover (accessed 31 December 2023).

[344] Smith E., Dwight H. G. O., and Conder J., Missionary Researches in Armenia (1834) p. 63. Available at: https://www.google.co.uk/books/edition/Missionary_Researches_in_Armenia/-c0NAAAAIAAJ? hl=en&gbpv=1&dq=kars+armenia&pg=PA81&printsec=frontcover (accessed 31 December 2023).

[345] Parker R. K., Travels in Georgia, Persia, Armenia, Ancient Babylonia, &c. &c. During the Years 1817, 1818, and 1820 (1822) p. 667. Available at: https://www.google.co.uk/books/edition/Travels_in_Georgia_Persia_Armenia_Ancien/1qdkXaifShsC? hl=en&gbpv=1&dq=armenian+dress&pg=PA832&printsec=frontcover (accessed 2 January 2024).

[346] Smith E., Dwight H. G. O., and Conder J., Missionary Researches in Armenia (1834) p. 64. Available at: https://www.google.co.uk/books/edition/Missionary_Researches_in_Armenia/-c0NAAAAIAAJ? hl=en&gbpv=1&dq=kars+armenia&pg=PA81&printsec=frontcover (accessed 31 December 2023).

[347] Smith E., Dwight H. G. O., and Conder J., Missionary Researches in Armenia (1834) p. 447. Available at: https://www.google.co.uk/books/edition/Missionary_Researches_in_Armenia/-c0NAAAAIAAJ? hl=en&gbpv=1&dq=kars+armenia&pg=PA81&printsec=frontcover (accessed 30 December 2023).

[348] Smith E., Dwight H. G. O., and Conder J., Missionary Researches in

Armenia (1834) p. 81. Available at:
https://www.google.co.uk/books/edition/Missionary_Researches_in_Arme
nia/-c0NAAAAIAAJ?
hl=en&gbpv=1&dq=kars+armenia&pg=PA81&printsec=frontcover
(accessed 30 December 2023).

[349] Tancoigne J. M., a narrative of a journey Into Persia and Residence at
Teheran (1820) pp. 336-337. Available at:
https://www.google.co.uk/books/edition/A_Narrative_of_a_Journey_Into_
Persia_and/LxD3tYJ6pTAC?
hl=en&gbpv=1&dq=trebizond&pg=PA332&printsec=frontcover (accessed
6 January 2024).

[350] Parker R. K., Travels in Georgia, Persia, Armenia, Ancient Babylonia,
&c. &c. During the Years 1817, 1818, and 1820 (1822) p. 666. Available
at:
https://www.google.co.uk/books/edition/Travels_in_Georgia_Persia_Arme
nia_Ancien/1qdkXaifShsC?
hl=en&gbpv=1&dq=armenian+dress&pg=PA832&printsec=frontcover
(accessed 1 January 2024).

[351] Parker R. K., Travels in Georgia, Persia, Armenia, Ancient Babylonia,
&c. &c. During the Years 1817, 1818, and 1820 (1822) p. 696. Available
at:
https://www.google.co.uk/books/edition/Travels_in_Georgia_Persia_Arme
nia_Ancien/1qdkXaifShsC?
hl=en&gbpv=1&dq=armenian+dress&pg=PA832&printsec=frontcover
(accessed 1 January 2024).

[352] Herculean, Trebizond, the last Greek Empire, Hellenic travels to the
past (2008), Available at:
https://herculean.wordpress.com/2008/01/29/trebizond-the-last-greek-
empire/ (accessed 4 January 2024).

[353] The Monthly Magazine, Or, British Register (1803) p. 33. Available
at:
https://www.google.co.uk/books/edition/Monthly_Magazine_of_Politics_
Literature/NL3a7toBe-4C?
hl=en&gbpv=1&dq=Trebizond&pg=PA33&printsec=frontcover (accessed
3 January 2024).

[354] Minority Rights, Laz. Available at:
https://minorityrights.org/minorities/laz/ (accessed 5 January 2024).

[355] Knight C., the English Cyclopedia, part 1, volume 1 (1866) p. 507.
Available at:
https://www.google.co.uk/books/edition/The_English_Cyclopedia/e589A
QAAMAAJ?

hl=en&gbpv=1&dq=laz+trebizond&pg=PA507&printsec=frontcover (accessed 5 January 2024).

[356] Matcham, M.E. (1911) The Nelsons of Burnham Thorpe: a record of a Norfolk family compiled from unpublished letters and notebooks, 1787-1842, p. 35.

[357] Wikipedia contributors, Sir Robert Ainslie, 1st Baronet. Available at: https://en.wikipedia.org/wiki/Sir_Robert_Ainslie,_1st_Baronet (accessed 6 January 2024).

[358] The British Museum, Baths of Cleopatra, at Alexandria, series: views in Egypt, Palestine and other parts of the Ottoman Empire. Available at: https://www.britishmuseum.org/collection/object/P_1948-1125-2 (accessed 7 January 2024).

[359] Watkins T., travels through Switzerland, Italy, Sicily, the Greek Islands to Constantinople... (1794) pp. 223–225. Available at: https://www.google.co.uk/books/edition/Travels_Through_Switzerland_Italy_Sicily/S-Y-AQAAMAAJ?hl=en&gbpv=1&dq=Robert+Ainslie&pg=PA223&printsec=frontcover (accessed 6 January 2024).

[360] Watkins T., travels through Switzerland, Italy, Sicily, the Greek Islands to Constantinople... (1794) p. 227. Available at: https://www.google.co.uk/books/edition/Travels_Through_Switzerland_Italy_Sicily/S-Y-AQAAMAAJ?hl=en&gbpv=1&dq=Robert+Ainslie&pg=PA223&printsec=frontcover (accessed 6 January 2024).

[361] Frost J., the panorama of nations (1853) p. 453. Available at: https://www.google.co.uk/books/edition/The_Panorama_of_Nations/dWkBAAAAYAAJ?hl=en&gbpv=1&dq=trebizond+vista&pg=PA453&printsec=frontcover (accessed 6 January 2024).

[362] Matcham, M.E. (1911) The Nelsons of Burnham Thorpe: a record of a Norfolk family compiled from unpublished letters and notebooks, 1787-1842, p. 36.

[363] Umasy, N., Ottoman Greece | Map and timeline (no date). Available at: https://history-maps.com/story/History-of-Greece/event/Ottoman-Greece (accessed 6 November 2023).

[364] Matcham, M.E. (1911) The Nelsons of Burnham Thorpe: a record of a Norfolk family compiled from unpublished letters and notebooks, 1787-1842, p. 36.

[365] Wikipedia contributors, William Hamilton (diplomat) (2023).

Available at: https://en.wikipedia.org/wiki/William_Hamilton_(diplomat) (accessed 7 January 2024).

[366] Contributors to Wikimedia projects, Dictionary of National Biography,1885-1900/Matcham, George(2020). Available at: https://en.wikisource.org/wiki/Dictionary_of_National_Biography,_1885-1900/Matcham,_George (accessed 27 October 2023).

[367] Wagnleitner, R.F., Schreyvogl, F. and Roider, K.A., Joseph II | Holy Roman Emperor, Enlightened Ruler & Reformer (1998). Available at: https://www.britannica.com/biography/Joseph-II (accessed 27 October 2023).

[368] Information kindly supplied by Abel Land, curatorial assistant of the Fashion History Museum in Cambridge, Ontario, and tailor of historical menswear. Private email correspondence in August 2023.

[369] Western fashion of men in 1775-1795 – HiSoUR – Hi So You Are (no date). Available at: https://www.hisour.com/western-fashion-of-men-in-1775-1795-32516/. (Accessed 13 July 2023)

[370] Matcham, M.E. (1911) The Nelsons of Burnham Thorpe: a record of a Norfolk family compiled from unpublished letters and notebooks, 1787-1842, p. 34

[371] Matcham, M.E. (1911) The Nelsons of Burnham Thorpe: a record of a Norfolk family compiled from unpublished letters and notebooks, 1787-1842, p. 30.

[372] Wiltshire and Swindon History Centre: Eyre-Matcham family of Newhouse, Whiteparish and Downton; 3 - deeds etc. Matcham family: not main estate, 1369/3/2: Copies of the marriage settlement of George Matcham of Enfield, Middlesex, and Catherine Nelson of Burnham Thorpe, Norfolk, 1787, with trust deeds.

[373] Matcham, M.E. (1911) The Nelsons of Burnham Thorpe: a record of a Norfolk family compiled from unpublished letters and notebooks, 1787-1842, p. 36.

[374] Coaching inns - the Westgate Bath - history (2014) Bath UK Tourism, Accommodation, Restaurants & Whats On. Available at: https://bath.co.uk/featured/coaching-inns-the-westgate-bath (Accessed: 12 July 2023).

[375] Cruttwell, R. (1780) Bath Guide. R. Cruttwell. Available at: https://www.google.co.uk/books/edition/The_New_Bath_Guide_Embellis hed_with_Five/mHm_jDiWuqQC?hl=en&gbpv=1. (Accessed 23 July 2023)

[376] Bath Journal, 11th December 1786, p. 4. Copyright British Library Board. Find My Past: https://search.findmypast.co.uk/bna/viewarticle?id=BL/0004012/17861211/004&stringtohighlight=mrs%20matcham

(accessed 30 August 2023).

[377] UNESCO World Heritage Centre, (no date) City of Bath, UNESCO. Available at: https://whc.unesco.org/en/list/428/ (Accessed: 12 July 2023).

[378] Manco, J. (no date) Bath past, Bath Past: Restoration Gaiety. Available at: http://www.buildinghistory.org/bath/tudor/restoration.shtml (Accessed: 12 July 2023).

[379] Bradley I., (2021) Why is 18th-century Bath considered the model for modern day spas?, Literary Hub. Available at: https://lithub.com/why-is-18th-century-bath-considered-the-model-for-modern-day-spas/ (Accessed: 12 July 2023).

[380] Egan, P. (1819) in Walks Through Bath, Describing Everything Worthy Of Interest. Meyler and Son, pp. 30–31. Available at: https://www.google.co.uk/books/edition/Walks_Through_Bath/jtVCAAAAIAAJ?hl=en&gbpv=1&dq=Pierce+Egan%27s+Walks+Through+Bath&printsec=frontcover (accessed: 12 July 2023).

[381] The Royal Crescent (no date) Visit Bath. Available at: https://visitbath.co.uk/things-to-do/the-royal-crescent-p56191 (Accessed: 11 July 2023).

[382] The Assembly Rooms (no date) Visit Bath. Available at: https://visitbath.co.uk/things-to-do/the-assembly-rooms-p23901 (Accessed: 12 July 2023).

[383] Young, A. (2019) G is for Gainsborough, Anne's Family History. Available at: https://anneyoungau.wordpress.com/2019/04/08/g-is-for-gainsborough/ (accessed 12 July 2023).

[384] Egan, P. (1819) in Walks Through Bath, Describing Everything Worthy Of Interest. Meyler and Son, pp. 129–128. Available at: https://www.google.co.uk/books/edition/Walks_Through_Bath/jtVCAAAAIAAJ?hl=en&gbpv=1&dq=Pierce+Egan%27s+Walks+Through+Bath&printsec=frontcover (accessed 12 July 2023).

[385] Matcham, M.E. (1911) in Nelsons of Burnham Thorpe: A record of a Norfolk family ... J. Lane, p. 30.

[386] The Assembly Rooms (no date) Visit Bath. Available at: https://visitbath.co.uk/things-to-do/the-assembly-rooms-p23901

(Accessed: 12 July 2023).

[387] RegencyDances.org - your index to 19th century dances (no date b). Available at: https://www.regencydances.org/paper011.php (accessed 14 July 2023).

[388] Bruce-Watt, M. (2023b) Reading the Rooms - The Bath Magazine. Available at: https://thebathmagazine.co.uk/reading-the-rooms/. (Accessed 13 July 2023).

[389] Ipswich Journal, 30th December 1786, p. 2. Copyright British Library Board. Find My Past: https://search.findmypast.co.uk/bna/viewarticle?id=BL/0000071/17861230/025&stringtohighlight=ball%20bath (accessed 12 July 2023).

[390] Bath Chronicle and Weekly Gazette, 28th December 1786, p. 3. Copyright British Library Board. Find My Past: Ipswich Journal, 30th December 1786, p. 2. Copyright British Library Board. Find My Past: https://search.findmypast.co.uk/bna/viewarticle?id=BL/0000071/17861230/025&stringtohighlight=ball%20bath (Accessed 12 July 2023).

[391] Timbrell Cockburn Cunha (no date) 17th, 18th and Early 19th Century Reproduction Perfumes and Colognes. Available at: https://tccunha.ca/products/17th-18th-and-early-19th-century-reproduction-perfumes-and-colognes. (Accessed 13 July 2023)

[392] Savage, V.A.P. by W. (2016) Georgian hair-care: Pomades. Available at: https://penandpension.com/2016/02/23/georgian-hair-care-pomades/. (Accessed 13 July 2023)

[393] Bruce-Watt, M. (2023) Reading the Rooms - The Bath Magazine. Available at: https://thebathmagazine.co.uk/reading-the-rooms/. (Accessed: 12 July 2023).

[394] Lesso, R. and Lesso, R. (2022) "Marie Antoinette: Rococo Queen - the thread," the thread - the thread is the FS online editorial embracing our sewing community and providing weekly inspiration, 13 June. Available at: https://blog.fabrics-store.com/2020/09/01/marie-antoinette-rococo-queen/. (Accessed 12 July 2023)

[395] Women's Hairstyles & Cosmetics of the 18th Century: France & England, 1750-1790 – Démodé (no date). Available at: http://demodecouture.com/hairstyles-cosmetics-18th-century/. (Accessed 13 July 2023)

[396] Majer, M. (no date b) 1780-1789 | Fashion History Timeline. Available at: https://fashionhistory.fitnyc.edu/1780-1789/. (Accessed 13 July 2023)

[397] Williams, K. (2006) in England's mistress: The infamous life of Emma Hamilton. London: Hutchinson, p. 95.

[398] Matcham, M.E. (1911) The Nelsons of Burnham Thorpe: a record of a Norfolk family compiled from unpublished letters and notebooks, 1787-1842, p. 36.

[399] H, C. (2014) Social Dancing – a matter of import II. Available at: https://historicinterpreter.wordpress.com/2014/12/15/social-dancing-a-matter-of-import-part-2/. (Accessed 14 July 2023)

[400] Matcham, M.E. (1911) The Nelsons of Burnham Thorpe: a record of a Norfolk family compiled from unpublished letters and notebooks, 1787-1842, p. 18

[401] Proceedings of the History of Bath Research Group (2017) Tracking Nelson Through Bath 1771–1798, p. 8. Available at: https://historyofbath.org/images/documents/e55f08aa-a773-43a8-aa3c-31168002fece.pdf (Accessed: 11 July 2023).

[402] Hibbert, C., Nelson: A personal history. London: Penguin (2002). P. 4.

[403] Matcham, M.E. (1911) The Nelsons of Burnham Thorpe: a record of a Norfolk family compiled from unpublished letters and notebooks, 1787-1842, p. 36.

[404] Matcham, M.E. (1911) The Nelsons of Burnham Thorpe: a record of a Norfolk family compiled from unpublished letters and notebooks, 1787-1842, p. 10.

[405] Matcham, M.E. (1911) The Nelsons of Burnham Thorpe: a record of a Norfolk family compiled from unpublished letters and notebooks, 1787-1842, p. 18.

[406] Matcham, M.E. (1911) The Nelsons of Burnham Thorpe: a record of a Norfolk family compiled from unpublished letters and notebooks, 1787-1842, p. 57.

[407] Matcham, M.E. (1911) The Nelsons of Burnham Thorpe: a record of a Norfolk family compiled from unpublished letters and notebooks, 1787-1842, p. 57.

[408] Ancestry.com. Somerset, England, Marriage Registers, Bonds and Allegations, 1754-1914 [database on-line]. Lehi, UT, USA: Ancestry.com Operations, Inc., 2016. Original data: Anglican Parish Registers. Marriage Bonds and Allegations. Somerset Archives & Local Studies, South West Heritage Trust, Taunton, England. Available at: https://www.ancestry.co.uk/imageviewer/collections/60858/images/ENGL B030D_D-D-CM-1787B_M_00313?pId=5105511 (Accessed 15 July

2023)

[409] Ancestry.com. Somerset, England, Marriage Registers, Bonds and Allegations, 1754-1914 [database on-line]. Lehi, UT, USA: Ancestry.com Operations, Inc., 2016. Original data: Anglican Parish Registers. Marriage Bonds and Allegations. Somerset Archives & Local Studies, South West Heritage Trust, Taunton, England. Available at: https://www.ancestry.co.uk/imageviewer/collections/60858/images/ENGL B030D_D-D-CM-1787B_M_00313?pId=5105511 (Accessed 15 July 2023)

[410] St James, Bath (no date). Available at: https://www.batharchives.co.uk/cemeteries/st-james-bath. (Accessed 15 July 2023)

[411] Marrying by licence: Marriage bonds and allegations (no date). Available at: https://www.york.ac.uk/media/borthwick/documents/5marriagebonds.pdf (Accessed: July 22, 2023).

[412] Ancestry.com. Somerset, England, Church of England Baptisms, Marriages, and Burials, 1531-1812 [database on-line]. Lehi, UT, USA: Ancestry.com Operations, Inc., 2016. Available at: https://www.ancestry.co.uk/discoveryui-content/view/903294788:60856? tid=82673375&pid=40467016918&queryId=23c0ba98c24f64725a75bc4e 1ca66e04&_phsrc=ECs1862&_phstart=successSource (Accessed 21 July 2023)

[413] Bath Chronicle and Weekly Gazette, 1st March 1787, p.3. Copyright British Library Board. Find My Past: https://search.findmypast.co.uk/bna/viewarticle? id=BL/0000221/17870301/013&stringtohighlight=matcham%20enfield (accessed 15 July 2023).

[414] The Royal Crescent (no date) Visit Bath. Available at: https://visitbath.co.uk/things-to-do/the-royal-crescent-p56191 (Accessed: 11 July 2023).

[415] Egan, P. (1819) in Walks Through Bath, Describing Everything Worthy Of Interest. Meyler and Son, pp. 156. Available at: https://www.google.co.uk/books/edition/Walks_Through_Bath/jtVCAAA AIAAJ?hl=en&gbpv=1&dq=Pierce+Egan %27s+Walks+Through+Bath&printsec=frontcover (Accessed: 23 July 2023).

[416] Place making areas: Walcot Street south (no date). Available at: https://www.bathnes.gov.uk/sites/default/files/sitedocuments/Planning-and-Building-Control/Planning-Policy/Evidence-Base/Urban-Design-

Landscape-and-Heritage/her_walcot_street_south_2014.pdf (Accessed: July 25, 2023).

[417] St Swithin's History (no date) "Our history". Available at: Available at: https://www.stswithinswalcot.org.uk/history.html (accessed 22 July 2023)

[418] Lathan, S. (2022) Regency Marriage ~ The Ceremony Preparation & Participants - Sharon Lathan, Novelist. Available at: https://sharonlathanauthor.com/regency-marriage-the-ceremony/ (accessed 22 July 2023)

[419] Bath daily photo (2007). Available at: https://www.flickr.com/photos/25058859@N00/558354701/ (accessed 16 November 2023).

[420] Information kindly supplied by Abel Land, curatorial assistant of the Fashion History Museum in Cambridge, Ontario, and tailor of historical menswear. Private email correspondence in August 2023.

[421] Lathan, S. (2022) Regency Marriage ~ The Ceremony Preparation & Participants - Sharon Lathan, Novelist. Available at: https://sharonlathanauthor.com/regency-marriage-the-ceremony/ (accessed 22 July 2023)

[422] Chertsey Museum – Brides Revisited (no date). Available at: https://chertseymuseum.org/brides-revisited (accessed 23 July 2023)

[423] Sugden, J. Nelson: The Sword of Albion. Random House (2012), p. 721.

[424] Ancestry.com. Somerset, England, Church of England Baptisms, Marriages, and Burials, 1531-1812 [database on-line]. Lehi, UT, USA: Ancestry.com Operations, Inc., 2016. Available at: https://www.ancestry.co.uk/discoveryui-content/view/903294788:60856?tid=82673375&pid=40467016918&queryId=23c0ba98c24f64725a75bc4e1ca66e04&_phsrc=ECs1862&_phstart=successSource (Accessed 22 July 2023)

[425] Samuel Finney | Thomas Bolton and Susannah Nelson (sister of Admiral Horatio Nelson) | MutualArt (no date). https://www.mutualart.com/Artwork/Thomas-Bolton-and-Susannah-Nelson--siste/111EC926EF158DFC5965C18E470DD05F?fbclid=IwAR0G16KKbZ9HojpL1iQUD7g7iVicYQbXqdakeyfrddU3LyDLBObQxwfh3-o (accessed 19 September 2023).

[426] Lathan, S. (2022b) Regency Marriage ~ The Vows & The Celebration! - Sharon Lathan, Novelist. Available at: https://sharonlathanauthor.com/regency-marriage-the-vows-the-

celebration/ (accessed 23 July 2023)

[427] https://www.jstor.org/stable/3678475

[428] https://www.nottingham.ac.uk/manuscriptsandspecialcollections/research guidance/deedsindepth/settlements/settlements.aspx

[429] Wiltshire and Swindon History Centre: Eyre-Matcham family of Newhouse, Whiteparish and Downton; 3 - deeds etc. Matcham family: not main estate, 1369/3/2: Copies of the marriage settlement of George Matcham of Enfield, Middlesex, and Catherine Nelson of Burnham Thorpe, Norfolk, 1787, with trust deeds.

[430] Private correspondence between Dr Tim Ridge and the author.

[431] Hibbert, C., Nelson: A personal history. London: Penguin (2002). P. 4.

[432] Matcham, M.E. (1911) The Nelsons of Burnham Thorpe: a record of a Norfolk family compiled from unpublished letters and notebooks, 1787-1842, pp. 284–288.

[433] Manley, G. (1974) Central England temperatures: monthly means 1659 to 1973. Available at: https://www.rmets.org/sites/default/files/papers/qj74manley.pdf (accessed 23 August 2023).

[434] Matcham, M.E. (1911) The Nelsons of Burnham Thorpe: a record of a Norfolk family compiled from unpublished letters and notebooks, 1787-1842, pp. 78–79.

[435] The rise of cities in the 18th century (2009). Available at: https://www.bl.uk/georgian-britain/articles/the-rise-of-cities-in-the-18th-century (accessed 25 August 2023).

[436] England, Pallot's Marriage Index, 1780 - 1837 (2001). Available at: https://www.ancestry.co.uk/family-tree/person/tree/82673375/person/40467016665/facts (accessed: August 24, 2023).

[437] Wikipedia contributors, St Pancras, London (2023). Available at: https://en.wikipedia.org/wiki/St_Pancras,_London (accessed 24 August 2023).

[438] History (no date d). Available at: https://www.britishmuseum.org/about-us/british-museum-story/history (accessed: August 23, 2023).

[439] Sugden, J. Nelson: The Sword of Albion. Random House (2012), p. 861.

[440] Historic England (no date a) Black Lives in England - Black British history in the 18th and 19th centuries | Historic England. Available at: https://historicengland.org.uk/research/inclusive-heritage/the-slave-trade-and-abolition/sites-of-memory/black-lives-in-england/ (accessed 24 August 2023).

[441] Historic England (no date b) Servants - Black British history in the 18th and 19th centuries | Historic England. Available at: https://historicengland.org.uk/research/inclusive-heritage/the-slave-trade-and-abolition/sites-of-memory/black-lives-in-england/servants/ (accessed 24 August 2023).

[442] British Library (no date). Available at: https://www.bl.uk/restoration-18th-century-literature/articles/abolition-of-the-slave-trade-and-slavery-in-britain (accessed 24 August 2023).

[443] British Library (no date b). Available at: https://www.bl.uk/collection-items/illustration-of-the-long-room-custom-house (accessed 25 August 2023).

[444] Ashworth, W. J., 'Life on the Waterfront', Customs and Excise: Trade, Production, and Consumption in England 1640-1845 (Oxford, 2003; online edn, Oxford Academic, 1 Jan. 2010), https://doi.org/10.1093/acprof:oso/9780199259212.003.0009 (accessed 22 August 2023).

[445] Warwick Leadlay Gallery (no date) The Custom house. Available at: https://warwickleadlay.com/products/the-custom-house (accessed 24 August 2023).

[446] Newtonian (2012) Pollution In The Thames – Reason, Romanticism, and Revolution. Available at: https://www.leeannhunter.com/humanities/2012/09/19/pollution-in-the-thames/. (accessed 25 August 2023).

[447] London, England, Land Tax Records, 1692-1932 (2011). Available at: https://www.ancestry.co.uk/family-tree/person/tree/82673375/person/40467016860/facts (accessed 24 August 2023).

[448] Sugden, J. Nelson: The Sword of Albion. Random House (2012), p. 19.

[449] Hibbert, C., Nelson: A personal history. London: Penguin (2002). P. 5.

[450] Hibbert, C., Nelson: A personal history. London: Penguin (2002). P. 5.

[451] Sugden, J. Nelson: The Sword of Albion. Random House (2012), p. 860.

[452] Savage, V.A.P. by W. (2016b) Traffic on Georgian roads in Norfolk. Available at: https://penandpension.com/2016/01/12/traffic-on-georgian-roads-in-norfolk/ (accessed 23 July 2023)

[453] Details derived from the author's visit to the house in 2017 with the kind permission of its current owner.

[454] Harrison, J. (1806) Life of Lord Nelson. London, p. 11. Available at: https://www.google.co.uk/books/edition/The_life_of_Horatio_lord_viscou nt_Nelson/cToIAAAAQAAJ? hl=en&gbpv=1&dq=nelson+grandmother+hilborough&pg=PA11&printse c=frontcover (accessed 25 July 2023)

[455] Sugden, J. Nelson: The Sword of Albion. Random House (2012), p. 486.

[456] Matcham, M.E. (1911) The Nelsons of Burnham Thorpe: a record of a Norfolk family compiled from unpublished letters and notebooks, 1787-1842, p. 37.

[457] Academic Dictionaries and Encyclopedias (2010) The Norfolk Burnhams. Available at: https://en-academic.com/dic.nsf/enwiki/952474 (accessed 29 July 2023)

[458] Gérin W., Horatia Nelson Oxford University Press (1970) p. 227.

[459] Howarth, D.A. and Howarth, S., Nelson: The immortal memory. London: Conway Maritime. (2004), p. 4.

[460] The Rectory, Burnham Thorpe, Norfolk (no date) Royal Museums Greenwich. Available at: https://www.rmg.co.uk/collections/objects/rmgc-object-13252 (Accessed: 11 July 2023).

[461] Farmstead and Landscape Statement: North West Norfolk. (2020). Available at: https://historicengland.org.uk/research/results/reports/8095/NorthWestNorf olkChalkandLimestoneMixed (accessed 29 July 2023)

[462] History of Holkham Hall & Estate | Visiting Holkham | The Earls (2023). Available at: https://www.holkham.co.uk/about-us/our-history/ (accessed 20 august 2023).

[463] Briscoe, K. (2022) "How Norfolk shaped agricultural history," Eastern Daily Press, 7 September. Available at: https://www.edp24.co.uk/news/21162226.norfolk-shaped-agricultural-history/ (accessed 29 July 2023).

[464] James, D. (2022) "Where the pines meet the sea on the north Norfolk coast," Eastern Daily Press, 23 August. Available at:

https://www.edp24.co.uk/lifestyle/20709570.pines-meet-sea-north-norfolk-coast/ (accessed 30th July 2023).

[465] Matcham, M.E. (1911) The Nelsons of Burnham Thorpe: a record of a Norfolk family compiled from unpublished letters and notebooks, 1787-1842, p. 37.

[466] Matcham, M.E. (1911) The Nelsons of Burnham Thorpe: a record of a Norfolk family compiled from unpublished letters and notebooks, 1787-1842, pp. 37–38.

[467] Matcham, M.E. (1911) The Nelsons of Burnham Thorpe: a record of a Norfolk family compiled from unpublished letters and notebooks, 1787-1842, p. 83.

[468] Hibbert, C., Nelson: A personal history. London: Penguin (2002). P. 5.

[469] Matcham, M.E. (1911) The Nelsons of Burnham Thorpe: a record of a Norfolk family compiled from unpublished letters and notebooks, 1787-1842, p. 24.

[470] Matcham, M.E. (1911) The Nelsons of Burnham Thorpe: a record of a Norfolk family compiled from unpublished letters and notebooks, 1787-1842, p, 58.

[471] Observations from the author's visit to Norfolk in August 2023.

[472] Irwin, E. (1787) A Series of Adventures in the Course of a Voyage Up the Red-Sea.... p. 293. Available at: https://www.google.co.uk/books/edition/A_Series_of_Adventures_in_the_Course_of/_VVWAAAAYAAJ?hl=en&gbpv=0 (accessed January 2022).

[473] Ross D., Britain Express (no date) Wells next the Sea, Norfolk - History, Travel, and accommodation information. Available at: https://www.britainexpress.com/attractions.htm?attraction=2988 (accessed 30 July 2023).

[474] Cross, A. (no date) Family life. Available at: https://nelson-society.com/life-of-nelson/family-life/ (accessed 26 July 2023)

[475] Samuel Finney | Thomas Bolton and Susannah Nelson (sister of Admiral Horatio Nelson) | MutualArt (no date). https://www.mutualart.com/Artwork/Thomas-Bolton-and-Susannah-Nelson--siste/111EC926EF158DFC5965C18E470DD05F?fbclid=IwAR0G16KKbZ9HojpL1iQUD7g7iVicYQbXqdakeyfrddU3LyDLBObQxwfh3-o (accessed 19 September 2023).

[476] Sugden, J. (2012) Nelson: A Dream of Glory. Random House. Kindle Edition. P. 206.

[477] Hibbert, C., Nelson: A personal history. London: Penguin (2002). P. 5.

[478] James, D. (2022) "Where the pines meet the sea on the north Norfolk coast," Eastern Daily Press, 23 August. Available at: https://www.edp24.co.uk/lifestyle/20709570.pines-meet-sea-north-norfolk-coast/ (accessed 30th July 2023).

[479] Norfolk Chronicle, 21st January 1786, p.3. Copyright British Library Board. Find My Past: https://search.findmypast.co.uk/bna/viewarticle?id=BL/0000246/17860121/015&stringtohighlight=thomas%20bolton%20wells (accessed 30 July 2023).

[480] The Nelson Touch (2013) Timeline. Available at: http://www.admiralnelson.info/Timeline.htm (accessed 30 July 2023)

[481] Matcham, M.E. (1911) The Nelsons of Burnham Thorpe: a record of a Norfolk family compiled from unpublished letters and notebooks, 1787-1842, p. 39.

[482] Matcham, M.E. (1911) The Nelsons of Burnham Thorpe: a record of a Norfolk family compiled from unpublished letters and notebooks, 1787-1842, p. 39.

[483] Broads Authority (no date) History. Available at: https://www.broads-authority.gov.uk/learning/for-students/history (accessed 30 July 2013)

[484] Matcham, M.E. (1911) The Nelsons of Burnham Thorpe: a record of a Norfolk family compiled from unpublished letters and notebooks, 1787-1842, p. 39.

[485] Norfolk Heritage Explorer (no date) Barton-Hall. Available at: https://www.heritage.norfolk.gov.uk/record-details?MNF23028-Barton-Hall&Index=21879&RecordCount=57339&SessionID=858014c7-56f1-4333-8d51-55b0ac2a5ddb (accessed 30 July 2023)

[486] Window tax: Tyne and Wear case study (no date) Parliament UK. Available at: https://www.parliament.uk/about/living-heritage/transformingsociety/towncountry/towns/tyne-and-wear-case-study/ (Accessed: 30 July 2023).

[487] Observations from the author's visit to Barton Hall, in 2017, when it was owned by Mrs. Jeanie Peel.

[488] Matcham, M.E. (1911) The Nelsons of Burnham Thorpe: a record of a Norfolk family compiled from unpublished letters and notebooks, 1787-1842, p. 58.

[489] Matcham, M.E. (1911) The Nelsons of Burnham Thorpe: a record of a Norfolk family compiled from unpublished letters and notebooks, 1787-

1842, p. 40.

[490] Norfolk Chronicle, 1st October 1791, p.2. Copyright British Library Board. Find My Past: https://search.findmypast.co.uk/bna/viewarticle?id=BL/0000246/17911001/003&stringtohighlight=matcham (accessed 19 August 2023).

[491] Matcham, M.E. (1911) The Nelsons of Burnham Thorpe: a record of a Norfolk family compiled from unpublished letters and notebooks, 1787-1842, p, 42.

[492] B, B. (1829) The Sporting Magazine. Volume 73. P. 164. Available at: https://www.google.co.uk/books/edition/The_Sporting_Magazine/Zqsrw_J N14IC?hl=en&gbpv=1 (accessed: August 7, 2023).

[493] Lubbock, R. (1845) Observations on the fauna of Norfolk: And More Particularly on the District of the Broads. Pp. 54–58. Available at: https://www.google.co.uk/books/edition/Observations_on_the_fauna_of_N orfolk_and/DRAAAAAAQAAJ?hl=en&gbpv=1&dq=norfolk+broads+sport&pg=PA51&printsec=frontcove r (accessed 7 August 2023).

[494] B, B. (1829) The Sporting Magazine. Volume 73. P. 163. Available at: https://www.google.co.uk/books/edition/The_Sporting_Magazine/Zqsrw_J N14IC?hl=en&gbpv=1 (accessed: August 7, 2023).

[495] The Sporting Magazine (1836) Volumes 10–11, Issues 57–68. P. 482. Available at: https://www.google.co.uk/books/edition/The_New_Sporting_Magazine/2 VWMQYPfpHsC?hl=en&gbpv=1 (accessed: August 7, 2023).

[496] Lubbock, R. (1845b) Observations on the fauna of Norfolk: And More Particularly on the District of the Broads. Pp. 51–52. Available at: https://www.google.co.uk/books/edition/Observations_on_the_fauna_of_N orfolk_and/DRAAAAAAQAAJ?hl=en&gbpv=1&dq=norfolk+broads+sport&pg=PA51&printsec=frontcove r (accessed 7 August 2023).

[497] Matcham, M.E. (1911) The Nelsons of Burnham Thorpe: a record of a Norfolk family compiled from unpublished letters and notebooks, 1787-1842, p. 59.

[498] Matcham, M.E. (1911) The Nelsons of Burnham Thorpe: a record of a Norfolk family compiled from unpublished letters and notebooks, 1787-1842, p. 58.

[499] Matcham, M.E. (1911) The Nelsons of Burnham Thorpe: a record of a Norfolk family compiled from unpublished letters and notebooks, 1787-1842, p. 45.

[500] Howarth, D.A. and Howarth, S., Nelson: The immortal memory. London: Conway Maritime. (2004). P. 87.

[501] Digital Library of the Caribbean (no date). Available at: https://www.dloc.com/UF00075409/00007/images/96 (accessed 6 August 2023).

[502] A history of St Kitts : the sweet trade : Hubbard, Vincent K : Free Download, Borrow, and Streaming : Internet Archive (2002). Available at: https://archive.org/details/historyofstkitts00vinc/page/102/mode/2up?q=nelson (accessed 14 October 2023).

[503] Hibbert, C., Nelson: A personal history. London: Penguin (2002). P. 35.

[504] Matcham, M.E. (1911) The Nelsons of Burnham Thorpe: a record of a Norfolk family compiled from unpublished letters and notebooks, 1787-1842, pp. 44–45.

[505] Sugden, J. (2012) Nelson: A Dream of Glory. Random House. Kindle Edition. P. 370.

[506] Matcham, M.E. (1911) The Nelsons of Burnham Thorpe: a record of a Norfolk family compiled from unpublished letters and notebooks, 1787-1842, pp. 52–53.

[507] Sugden, J. (2012) Nelson: A Dream of Glory. Random House. Kindle Edition. Pp. 376-7.

[508] Sugden, J. (2012) Nelson: A Dream of Glory. Random House. Kindle Edition. Pp. 376-377.

[509] Matcham, M.E. (1911) The Nelsons of Burnham Thorpe: a record of a Norfolk family compiled from unpublished letters and notebooks, 1787-1842, p. 285.

[510] Miniature portrait of young Nelson formerly in the possession of the Style Ward family.

[511] Sugden, J. (2012) Nelson: A Dream of Glory. Random House. Kindle Edition. P. 221.

[512] Sugden, J. (2012) Nelson: A Dream of Glory. Random House. Kindle Edition. P. 312.

[513] Fraser F., Beloved Emma. Weidenfield and Nicholson. London (1986). P. 281.

[514] Frances Nisbet (no date). Available at: https://www.rmg.co.uk/stories/topics/frances-nisbet (accessed 16 October

2023).

[515] Matcham, M.E. (1911) The Nelsons of Burnham Thorpe: a record of a Norfolk family compiled from unpublished letters and notebooks, 1787-1842, pp. 60–61.

[516] Sugden, J. (2012) Nelson: A Dream of Glory. Random House. Kindle Edition. P. 377.

[517] Sugden, J. (2012) Nelson: A Dream of Glory. Random House. Kindle Edition. P. 377.

[518] Sugden, J. (2012) Nelson: A Dream of Glory. Random House. Kindle Edition. P. 381.

[519] Sugden, J. (2012) Nelson: A Dream of Glory. Random House. Kindle Edition. P. 380.

[520] Matcham, M.E. (1911) The Nelsons of Burnham Thorpe: a record of a Norfolk family compiled from unpublished letters and notebooks, 1787-1842, pp. 64-55.

[521] Royal Museums Greenwich (no date) French Revolution. Available at: https://www.rmg.co.uk/stories/topics/french-revolution (accessed 29 July 2023)

[522] Bath Chronicle and Weekly Gazette, 10th December 1789, p.3. Copyright British Library Board. Find My Past: https://search.findmypast.co.uk/bna/viewarticle?id=BL/0000221/17891210/013&stringtohighlight=matcham%20bath (accessed 30 August 2023).

[523] Matcham, M.E. (1911) The Nelsons of Burnham Thorpe: a record of a Norfolk family compiled from unpublished letters and notebooks, 1787-1842, pp. 78–79.

[524] Lipscomb, G. (1799) A Journey Into Cornwall, Through the Counties of Southampton, Wilts, Dorset, Somerset & Devon. P. 87. Available at: https://www.google.co.uk/books/edition/A_Journey_Into_Cornwall_Through_the_Coun/i8QuAAAAMAAJ?hl=en&gbpv=0 (accessed 3 September 2023).

[525] Matcham, M.E. (1911) The Nelsons of Burnham Thorpe: a record of a Norfolk family compiled from unpublished letters and notebooks, 1787-1842, p. 135.

[526] Cary, J. (1798) Cary's New Itinerary Or, An Accurate Delineation of the Great Roads, Both Direct and Cross, Throughout England and Wales. P. 61. Available at:

https://www.google.co.uk/books/edition/Cary_s_New_Itinerary/iF6NInA-1ooC?hl=en&gbpv=0 (accessed 3 September 2023).

[527] Matcham, M.E. (1911) The Nelsons of Burnham Thorpe: a record of a Norfolk family compiled from unpublished letters and notebooks, 1787-1842, p. 82.

[528] Wiltshire and Swindon History Centre: Eyre-Matcham family of Newhouse, Whiteparish and Downton; 3 - deeds etc. Matcham family: not main estate, 1369/3/2, Copies of the marriage settlement of George Matcham of Enfield, Middlesex, and Catherine Nelson of Burnham Thorpe, Norfolk, 1787, with trust deeds.

[529] Norfolk Chronicle, 1st October 1791, p.2. Copyright British Library Board. Find My Past: https://search.findmypast.co.uk/bna/viewarticle?id=BL/0000246/17911001/003&stringtohighlight=matcham (accessed 19 August 2023).

[530] Ramsay, Allan. (1790) The Gentle Shepherd, a Scotch Pastoral. by Allan Ramsay. Attempted in English by Margaret Turner. Available at: https://www.google.co.uk/books/edition/The_Gentle_Shepherd/E8cIAAAAQAAJ?hl=en&gbpv=1&dq=%22george+matcham%22&pg=PP21&printsec=frontcover (accessed 24 September 2023).

[531] Ibid.

[532] Matcham, M.E. (1911) The Nelsons of Burnham Thorpe: a record of a Norfolk family compiled from unpublished letters and notebooks, 1787-1842, p. 86.

[533] Matcham, M.E. (1911) The Nelsons of Burnham Thorpe: a record of a Norfolk family compiled from unpublished letters and notebooks, 1787-1842, p. 91.

[534] Matcham, M.E. (1911) The Nelsons of Burnham Thorpe: a record of a Norfolk family compiled from unpublished letters and notebooks, 1787-1842, p. 92.

[535] Forum Auctions: LOT:160 | Travel Diary.- Armstrong (Harriet, of Castle Armstrong, Co. Offaly, Ireland, fl. 1792) [Journal of a journey from Ringwood, Hampshire to Holyhead], autograph manuscript, stains slightly affecting some text, original marbled wrappers, 12mo, 1792. Available at: https://www.forumauctions.co.uk/29412/Harriet-Armstrong.-Travel-journal-manuscript-12mo-1792?auction_no=1008&view=lot_detail (accessed 27 August 2023).

[536] Matcham, M.E. (1911) The Nelsons of Burnham Thorpe: a record of a Norfolk family compiled from unpublished letters and notebooks, 1787-1842, pp. 98-99.

[537] Sotheby's and Co, S.P.B.A., Nelson and the Napoleonic Wars ; Including the Matcham Collection, Trafalgar, (2005) item 2, NELSON, HORATIO, Lord. Autograph letter signed ("Horatio Nelson"), with his right hand, to his sister Catherine Matcham on FAMILY BUSINESS AND LOCAL GOSSIP, p. 20.

[538] Matcham, M.E. (1911) The Nelsons of Burnham Thorpe: a record of a Norfolk family compiled from unpublished letters and notebooks, 1787-1842, p. 96.

[539] Harrison, C. (no date) Find a ship. Available at: https://threedecks.org/index.php?display_type=ships_search (accessed 7 August 2023).

[540] Cross, A. (no date a) Chronology. Available at: https://nelson-society.com/life-of-nelson/chronology/ (accessed 6 August 2023).

[541] Watson, J.R. (2003) "1793," in *Palgrave Macmillan UK eBooks*, pp. 39–51. Available at: https://doi.org/10.1057/9780230514539_3 (accessed 28 August 2023).

[542] Howarth, D.A. and Howarth, S., Nelson: The immortal memory. London: Conway Maritime. (2004). P. 93.

[543] Hibbert, C., Nelson: A personal history. London: Penguin (2002). P. 66.

[544] Howarth, D.A. and Howarth, S., Nelson: The immortal memory. London: Conway Maritime. (2004). P. 127.

[545] Matcham, M.E. (1911) The Nelsons of Burnham Thorpe: a record of a Norfolk family compiled from unpublished letters and notebooks, 1787-1842, p. 103.

[546] Matcham, M.E. (1911) The Nelsons of Burnham Thorpe: a record of a Norfolk family compiled from unpublished letters and notebooks, 1787-1842, p. 153.

[547] Cary, J. (1798) Cary's New Itinerary Or, An Accurate Delineation of the Great Roads, Both Direct and Cross, Throughout England and Wales. P. 61. Available at: https://www.google.co.uk/books/edition/Cary_s_New_Itinerary/iF6NInA-1ooC?hl=en&gbpv=0 (accessed 3 September 2023).

[548] Matcham, M.E. (1911) The Nelsons of Burnham Thorpe: a record of a Norfolk family compiled from unpublished letters and notebooks, 1787-1842, p. 34.

[549] Thomas William Coke, the first Earl of Leicester, lived in Holkham

Hall whose estates bordered Burnham Thorpe. Coke's innovations had revolutionised agriculture.

[550] Matcham, M.E. (1911) The Nelsons of Burnham Thorpe: a record of a Norfolk family compiled from unpublished letters and notebooks, 1787-1842, p. 86.

[551] Matcham, M.E. (1911) The Nelsons of Burnham Thorpe: a record of a Norfolk family compiled from unpublished letters and notebooks, 1787-1842, pp. 89-90.

[552] The St Leonards & St Ives Directory - October 2017 (2017). Available at: https://issuu.com/dorsetpublications/docs/slsid_october_2017_-_web (accessed 27 August 2023).

[553] Ordnance Survey (2023) "GetOutside: do more in the British Outdoors," OS GetOutside [Preprint]. Available at: https://getoutside.ordnancesurvey.co.uk/local/plumley-wood-new-forest (accessed 3 September 2023).

[554] Wiltshire and Swindon History Centre: Eyre-Matcham family of Newhouse, Whiteparish and Downton; 3 - deeds etc. Matcham family: not main estate, 1369/7/2/1, Correspondence to George Matcham family and business including East India Company affairs (1777-1801): letter to George Matcham from Henry Oake of Ringwood dated 23rd May 1799.

[555] Hampshire Chronicle, 30th September 1793, p.4. Copyright British Library Board. Find My Past: https://search.findmypast.co.uk/bna/viewarticle?id=bl%2f0000230%2f17930930%2f014&stringtohighlight=matcham (accessed 17 August 2023).

[556] Sporting Magazine (1793). P. 276. Available at: https://www.google.co.uk/books/edition/Sporting_Magazine/Y5saAQAAMAAJ?hl=en&gbpv=1&dq=new+forest+game&pg=PA276&printsec=frontcover (accessed 3 September 2023).

[557] Strutt, J. (1903) The Sports and Pastimes of the People of England from the Earliest Period: Including the Rural and Domestic Recreations, May Games, Mummeries, Pageants, Processions and Pompous Spectacles, p. 228. Available online: https://www.google.co.uk/books/edition/The_Sports_and_Pastimes_of_the_People_of/eJwSAAAAYAAJ?hl=en&gbpv=1&dq=hunting+new+forest&pg=PA228&printsec=frontcover (accessed 3 September 2023).

[558] Sporting Magazine (1793). P. 248. Available at:
https://www.google.co.uk/books/edition/Sporting_Magazine/Vr0CAAAAY
AAJ?hl=en&gbpv=1&dq=ringwood&pg=PA248&printsec=frontcover
(accessed 3 September 2023).

[559] Matcham, M.E. (1911) The Nelsons of Burnham Thorpe: a record of
a Norfolk family compiled from unpublished letters and notebooks, 1787-
1842, p. 135.

[560] Wiltshire and Swindon History Centre: Eyre-Matcham family of
Newhouse, Whiteparish and Downton; 3 - deeds etc. Matcham family: not
main estate, 1369/7/2/1, Correspondence to George Matcham family and
business including East India Company affairs (1777-1801): letter to
George Matcham from an East India Company agent in Soho, London,
dated 26th September 1794.

[561] Bournemouth Local History (2022) The Bournemouth Pines.
Available at:
https://www.facebook.com/bournemouthlocalhistory/posts/pfbid0kFeHuX
z8HwwxVrp1FpH9uTf14aYydxziEmDfjwRAw3QBSXPzm698gkKbQeE
2G1nyl?
comment_id=304020428807087&reply_comment_id=205761905809097¬
if_id=1691077562793271¬if_t=comment_mention&ref=notif (accessed
August 29, 2023).

[562] Additional information provided by Bournemouth Local History via
their Facebook post (2023) The Bournemouth Pines. Available at:
https://www.facebook.com/bournemouthlocalhistory/posts/pfbid0kFeHuX
z8HwwxVrp1FpH9uTf14aYydxziEmDfjwRAw3QBSXPzm698gkKbQeE
2G1nyl?
comment_id=304020428807087&reply_comment_id=205761905809097¬
if_id=1691077562793271¬if_t=comment_mention&ref=notif (accessed
August 29, 2023).

[563] Matcham, M.E. (1911) The Nelsons of Burnham Thorpe: a record of
a Norfolk family compiled from unpublished letters and notebooks, 1787-
1842, p. 135.

[564] Matcham, M.E. (1911) The Nelsons of Burnham Thorpe: a record of
a Norfolk family compiled from unpublished letters and notebooks, 1787-
1842, p. 136.

Horatio Nelson, and inventiveness in Bath

[565] Mechtraveller (2022) *Where did Admiral Nelson lose his eye? -
Mechtraveller.* Available at https://mechtraveller.com/where-did-admiral-

nelson-lose-his-eye (accessed 30 September 2023).

[566] BATH GUIDE REF 17 NEW KING STREET 1797

[567] Howarth, D.A. and Howarth, S., Nelson: The immortal memory. London: Conway Maritime. (2004). Pp. 181–182

[568] https://thebathmagazine.co.uk/nelson-war-hero/

[569] Lambourn Website (2021) Hair powder tax | Lambourn. Available at: https://lambourn.org/hair-powder-tax (accessed 5 September 2023).

[570] French Revolution (no date b). Available at: https://www.rmg.co.uk/stories/topics/french-revolution (accessed 4 September 2023).

[571] Rauser, A.F. (2015) Living statues and neoclassical dress in late Eighteenth-Century Naples. Available at: https://www.semanticscholar.org/paper/Living-Statues-and-Neoclassical-Dress-in-Late-Rauser/2f9ae749e1b5b07856ca936e5fdaf641572a0ca8.

[572] Colville, Q. and Russell, G. (2016) Seduction and celebrity. National Geographic Books, p. 139.

[573] Williams, K. (2006) in England's mistress: The infamous life of Emma Hamilton. London: Hutchinson, p. 172

[574] Majer, M. (no date c) 1790-1799 | Fashion History Timeline. Available at: https://fashionhistory.fitnyc.edu/1790-1799/ (accessed 4 September 2023).

[575] Matcham, M.E. (1911) The Nelsons of Burnham Thorpe: a record of a Norfolk family compiled from unpublished letters and notebooks, 1787-1842, p. 145.

[576] Matcham, M.E. (1911) The Nelsons of Burnham Thorpe: a record of a Norfolk family compiled from unpublished letters and notebooks, 1787-1842, p. 148.

[577] Matcham, M.E. (1911) The Nelsons of Burnham Thorpe: a record of a Norfolk family compiled from unpublished letters and notebooks, 1787-1842, p. 154.

[578] Bath daily photo. Walcot, History of St. Swithin's (2007). Available at: https://bathdailyphoto.wordpress.com/2007/06/18/070618walcot-history-of-st-swithins (accessed 24 September 2023).

[579] The Gloucester Journal, 5th September 1796, p.4. Copyright British Library Board. Find My Past: https://www.findmypast.co.uk/image-viewer?issue=BL

%2F0000073%2F17981229&page=4&article=022&stringtohighlight=will iam+suckling (accessed 1 September 2023).

[580] 15 Kensington Place, Walcot, Bath (no date). Available at: https://www.bath-preservation-trust.org.uk/planning-application/15-kensington-place-walcot-bath/ (accessed 1 September 2023).

[581] Chapman, M., BA AIFA (2010) Kensington Meadows Local Nature Reserve, Bath A DESK BASED HISTORICAL ASSESSMENT. Available at: https://www.bathnes.gov.uk/sites/default/files/sitedocuments/Sport-Leisure-and-Parks/Parks-opening-times-and-Locations/kensington_meadows_historical_study_copyright_bnes_and_mi ke_chapman2.pdf (accessed 2 September 2023).

[582] British interior design – Jane Austen's World (no date). Available at: https://janeaustensworld.com/tag/british-interior-design/ (accessed 15 September 2023).

[583] Avis-Riordan, K. (2023) "Which house do you live in? 13 illustrations depict British houses through the ages," Country Living, 2 February. Available at: https://www.countryliving.com/uk/homes-interiors/property/news/a2387/british-houses-through-ages-illustrations/ (accessed 15 September 2023).

[584] Characteristics of the Georgian town House (2009). Available at: https://janeaustensworld.com/2009/06/03/characteristics-of-the-georgian-town-house/.

[585] Slurrp Editorial (2023) When aristocrats went (B)Ananas over Pineapples. Available at: https://www.slurrp.com/article/pineapple-privilege-when-aristocrats-went-b-ananas-over-an-excellent-fruit-1687943502340 (accessed 15 September 2023).

[586] Characteristics of the Georgian town House (2009). Available at: https://janeaustensworld.com/2009/06/03/characteristics-of-the-georgian-town-house/.

[587] Booyens, L. (2023) "Interior Design Style - Georgian," Mysite, 27 August. Available at: https://www.louisebooyens.com/post/interior-design-style-georgian (accessed 16 September 2023).

[588] Egan, P. (1819) in Walks Through Bath, Describing Everything Worthy Of Interest. Meyler and Son, p. 32. Available at: https://www.google.co.uk/books/edition/Walks_Through_Bath/jtVCAAA AIAAJ?hl=en&gbpv=1&dq=Pierce+Egan %27s+Walks+Through+Bath&printsec=frontcover (Accessed: 9 September 2023).

[589] Berkshire marriages index image, p.92. Copyright British Library

Board. Find My Past: https://search.findmypast.co.uk/record?
id=S2%2FGBPRS%2FPHILLIMOREBERKS
%2FBRKV2%2F0092&parentid=GBPRS%2FPHILLIMOREBERKS
%2FMAR%2F000006306%2F1 (accessed 9 September 2023).

[590] Author's private correspondence with her brother, David Bullock,
who lives in Bath. September 2023.

[591] The National Archives; Kew, England; Prerogative Court of
Canterbury and Related Probate Jurisdictions: Will Registers; Class:
PROB 11; Piece: 1552. Available at:
https://www.ancestry.co.uk/imageviewer/collections/5111/images/40611_3
11071-00327?pId=373416 (accessed 9 September 2023).

[592] Bathford tomb inscription, visited in 2 October 2019.

[593] Blanckley Family Papers, Box B-000820; Folder 8, Manuscripts
Division, Department of Rare Books and Special Collections, Princeton
University Library.

[594] Broughton, E., Six years residence in Algiers, Saunders and Oatley,
London (1839), p. 323. Available online at:
https://books.google.co.uk/books?
id=a3sEAAAAQAAJ&printsec=frontcover&dq=six+years+residence+in+
algiers&hl=en&newbks=1&newbks_redir=0&sa=X&redir_esc=y#v=snipp
et&q=venerable&f=false (accessed 10 September 2023).

[595] Fawcett, T. (2005) Coffee-Houses in bath. Available at:
https://www.buildinghistory.org/bath/georgian/coffeehouses.shtml
(accessed 10 September 2023).

[596] Wikipedia contributors (2023c) "Henry Stanyford Blanckley,"
Wikipedia [Preprint]. Available at:
https://en.wikipedia.org/wiki/Henry_Stanyford_Blanckley (accessed 10
September 2023).

[597] Matcham, M.E. (1911) The Nelsons of Burnham Thorpe: a record of
a Norfolk family compiled from unpublished letters and notebooks, 1787-
1842, p. 156.

[598] Matcham, M.E. (1911) The Nelsons of Burnham Thorpe: a record of
a Norfolk family compiled from unpublished letters and notebooks, 1787-
1842, pp. 159–160.

[599] Matcham, M.E. (1911) The Nelsons of Burnham Thorpe: a record of
a Norfolk family compiled from unpublished letters and notebooks, 1787-
1842, p. 159.

[600] The Editors of Encyclopaedia Britannica (2023) Battle of the Nile |

French-British Naval Conflict, 1798. Available at:
https://www.britannica.com/event/Battle-of-the-Nile (accessed 2 September 2023).

[601] Coleman, T. (2004) The Nelson Touch: The Life and Legend of Horatio Nelson. Oxford University Press, pp. 166-167.

[602] The Chester Courant, 18th December 1798, p.4. Copyright British Library Board. Find My Past: https://www.findmypast.co.uk/image-viewer?issue=BL%2F0000388%2F17981218&page=4&article=017&stringtohighlight=horatio+nelson+hero (accessed 4 September 2023).

[603] Matcham, M.E. (1911) The Nelsons of Burnham Thorpe: a record of a Norfolk family compiled from unpublished letters and notebooks, 1787-1842, p. 162.

[604] Matcham, M.E. (1911) The Nelsons of Burnham Thorpe: a record of a Norfolk family compiled from unpublished letters and notebooks, 1787-1842, p. 163.

[605] Wiltshire and Swindon History Centre: Eyre-Matcham family of Newhouse, Whiteparish and Downton; 3 - deeds etc. Matcham family: not main estate, 1369/7/2/1, Correspondence to George Matcham family and business including East India Company affairs (1777-1801): letter to George Matcham from Henry Oake of Ringwood dated 23rd May 1799.

[606] Matcham, M.E. (1911) The Nelsons of Burnham Thorpe: a record of a Norfolk family compiled from unpublished letters and notebooks, 1787-1842, pp. 168-169.

[607] Williams, K. (2006) in England's mistress: The infamous life of Emma Hamilton. London: Hutchinson, p. 205.

[608] Augusta Sophia (no date) Wikipedia. Wikimedia Foundation. Available at: https://tr.wikipedia.org/wiki/Augusta_Sophia_(Birle%C5%9Fik_Krall%C4%B1k_prensesi)#/media/Dosya:Princess_Augusta.jpg (Accessed: March 27, 2023).

[609] The Hampshire Chronicle, 26th November 1798, p.4. Copyright British Library Board. Find My Past: https://www.findmypast.co.uk/image-viewer?issue=BL%2F0000230%2F17981126&page=4&article=027&stringtohighlight=nelson+baron

[610] Manley, G. (1974) Central England temperatures: monthly means 1659 to 1973. Available at: https://www.rmets.org/sites/default/files/papers/qj74manley.pdf (accessed

11 September 2023).

[611] Northampton Mercury, 26th February 1799, p.4. Copyright British Library Board. Find My Past: https://www.findmypast.co.uk/image-viewer?issue=BL%2F0000317%2F17990216&page=4&article=023&stringtohighlight=snow (accessed 11 September 2023).

[612] Kentish Gazette, 10th August 1798, p.4. Copyright British Library Board. Find My Past: https://www.findmypast.co.uk/image-viewer?issue=BL%2F0000235%2F17980810&page=4&article=014&stringtohighlight=lady+hamilton (accessed 12 September 2023).

[613] Sugden, J. (2012) Nelson: A Dream of Glory. Random House. Kindle Edition.

[614] Robinson S. K., in defence of Emma (2015) p. 391.

[615] Williams, K. (2006) in England's mistress: The infamous life of Emma Hamilton. London: Hutchinson, p. 205.

[616] Oxford Journal, 29th October 1799, p.4. Copyright British Library Board. Find My Past: https://www.findmypast.co.uk/image-viewer?issue=BL%2F0000532%2F17960905&page=1&article=005&stringtohighlight=kensington+place+bath (accessed 1 September 2023).

[617] Staffordshire Advertiser, 26th January 1799, p. 4. Copyright British Library Board. Find My Past: https://www.findmypast.co.uk/image-viewer?issue=BL%2F0000215%2F17990126&page=4&article=030&stringtohighlight=naples+french (accessed 14 Septwmber 2023).

[618] The Kentish Gazette, 8th February 1799, p. 3. Copyright British Library Board. Find My Past: https://www.findmypast.co.uk/image-viewer?issue=BL%2F0000235%2F17990208&page=3&article=017&stringtohighlight=lady+hamilton (accessed 14 September 2023).

[619] Sugden, J. (2012) Nelson: A Dream of Glory. Random House. Kindle Edition.

[620] Sugden, J. (2012) Nelson: The Sword of Albion. Random House. Kindle Edition. P. 266.

[621] Chester Chronicle, 23rd August 1799, p.2. Copyright British Library Board. Find My Past: https://www.findmypast.co.uk/image-viewer?issue=BL

%2F0000341%2F17990823&page=2&article=002&stringtohighlight=nels on+rebels (accessed 16 September 2023).

[622] The Chester Courant, 29th December 1798, p.1. Copyright British Library Board. Find My Past: https://www.findmypast.co.uk/image-viewer?issue=BL %2F0000388%2F17991029&page=4&article=012&stringtohighlight=lady +hamilton (accessed 6 September 2023).

[623] London, England, Church of England Marriages and Banns, 1754-1938 (2010). Available at: https://www.ancestry.co.uk/discoveryui-content/view/1718649:1623? tid=&pid=&queryId=371055fdea31515be91342979cedc2e7&_phsrc=ECs 2297&_phstart=successSource (accessed 4 November 2023).

[624] Manley, G. (1974) Central England temperatures: monthly means 1659 to 1973. Available at: https://www.rmets.org/sites/default/files/papers/qj74manley.pdf (accessed 11 September 2023).

[625]

Hamilton, W., Nelson, H. N., Hamilton, E., Pettigrew, T. J. (1894). The Hamilton & Nelson Papers ... 1756-[1815]: 1798-1815. United Kingdom: private circulation, p. 81. Available at: https://www.google.co.uk/books/edition/The_Hamilton_Nelson_Papers_1 756_1815_179/qDeIqic5uwAC?hl=en&gbpv=1&dq=matcham+shepherd %27s+spring&pg=PA81&printsec=frontcover (accessed 8 September 2023).

[626] Grose J. H., A Voyage to the East Indies (1772) p. 250. Available at: https://www.google.co.uk/books/edition/A_Voyage_to_the_East_Indies/Rr A2AAAAMAAJ? hl=en&gbpv=1&dq=barbeers&pg=PA250&printsec=frontcover (accessed 16 November 2023).

[627] Cerny T., et al, the range of neurological complications in chikungunya fever, Neurocritical Care, 27(3), pp. 447–457 (2017). Available at: https://doi.org/10.1007/s12028-017-0413-8 (accessed 16 November 2023).

[628] Mehta, R., P., et al, The neurological complications of chikungunya virus: A systematic review,' Reviews in Medical Virology, 28(3) (2018). Available at: https://doi.org/10.1002/rmv.1978 (accessed 16 November 2023).

[629]

Hamilton, W., Nelson, H. N., Hamilton, E., Pettigrew, T. J. (1894). The Hamilton & Nelson Papers ... 1756-[1815]: 1798-1815. United

Kingdom: private circulation, p. 81. Available at: https://www.google.co.uk/books/edition/The_Hamilton_Nelson_Papers_1 756_1815_179/qDeIqic5uwAC?hl=en&gbpv=1&dq=matcham+shepherd %27s+spring&pg=PA81&printsec=frontcover (accessed 8 September 2023).

[630] Sugden, J. (2012) Nelson: The Sword of Albion. Random House. Kindle Edition. P. 361.

[631]

Hamilton, W., Nelson, H. N., Hamilton, E., Pettigrew, T. J. (1894). The Hamilton & Nelson Papers ... 1756-[1815]: 1798-1815. United Kingdom: private circulation, p. 81. Available at: https://www.google.co.uk/books/edition/The_Hamilton_Nelson_Papers_1 756_1815_179/qDeIqic5uwAC?hl=en&gbpv=1&dq=matcham+shepherd %27s+spring&pg=PA81&printsec=frontcover (accessed 8 September 2023).

[632] Matcham, M.E. (1911) The Nelsons of Burnham Thorpe: a record of a Norfolk family compiled from unpublished letters and notebooks, 1787-1842, p. 174.

[633] Staffordshire Advertiser, 19th April 1800, p. 2. Copyright British Library Board. Find My Past: https://www.findmypast.co.uk/image-viewer?issue=BL %2F0000215%2F18000419&page=2&article=002&stringtohighlight=lady +hamilton (accessed 13 September 2023).

[634] The Cambridge Chronicle, 8th March 1800, p. 2. Copyright British Library Board. Find My Past: https://www.findmypast.co.uk/image-viewer?issue=BL %2F0000419%2F18000308&page=2&article=002&stringtohighlight=nels on (accessed 16 September 2023).

[635] The Kentish Gazette, 14th March 1800, p .4. Copyright British Library Board. Find My Past: https://www.findmypast.co.uk/image-viewer?issue=BL %2F0000235%2F18000314&page=4&article=019&stringtohighlight=lady +hamilton (accessed 16 September 2023).

[636] The Chester Courant, 25th March 1800, p. 3. Copyright British Library Board. Find My Past: https://www.findmypast.co.uk/image-viewer?issue=BL %2F0000388%2F18000325&page=3&article=008&stringtohighlight=lady +hamilton (accessed 16 September 2023).

[637] The Hampshire Chronicle, 31st March 1800, p. 3. Copyright British Library Board. Find My Past: https://www.findmypast.co.uk/image-

viewer?issue=BL
%2F0000230%2F18000331&page=3&article=007&stringtohighlight=nels
on (accessed 17 September 2023).

[638] The Hampshire Chronicle, 7th April 1800, p. 3. Copyright British
Library Board. Find My Past: https://www.findmypast.co.uk/image-
viewer?issue=BL
%2F0000230%2F18000407&page=3&article=007&stringtohighlight=nels
on (accessed 17 September 2023).

[639] The Caledonian Mercury, 19th May 1800, p. 2. Copyright British
Library Board. Find My Past:
https://search.findmypast.co.uk/bna/viewarticle?id=BL
%2F0000045%2F18000519/005&stringtohighlight=lady%20hamilton
(accessed 17 September 2023).

[640] The Hampshire Chronicle, 19th May 1800, p. 3. Copyright British
Library Board. Find My Past: https://www.findmypast.co.uk/image-
viewer?issue=BL
%2F0000230%2F18000519&page=3&article=007&stringtohighlight=ham
ilton+nelson (accessed 17 September 2023).

[641] The Cambridge Chronicle, 14th June 1800, p. 2. Copyright British
Library Board. Find My Past: https://www.findmypast.co.uk/image-
viewer?issue=BL
%2F0000419%2F18000614&page=2&article=002&stringtohighlight=nels
on+hamilton (accessed 13 September 2023).

[642] Sugden, J. (2012) Nelson: A Dream of Glory. Random House. Kindle
Edition.

[643] Nerots Hotel, 15 Clifford street, Bond street, St George Hanover
Square W1S (2022). Available at:
https://pubwiki.co.uk/LondonPubs/StGeorgeHanoverSquare/NerotsHotel.s
html (accessed 12 September 2023).

[644] Matcham, M.E. (1911) The Nelsons of Burnham Thorpe: a record of
a Norfolk family compiled from unpublished letters and notebooks, 1787-
1842, pp. 179–180.

[645] The Porcupine, 11th November 1800, p. 3. Copyright British Library
Board. Find My Past: https://www.findmypast.co.uk/image-viewer?
issue=BL
%2F0002586%2F18001111&page=3&article=009&stringtohighlight=nels
on+nerot (accessed 10 September 2023).

[646] Matcham, M.E. (1911) The Nelsons of Burnham Thorpe: a record of
a Norfolk family compiled from unpublished letters and notebooks, 1787-

1842, p. 180.

[647] Matcham, M.E. (1911) The Nelsons of Burnham Thorpe: a record of a Norfolk family compiled from unpublished letters and notebooks, 1787-1842, p. 181.

[648] https://landfordhistory.files.wordpress.com/2018/12/A-History-of-Landford-Part-10-Newhouse.pdf P. 17

[649] Hampshire Chronicle 8th December 1800, p. 2. Accessed via Find My Past https://search.findmypast.co.uk/bna/viewarticle?id=bl%2f0000230%2f18001208%2f004&stringtohighlight=nelson%20east%20india (accessed 10 September 2023).

[650] Nelson's Lost Jewel: The Extraordinary Story of the Lost Diamond Chelengk - Napoleon.org (no date). Available at: https://www.napoleon.org/en/magazine/publications/nelsons-lost-jewel-extraordinary-story-lost-diamond-chelengk/

[651] Kennedy, M. (2018) "Lord Nelson's rotating gems recreated decades after original was stolen," The Guardian, 22 February. Available at: https://www.theguardian.com/world/2017/oct/20/lord-admiral-horatio-nelson-rotating-gems-chelengk-recreated-decades-after-original-stolen

[652] Information supplied to the author by Christopher A. Sorensen, Historical Consultant | Maritime Heritage.

[653] Coleman, T. (2004) The Nelson Touch: The Life and Legend of Horatio Nelson. Oxford University Press, p. 233.

[654] Dutt, R. (2017) 'Beau Brummell: The man who invented style,' Savile Row Style [Preprint]. https://savilerow-style.com/news/the-man-who-invented-style (accessed 26 September 2023).

[655] Franklin, H. (2020) 1800-1809 | Fashion History Timeline. Available at: https://fashionhistory.fitnyc.edu/1800-1809/ (accessed 12 September 2023).

[656] Hibbert, C., Nelson: A personal history. London: Penguin (2002). P. 228.

[657] Hidden London (2022) Bishopsgate | Hidden London. Available at: https://hidden-london.com/gazetteer/bishopsgate/ (accessed 10 September 2023).

[658] Wikipedia contributors (2023d) "London Tavern," Wikipedia [Preprint]. Available at: https://en.wikipedia.org/wiki/London_Tavern (accessed 10 September 2023).

[659] Hampshire Chronicle, 8 December 1800, p. 3. Accessed via Find My

Past https://search.findmypast.co.uk/bna/viewarticle?id=bl%2f0000230%2f18001208%2f004&stringtohighlight=nelson%20east%20india (accessed 10 September 2023).

[660] The Porcupine, 2 December 1800, p. 2. Accessed via Find My Past https://www.findmypast.co.uk/image-viewer?issue=BL%2F0002586%2F18001202&page=3&article=014&stringtohighlight=london+tavern+dinner (accessed 10 September 2023).

[661] The Porcupine, 2 December 1800, p. 2. Accessed via Find My Past https://www.findmypast.co.uk/image-viewer?issue=BL%2F0002586%2F18001202&page=3&article=014&stringtohighlight=london+tavern+dinner (accessed 10 September 2023).

[662] The Porcupine, 12 December 1800, p. 3. Accessed via Find My Past https://www.findmypast.co.uk/image-viewer?issue=BL%2F0002586%2F18001212&page=3&article=015&stringtohighlight=lady+hamilton+nelson (accessed 12 September 2023).

[663] Peakman J., Emma Hamilton. Haus Publishing, London (2005). P 109.

[664] Keynes, M. (1998). The Portland Vase: Sir William Hamilton, Josiah Wedgwood and the Darwins. Notes and Records of the Royal Society of London, 52(2), pp. 237–259. Available at: http://www.jstor.org/stable/531859 (accessed 17 September 2023).

[665] Hibbert, C., Nelson: A personal history. London: Penguin (2002). P. 79.

[666] Matcham, M.E. (1911) The Nelsons of Burnham Thorpe: a record of a Norfolk family compiled from unpublished letters and notebooks, 1787-1842, p. 19.

[667] Anonymous (1743) The Lady's Companion or an Infallible Guide to the Fair Sex, pp. 13-14. Available online: https://archive.org/details/ladyscompaniono00ladygoog/page/n17/mode/2up?q=beaft (accessed 18 September 2023).

[668] The Gloucester Journal, 15 December 1800, p. 4. Accessed via Find My Past https://www.findmypast.co.uk/image-viewer?issue=BL%2F0000532%2F18001215&page=4&article=017&stringtohighlight=lady+hamilton (accessed 17 September 2023).

[669] Ipswich Journal, 27 December 1800, p. 2. Accessed via Find My Past https://www.findmypast.co.uk/image-viewer?issue=BL%2F0000191%2F18001227&page=2&article=004&stringtohighlight=lady+hamilton (accessed 17 September 2023).

[670] Sugden, J. Nelson: The Sword of Albion. Random House (2012), p. 381.

[671] A breakdown of evidence for George Matcham's relationship to Mary Pitt is provided in appendix 6.

[672] Trench, P., The Worst Country in the World: the true story of an Australian pioneer family, Prefab Publications (2012), p. 33.

[673] Matcham, M.E. (1911) The Nelsons of Burnham Thorpe: a record of a Norfolk family compiled from unpublished letters and notebooks, 1787-1842, p. 197.

[674] Trench, P., The Worst Country in the World: the true story of an Australian pioneer family, Prefab Publications (2012), pp. 42-43.

[675] Matcham, M.E., The Nelsons of Burnham Thorpe: a record of a Norfolk family compiled from unpublished letters and notebooks, 1787-1842 (1911), p. 154.

[676] Fraser F., Beloved Emma. Weidenfield and Nicholson. London (1986), p. 277.

[677] Sugden, J. Nelson: The Sword of Albion. Random House (2012), p. 493.

[678] Sugden, J. Nelson: The Sword of Albion. Random House (2012), p. 921.

[679] The Oracle and the Daily Advertiser, 9 January 1801, p. 2. Accessed via Find My Past https://www.findmypast.co.uk/image-viewer?issue=BL%2F0002428%2F18010109&page=2&article=011&stringtohighlight=font-hill (accessed 18 September 2023).

[680] Bury and Norwich Post, 7 January 1801, p. 2. Accessed via Find My Past https://www.findmypast.co.uk/image-viewer?issue=BL%2F0000156%2F18010107&page=2&article=004&stringtohighlight=lady+hamilton (accessed 18 September 2023).

[681] Whitehall Evening Post, 9 April 1801, p. 4. Accessed via Find My Past https://www.findmypast.co.uk/image-viewer?issue=BL%2F0002776%2F18010409&page=4&article=021&stringtohighlight=lady+hamilton (accessed 18 September 2023).

[682] Cross, A. (2023) Chronology of Nelson. Available at: https://nelson-society.com/life-of-nelson/chronology/ (accessed 18 September 2023).

[683] James Gillray: Dido in Despair (no date). Available at: https://www.james-gillray.org/pop/dido-despair.html (accessed 18 September 2023).

[684] Matcham, M.E. (1911) The Nelsons of Burnham Thorpe: a record of a Norfolk family compiled from unpublished letters and notebooks, 1787-1842, p. 187.

[685] Matcham, M.E. (1911) The Nelsons of Burnham Thorpe: a record of a Norfolk family compiled from unpublished letters and notebooks, 1787-1842, p. 188.

[686] Sugden, J. Nelson: The Sword of Albion. Random House (2012), p. 476.

[687] Edmund Nelson to Davison, no date, with a PS of 26 April, (postmark 27 April 1801, Bath), with black seal, on arrangements for Maurice Nelson's funeral at Burnham Thorpe. | Royal Museums Greenwich (no date). https://www.rmg.co.uk/collections/archive/rmgc-object-484283 (accessed 19 September 2023).

[688] Edmund Nelson to Davison, Bath, 27 April [1801], on his wish for the burial at Burnham Thorpe, the black servant to attend, and Mr Bolton [brother in law of Maurice]. | Royal Museums Greenwich (no date). https://www.rmg.co.uk/collections/archive/rmgc-object-484284 (accessed 19 September 2023).

[689] Sugden, J. Nelson: The Sword of Albion. Random House (2012), p. 476.

[690] Star, 6 May 1801, p. 3. Accessed via Find My Past https://www.findmypast.co.uk/image-viewer?issue=BL%2F0002646%2F18010506&page=3&article=012&stringtohighlight=maurice+nelson (accessed 19 September 2023).

[691] Trench, P., The Worst Country in the World: the true story of an Australian pioneer family, Prefab Publications (2012), pp. 49-50.

[692] Hampshire Chronicle, 29 June 1801, p. 4. Accessed via Find My Past https://www.findmypast.co.uk/image-viewer?issue=BL%2F0000230%2F18010629&page=4&article=014&stringtohighlight=canada+portsmouth (accessed 22 October 2023).

[693] The National Archives (2005) The National Archives | Exhibitions | Nelson, Trafalgar, and those who served. https://www.nationalarchives.gov.uk/nelson/gallery6/copenhagen.htm

[694] Bath Chronicle, 6 August 1801, p. 3. Accessed via Find My Past https://www.findmypast.co.uk/image-viewer?issue=BL%2F0000221%2F18010806&page=3&article=010&stringtohighlight=matcham (accessed 14 September 2023).

[695] The Daily Post, 17 July 1801, p. 2. Accessed via Find My Past

https://www.findmypast.co.uk/image-viewer?issue=BL
%2F0000175%2F18010717&page=2&article=005&stringtohighlight=she
pperton+nelson (accessed 19 September 2023).

[696] Pocock, T. Horatio Nelson: The story of the man who saved Britain from invasion, Lume Books, p. 360.

[697] Harrison, C. (no date b) Lord Horatio Nelson (1758-1805). Available at: https://threedecks.org/index.php?
display_type=show_crewman&id=1450 (accessed 19 September 2023).

[698] Peakman J., Emma Hamilton. Haus Publishing, London (2005), p. 124.

[699] Warwick, P. (1995) Here was paradise - A description of Merton Place, by Peter Warwick. Available at:
https://wandle.org/aboutus/nelson2005/paradise.htm (accessed 19 September 2023).

[700] The Salisbury and Winchester Journal, 21 September 1801, p. 2. Accessed via Find My Past https://www.findmypast.co.uk/image-viewer?
issue=BL
%2F0000361%2F18010921&page=2&article=021&stringtohighlight=mat cham (accessed 21 September 2023).

[701] The Hampshire Chronicle, 20 September 1802, p. 3. Accessed via Find My Past https://www.findmypast.co.uk/image-viewer?issue=BL
%2F0000230%2F18020920&page=3&article=021&stringtohighlight=mat cham (accessed 21 September 2023).

[702] Matcham, M.E. (1911) The Nelsons of Burnham Thorpe: a record of a Norfolk family compiled from unpublished letters and notebooks, 1787-1842, p. 192.

[703] Sugden, J. Nelson: The Sword of Albion. Random House (2012), p. 921.

[704] Matcham, M.E. (1911) The Nelsons of Burnham Thorpe: a record of a Norfolk family compiled from unpublished letters and notebooks, 1787-1842, p. 193.

[705] Matcham, M.E. (1911) The Nelsons of Burnham Thorpe: a record of a Norfolk family compiled from unpublished letters and notebooks, 1787-1842, p. 193.

[706] Gérin W., Horatia Nelson Oxford University Press (1970), p. 43.

[707] The Nelson Society (2004) Bath and Admiral Nelson. Quay Digital, Pp. 104.

[708] Great Pulteney Street (no date). https://visitbath.co.uk/things-to-do/great-pulteney-street-p1704883 (accessed 22 September 2023).

[709] Gérin W., Horatia Nelson Oxford University Press (1970) p. 43.

[710] Peakman J., Emma Hamilton. Haus Publishing, London (2005), p 126

[711] Peakman J., Emma Hamilton. Haus Publishing, London (2005), pp. 52-53.

[712] Gérin W., Horatia Nelson Oxford University Press (1970), p. 43.

[713] Gérin W., Horatia Nelson Oxford University Press (1970), p. 43.

[714] Dog collar | Royal Museums Greenwich (no date). Available at: https://www.rmg.co.uk/collections/objects/rmgc-object-62045 (accessed 23 October 2023).

[715] Matcham, M.E. (1911) The Nelsons of Burnham Thorpe: a record of a Norfolk family compiled from unpublished letters and notebooks, 1787-1842, p. 193.

[716] Matcham, M.E. (1911) The Nelsons of Burnham Thorpe: a record of a Norfolk family compiled from unpublished letters and notebooks, 1787-1842, p. 193.

[717] Matcham, M.E. (1911) The Nelsons of Burnham Thorpe: a record of a Norfolk family compiled from unpublished letters and notebooks, 1787-1842, p. 194.

[718] The Editors of Encyclopaedia Britannica (1998) Treaty of Amiens | Napoleonic Wars, Peace, Britain. Available at: https://www.britannica.com/event/Treaty-of-Amiens-1802 (accessed 17 October 2023).

[719] Wiltshire and Swindon History Centre: Eyre-Matcham family of Newhouse, Whiteparish and Downton; 3 - deeds etc. Matcham family: not main estate, 1369/7/2/1, correspondence to George Matcham family and business including East India Company affairs.

[720] Patent amendment kindly supplied by the British Library in 2023. For full text, please see appendix 4.

[721] Encyclopaedia Britannica (2023) Steam engine | Definition, History, Impact, & Facts. Available at https://www.britannica.com/technology/steam-engine (accessed 4 October 2023).

[722] Richard Trevithick 1804 penydarren (2022). Available at https://preservedbritishsteamlocomotives.com/richard-trevithick-1804-

penydarren (accessed 6 October 2023).

[723] Bath Journal, 31 December 1801, p. 2. Accessed via Find My Past https://www.findmypast.co.uk/image-viewer?issue=BL %2F0004012%2F18011221&page=2&article=002&stringtohighlight=mat cham (accessed 6 October 2023).

[724] About us - Avon Navigation Trust (2022). Available at https://www.avonnavigationtrust.org/about-us (accessed 5 October 2023).

[725] Hungerford Virtual Museum (2022) Building the Kennet & Avon Canal. Available at https://www.hungerfordvirtualmuseum.co.uk/? view=article&id=826&catid=36 (accessed 4 October 2023).

[726] Patent amendment kindly supplied by the British Library in 2023. For full text, please see appendix 4.

[727] Wiltshire and Swindon History Centre: Eyre-Matcham family of Newhouse, Whiteparish and Downton; 3 - deeds etc. Matcham family: not main estate, 1369/7/2/1, correspondence to George Matcham family and

business including East India Company affairs.

[728] Sugden, J. Nelson: The Sword of Albion. Random House (2012), p. 553.

[729] Matcham, M.E. (1911) The Nelsons of Burnham Thorpe: a record of a Norfolk family compiled from unpublished letters and notebooks, 1787-1842, pp. 194-195.

[730] The Nelson Society (2004) Bath and Admiral Nelson. Quay Digital, Pp. 104.

[731] Matcham, M.E. (1911) The Nelsons of Burnham Thorpe: a record of a Norfolk family compiled from unpublished letters and notebooks, 1787-1842, pp. 196-197.

[732] Bury and Norwich Post, 5 May 1802, p. 3. Accessed via Find My Past https://www.findmypast.co.uk/image-viewer?issue=BL %2F0000156%2F18020505&page=3&article=007&stringtohighlight=edm und+nelson (accessed 24 September 2023).

[733] Norfolk Burials (1662-1812) © Norfolk Records Office. Available at: https://search.findmypast.co.uk/record?id=GBPRS%2FNORFOLK %2FPD_571-2%2F01572&parentid=GBPRS%2FNORFOLK%2FBUR %2F002962479 (accessed 15 October 2023).

[734] Matcham, M.E. (1911) The Nelsons of Burnham Thorpe: a record of a Norfolk family compiled from unpublished letters and notebooks, 1787-1842, p. 198.

[735] Sotheby's and Co, S.P.B.A., Nelson and the Napoleonic Wars ; Including the Matcham Collection, Trafalgar, (2005) item 17, NELSON, HORATIO, Lord. Autograph letter signed ("Nelson & Bronte") to George Matcham, p. 42.

[736] Gérin W., Horatia Nelson Oxford University Press (1970) p. 50.

[737] Sugden, J. Nelson: The Sword of Albion. Random House (2012), p. 555.

[738] Gérin W., Horatia Nelson Oxford University Press (1970) pp. 49-50.

[739] Here was paradise - A description of Merton Place, by Peter Warwick. (1995). Available at: https://wandle.org/aboutus/nelson2005/footnotes.htm (accessed 11 October 2023).

[740] Pocock, Tom. Horatio Nelson: The story of the man who saved Britain from invasion (p. 384). Lume Books. Kindle Edition.

[741] Morning Herald, 14 July 1802, p. 2. Accessed via Find My Past https://www.findmypast.co.uk/image-viewer?issue=BL%2F0002408%2F18020714&page=2&article=008&stringtohighlight=nelson (accessed 25 September 2023).

[742] Matcham, M.E. (1911) The Nelsons of Burnham Thorpe: a record of a Norfolk family compiled from unpublished letters and notebooks, 1787-1842, p. 200.

[743] Manley, G. (1974) Central England temperatures: monthly means 1659 to 1973. Available at: https://www.rmets.org/sites/default/files/papers/qj74manley.pdf (accessed 25 September 2023).

[744] Boyle, L. and Boyle, L. (2023) 'A tour of regency fashion: day and evening dress,' *JaneAusten.co.uk* [Preprint]. https://janeausten.co.uk/blogs/womens-regency-fashion-articles/a-tour-of-regency-fashion-day-and-evening-dress (accessed 27 September 2023).

[745] Knowles, R. (2012) The rise and fall of Beau Brummell (1778-1840). https://www.regencyhistory.net/2012/11/the-rise-and-fall-of-beau-brummell-1778.html (accessed 25 September 2023).

[746] Robinson S. K., in defence of Emma (2015) p. 296.

[747] Information supplied to the author by Christopher A. Sorensen, Historical Consultant | Maritime Heritage.

[748] Matcham, M.E. (1911) The Nelsons of Burnham Thorpe: a record of a Norfolk family compiled from unpublished letters and notebooks, 1787-

1842, p. 88.

[749] Robinson S. K., in defence of Emma (2015) p. 296.

[750] Peakman J., Emma Hamilton. Haus Publishing, London (2005). P 129.

[751] Jenkins, S. (2023) *The High, Oxford: Angel Inn*. https://www.oxfordhistory.org.uk/high/tour/south/angel_hotel.html (accessed 25 September 2023).

[752] Schmid, S. (no date) Inns. https://www.digitens.org/en/notices/inns.html (accessed 26 September 2023).

[753] The Grand Cafe - A Little History - The Grand Café - Oxford (2015). https://www.thegrandcafe.co.uk/grand-cafe-history (accessed 26 September 2023).

[754] Jenkins, S. (no date) Inns and hotels of Oxford. Available at https://www.oxfordhistory.org.uk/old_oxford/inns/index.html (accessed 5 October 2023).

[755] S7hauhe (2011) Late English Georgian. Available at https://s7hauhe.wordpress.com/2011/07/17/late-english-georgian/ (accessed 5 October 2023).

[756] Williams, K. (2006) in England's mistress: The infamous life of Emma Hamilton. London: Hutchinson, p. 280.

[757] Fraser F., Beloved Emma. Weidenfield and Nicholson. London (1986). P. 277.

[758] Miss Emma Woodhouse and Lady Emma Hamilton: two beautiful Emmas (2007). https://janeaustensworld.com/2007/12/07/beautiful-emma (accessed 27 September 2023).

[759] Sugden, J. Nelson: The Sword of Albion. Random House (2012), p. 486.

[760] Information supplied to the author by Christopher A. Sorensen, Historical Consultant | Maritime Heritage.

[761] Hibbert, C., Nelson: A personal history. London: Penguin (2002). P. 216.

[762] Chesters, L. (2017) 'News Article: The case of the missing eyebrow – rediscovery of 'lost' painting reveals Nelson's battle scars,' *Antiques Trade Gazette*, 13 November. Available at https://www.antiquestradegazette.com/news/2017/the-case-of-the-missing-

eyebrow-rediscovery-of-lost-painting-reveals-nelsons-battle-scars (accessed 30 September 2023).

[763] The Gloucester Journal, 26 July 1802, p. 3. Accessed via Find My Past https://www.findmypast.co.uk/image-viewer?issue=BL %2F0000532%2F18020726&page=3&article=022&stringtohighlight=will iam+nelson (accessed 27 September 2023).

[764] Bath Chronicle, 15 July 1802, p. 4. Accessed via Find My Past https://www.findmypast.co.uk/image-viewer?issue=BL %2F0000221%2F18020715&page=4&article=007&stringtohighlight=nels on (accessed 5 October 2023).

[765] Mealtimes | The Regency Town House (no date). http://www.rth.org.uk/regency-period/family-life/mealtimes (accessed 27 September 2023).

[766] Gilbert, L., The scent of sandalwood (2015). Available at: https://englishhistoryauthors.blogspot.com/2015/02/the-scent-of-sandalwood.html (accessed 27 September 2023).

[767] Gérin W., Horatia Nelson Oxford University Press (1970) p. 96.

[768] Peakman J., Emma Hamilton. Haus Publishing, London (2005). P 63.

[769] Hibbert, C., Nelson: A personal history. London: Penguin (2002). P. 212.

[770] Hunter, W., Esq. Travels in the year 1792 through France, Turkey and Hungary, to Vienna (1796). Pp. 430-432. Available at: https://www.google.co.uk/books/edition/Travels_in_the_Year_1792_Throu gh_France/thNgAAAAcAAJ? hl=en&gbpv=1&dq=vienna&printsec=frontcover (accessed 15 October 2023).

[771] Hibbert, C., Nelson: A personal history. London: Penguin (2002). Pp. 217-218.

[772] Hibbert, C., Nelson: A personal history. London: Penguin (2002). Pp. 220-221.

[773] Matcham, M.E. (1911) The Nelsons of Burnham Thorpe: a record of a Norfolk family compiled from unpublished letters and notebooks, 1787-1842, p. 292.

[774] National Trust (no date) George Nelson Matcham (1789-1877) 730971. Available at: https://www.nationaltrustcollections.org.uk/object/730971 (accessed 4 October 2023).

[775] Matcham, M.E. (1911) The Nelsons of Burnham Thorpe: a record of a Norfolk family compiled from unpublished letters and notebooks, 1787-1842, p. 266.

[776] Sugden, J. Nelson: The Sword of Albion. Random House (2012), p. 759.

[777] Sugden, J. Nelson: The Sword of Albion. Random House (2012), p. 550.

[778] Matcham, M.E. (1911) The Nelsons of Burnham Thorpe: a record of a Norfolk family compiled from unpublished letters and notebooks, 1787-1842, p. 287.

[779] (#10) # - Oliver, F. (no date). Available at: https://www.sothebys.com/en/auctions/ecatalogue/2008/english-literature-history-childrens-books-illustrations-l08405/lot.10.html (accessed 13 October 2023).

[780] White, C. (2005) The Nelson Companion. Available at: https://www.google.co.uk/books/edition/The_Nelson_Companion/9bY7A wAAQBAJ?hl=en&gbpv=1&dq=%22francis+oliver %22+william+hamilton&pg=PT235&printsec=frontcover (accessed 14 October 2023).

[781] Fraser F., Beloved Emma. Weidenfield and Nicholson. London (1986), p. 267.

[782] White C. (2005) Nelson, The New Letters. Boydell Press, p. 73.

[783] Sugden, J. Nelson: The Sword of Albion. Random House (2012), p. 544.

[784] Howarth, D.A. and Howarth, S., Nelson: The immortal memory. London: Conway Maritime. (2004). Pp. 239-240.

[785] Hibbert, C., Nelson: A personal history. London: Penguin (2002). P. 243.

[786] London, England, Church of England Baptisms, Marriages and Burials, 1538-1812 (2010). Available at: https://www.ancestry.co.uk/imageviewer/collections/1624/images/31280_1 94652-00352?pId=709315 (accessed 12 October 2023).

[787] Idea supplied to the author by Christopher A. Sorensen, Historical Consultant | Maritime Heritage.

[788] Matcham, M.E. (1911) The Nelsons of Burnham Thorpe: a record of a Norfolk family compiled from unpublished letters and notebooks, 1787-1842, p. 200.

[789] *Google Books* (no date). Available at: https://www.google.co.uk/books/edition/Letters_from_England_First_American_Edit/0ifD0mYVZR8C?hl=en&gbpv=1&dq=angel+inn+oxford&pg=PA167&printsec=frontcover. Pp. 166-168 (accessed 2 October 2023).

[790] Journal of the Royal United Service Institution (1921), p. 569. Available at: https://www.google.co.uk/books/edition/Journal_of_the_Royal_United_Service_Inst/OcJMAAAAYAAJ?hl=en&gbpv=1&dq=Admiralty-Office,+June+1795+lappells&pg=PA568&printsec=frontcover (accessed 2 October 2023).

[791] Robe of a Knight Grand Cross of the Order of the Bath | Royal Museums Greenwich (no date). https://www.rmg.co.uk/collections/objects/rmgc-object-71382 (accessed 2 October 2023).

[792] Robert, M.A.E. [i. E. (1808) Letters from England ... First American Edition. Available at https://www.google.co.uk/books/edition/Letters_from_England_First_American_Edit/0ifD0mYVZR8C?hl=en&gbpv=1&dq=angel+inn+oxford&pg=PA167&printsec=frontcover (accessed 26 September 2023).

[793] Information supplied to the author by Christopher A. Sorensen, Historical Consultant | Maritime Heritage.

[794] Old Town Hall, Oxford (no date). http://www.oxfordhistory.org.uk/mayors/town_hall/old.html (accessed 2 October 2023).

[795] The New Oxford Guide; or, companion through the University ... To which is added, a tour to Blenheim, Ditchley, and Stow ... By a Gentleman of Oxford (1765), p. t. Available at https://www.google.co.uk/books/edition The_New_Oxford_Guide_Or_Companion_Throug/vIEHAAAAQAAJ?hl=en&gbpv=1&dq=oxford+guide+town+hall&printsec=frontcover (accessed 2 October 2023).

[796] Old Town Hall, Oxford (no date). http://www.oxfordhistory.org.uk/mayors/town_hall/old.html (accessed 2 October 2023).

[797] The Oxford university and city guide. To which is added, a guide to Blenheim, Nuneham... (1828), p. 131. Available at https://www.google.co.uk/books/edition/The_Oxford_university_and_city_guide_To/SoAHAAAAQAAJ?

hl=en&gbpv=1&dq=oxford+guide+town+hall&pg=PA131&printsec=front cover (accessed 2 October 2023).

[798] Morning Herald, 26 July 1802, p. 3. Accessed via Find My Past https://www.findmypast.co.uk/image-viewer?issue=BL %2F0002408%2F18020726&page=3&article=020&stringtohighlight=lord +nelson (accessed 2 October 2023).

[799] The Gloucester Journal, 26 July 1802, p. 3. Accessed via Find My Past https://www.findmypast.co.uk/image-viewer?issue=BL %2F0000532%2F18020726&page=3&article=022&stringtohighlight=will iam+nelson (accessed 27 September 2023).

[800] The Gloucester New Guide... (1802). R Raikes. Pp. 1, 14, 17. Available at: https://www.scribbr.co.uk/referencing/generator/folders/XvHQtcefA2SoR GHGOFkiY/lists/7fw7kFCQ6MsoF7rv7Y06Bp (accessed 12 October 2023).

[801] Pocock, Tom. Horatio Nelson: The story of the man who saved Britain from invasion (pp. 407-408). Lume Books. Kindle Edition

[802] Morning Post, 31 July 1802, p. 3. Accessed via Find My Past https://www.findmypast.co.uk/image-viewer?issue=BL %2F0002408%2F18020726&page=3&article=020&stringtohighlight=lord +nelson (accessed 5 October 2023).

[803] Morning Post, 30 July 1802, p. 2. Accessed via Find My Past https://www.findmypast.co.uk/image-viewer?issue=BL %2F0000175%2F18020730&page=2&article=005&stringtohighlight=nels on (accessed 5 October 2023).

[804] Matcham, M.E. (1911) The Nelsons of Burnham Thorpe: a record of a Norfolk family compiled from unpublished letters and notebooks, 1787-1842, p. 216.

[805] Sugden, J. Nelson: The Sword of Albion. Random House (2012), p. 539–541.

[806] Here was paradise - A description of Merton Place, by Peter Warwick. (1995). Available at: https://wandle.org/aboutus/nelson2005/footnotes.htm (accessed 21 October 2023).

[807] Sotheby's and Co, S.P.B.A., Nelson and the Napoleonic Wars ; Including the Matcham Collection, Trafalgar, (2005) item 29, HAMILTON, EMMA. Autograph letter to Catherine Matcham, p. 62.

[808] The Hampshire Chronicle, 20 September 1802, p. 3. Accessed via Find My Past https://www.findmypast.co.uk/image-viewer?issue=BL

%2F0000175%2F18020731&page=3&article=010&stringtohighlight=nels on (accessed 5 October 2023).

[809] NELSON | Autograph letter signed, to Matcham, together with enclosure, 1802 | The Collection of a Connoisseur: History in Manuscript | 2020 | Sotheby's (no date). https://www.sothebys.com/en/buy/auction/2020/the-collection-of-a-connoisseur-history-in-manuscript/nelson-autograph-letter-signed-to-matcham-together (accessed 7 October 2023).

[810] Robinson S. K., in defence of Emma (2015) p. 302.

[811] Here was paradise - A description of Merton Place, by Peter Warwick. (1995). Available at: https://wandle.org/aboutus/nelson2005/footnotes.htm (accessed 19 September 2023).

[812] Sugden, J. Nelson: The Sword of Albion. Random House (2012), p. 541.

[813] (#10) # - Oliver, F. (no date). Available at: https://www.sothebys.com/en/auctions/ecatalogue/2008/english-literature-history-childrens-books-illustrations-l08405/lot.10.html (accessed 13 October 2023).

[814] Matcham, M.E. (1911) The Nelsons of Burnham Thorpe: a record of a Norfolk family compiled from unpublished letters and notebooks, 1787-1842, p. 205.

[815] Matcham, M.E. (1911) The Nelsons of Burnham Thorpe: a record of a Norfolk family compiled from unpublished letters and notebooks, 1787-1842, pp. 205-206.

[816] Sugden, J. Nelson: The Sword of Albion. Random House (2012), p. 555.

[817] Sugden, J. Nelson: The Sword of Albion. Random House (2012), p. 555.

[818] Hibbert, C., Nelson: A personal history. London: Penguin (2002). P. 275.

[819] Sugden, J. Nelson: The Sword of Albion. Random House (2012), p. 555.

[820] Fraser F., Beloved Emma. Weidenfield and Nicholson. London (1986). P. 281.

[821] Williams, K. (2006) in England's mistress: The infamous life of Emma Hamilton. London: Hutchinson, p. 249.

[822] The essential mistress (2017). Available at: https://regencyromancewithatwist.com/2017/04/09/the-essential-mistress (accessed 19 October 2023).

[823] Wolfram, S., Divorce in England 1700-1857, Oxford Journal of Legal Studies 5, no. 2 (1985): 155–86. Available at: http://www.jstor.org/stable/764190 (accessed 19 October 2023).

[824] Fraser F., Beloved Emma. Weidenfield and Nicholson. London (1986), pp. 286-287.

[825] Howarth, D.A. and Howarth, S., Nelson: The immortal memory. London: Conway Maritime. (2004), p. 93.

[826] Information supplied to the author by Christopher A. Sorensen, Historical Consultant | Maritime Heritage.

[827] Fraser F., Beloved Emma. Weidenfield and Nicholson. London (1986). P. 221.

[828] (#10) # - Oliver, F. (no date). Available at: https://www.sothebys.com/en/auctions/ecatalogue/2008/english-literature-history-childrens-books-illustrations-l08405/lot.10.html (accessed 13 October 2023).

[829] Underwood, T. and Underwood, G. (1803) The Repertory of Patent Inventions And Other Discoveries and Improvements in Arts, Manufactures, and Agriculture ... Available at: https://www.google.co.uk/books/edition/The_Repertory_of_Patent_Inventions/O9Y0AAAAMAAJ?hl=en&gbpv=1&dq=george+matcham+patent&pg=PA320&printsec=frontcover (accessed 15 October 2023).

[830] Matcham, M.E. (1911) The Nelsons of Burnham Thorpe: a record of a Norfolk family compiled from unpublished letters and notebooks, 1787-1842, pp. 30-31.

[831] Somerset Heritage Service; Taunton, Somerset, England; Somerset Parish Records, 1538-1914; Reference Number: D\p\bafd/2/1/2. Available at: https://www.ancestry.co.uk/imageviewer/collections/60856/images/engl78030_d-p-bafd-2-1-2_m_00030?pId=1403747 (accessed 13 October 2023).

[832] Peakman J., Emma Hamilton. Haus Publishing, London (2005). P 131.

[833] Matcham, M.E. (1911) The Nelsons of Burnham Thorpe: a record of a Norfolk family compiled from unpublished letters and notebooks, 1787-1842, p. 207.

[834] Somerset Heritage Service; Taunton, Somerset, England; Somerset Parish Records, 1538-1914; Reference Number: D\p\bafd/2/1/2. Available at: https://www.ancestry.co.uk/imageviewer/collections/60856/images/engl78 030_d-p-bafd-2-1-2_m_00030?pId=1403747 (accessed 13 October 2023).

[835] https://www.ancestry.co.uk/discoveryui-content/view/52597;5111? ssrc=pt&tid=82673375&pid=40467016521

[836] The Peace of Amiens, 1802 | napoleonic wars (no date). Available at: https://www.thenapoleonicwars.net/peace-of-amiens-overview (accessed 17 October 2023).

[837] Cross, A. (no date) Chronology of Nelson. Available at: https://nelson-society.com/life-of-nelson/chronology/ (accessed 17 October 2023).

[838] Matcham, M.E. (1911) The Nelsons of Burnham Thorpe: a record of a Norfolk family compiled from unpublished letters and notebooks, 1787-1842, pp. 207-208.

[839] Patent amendment kindly supplied by the British Library in 2023.

[840] Bath and West of England Society list of members... (1801). Available at: https://www.google.co.uk/books/edition/Rules_orders_and_premiums_of_ the_Bath_an/ZWVpAAAAcAAJ? hl=en&gbpv=1&dq=Bath+and+West+of+England+Society&printsec=fron tcover (accessed 16 October 2023).

[841] Sugden, J. Nelson: The Sword of Albion. Random House (2012), p. 544.

[842] Bath Chronicle and Weekly Gazette 31 December 1807

https://search.findmypast.co.uk/bna/viewarticle?id=bl %2f0000221%2f18071231%2f021&stringtohighlight=matcham

[843] Bath Chronicle and Weekly Gazette, 6 October 1803, p. 4. Available at: Find My Past https://www.findmypast.co.uk/image-viewer?issue=BL %2F0000221%2F18031006&page=4&article=009&stringtohighlight=wea ther (accessed 17 October 2023).

[844] The Salisbury and Winchester Journal, 1 October 1803, p. 2. Accessed via Find My Past https://www.findmypast.co.uk/image-viewer? issue=BL %2F0000361%2F18041001&page=2&article=020&stringtohighlight=mat cham (accessed 17 October 2023).

[845] Lynn, The Anglo-Spanish War of 1796: on this day in history (2017). Available at: http://www.lynnbryant.co.uk/the-anglo-spanish-war-of-1796 (accessed 26 October 2023).

[846] Matcham, M.E. (1911) The Nelsons of Burnham Thorpe: a record of a Norfolk family compiled from unpublished letters and notebooks, 1787-1842, pp. 213-214.

[847] Matcham, M.E. (1911) The Nelsons of Burnham Thorpe: a record of a Norfolk family compiled from unpublished letters and notebooks, 1787-1842, p. 214.

[848] Matcham, M.E. (1911) The Nelsons of Burnham Thorpe: a record of a Norfolk family compiled from unpublished letters and notebooks, 1787-1842, p. 10.

[849] Matcham, M.E. (1911) The Nelsons of Burnham Thorpe: a record of a Norfolk family compiled from unpublished letters and notebooks, 1787-1842, p. 219.

[850] British Museum Department of Manuscripts, List of additions to the manuscripts in the British Museum (1901), p. 1259. Available at: https://www.google.co.uk/books/edition/List_of_Additions_to_the_Manuscripts_in/RqFDAQAAMAAJ?hl=en&gbpv=1&bsq=felipe+Ramirez+minorca&dq=felipe+Ramirez+minorca&printsec=frontcover (accessed 25 October 2023).

[851] Six Years Residence in Algiers by Elizabeth Broughton, (1839) p. 321. Available at: https://books.google.co.uk/books?id=a3sEAAAAQAAJ&printsec=frontcover&dq=six+years+residence+in+algiers&hl=en&newbks=1&newbks_redir=0&sa=X&redir_esc=y#v=onepage&q=bayonet&f=false (accessed 25 October 2023).

[852] The Daily Advertiser and Oracle, 14 April 1804, p. 2. Accessed via Find My Past https://www.findmypast.co.uk/image-viewer?issue=BL%2F0002429%2F18040414&page=2&article=019&stringtohighlight=lady+hamilton (accessed 17 October 2023).

[853] The Lincoln, Rutland and Stamford Mercury, etc., 6 April 1804, p. 3. Available at: https://www.findmypast.co.uk/image-viewer?issue=BL%2F0000237%2F18040406&page=3&article=003&stringtohighlight=nelson (accessed 20 January 2024).

[854] The Morning Post, 10 May 1804, p. 3. Accessed via Find My Past https://search.findmypast.co.uk/bna/viewarticle?id=BL%2F0000174%2F18040510%2F007%2F0003 (accessed 17 October 2023).

[855] Shee, Sir George | Dictionary of Irish Biography (no date). Available

at: https://www.dib.ie/biography/shee-sir-george-a5350 (accessed 25 October 2023).

[856] Matcham, M.E. (1911) The Nelsons of Burnham Thorpe: a record of a Norfolk family compiled from unpublished letters and notebooks, 1787-1842, pp. 219-220.

[857] Saint James's Chronicle, 17 July 1804, p. 1. Available at: https://www.findmypast.co.uk/image-viewer?issue=BL%2F0002193%2F18040717&page=1&article=007&stringtohighlight=nelson (accessed 20 January 2024).

[858] Saint James's Chronicle, 14 July 1804, p. 1. Available at: Find My Past https://www.findmypast.co.uk/image-viewer?issue=BL%2F0002193%2F18040714&page=1&article=006&stringtohighlight=lady+hamilton+nelson (accessed 17 October 2023).

[859] Matcham, M.E. (1911) The Nelsons of Burnham Thorpe: a record of a Norfolk family compiled from unpublished letters and notebooks, 1787-1842, p. 220.

[860] London Courier and Evening Gazette, 10 August 1804, p. 4. Available at: Find My Past https://www.findmypast.co.uk/image-viewer?issue=BL%2F0002193%2F18040714&page=1&article=006&stringtohighlight=lady+hamilton+nelson (accessed 17 October 2023).

[861] The Morning Post, 7 September 1804, p. 3. Accessed via Find My Past https://www.findmypast.co.uk/image-viewer?issue=BL%2F0000174%2F18040907&page=3&article=010&stringtohighlight=lady+hamilton (accessed 26 October 2023).

[862] Kentish Gazette, 11 September 1804, p. 3. Accessed via Find My Past https://www.findmypast.co.uk/image-viewer?issue=BL%2F0000235%2F18040911&page=3&article=005&stringtohighlight=lord+nelson (accessed 26 October 2023).

[863] The Salisbury and Winchester Journal, 1 October 1804, p. 2. Accessed via Find My Past https://www.findmypast.co.uk/image-viewer?issue=BL%2F0000361%2F18041001&page=2&article=020&stringtohighlight=plumley (accessed 25 October 2023).

[864] The London Chronicle, 11 December 1804, p. 6. Accessed via Find my Past https://www.findmypast.co.uk/image-viewer?issue=BL%2F0002634%2F18041211&page=6&article=025&stringtohighlight=lady+hamilton (accessed 10 January 2024).

[865] Morning Herald (London) 25 December 1804, p. 2. Accessed via Find my Past https://www.findmypast.co.uk/image-viewer?issue=BL

%2F0002408%2F18041225&page=2&article=005&stringtohighlight=lady +hamilton (accessed 10 January 2024).

[866] Oracle and the Daily Advertiser, 14 January 1805, p. 2. Accessed via Find my Past https://www.findmypast.co.uk/image-viewer?issue=BL %2F0002430%2F18050114&page=2&article=012&stringtohighlight=lady +hamilton (accessed 10 January 2024).

[867] Sun (London), 26 January 1805, p. 2. Accessed via Find my Past https://www.findmypast.co.uk/image-viewer?issue=BL %2F0002194%2F18050126&page=2&article=011&stringtohighlight=nels on (accessed 21 January 2024).

[868] Morning Post, 20 February 1805, p. 3. Accessed via Find my Past https://www.findmypast.co.uk/image-viewer?issue=BL %2F0000174%2F18050220&page=3&article=007&stringtohighlight=lady +hamilton (accessed 10 January 2024).

[869] Morning Post, 5 March 1805, p. 3. Accessed via Find my Past https://www.findmypast.co.uk/image-viewer?issue=BL %2F0000174%2F18050305&page=3&article=006&stringtohighlight=lady +hamilton (accessed 10 January 2024).

[870] Matcham, M.E. (1911) The Nelsons of Burnham Thorpe: a record of a Norfolk family compiled from unpublished letters and notebooks, 1787-1842, p. 227.

[871] Oracle and the Daily Advertiser, 18 May 1805, p. 2. Accessed via Find My Past https://www.findmypast.co.uk/image-viewer?issue=BL %2F0002430%2F18050518&page=2&article=014&stringtohighlight=nels on (accessed 20 January 2024).

[872] Morning Post, 27 May 1805, p. 3. Accessed via Find my Past https://www.findmypast.co.uk/image-viewer?issue=BL %2F0000174%2F18050527&page=3&article=010&stringtohighlight=lady +hamilton (accessed 10 January 2024).

[873] Matcham, M.E. (1911) The Nelsons of Burnham Thorpe: a record of a Norfolk family compiled from unpublished letters and notebooks, 1787-1842, pp. 220-221

[874] Matcham, M.E. (1911) The Nelsons of Burnham Thorpe: a record of a Norfolk family compiled from unpublished letters and notebooks, 1787-1842, pp. 220-221

[875] Chester Courant, 11 June 1805, p.1. Accessed via Find my Past https://www.findmypast.co.uk/image-viewer?issue=BL %2F0000388%2F18050611&page=1&article=001&stringtohighlight=nels on (accessed 20 January 2024).

[876] London Chronicle, 8 June 1805, p. 1. Accessed via Find my Past https://www.findmypast.co.uk/image-viewer?issue=BL %2F0002634%2F18050608&page=1&article=001&stringtohighlight=lady +hamilton (accessed 10 January 2024).

[877] Matcham, M.E. (1911) The Nelsons of Burnham Thorpe: a record of a Norfolk family compiled from unpublished letters and notebooks, 1787-1842, p. 223.

[878] DB Pedia, Sir Charles Warre Mallet. Available at: https://dbpedia.org/page/Sir_Charles_Malet,_1st_Baronet (accessed 31 January 2024).

[879] Chester Courant, 16 July 1805, p. 1. Accessed via Find My Past https://www.findmypast.co.uk/image-viewer?issue=BL %2F0000388%2F18050716&page=1&article=001&stringtohighlight=nels on (accessed 20 January 2024).

[880] Saint James's Chronicle, 10 August 1805, p. 4. Accessed via Find My Past https://www.findmypast.co.uk/image-viewer?issue=BL %2F0002193%2F18050810&page=4&article=020&stringtohighlight=nels on (accessed 20 January 2024).

[881] Cross, A. (no date) Chronology of Nelson. Available at: https://nelson-society.com/life-of-nelson/chronology/ (accessed 17 January 2024).

[882] The News (London), 25 August 1805, p. 7. Accessed via Find My Past https://www.findmypast.co.uk/image-viewer?issue=BL %2F0002257%2F18050825&page=7&article=029&stringtohighlight=nels on (accessed 21 January 2024).

[883] Matcham, M.E. (1911) The Nelsons of Burnham Thorpe: a record of a Norfolk family compiled from unpublished letters and notebooks, 1787-1842, pp. 226-227.

[884] Matcham, M.E. (1911) The Nelsons of Burnham Thorpe: a record of a Norfolk family compiled from unpublished letters and notebooks, 1787-1842, pp. 227-228.

[885] Somerset burials, Bathford, Somerset, England, copyright Find My Past. Available at: https://www.findmypast.co.uk/transcript?id=GBPRS %2FSOMERSET%2FBUR%2F003536016 (accessed 21 January 2024).

[886] Sotheby's and Co, S.P.B.A., Nelson and the Napoleonic Wars ; Including the Matcham Collection, Trafalgar, (2005) item 49, NELSON, HORATIO, Lord and EMMA HAMILTON. Two autograph letters signed, WRITTEN DURING NELSON'S LAST SHORE LEAVE TWO MONTHS BEFORE TRAFALGAR, pp. 96-97.

[887] Sugden, J. Nelson: The Sword of Albion. Random House (2012), p. 541.

[888] Matcham, M.E. (1911) The Nelsons of Burnham Thorpe: a record of a Norfolk family compiled from unpublished letters and notebooks, 1787-1842, p. 228.

[889] Gérin W., Horatia Nelson Oxford University Press (1970) p. 6.

[890] Matcham, M.E. (1911) The Nelsons of Burnham Thorpe: a record of a Norfolk family compiled from unpublished letters and notebooks, 1787-1842, p. 230.

[891] Sugden, J. Nelson: The Sword of Albion. Random House (2012), p. 759.

[892] Matcham, M.E. (1911) The Nelsons of Burnham Thorpe: a record of a Norfolk family compiled from unpublished letters and notebooks, 1787-1842, p. 285.

[893] Matcham, M.E. (1911) The Nelsons of Burnham Thorpe: a record of a Norfolk family compiled from unpublished letters and notebooks, 1787-1842, p. 233.

[894] Matcham, M.E. (1911) The Nelsons of Burnham Thorpe: a record of a Norfolk family compiled from unpublished letters and notebooks, 1787-1842, p. 272.

[895] Matcham, M.E. (1911) The Nelsons of Burnham Thorpe: a record of a Norfolk family compiled from unpublished letters and notebooks, 1787-1842, p. 230.

[896] Howarth, D.A. and Howarth, S., Nelson: the immortal memory. London: Conway Maritime. (2004), p. 309.

[897] Robinson S. K., in defence of Emma (2015) p. 352.

[898] Gérin W., Horatia Nelson Oxford University Press (1970) p. 100.

[899] Hibbert, C., Nelson: A personal history. London: Penguin (2002). P. 353.

[900] Sotheby's and Co, S.P.B.A., Nelson and the Napoleonic Wars; Including the Matcham Collection, Trafalgar, (2005) p. 10.

[901] Matcham, M.E. (1911) The Nelsons of Burnham Thorpe: a record of a Norfolk family compiled from unpublished letters and notebooks, 1787-1842, p. 285.

[902] Matcham, M.E. (1911) The Nelsons of Burnham Thorpe: a record of

a Norfolk family compiled from unpublished letters and notebooks, 1787-1842, p. 266.

[903] Sugden, J. Nelson: The Sword of Albion. Random House (2012), p. 759.

[904] Robinson S. K., in defence of Emma (2015) pp. 378-379.

[905] Robinson S. K., in defence of Emma (2015) p. 380.

[906] Fraser F., Beloved Emma. Weidenfield and Nicholson. London (1986), p. 367.

[907] Robinson S. K., in defence of Emma (2015) p. 379.

[908] Morning Post, 2 February 1813, p. 3. Accessed via Find My Past https://www.findmypast.co.uk/image-viewer?issue=BL%2F0000215%2F18051221&page=4&article=007&stringtohighlight=earl+nelson (accessed 9 February 2024).

[909] Robinson S. K., in defence of Emma (2015) p. 382.

[910] Pettigrew T. J., memoirs of the life of Vice-Admiral Lord Viscount Nelson, volume 2 (1849), pp. 625-626. Available at: https://www.google.co.uk/books/edition/Memoirs_of_the_Life_of_Vice_Admiral_Lord/ETXIvvN5VW4C?hl=en&gbpv=1&dq=lady+hamilton+clarges+street&pg=PA625&printsec=frontcover (accessed 9 February 2024).

[911] Staffordshire Advertiser, etc, 21 December 1805, p. 4. Accessed via Find My Past https://www.findmypast.co.uk/image-viewer?issue=BL%2F0000174%2F18130202&page=3&article=013&stringtohighlight=lady+hamilton+nelson (accessed 9 February 2024).

[912] Oracle and the Daily Advertiser, 6 January 1806, p. 3. Accessed via Find My Past https://www.findmypast.co.uk/image-viewer?issue=BL%2F0002430%2F18051225&page=3&article=013&stringtohighlight=earl+nelson (accessed 9 February 2024).

[913] Nelson's funeral (no date). Available at: https://www.rmg.co.uk/stories/topics/nelsons-funeral (accessed 17 October 2023).

[914] Oracle and the Daily Advertiser, 25 December 1805, p. 3. Accessed via Find My Past https://www.findmypast.co.uk/image-viewer?issue=BL%2F0000174%2F18060106&page=3&article=012&stringtohighlight=nelson+funeral (accessed 13 February 2024).

[915] Fraser F., Beloved Emma. Weidenfield and Nicholson. London (1986), p. 335.

[916] Morning Post, 2 February 1813, p. 3. Accessed via Find My Past https://www.findmypast.co.uk/image-viewer?issue=BL %2F0000215%2F18051221&page=4&article=007&stringtohighlight=earl +nelson (accessed 9 February 2024).

[917] Fraser F., Beloved Emma. Weidenfield and Nicholson. London (1986), p. 334.

[918] Information kindly supplied by Abel Land, curatorial assistant of the Fashion History Museum in Cambridge, Ontario, and tailor of historical menswear. Private email correspondence in August 2023.

[919] Morning Chronicle, 10 January 1806, p. 3. Accessed via Find My Past https://www.findmypast.co.uk/image-viewer?issue=BL %2F0000082%2F18060110&page=3&article=005&stringtohighlight=nels on+funeral (accessed 14 February 2024).

[920] Morning Chronicle, 10 January 1806, p. 3. Accessed via Find My Past https://www.findmypast.co.uk/image-viewer?issue=BL %2F0000082%2F18060110&page=3&article=005&stringtohighlight=nels on+funeral (accessed 14 February 2024).

[921] Fairburn J., the funeral of Admiral Lord Nelson, 2nd edition (1806) p. 89. Available at: https://www.google.co.uk/books/edition/Fairburn_s_2nd_edition_of_the_f uneral_of/XzwIAAAAQAAJ?hl=en&gbpv=1&dq=nelson %27s+funeral&printsec=frontcover (accessed 15 February 2024).

[922] Morning Chronicle, 10 January 1806, p. 3. Accessed via Find My Past https://www.findmypast.co.uk/image-viewer?issue=BL %2F0000082%2F18060110&page=3&article=005&stringtohighlight=nels on+funeral (accessed 14 February 2024).

[923] Oracle and the Daily Advertiser, 3 January 1806, p. 3. Accessed via Find My Past https://www.findmypast.co.uk/image-viewer?issue=BL %2F0002430%2F18060103&page=3&article=030&stringtohighlight=nels on+procession (accessed 13 February 2024).

[924] Morning Chronicle, 10 January 1806, p. 3. Accessed via Find My Past https://www.findmypast.co.uk/image-viewer?issue=BL %2F0000082%2F18060110&page=3&article=005&stringtohighlight=nels on+funeral (accessed 14 February 2024).

[925] Fairburn J., the funeral of Admiral Lord Nelson, 2nd edition (1806) p. 90. Available at: https://www.google.co.uk/books/edition/Fairburn_s_2nd_edition_of_the_f uneral_of/XzwIAAAAQAAJ?hl=en&gbpv=1&dq=nelson %27s+funeral&printsec=frontcover (accessed 15 February 2024).

[926] Nelson's funeral, Royal Museums Greenwich Available at: https://www.rmg.co.uk/stories/topics/nelsons-funeral (accessed 10 February 2024).

[927] Oracle and the Daily Advertiser, 11 January 18065, p. 2. Accessed via Find My Past https://www.findmypast.co.uk/image-viewer?issue=BL%2F0002430%2F18060111&page=2&article=007&stringtohighlight=nelson+funeral (accessed 14 February 2024).

[928] Fairburn J., the funeral of Admiral Lord Nelson, 2nd edition (1806) p. 91. Available at: https://www.google.co.uk/books/edition/Fairburn_s_2nd_edition_of_the_funeral_of/XzwIAAAAQAAJ?hl=en&gbpv=1&dq=nelson%27s+funeral&printsec=frontcover (accessed 15 February 2024).

[929] Sun (London), 10 January 1806, p. 3. Accessed via Find My Past https://search.findmypast.co.uk/bna/viewarticle?id=bl/0002194/18060110/007&stringtohighlight=matcham (accessed 10 February 2024).

[930] Fairburn J., the funeral of Admiral Lord Nelson, 2nd edition (1806) p. 93. Available at: https://www.google.co.uk/books/edition/Fairburn_s_2nd_edition_of_the_funeral_of/XzwIAAAAQAAJ?hl=en&gbpv=1&dq=nelson%27s+funeral&printsec=frontcover (accessed 15 February 2024).

[931] Robinson S. K., in defence of Emma (2015) p. 385.

[932] Matcham, M.E. (1911) The Nelsons of Burnham Thorpe: a record of a Norfolk family compiled from unpublished letters and notebooks, 1787-1842, pp. 250-251.

[933] Gloucester Journal, 19 May 1806, p. 4. Accessed via Find My Past https://www.findmypast.co.uk/image-viewer?issue=BL%2F0000532%2F18060519&page=4&article=019&stringtohighlight=nelson (accessed 9 February 2024).

[934] Fraser F., Beloved Emma. Weidenfield and Nicholson. London (1986), p. 342.

[935] Lower M. A., a compendious history of Sussex (1780) p. 164. Available at: https://www.google.co.uk/books/edition/A_Compendious_History_of_Sussex/CLEHAAAAQAAJ?hl=en&gbpv=1&dq=slaugham&pg=PA164&printsec=frontcover (accessed 22 February 2024)

[936] Email correspondence with Barry Ray of Slaugham Archive. 6 March 2023.

[937] Matcham, M.E. (1911) The Nelsons of Burnham Thorpe: a record of a Norfolk family compiled from unpublished letters and notebooks, 1787-1842, p. 244.

[938] The king's candlesticks, William Haslewood (2024). Available at: http://www.thekingscandlesticks.com/webs/pedigrees/22131.html (accessed 27 april 2024).

[939] Ancestry.com. London, England, Church of England Baptisms, Marriages and Burials, 1538-1812. Available at: https://www.ancestry.co.uk/discoveryui-content/view/3207:1624?tid=&pid=&queryId=63bae691-7d5e-4142-b47d-1be99e806164&_phsrc=ECs5532&_phstart=successSource (accessed 27 April 2024).

[940] Slaugham Archives, document #61. Available at: https://slaughamarchives.org/pictures/document/61.pdf?r=129050 (accessed 3 March 2024).

[941] Morning Herald (London), 23 November 1822, p. 3. Accessed via Find My Past https://www.findmypast.co.uk/image-viewer?issue=BL%2F0002408%2F18221123&page=1&article=002&stringtohighlight=ashfold+slaugham (accessed 20 February 2024).

[942] Lower M. A., a compendious history of Sussex (1870) p. 164. Available at: https://www.google.co.uk/books/edition/A_Compendious_History_of_Sussex/CLEHAAAAQAAJ?hl=en&gbpv=1&dq=slaugham&pg=PA164&printsec=frontcover (accessed 9 March 2024).

[943] Email correspondence with Barry Ray of Slaugham Archive. 2 March 2023.

[944] Sickelmore R., The history of Brighton from the earliest period to the present time… (1823) pp. 115-116. Available at: https://www.google.co.uk/books/edition/The_history_of_Brighton_from_the_earlies/lK4HAAAAQAAJ?hl=en&gbpv=1&dq=handcross&pg=PA115&printsec=frontcover (accessed 5 March 2024).

[945] Attree H. R., Attree's Topography of Brighton (1809) p. 16. Available at: https://www.google.co.uk/books/edition/Attree_s_Topography_of_Brighton/e64HAAAAQAAJ?hl=en&gbpv=1&dq=handcross&pg=RA2-PA16&printsec=frontcover (accessed 5 March 2024).

[946] Hamilton E., Lady, his capital messuage at Merton in the county of Surry (1807). Available at Bonhams:

https://www.bonhams.com/auctions/11430/lot/279/ (accessed 9 March 2024).

[947] Matcham, M.E. (1911) The Nelsons of Burnham Thorpe: a record of a Norfolk family compiled from unpublished letters and notebooks, 1787-1842, p. 258.

[948] The Kentish Weekly Post or Canterbury Journal, 18 August 1807, p. 4. Accessed via Find My Past https://www.findmypast.co.uk/image-viewer?issue=BL%2F0001409%2F18070818&page=4&article=018&stringtohighlight=earl+nelson (accessed 10 March 2024).

[949] Peakman J., Emma Hamilton. Haus Publishing, London (2005). P 148.

[950] Worthing history, wherefore art thou Shakespeare? (no date). Available at: https://worthinghistory.com/?page_id=561 (accessed 10 March 2024).

[951] Matcham, M.E. (1911) The Nelsons of Burnham Thorpe: a record of a Norfolk family compiled from unpublished letters and notebooks, 1787-1842, p. 259.

[952] Editors of Wikipedia, list of royal visits to Worthing (2018). Available at: https://en.wikipedia.org/wiki/List_of_royal_visits_to_Worthing (accessed 10 March 2024).

[953] Morning Herald (London), 12 August 1807, p. 3. Accessed via Find My Past https://www.findmypast.co.uk/image-viewer?issue=BL%2F0002408%2F18070812&page=3&article=015&stringtohighlight=worthing+theatre (accessed 10 March 2024).

[954] Fraser F., Beloved Emma. Weidenfield and Nicholson. London (1986). P. 344.

[955] Matcham, M.E. (1911) The Nelsons of Burnham Thorpe: a record of a Norfolk family compiled from unpublished letters and notebooks, 1787-1842, p. 259.

[956] Gérin W., Horatia Nelson Oxford University Press (1970) p. 142.

[957] Ross D., follies in the English landscape, Britain Express (no date). Available at: https://www.britainexpress.com/History/follies.htm (accessed 10 January 2024).

[958] Star (London), 22 September 1807, p. 3. Accessed via Find My Past: https://www.findmypast.co.uk/image-viewer?issue=BL%2F0001254%2F18070829&page=2&article=007&stringtohighlight=cuc

kfield (accessed 28 February 2024).

[959] Public Ledger and Daily Advertiser, 29 August 1807, p. 2. Accessed via Find My Past: https://www.findmypast.co.uk/image-viewer?issue=BL%2F0002646%2F18070922&page=3&article=017&stringtohighlight=cuckfield (accessed 28 February 2024).

[960] London Metropolitan Archives: ROYAL AND SUN ALLIANCE INSURANCE GROUP; Reference Code: CLC/B/192/F/001/MS11936/434/785712

(1806 Jan 14). Available at: https://search.lma.gov.uk/scripts/mwimain.dll/144/LMA_OPAC/web_detail?SESSIONSEARCH&exp=refd%20CLC/B/192/F/001/MS11936/437/795665 (viewed 28 February 2024)

[961] Wiltshire and Swindon History Centre: Eyre-Matcham family of Newhouse, Whiteparish and Downton; 3 - deeds etc. Matcham family: not main estate, 1369/7/2/6, Correspondence to George Matcham family and business including East India Company affairs (1777-1801): letter to George Matcham from J. Lawrence dated 6th December 1810.

[962] Matcham, M.E. (1911) The Nelsons of Burnham Thorpe: a record of a Norfolk family compiled from unpublished letters and notebooks, 1787-1842, p. 256.

[963] Wiltshire and Swindon History Centre: Eyre-Matcham family of Newhouse, Whiteparish and Downton; 3 - deeds etc. Matcham family: not main estate, 1369/7/2/6, Correspondence to George Matcham family and business including East India Company affairs (1777-1801): letter to George Matcham from J. Lawrence dated 6th December 1810.

[964] Star (London), 29 December 1807, p. 4. Accessed via Find My Past: https://www.findmypast.co.uk/image-viewer?issue=BL%2F0002646%2F18071229&page=4&article=023&stringtohighlight=matcham+sussex (accessed 16 March 2024).

[965] Norfolk Chronicle, 23 January 1808, p. 2. Accessed via Find My Past: https://www.findmypast.co.uk/image-viewer?issue=BL%2F0000246%2F18080123&page=2&article=013&stringtohighlight=trafalgar (accessed 16 March 2024).

[966] Matcham, M.E. (1911) The Nelsons of Burnham Thorpe: a record of a Norfolk family compiled from unpublished letters and notebooks, 1787-1842, p. 262.

[967] London Chronicle, 27 January 1808, p. 3. Accessed via Find My Past: https://www.findmypast.co.uk/image-viewer?issue=BL%2F0002634%2F18080127&page=3&article=010&stringtohighlight=hor

atio+nelson (accessed 17 March 2024).

[968] Matcham, M.E. (1911) The Nelsons of Burnham Thorpe: a record of a Norfolk family compiled from unpublished letters and notebooks, 1787-1842, pp. 263-4.

[969] Family Search, burial record image, film number 004428016. Image courtesy of West Sussex Council. Available at: https://www.familysearch.org/ark:/61903/3:1:S3HY-D1D7-F5?i=173&cc=1465706 (accessed 16 March 2024).

[970] Clark J. S. and Jones S., the naval chronicle, volume 19 (1808) p. 263. Available at: https://www.google.co.uk/books/edition/The_Naval_Chronicle/DHbgHzUWfFwC?hl=en&gbpv=1&dq=T+matcham&pg=PA263&printsec=frontcover (accessed 16 March 2024).

[971] Owen W., Owen's new book of fairs (1813) p. 73. Available at: https://www.google.co.uk/books/edition/Owen_s_New_Book_of_Fairs_A_new_edition_e/lrdVAAAAcAAJ?hl=en&gbpv=1&dq=slaugham&pg=PA144&printsec=frontcover (viewed 9 March 2024).

[972] Long W. H., memoirs of Emma, Lady Hamilton (1892) p. 294. Available at hhttps://www.google.co.uk/books/edition/Memoirs_of_Emma_Lady_Hamilton/-9wxAQAAIAAJ?hl=en&gbpv=1 (accessed 26 February 2024).

[973] Borrelli-Persson, L. (2016) 'The Empire Silhouette: Tracing the trend,' Vogue, 11 July. https://www.vogue.com/article/fall-2016-couture-empire-trend-gisele-bundchen-rihanna (accessed 27 September 2023).

[974] Peakman J., Emma Hamilton. Haus Publishing, London (2005). P 147

[975] Robinson S. K., in defence of Emma (2015) P. 438.

[976] Warwick, P. (1995) Here was paradise - A description of Merton Place, by Peter Warwick. Available at: https://wandle.org/aboutus/nelson2005/paradise.htm (accessed 27 April 2024).

[977] Peakman J., Emma Hamilton. Haus Publishing, London (2005), p. 148.

[978] Matcham G. (junior), character of admiral ord nelson naval history the author's copy (1861). eBay sale item: https://rb.gy/nzgtzp (accessed 15 March 2024).

[979] Matcham, M.E. (1911) The Nelsons of Burnham Thorpe: a record of

a Norfolk family compiled from unpublished letters and notebooks, 1787-1842, p. 267.

[980] Robinson S. K., in defence of Emma (2015) P. 404.

[981] Gérin W., Horatia Nelson Oxford University Press (1970) p. 219.

[982] Journals of the House of Commons, volume 75 (1819) p. 951. Available at https://www.google.co.uk/books/edition/Journals_of_the_House_of_Commons/gR5DAAAAcAAJ?hl=en&gbpv=1&dq=george+matcham+journals&pg=PA951&printsec=frontcover (accessed 15 March 2024).

[983] Matcham, M.E. (1911) The Nelsons of Burnham Thorpe: a record of a Norfolk family compiled from unpublished letters and notebooks, 1787-1842, p. 272.

[984] Fraser F., Beloved Emma. Weidenfield and Nicholson. London (1986). P. 351.

[985] Peakman J., Emma Hamilton. Haus Publishing, London (2005), p. 153.

[986] Gérin, W., Horatia Nelson Oxford University Press (1970) p. 184.

[987] The British and Foreign Bible Society, report (1812). Available at: https://www.google.co.uk/books/edition/The_Report_of_the_British_and_Foreign_Bi/UhvLQ2yCREgC?hl=en&gbpv=1&dq=sussex+matcham&pg=RA25-PA7&printsec=frontcover (accessed 15 March 2024).

[988] Matcham, M.E. (1911) The Nelsons of Burnham Thorpe: a record of a Norfolk family compiled from unpublished letters and notebooks, 1787-1842, p. 299.

[989] Wiltshire and Swindon History Centre: Eyre-Matcham family of Newhouse, Whiteparish and Downton; 3 - deeds etc. Matcham family: not main estate, 1369/7/2/6, Correspondence to George Matcham family and business including East India Company affairs (1777-1801): letter to George Matcham from J. Lawrence dated 27th March 1812.

[990] Matcham, M.E. (1911) The Nelsons of Burnham Thorpe: a record of a Norfolk family compiled from unpublished letters and notebooks, 1787-1842, p. 300.

[991] Wikipedia contributors (2023e) St James's Park, Wikipedia [Preprint]. Available at: https://en.wikipedia.org/wiki/St_James%27s_Park (accessed 17 October 2023).

[992] Matcham, M.E. (1911) The Nelsons of Burnham Thorpe: a record of a Norfolk family compiled from unpublished letters and notebooks, 1787-1842, pp. 286-289.

[993] Gérin, W., Horatia Nelson Oxford University Press (1970) p. 181-182.

[994] Matcham, M.E. (1911) The Nelsons of Burnham Thorpe: a record of a Norfolk family compiled from unpublished letters and notebooks, 1787-1842, p. 273.

[995] National Register (London), 7 February 1813, p. 12. Accessed via Find My Past https://www.findmypast.co.uk/image-viewer?issue=BL%2F0002644%2F18130207&page=12&article=032&stringtohighlight=lady+hamilton (accessed 18 March 2024).

[996] The Globe, 31 October 1812, p. 3. Accessed via Find My Past https://search.findmypast.co.uk/bna/viewarticle?id=bl%2f0001651%2f18121031%2f007 (accessed 15 March 2024).

[997] Matcham, M.E. (1911) The Nelsons of Burnham Thorpe: a record of a Norfolk family compiled from unpublished letters and notebooks, 1787-1842, p. 274.

[998] Matcham, M.E. (1911) The Nelsons of Burnham Thorpe: a record of a Norfolk family compiled from unpublished letters and notebooks, 1787-1842, p. 274.

[999] Robinson S. K., in defence of Emma (2015) P. 438.

[1000] Robinson S. K., in defence of Emma (2015) P. 446.

[1001] Robinson S. K., in defence of Emma (2015) P. 445.

[1002] Bury and Norwich Post, 6 April 1814, p. 3. Accessed via Find My Past https://www.findmypast.co.uk/image-viewer?issue=BL%2F0000156%2F18140406&page=2&article=010&stringtohighlight=matcham (accessed 15 March 2024).

[1003] Saint James's Chronicle, 12 April 1814, p. 2. Accessed via Find My Past https://www.findmypast.co.uk/image-viewer?issue=BL%2F0002193%2F18140412&page=2&article=010&stringtohighlight=napoleon (accessed 19 March 2024).

[1004] Robinson S. K., in defence of Emma (2015) P. 447.

[1005] Robinson S. K., in defence of Emma (2015) P. 448.

[1006] Robinson S. K., in defence of Emma (2015) P. 449.

[1007] Matcham, M.E. (1911) The Nelsons of Burnham Thorpe: a record of a Norfolk family compiled from unpublished letters and notebooks, 1787-1842, p. 279.

[1008] Handwritten notes in the Matcham family's copy of Walter Sichel's 1905 Emma Lady Hamilton. Shown to the author by Matcham descendant, George Jeffreys, in October 2017. The author's photo is included in Appendix 9.

[1009] Gérin W., Horatia Nelson Oxford University Press (1970) p. 219.

[1010] Matcham, M.E. (1911) The Nelsons of Burnham Thorpe: a record of a Norfolk family compiled from unpublished letters and notebooks, 1787-1842, p. 277.

[1011] Wikipedia contributors, Sir Charles Malet, 1st Baronet (2023). Available at: https://en.wikipedia.org/wiki/Sir_Charles_Malet,_1st_Baronet (accessed 4 November 2023).

[1012] Gérin W., Horatia Nelson Oxford University Press (1970) p. 219.

[1013] Wikipedia contributors, Napoleon, (2024). Available at: https://en.wikipedia.org/wiki/Napoleon (accessed 19 March 2024).

[1014] Gérin W., Horatia Nelson Oxford University Press (1970) p. 220.

[1015] Gérin W., Horatia Nelson Oxford University Press (1970) p. 219.

[1016] Morning Post, 18 August 1815, p. 3. Accessed via Find My Past https://www.findmypast.co.uk/image-viewer?issue=BL%2F0000174%2F18150818&page=3&article=011&stringtohighlight=wellington+paris (accessed 22 March 2024).

[1017] Thompson P., Henry Stanyford Blanckley (1785-1819), (2023) p. 107. Available at: https://www.lilystyle.co.uk/download/hsb-spy.pdf (accessed 22 March 2024).

[1018] Royal Museums Greenwich, Horatia Nelson, 1801-1881. Available at: https://www.rmg.co.uk/collections/objects/rmgc-object-14359 (accessed 20 March 2024).

[1019]

Hamilton, W., Nelson, H. N., Hamilton, E., Pettigrew, T. J. (1894). The Hamilton & Nelson Papers ... 1756-[1815]: 1798-1815. United Kingdom: private circulation, p. 81. Available at: https://www.google.co.uk/books/edition/The_Hamilton_Nelson_Papers_1756_1815_179/qDeIqic5uwAC?hl=en&gbpv=1&dq=matcham+shepherd%27s+spring&pg=PA81&printsec=frontcover (accessed 19 March 2024).

[1020] London Courier and Evening Gazette, 15 May 1816, p. 1. Accessed via Find My Past: https://www.findmypast.co.uk/image-viewer?issue=BL%2F0001476%2F18160515&page=1&article=002&stringtohighlight=matcham (accessed 22 March 2024).

[1021] Gérin, W., Horatia Nelson, Oxford: Clarendon (1970). P. 221.

[1022] Encyclopaedia Britannica, Beau Brummell English dandy (2024). Available at: https://www.britannica.com/biography/Beau-Brummell-English-dandy (accessed 19 March 2024).

[1023] Wikipedia contributors, History of Portugal (2024). Available at: https://en.wikipedia.org/wiki/History_of_Portugal (accessed 23 March 2024).

[1024] Fashion history timeline, 1810-1819 (2020). Available at: https://fashionhistory.fitnyc.edu/1810-1819/ (accessed 22 March 2024).

[1025] Gérin, W., Horatia Nelson, Oxford: Clarendon (1970). P. 222.

[1026] Ancestry.com. Wiltshire, England, Church of England Marriages and Banns, 1754-1916. Available at: https://www.ancestry.co.uk/imageviewer/collections/61189/images/45582_263021009496_1063-00014?pId=2872042 (accessed 24 March 2024).

[1027] Blanckley Family Papers, Box B-000820; Folder 8, Manuscripts Division, Department of Rare Books and Special Collections, Princeton University Library

[1028] Gérin, W., Horatia Nelson, Oxford: Clarendon (1970). P. 224.

[1029] Wikipedia contributors, Ahmed bin Ali Khodja (2024). Available at: https://en.wikipedia.org/wiki/Ahmed_bin_Ali_Khodja (accessed 28 March 2024).

[1030] Royal Marines history, bombardment of Algiers - fighting slavery (2021) Available at: https://www.royalmarineshistory.com/post/bombardment-of-algiers-fighting-slavery (accessed 28 March 2024).

[1031] Broughton, E., Six years residence in Algiers, Saunders and Oatley, London (1839), pp. 3-4. Available online at: https://books.google.co.uk/books?id=a3sEAAAAQAAJ&printsec=frontcover&dq=six+years+residence+in+algiers&hl=en&newbks=1&newbks_redir=0&sa=X&redir_esc=y#v=snippet&q=venerable&f=false (accessed 10 September 2023).

[1032] Blanckley Family Papers, Box B-000820; Folder 8, Manuscripts Division, Department of Rare Books and Special Collections, Princeton

University Library. Fully transcribed in appendix 10.

[1033] Hugill R. (2021). Available at: https://www.planethugill.com/2021/08/admired-by-berlioz-and-wagner-operas-of.html (accessed 25 March 2024).

[1034] Wikipedia contributors, Paris during the Bourbon Restoration (2024). Available at: https://en.wikipedia.org/wiki/Paris_during_the_Bourbon_Restoration (accessed 20 March 2024).

[1035] Gérin, W., Horatia Nelson, Oxford: Clarendon (1970). P. p. 231-232.

[1036] Dictionary of National Biography, Volumes 1-22 for George Matcham. https://www.ancestry.co.uk/imageviewer/collections/1981/images/31205_Vol13-00047?pId=41046

[1037] Matcham G., Anecdotes of a Croat (1821) Pp. 257-258. Available at: https://play.google.com/books/reader?id=rcABAAAAQAAJ&pg=GBS.PA258&hl=en (accessed 26 March 2024).

[1038] Gérin, W., Horatia Nelson, Oxford: Clarendon (1970). P. 232.

[1039] Gérin, W., Horatia Nelson, Oxford: Clarendon (1970). P. 234.

[1040] Wikipedia contributors, William à Court, 1st Baron Heytesbury (2024). Available at: https://en.wikipedia.org/wiki/William_%C3%A0_Court,_1st_Baron_Heytesbury (accessed 27 March 2024).

[1041] Wiltshire and Swindon History Centre: Eyre-Matcham family of Newhouse, Whiteparish and Downton; 3 - deeds etc. Matcham family: not main estate, 1369/3/20, Undated copy of an agreement by George Matcham to make a financial settlement on the marriage of his daughter Harriet with Edward Blanckley.

[1042] Matcham, M.E. (1911) The Nelsons of Burnham Thorpe: a record of a Norfolk family compiled from unpublished letters and notebooks, 1787-1842. Pp. 289-290.

[1043] Matcham, M.E. (1911) The Nelsons of Burnham Thorpe: a record of a Norfolk family compiled from unpublished letters and notebooks, 1787-1842. Pp. 289-291.

[1044] Ancestry.com. UK, British Army and Navy Birth, Marriage and Death Records, 1730-1960. Available at: https://www.ancestry.co.uk/discoveryui-content/view/348508:60931?ssrc=pt&tid=82673375&pid=40467016630 (accessed 29 March 2024).

[1045] Morning Post, 22 February 1819, p. 2. Accessed via Find My Past https://search.findmypast.co.uk/bna/viewarticle?id=bl/0000174/18190222/006 (accessed 29 March 2024).

[1046] Wiltshire and Swindon History Centre: Eyre-Matcham family of Newhouse, Whiteparish and Downton; 3 - deeds etc. Matcham family: not main estate, 1369/7/2/12, Correspondence to George and Nelson Matcham with Thomas Delisle & Co of Paris, France, on family matters in Europe and the Near East, with cash accounts. 1825 letter sent from Paris to George Matcham junior concerning the Blanckley relinquishing their property in Dieppe.

[1047] Anecdotes of a Croat - Google Play (no date). https://play.google.com/books/reader?id=rcABAAAAQAAJ&pg=GBS.PP10&hl=en (accessed 30 September 2023).

[1048] Matcham, M.E. (1911) The Nelsons of Burnham Thorpe: a record of a Norfolk family compiled from unpublished letters and notebooks, 1787-1842, p. 294.

[1049] Matcham, M.E. (1911) The Nelsons of Burnham Thorpe: a record of a Norfolk family compiled from unpublished letters and notebooks, 1787-1842, p. 294.

[1050] Matcham, M.E. (1911) The Nelsons of Burnham Thorpe: a record of a Norfolk family compiled from unpublished letters and notebooks, 1787-1842, p. 295.

[1051] Exmouth News Hub, local historian: Exmouth's connection to the wife of Lord Nelson (2022). Available at: https://exmouth.nub.news/news/local-news/local-historian-exmouths-connection-to-the-wife-of-lord-nelson-150338 (accessed 13 April 2024).

[1052] Hobart history, will the real Lady Nelson please stand up (2020). Available at: See Facebook for details. (accessed 13 April 2024).

[1053] Gérin, W., Horatia Nelson, Oxford: Clarendon (1970). P. 258.

[1054] Ancestry, Yvelines, France, Births, Marriages and Deaths 1734-1996. Available at: https://www.ancestry.co.uk/discoveryui-content/view/383515:62009?ssrc=pt&tid=82673375&pid=392476861817 (accessed 29 March 2024).

[1055] Matcham, M.E. (1911) The Nelsons of Burnham Thorpe: a record of a Norfolk family compiled from unpublished letters and notebooks, 1787-1842, p. 78.

[1056] Matcham, M.E. (1911) The Nelsons of Burnham Thorpe: a record of

a Norfolk family compiled from unpublished letters and notebooks, 1787-1842, p. 323.

[1057] British listed buildings, 18-26, Holland Street W8. Available at: https://britishlistedbuildings.co.uk/101080594-18-26-holland-street-w8-campden-ward (accessed 12 April 2024).

[1058] Dictionary of National Biography, Volumes 1-22 for George Matcham. https://www.ancestry.co.uk/imageviewer/collections/1981/images/31205_Vol13-00047?pId=41046

[1059] Anecdotes of a Croat by Croat - books on Google Play (1821). https://play.google.com/store/books/details?id=rcABAAAAQAAJ&rdid=book-rcABAAAAQAAJ&rdot=1 (accessed 30 September 2023).

[1060] Sotheby's and Co, S.P.B.A., Nelson and the Napoleonic Wars ; Including the Matcham Collection, Trafalgar, (2005) item 2, NELSON, HORATIO, Lord. Autograph letter signed ("Horatio Nelson"), with his right hand, to his sister Catherine Matcham on FAMILY BUSINESS AND LOCAL GOSSIP, p. 20.

[1061] Black and white copy of a portrait with the inscription "Captain Arthur Davis RN" shared on Ancestry.com. Available at: https://www.ancestry.co.uk/sharing/12276691?mark=7b22746f6b656e223a2253706e73353533454368487352775272724e595a4d387a70424e685764324e516f61454649635a2f6e6e30493d222c22746f6b656e5f76657273696f6e223a225632227d (accessed 9 April 2024).

[1062] Ancestry, London, England, Church of England Marriages and Banns, 1754-1938. Available at: https://www.ancestry.co.uk/discoveryui-content/view/5989826:1623?ssrc=pt&tid=82673375&pid=40510097693 (accessed 9 April 2024).

[1063] Morning Post, 7 May 1824, p. 4. Accessed via Find My Past https://www.findmypast.co.uk/image-viewer?issue=BL%2F0000174%2F18240507&page=4&article=023&stringtohighlight=matcham (accessed 9 April 2024).

[1064] Matcham (no date) Parental Chitchat. Not published. 26 ... https://www.abebooks.de/Parental-Chitchat-published-26-december-1826/31174596581/bd#&gid=1&pid=5 (accessed 30 September 2023).

[1065] Portrait of Professor John Wilson of Ellerey, (nom de plume "Christopher North") 1785 - 1854. Available at: https://www.artwarefineart.com/gallery/portrait-professor-john-wilson-ellerey-nom-de-plume-christopher-north-1785-1854 (accessed 11 January

2024).

[1066] North C., Blackwood's Edinburgh Magazine, (1827) vol. 21, p. 343. Available at: https://archive.org/details/sim_blackwoods-magazine_1827-03_21_123/page/342/mode/2up?q=india (accessed 11 January 2024).

[1067] Matcham (no date) Parental Chitchat. Not published. 26 ... https://www.abebooks.de/Parental-Chitchat-published-26-december-1826/31174596581/bd#&gid=1&pid=5 (accessed 30 September 2023).

[1068] Matcham C. H. N., personal journal placed for sale on eBay in 2023 with ome pages legible in sales photos, including Charles Matcham's note of anchoring in Plymouth Sound on 23 August 1828.

[1069] Ancestry.com. UK, England & Wales, Prerogative Court of Canterbury Wills, 1384-1858, PROB 11: Will Registers, 1832-1834, Piece 1812: Farquhar, Quire Numbers 101-150 (1833). Available at: https://www.ancestry.co.uk/imageviewer/collections/5111/images/40611_3 10472-00065?pId=146589 (accessed 13 April 2024).

[1070] Strutt and Parker (estate agents) Redlynch (©2024). Available at: https://www.struttandparker.com/properties/redlynch-1 (accessed 13 April 2024).

[1071] Matcham, M.E. (1911) The Nelsons of Burnham Thorpe: a record of a Norfolk family compiled from unpublished letters and notebooks, 1787-1842, p. 323.

[1072] Matcham, M.E. (1911) The Nelsons of Burnham Thorpe: a record of a Norfolk family compiled from unpublished letters and notebooks, 1787-1842, pp. 296–297.

[1073] Dictionary of National Biography, Volumes 1-22 for George Matcham. Available at: https://www.ancestry.co.uk/imageviewer/collections/1981/images/31205_Vol13-00047?pId=41046 (accessed January 2022).

[1074] George Matcham 3 February 1833 in BillionGraves GPS Headstones | BillionGraves (no date). https://billiongraves.com/grave/George-Matcham/16889703 (accessed 30 September 2023).

[1075] Matcham, M.E. (1911) The Nelsons of Burnham Thorpe: a record of a Norfolk family compiled from unpublished letters and notebooks, 1787-1842, p. 287.

[1076] Matcham, M.E. (1911) The Nelsons of Burnham Thorpe: a record of a Norfolk family compiled from unpublished letters and notebooks, 1787-1842, pp. 286-287.

[1077] Howarth, D.A. and Howarth, S. (2004) in Nelson: The immortal memory. London: Conway Maritime, p. 205.

[1078] Chamber, W. and Chamber, R. (1864) "NELSON, Horatio," in Chamber's Encyclopaedia. London, England: Chamber's, pp. 702–703.

[1079] Williams, K. (2006) in England's mistress: The infamous life of Emma Hamilton. London: Hutchinson, p. 281.

[1080] Williams, K. (2006) in England's mistress: The infamous life of Emma Hamilton. London: Hutchinson, p. 381.

[1081] Williams, K. (2006) in England's mistress: The infamous life of Emma Hamilton. London: Hutchinson, p. 329.

[1082] Personal correspondence from John Hawkin to Lily Style in 2015.

[1083] Institution of Civil Engineers, Devonport Royal Dockyard, Plymouth, United Kingdom (2024). Available at: https://www.ice.org.uk/what-is-civil-engineering/what-do-civil-engineers-do/devonport-royal-dockyard (accessed 13 April 2024).

[1084] Wiltshire and Swindon History Centre: Eyre-Matcham family of Newhouse, Whiteparish and Downton; 3 - deeds etc. Matcham family: not main estate, 1369/3/1, Probate of the will of Simon Matcham of Bombay, India (proved in Bombay) 1776; will made 1758.

[1085] Patent amendment kindly supplied by the British Library in 2023.

[1086] Liberto, D. (2023) 'Locus Sigilli: Meaning, examples, and history,' Investopedia [Preprint]. Available at: https://www.investopedia.com/terms/l/locus-sigilli.asp (accessed 16 October 2023).

[1087] Millman, J. (no date) THE JERMYs OF GUNTON (2). Available at: http://www.jermy.org/jm-tripartite/THE%20JERMYs%20OF%20GUNTON%20(2).htm (accessed 16 October 2023).

[1088] Trench, P., The Worst Country in the World: the true story of an Australian pioneer family, Prefab Publications (2012), p. 9.

[1089] Trench, P., The Worst Country in the World: the true story of an Australian pioneer family, Prefab Publications (2012), pp. 24-25.

[1090] Trench, P., The Worst Country in the World: the true story of an Australian pioneer family, Prefab Publications (2012), p. 25.

[1091] Trench, P., The Worst Country in the World: the true story of an Australian pioneer family, Prefab Publications (2012), p. 26.

[1092] Wiltshire and Swindon History Centre: Eyre-Matcham family of Newhouse, Whiteparish and Downton; 3 - deeds etc. Matcham family: not main estate, 1369/13/1: Genealogy notes and material on the Eyre, Matcham and Nelson families (1823-1897).

[1093] Matcham, M.E. (1911) The Nelsons of Burnham Thorpe: a record of a Norfolk family compiled from unpublished letters and notebooks, 1787-1842, pp. 183–184.

[1094] Trench, P., The Worst Country in the World: the true story of an Australian pioneer family, Prefab Publications (2012), p. 10.

[1095] Trench, P., The Worst Country in the World: the true story of an Australian pioneer family, Prefab Publications (2012), pp. 42, 149.

[1096] Trench, P., The Worst Country in the World: the true story of an Australian pioneer family, Prefab Publications (2012), pp. 52-53.

[1097] Hampshire Chronicle, 29 June 1801, p. 4. Accessed via Find My Past https://www.findmypast.co.uk/image-viewer?issue=BL %2F0000230%2F18010629&page=4&article=014&stringtohighlight=canada+portsmouth (accessed 22 October 2023).

[1098] Spranklen, A., Historic New Forest Newhouse Estate Hits The Market for £18 Million, Tatler, (2021). Available at: https://www.tatler.com/article/newhouse-estate-for-sale (accessed 23 October 2023).

[1099] Matcham, M.E. (1911) The Nelsons of Burnham Thorpe: a record of a Norfolk family compiled from unpublished letters and notebooks, 1787-1842, p. 184.

[1100] Wiltshire and Swindon History Centre: Eyre-Matcham family of Newhouse, Whiteparish and Downton; 3 - deeds etc. Matcham family: not main estate, 1369/7/2/4: Various family letters including a letter to Lord Nelson 1803 from Governor King in Sydney.

Acknowledgements

My thanks go to Abel Land, curatorial assistant of the Fashion History Museum in Cambridge, Ontario, and tailor of historical menswear.

I'd like to thank my brother, David Bullock, for his invaluable knowledge of Matcham, Nelson and Blanckley addresses in Bath. Also, David Bullock and Meron Kassa of the British Library for locating George Matcham's 1803 patent amendment.

I am firther indebted to Christopher A. Sorensen, Historical Consultant | Maritime Heritage, for information about contemporary Royal Navy uniform customs and regulations.

I extend additional thanks to Bournemouth Local History and to Barry Ray of Slaugham Archive. Also to Adam Preston for the photograph of his fifth great-grandfather, Thomas Bolton's invitation to attend Nelson's funeral procession; Tim Ridge for sharing his family story of descent from Ann Nelson and to Dee Marley of Historium Press for her professional support and instantly seeing this book's seedling potential.

Lastly, but by no means least, I am heartly grateful to the generosity of people who donated funds to enable this book's publication. These are, Sylvia K. Robinson, author of the invaluable In Defense of Emma, who very kindly stood as an advocate. Tony Rea and Rebecca Budd who contributed as supporting partners. Alison Huntingord, Dotlyall, Ray Mayhew, Bob and Marilyn Morrison, Carolyn M Osborne and Jonathan Smith as additional supporters.

About the Author

Lily Style is a keen historical author, of both fiction and nonfiction.

Her writing took off after she explored her colourful lineage, which includes the famous lovers, Admiral Lord Nelson and Emma Hamilton, who are her 4th great-grandparents. In researching them, and other ancestors, she noticed things others seem to have missed. She believes this is because of an affectionate, protective family connection.

Real human stories are everything, even in her fiction.

Her interest is in piecing together the real human stories that lie beneath dry facts. Her historical fiction, Somerswood, is the bronze winner of The Historical Fiction Company's 2023 short story category.

Her *George Matcham biography, A Most Unsettled Man* is being published by Historium Press in July 2024.

She writes regularly for Nelson-related publications, and have recently signed a contract with Historium Press for a full-length biography of George Matcham; which will expand from a short piece she wrote for Trafalgar Chronicle in 2022.

Lily Style wrote her first historical novel, Horatia's Secret to communicate her strong intuition about why Nelson & Emma's only child, Horatia, claimed not to know who her mother was.

She is the creator and webmaster of the Emma Hamilton Society, whose purpose is to provide positive and deserved press to Dame Emma

Hamilton (her correct title is Dame as she was awarded the Maltese Cross). Dame Emma Hamilton has been unfairly maligned because of prevailing sexism and snobbery: she had unwedded relationships (but not promiscuously) and spoke with a common accent.

Her keen interest in Mediterranean history has been rekindled by her research for the George Matcham biography. Having visited Turkey, particularly the central region of Cappadocia, over 30 times, from 1994 onwards, she has a strong affinity with Anatolian history. Her article about the history of the Islamic crescent moon and star symbol was published by Historical Times magazine in 2023, and she is currently researching the neolithic site of Çatalhöyük near Konya.

She is a volunteer for South Hams Authors Network and created their website and the logo for the 2023 South Hams Literary Festival.

Visit her website at www.lilystyle.co.uk

www.historiumpress.com